BY TOM BOWER

SWEET REVENGE

SWEET REVENGE

THE INTIMATE LIFE OF
SIMON COWELL

TOM BOWER

BALLANTINE BOOKS · NEW YORK

Published in the United States by Ballantine Books, an imprint of
The Random House Publishing Group, a division of Random House, Inc., New York.

BALLANTINE and colophon are registered trademarks of Random House, Inc.

Simultaneously published in the United Kingdom by Faber and Faber, London.

ISBN 978-0-345-53394-4
eBook ISBN 978-0-345-53395-1

Printed in the United States of America on acid-free paper

www.ballantinebooks.com

2 4 6 8 9 7 5 3 1

First U.S. Edition

Book design by Liz Cosgrove

To Veronica

HE WHO SEEKS REVENGE

SHOULD REMEMBER TO DIG TWO GRAVES.

—proverb

CONTENTS

———

INTRODUCTION

———

MARVIN GAYE'S "AIN'T NO MOUNTAIN HIGH ENOUGH" WAS BLARING across the dark Mediterranean. Simon Cowell pulled on his Kool cigarette. "Today was an eye-opener," he said, gritting and swigging a freezing Sapporo beer. "I'm disappointed."

At 2:30 A.M. on August 5, 2011, Cowell had returned to *Slipstream,* his 193-foot chartered yacht, from Bâoli, a brash restaurant in Cannes's harbor. "I hate this place," Cowell had told his friends. "Getting in was trouble. I expected an elbow in my eye." Offensive doormen had temporarily blocked his entrance after failing to recognize their famous guest.

After eating only a single course, Cowell unexpectedly rose and declared, "Let's go." His exit was delayed by a dozen tourists asking for a photograph. As usual, Cowell politely obliged—some would say his politeness was manipulation, but he believed in being pleasant to everyone—and then strode past the restaurant's bouncers, across the quay, and stepped onto *Take Five,* a new VanDutch speedboat, his summer toy. Taking control from the ship hand, he sharply levered the throttle. Speed was an easy cure to his stress. Zooming across the flat sea at 45 mph, he steered into the darkness beyond the harbor walls. The exhilaration provoked a smile and he swung back toward his gleaming pleasure craft, a haven of privacy from the mobs.

Sitting on *Slipstream*'s spacious aft deck, Cowell glanced at the latest text messages from Los Angeles. "Not good," he announced. Casting aside the nearly full bottle—"Another cold one," he ordered—he took a swig and headed for his suite. In Los Angeles, everyone was still awake. He needed a postmortem. He anticipated making telephone calls until daybreak.

Seven hours earlier, Cowell had been linked by satellite from the yacht's lounge to Los Angeles, where two hundred fifty television critics had gathered for the industry's showcase of the autumn season. "This is the Big One," Cowell had told Fox TV's executives. After thirty years in the music business, Cowell was gambling his fate on *The X Factor*'s successful launch in America.

"I only play to win," he volunteered. Repeatedly, he had reedited a glitzy twelve-minute promotion tape highlighting the *X Factor* auditions recently held in Pasadena, California. His pursuit of the tape's editors in Los Angeles was a foretaste of the pressure he put on himself and others to produce flawless programs. "They'll get it in the neck," he promised. Perfectionism and unpredictability were his trademark.

"We all love this tape and this is going to be a great launch," he enthused about the mixture of tantrums, tears, and seductive singing to be shown to the journalists.

In Pasadena, he had picked Stacy Francis, a forty-two-year-old single mother, as the competition's probable winner. "She'll be bigger than Susan Boyle," he privately predicted. And if not Stacy, his next favorite was Rachel Crow, a frizzy-haired thirteen-year-old from a remote farm in Colorado. "Both backstories are special," he said with daunting self-confidence, adding to his friends on the yacht, "I'll be worried if the audience doesn't get to thirty million plus." His ambitious target for *The X Factor,* he predicted, would humble *American Idol*'s 2011 average of twenty-three million viewers.

Attacking *Idol* was not a publicity stunt. Ridiculing the program that made him famous in America had become an all-consuming passion. To keep him happy, Fox had just broadcast a controversial promotional teaser for *The X Factor* in the middle of the All-Star baseball game. The commercial featured Cowell waking from a nightmare in which he was still working on *American Idol*. The promise was that *The X Factor* would push the "bland" *Idol* aside. Many viewers were baffled, but not more than *Idol*'s producers. Their program, after all, was also broadcast by Fox. Fevered critics spoke about cannibalism and self-destruction as they witnessed the calculated gamble taken by Fox executives to stage *The X Factor*.

With glee, Fox's rivals had watched the recent turmoil about the judge Cheryl Cole's acrimonious departure from the U.S. *X Factor* and intensified their plots to usurp Cowell's supremacy. Fractured relationships always undermined self-confidence and the promo tape during the baseball game had just flopped. "I felt zero when I·saw it," admitted Cowell two months later. "It was too clever and aimed at women when the audience was all male." Three months after that, he would describe his strategy as "a blunder." That afternoon's satellite presentation from the yacht to journalists in Los Angeles was a premonition of things to come.

"*X Factor* is like nothing you've seen before," Cowell began. "We're throwing everything in to win—to make the best TV show in the world." *The X Factor,* he declared unambiguously, would be better than *American Idol*. "We're looking for contestants with star quality who we can turn into stars." *The X Factor* had not been launched, he answered one journalist, "to win the silver medal," and there was an unprecedented five-million-dollar prize. "I want to show that the process is honest—warts and all," he declared, aiming to silence the repeated accusations about behind-the-scenes manipulation and deception. The journalists were not told that he was broadcasting from the Mediterranean. As he spoke, Cowell cursed the three-second delay of his voice. "Are you the PR puppet meister?" asked a woman. "No," he replied. "It's not our intention to be mean. That's just within us."

Paula Abdul, the star singer and dancer, sitting in the Los Angeles studio, described her reaction after being invited by Cowell to become an *X Factor* judge. "I felt harrowed and elated and I cried for days after," she said. For Abdul, who had left *American Idol* after its eighth season, it was the end of three years in the wilderness. "Well, I give everyone a third chance," cut in Cowell smugly. The voice of Nicole Scherzinger, Cheryl Cole's replacement, followed, but her words were incomprehensible down a deteriorating sound feed. "Nicole's selfish," Cowell chimed in, reflecting his suspicion that the former Pussycat Doll was focused solely on self-glorification. He also happened to take pleasure in expressing blunt truths.

"We've got a problem," rattled the TV technician's voice across the yacht's plush interior. The sound had been cut. Next, the screen went black. Technology was sabotaging the master of control. "That's it," announced the production manager on the yacht. To Cowell's disgust, this same production manager, despite being responsible for the wreck of the presentation, now asked for a photograph of the two together. But, always gracious, he smoothly agreed, fulfilled the chore, and then hurried to his private suite. "The feed was bad, the production was bad and we had no leadership," Cowell said, lambasting his producers in Los Angeles. The happy spell on the pristine yacht had been broken. Doubtless, all would be forgotten after a good night's sleep, but new problems were certain to arise the following day, because every day brought problems.

Cowell had arrived at the Côte d'Azur on a private jet from Los Angeles after stopping in New York to collect his favorite holiday companions. Three couples were invited to care for his needs and join the fun.

One guest was his best friend, Paul McKenna, the hypnotist and self-improvement guru, who was accompanied by Sam, an attractive Englishwoman. The others were Andrew Silverman, a New York property developer and the owner of a casino in Panama, with his wife, Lauren, and Kelly Bergantz, who is employed by Cowell as an executive producer on *The X Factor,* with her boyfriend, a hedge-fund manager. All the women were glamorous, high-octane players willing to pander to Cowell's innocent whims. They were joined by Sinitta, a former girlfriend, whose song "So Macho" was Cowell's first hit, in 1986. To widespread bewilderment, including that of Julie Cowell, his eighty-six-year-old mother, Cowell's former girlfriends remained his closest friends, united by their jealousy toward one another while competing for his attention.

The notable absentee from the party was Mezhgan Hussainy, Cowell's Afghani fiancée. To his mother's relief, he had quietly canceled his wedding to the makeup artist. "I'm shattered by the way she behaves," Julie Cowell had told her son after an incident when Hussainy had stormed from the dining room in his Los Angeles house and slammed the bedroom door. Although Hussainy had worked with Cowell in the studio, she had not understood the stresses in his life. She was unsympathetic, both Julie and Simon agreed, to his love of uncertainty, change, and his "relentless, relentless, relentless" competitiveness.

"We came to the conclusion that I'm a hopeless boyfriend and I don't blame her," he said, gazing across the Mediterranean. There would have to be compensation, he had agreed. "When you make a promise to someone you have to support her." To minimize any damage, he was reluctantly considering the gift of his eight-million-dollar hilltop home in Beverly Hills. For the moment, their separation remained unpublicized. Although he had found another woman who would board the yacht later, Cowell was mindful that any paparazzi photograph would embarrass the proud Hussainy. To frustrate the intruding cameras along the Riviera, he would party—and sleep—alone until he reached Sardinia.

The breakup did not surprise Paul McKenna, who at forty-seven was another unmarried Los Angeles personality. "We've got commitment phobia," McKenna concluded about his and Cowell's common resistance to permanent relationships and children. Loving dogs and the "people business"—or, more pertinently, "people deconstruction"—was their common interest. Another was just having fun.

"I want to be happy, have good people around me," agreed Cowell. "I want to be free and I don't want to be bored." After McKenna disappeared into his cabin, Cowell reflected on his unwillingness to marry: "I'm attracted to crazy women. I encourage crazy behavior and I make them crazy. I'm attracted to certain personalities who are difficult to control, so there are tantrums, tears, and fights, which is all part of the drama. My life is really odd. Every girl wants to be number one, and is very territorial. I like the fight because otherwise I'd have a dull group of girlfriends."

To his most intimate friends on the yacht, Cowell was not only a world-famous icon but a most generous friend and also, occasionally, an insecure, lonely man whose greatest comfort was lying on a couch between Lauren Silverman and Kelly Bergantz watching a film and grazing on simple food suitable for kids in a nursery.

The fifty-one-year-old's career had reached a crossroads. Chartering *Slipstream* for one month at a cost of two million pounds reflected his new tastes. During his first twenty years in the music business, Cowell had been regarded as an amusing sideshow, renowned for surviving endless humiliations, before eventually emerging as a successful producer. Only in the spring of 2001, after moving hesitantly out of the record industry's shadows to become a television personality, did he finally achieve his ambition: to become the godfather of celebrity culture.

Six months earlier, in winter 2011, he had felt exhausted and on the verge of giving up. "Then I got my mojo back and decided to crack on," he said, taking a cigarette, which was lit by a member of the crew. Describing himself as a rebel, and keen to define the vitality of his own era, he spoke energetically about his search for immortality.

Celebrity and shameless vanity have become Cowell's vehicles of subversion. On the yacht, he flaunted his self-love and his personal admiration of those who were equally self-indulgent. Between beers, he revealed his negotiations with a Swiss company to freeze and store his corpse for one hundred thousand pounds in the expectation that science will invent rejuvenation. "I trust them," he said. In the meantime, he spared no expense to prolong his life and looks. Stubbing out his cigarette, he headed for sleep at four A.M.

"The best tomato sauce in the world on a pizza was Pizzaland's in Windsor," Cowell declared soon after emerging for the first time the following day at three o'clock in the afternoon. McKenna nodded. "I wonder if Geoff can make it for us," continued Cowell, summoning the yacht's chef. Cowell expected the yacht's crew of fourteen to satisfy his every whim. Geoff agreed to make some calls. Twenty minutes later he returned. Pizzaland, Geoff reported, was defunct, but he had tracked down the franchise's owner in Abu Dhabi. "He's giving nothing away but that's no problem." On the basis that the charterer's request had to be satisfied, Geoff emerged forty minutes later with a fresh pizza inside a box decorated with Pizzaland's colored motif copied from the Internet. "Brilliant," said Cowell, handing the shriveled pie to McKenna. "Now, our favorite meal," he announced as three hostesses brought Cumberland sausages, mashed potatoes, and Daddies, a strongly flavored sauce. "PG Tips with a dash of cardamom," requested Cowell as his favorite brand of tea. Scones with cream and cucumber sandwiches on sliced white bread were being piled onto the table.

He and McKenna discussed the latest gossip—a competition the previous night between two billionaires' sons at a St. Tropez nightclub over how many bottles of champagne they could order. An Indonesian had won with twenty-two magnums, costing $1.2 million (£800,000). "I hate that," said Cowell, who dislikes vulgarity and whose annual income was rising toward $70 million (£45 million). He turned the conversation to what he called "my life balance"— pumping himself with vitamins to cancel the damage caused by nicotine. Twice every year, Dr. Jean-Louis Sebagh, a French doctor in London, injects Cowell with Botox. "This is better than vitamins," the doctor had advised. "To me, Botox is no more unusual than toothpaste," Cowell said to his friends, who shared his obsession. "It simply works. You do it twice a year. Who cares, and it balances my smoking and drinking."

Cowell travels everywhere with at least two large suitcases filled with potions—eye drops, face creams, bath salts, milk lotions, and "wash-and-go" shampoo. Regularly he visits Harrods to buy the latest products. Women in his entourage always know his bathroom contains the best selection of cosmetics, which they are welcome to borrow. "I am definitely vain," Cowell admitted, "but to be honest with you I can't think of one person on TV who isn't." No one is allowed to spot him with "bed head," and when he awakes he equally dislikes seeing his girlfriends before they are properly groomed. Appearances are critical and he likes to see women with their face "done."

Always willing to try a new idea to prolong his youthful appearance, until recently he had a half-deaf woman visit weekly to cover him with oil, wrap him in cellophane, and squeeze him into a tube with the promise that the paralyzing discomfort and itching were guaranteed to detoxify and oxidize him. After he tired of her loud, monosyllabic pitches for a new TV show, he fired her and seized on another passing recommendation: the HB Health antiaging clinic on Beauchamp Place, in Knightsbridge, London. A friend's half-sentence description was sufficient to prompt Cowell to commission one hour's treatment in a "bubble," the whole treatment costing five thousand pounds that promised to detox, help weight loss, and prolong life. Three men carried the contraption to his bedroom on the first floor of his London house. "I hated it," Cowell exclaimed, complaining that the German applying the treatment had spent the entire hour promoting his ideas for new TV shows, and the captive patient had been forced to listen.

The ultimate treatment was introduced to Cowell by the Australian actress and singer Dannii Minogue, a fellow *X Factor* judge, in 2008. An attractive British general practitioner who advertises her speciality as "the integration of traditional and complementary medicine," recommended that Cowell have blood tests four times a year, "the full blood work" every six months during his health checks at UCLA Medical Center in Los Angeles, and injections once a week of magnesium, all the B vitamins, and pure vitamin C. Whenever he lives in America, Cowell receives the same mixture by a thirty-minute intravenous drip on Saturday afternoons in his bedroom. On her recommendation, he takes a saucer of pills daily, travels with bottles of supplements, and daily drinks two smoothies—one red and one green—made from expensive rare fruits.

Plates of untouched food were cleared and the group started to play Balderdash, described on the box as "the bluffing game, the game you can win without knowing anything." Next, Cowell and McKenna checked Facebook. One year earlier, both had invented characters and made a bet as to who would have the fewest friends after six months. Cowell's character was Derek Bates, whose password was "hairyballs69." Clicking on, he discovered no "friends." McKenna's invention, Jeremy Pipkin, had one friend, another person invented by McKenna. Both were genuinely disappointed by the failure of their ruse.

Immersed over the next four weeks in his billionaire's splendor, Cowell and his friends sailed across the Mediterranean from St. Tropez, searching for fun. First to Portofino and next to Sardinia to enjoy Flavio Briatore's Billionaire Club, one of the Mediterranean's best sanctuaries for the rich and famous to meet and mix with beautiful people.

Cowell's entrance with his friends provoked a frisson among the diners and dancers. Good looking, rich, famous, and, above all, unmarried, he was a potential catch for glamorous hunters. And most important, he was a willing target for a particular type. He certainly wasn't looking for intellect or strong characters. Just uncomplicated, uninhibited, sometimes trashy girls. Classy vulgarity excites him despite his fastidious concern about personal hygiene. In his quest for transitory enjoyment, those defects are tolerated. His search is rarely in vain. Quite literally, women throw themselves in his path. One-night stands are ideal for a man resistant to commitment, even when they occasionally end with theft or, worse, by girls whose motives are initially disguised. The stop in the Billionaire Club, however, had no such dramatic outcome.

After two days, *Slipstream* headed to Capri. Philip Green, the billionaire retailer, a close friend and advisor, was racing on his yacht from Turkey, and at the same time, Natalie Imbruglia, an exciting, sexy Australian singer and songwriter, was waiting for Cowell to pick her up at a hotel. The sassy entertainer, who had starred as a judge on Australia's *X Factor,* came on board, it seemed to Cowell, intent on "hooking up with Cowell after an earlier fling." For his part, Cowell also hoped to forge a relationship. His female friends were puzzled. "Natalie's not very interesting," whispered one. Cowell's charisma and fame, she knew, often suppressed the women he dated, not least because he rarely chased self-confident women who could resist the attractions of celebrity. Imbruglia, Cowell thought, was among the few who could spark something real. Instead, unsure about her host's fleeting intentions and his unwillingness to offer a relationship, she decided after four days to disembark.

"It didn't go anywhere," Lauren Silverman concluded.

"Just a K & C," agreed another, meaning "a kiss and a cuddle."

"I wanted another fling and she didn't," Cowell laughed. Rejection was irrelevant. He felt remarkably liberated.

"I don't care," he announced at dinner soon after. "This year I've cut out the darkness. I've cut out all the people I've hated."

Lauren Silverman understood. For too long, Cowell had been shackled to his former partner turned rival and the owner of the *American Idol* format, Simon Fuller, and, as Cowell put it, his "Moonies."

"All day, every day," Cowell recounted about his years on *American Idol,* "they'd be watching me. Watching and watching. And then tapping and tapping, all day long, sending Moonie reports back to Fuller. It was disgusting." Lauren Silverman, his closest confidant, nodded sympathetically.

Even while on vacation, Cowell spent no less than six hours on the telephone to London, New York, and Los Angeles daily. In between calls, he spent hours watching DVDs of *The X Factor* and the programs based on the *Britain's Got Talent* format, which are broadcast in more than forty countries. By any reckoning Cowell ranks as unrivaled among the world's TV and music producers. His priority during August was *The X Factor*'s launch in America on September 21. Each episode would cost a record three million dollars to produce, but in return, advertisers were agreeing to pay Fox four hundred thousand dollars for a thirty-second spot on the basis of guaranteed audiences. His focus was to reach the stratosphere as America's most powerful TV star, a quest that was electrified by events on July 20.

In the Houses of Parliament in London, Rupert and James Murdoch had just been humiliated by politicians investigating their employees' illegal hacking of celebrities' telephone messages. Sensing weakness, Simon Fuller, Cowell's bitterest enemy, chose that day to commence a lawsuit in the Los Angeles Superior Court against Fox

Broadcasting, which is part of the Murdochs' News Corporation. Carefully choreographed publicity ensured that Fuller's lawsuit produced headlines from Los Angeles to London. The former owner of *American Idol* was suing his partner. Fuller's declaration of war against Fox and also indirectly against Cowell, his erstwhile partner, demonstrated the British producer's bid to reassert his influence over the music industry.

Greed, ego, and money are what make Hollywood tick, and causing conflict can often bring rich rewards. On *Slipstream,* Cowell spotted Fuller's only weakness. "My fame is driving him crazy," he said, smiling. For ten years, Fuller had waged legal and psychological warfare to confirm his supremacy over Cowell. He had successfully extracted Cowell's meek acquiescence that *American Idol* had been Fuller's sole and exclusive creation. For ten years, Cowell had gone along with what he believed to be a lie, and now Fuller wanted to extract more blood. He wanted a credit on *The X Factor* as "executive producer" although he had not participated in any aspect of the program. "No one asks for a credit on a failure," John Ferriter, a Hollywood agent, reassured Cowell, reporting on Fuller's anguish. "Desperate publicity seeking," was Cowell's judgment.

There was no coincidence that the same issue of *Variety,* Hollywood's bible, reporting Fuller's demand to be given an executive producer credit, was dominated by twelve pages of congratulations to Jamie King, the choreographer who had teamed up with Fuller to find talented musicians for a new show to be called *Q'Viva! The Chosen,* described as "a search across the Americas for Latino artistry." So far Fuller had not found a major American network to finance his prospective show, instantly stymied by the announcement that its stars, Jennifer Lopez and Marc Anthony, were divorcing. In a city where a lawsuit is used as a negotiator's tool and both sides in a dispute can be seen eating amicably in the same restaurant, Fuller's blast was nevertheless regarded as exceptional. "We won't pay and we won't negotiate," Cowell was told by Fox executives. Fuller, he said, smiling, had shot himself in the foot. Their ten-year feud was coming to a climax. Andrew Lloyd Webber's famous response to the question "Which Simon do you love more?" was, "My money is on Simon."

Cowell hoped the equivocation would soon be over. His revenge would be complete.

With little effort, Cowell's mask concealed any hint of violent emotions. Despite endless media scrutiny, his critics' attempts to penetrate his defenses and expose the reality of his passion and jealousy, or the existence of self-doubt and decadence, had proven fruitless. Fearing exposure, Cowell presented himself as the antithesis of debauchery: a man who never pronounced on morality and seemingly never committed a moral wrong. To some, he inhabited an identity but resisted being defined by it.

High-minded critics have dismissed Cowell's world of mindless pleasure as middle-class philistinism. Such debunkers have portrayed his pedestrian disregard of human complexity as proof of a man who is neither moral nor immoral, just superbly sterile. Yet behind the mask, his confidants listen to confessions of torment, not least about his public image.

Like all subversives, he is terrified of others adopting his own armory against him. Troubled by the hatred he has generated, he has grasped that his own fortune rests on resisting the same humiliation as he had heaped on others. For years, he suffered mockery and for the past eleven years has sought revenge against those sneerers. "This is the make-or-break year," he admitted on *Slipstream.* By Christmas, he would know whether he had scaled new heights or been universally lampooned.

At the end of the trip he had also decided against freezing his corpse after all. A chance conversation during the voyage had revealed that the Swiss "clinic," after receiving the corpse of a basketball player, had cut off and frozen only the head. "Imagine," said Cowell laughing uncontrollably, "what all my ex-girlfriends would do if they just looked at my dead head? No way!"

SWEET REVENGE

1

THE CREATION

LAUGHTER AND PARTIES WERE THE BEDROCK OF SIMON COWELL'S childhood. Both his mother, Julie, a former Soho showgirl, and his father, Eric, a property manager, were generous hosts who promoted enjoyment rather than academic study for their children. Guests at their successive homes on the western fringes of London could not have imagined that the Cowells were concealing a tangled succession of relationships preceding their own happy union. Once the dust had settled, among those invited for long Sunday lunches were not only their two children together but four children from their previous relationships and various grandchildren. They all would later be acknowledged in Eric's last will.

Eric Cowell, born in February 1918 in London's East End, could trace his father's family back to the eighteenth century. In 1770, William Cowell had been a rope manufacturer. The family business continued in the East End for more than a hundred years until it was inherited by Joseph Cowell, Simon Cowell's great-grandfather. In 1890, Joseph, an Anglican, married Nancy Levy, a Jew, in Whitechapel. Their eldest son, also named Joseph, was born the following year and because of his mother's religion automatically became a Jew. The family business ended in the early twentieth century.

Soon after the outbreak of the First World War, in 1914, Joseph Cowell, then twenty-three years old, volunteered to join the Middle-sex Regiment of the British Army, serving as a private. The following year, Joseph married Esther Malinsky, a twenty-nine-year-old Jew who had been born in Poland. Malinsky's father, a cap maker, had fled to England to escape the Polish government's persecution of the Jews and set up his business in the premises of a mantle maker in the East End. The family home was two rooms at 22 Pelham Street, in a Jewish quarter in Spitalfields.

After the war, Joseph Cowell became an office clerk and moved with Esther to Ilford, an east London suburb. When the second of their three sons—Eric Selig Philip Cowell—was born, Joseph was em-ployed as an "inspector" on London's buses, checking passengers' tickets. On subsequent legal documents, Eric would describe his fa-ther as a "transport manager."

By 1939, Eric Cowell had qualified as a chartered surveyor. Soon after the outbreak of the Second World War, he joined the Middlesex Regiment and was posted to Calcutta, India, as a commercial clerk. In 1943, promoted by then to captain in the 19th Hyderabad Regiment, he married Enid Proudfoot in Bombay's Anglican cathedral. Proud-foot, the granddaughter of Emily da Costa, a native Indian, was un-aware that her husband was Jewish. Misleadingly, he had described himself on the marriage certificate as Congregational.

Life for British officers in India, the jewel of the British Empire, was relatively blissful, and Eric made the last year of the war even more comfortable by serving as a magistrate in Calcutta. His leisurely life of parties, privilege, and servants ended in August 1946. He re-tired from the army as an honorary major and returned alone to Brit-ain to set up business as a surveyor living near his mother, by then a widow, in Ilford. Enid, his wife, arrived in Britain some months later, but the marriage broke down and she returned to India.

Eric had already embarked on a relationship with Jeanette Sevier, a baker's daughter eight years younger than himself who occasion-ally modeled in Bristol. Renting a flat in Kensington, they remained unmarried, but in 1948 they had a son called Anthony, who was later known as John. Soon after, Eric was employed as a property manager by Barratts, the shoe manufacturer and retailer, and they moved temporarily to Stafford. In 1950 their daughter June was born. Two years later, after returning to Kensington, Eric apparently obtained a divorce from Enid Proudfoot—no official British record can be found—and married Jeanette in Fulham. Within one year, their marriage was floundering.

As part of his work, Eric traveled regularly on weekends between London and Northampton. Returning on the same train to London every Monday, he spotted an attractive woman, Julie Dalglish.

Born in November 1925, Julie was the only child of Robert Dalglish, a Birmingham garage mechanic and chauffeur, whose Scottish family had for generations been lithographers. In 1937, despite her strict father's opposition, Julie, accompanied by her mother, Winifred, had successfully auditioned to dance on the West End stage in London. Aged twelve, she left Birmingham with three other girls for six weeks of rehearsals of *Goody Two Shoes* before the performances began at Christmas, running until Easter 1938. Living with the group in west London, she passed the exams for the Royal Academy of Dance and continued during the war as a member of a dance troupe, touring Britain's seaside resorts to entertain tourists and the military.

After the war, using the stage name Josie Brett, she returned to London to work twice every night as the lead dancer in *Can-Can* at a nightclub off Piccadilly. At age twenty, she fell in love with Bertram Scrase, an actor, dancer, and singer who was married to another dancer. Scrase's charm, looks, and stories had seduced endless women. Performing together, Julie and Bertram toured Britain until Julie became pregnant. In 1946, while traveling with Bertram to Dublin, she gave birth to a son, Michael Scrase. To Julie's fury, Bertram's wife, Elaine, refused his request for a divorce.

Over the next years, troubled by Bertram's endless affairs, Julie left Michael with her parents in Birmingham and continued dancing in London. In 1950, although their relationship had disintegrated, she had a second son with Bertram named Tony. Some said that Scrase disappeared with another woman while others suggested that

Julie had met another man. Julie would later say that her relationship with Bertram Scrase was "disastrous" and to some she would add, "It didn't work. I thought, why did I get into marriage?"

Amid the austerity of the postwar era, the task of simultaneously bringing up two children while working to become a famous dancer was exhausting, not least because Bertram Scrase was financially unreliable and, having set up a new home with a waitress in Bognor Regis, abandoned contact with his two sons.

To avoid destitution, Julie left her sons with her mother in Birmingham while she continued to dance at the Pigalle Club in Piccadilly. Every weekend, she traveled by train to the Midlands, returning to London on Monday evenings. During those regular journeys, Julie spotted Eric Cowell boarding the same train at Northampton after his regular visit to Barratts' headquarters. In 1954, after entering the dining car he approached her.

"Would you care for a drink with me?" he asked.

"It's my birthday," she replied, "so yes."

It was the start, she would say, of "a long platonic relationship in London," which developed because he was "very interesting, well read, and had a sense of humor." Unhappy in his marriage, Eric abandoned his wife to pursue Julie.

Julie had every reason to succumb to a man offering a solid relationship. But he wanted more. Soon after they moved into a flat in Richmond, she came under pressure to have more children. "I thought we had four between us and that was enough," she said, "but Eric delivered an ultimatum." After successive miscarriages, a son was born in Brighton in 1958. Due to complications in the last weeks of pregnancy, the child, registered as "Stephen Cowell/Scrase," died three weeks later. The following year, on October 7, 1959, Simon Cowell was born in south London. His parents were unmarried, because according to Julie, "I was scared."

Soon after Simon's birth, Eric introduced Julie Dalglish to his sixty-nine-year-old mother. Unusually, Julie and her mother were invited to stay in the Cowells' Richmond home.

"My mother's from Poland," said Eric, without providing any more information.

"Eric's family is Jewish," Winifred told her daughter during that visit.

"Do you think you're Jewish?" Julie challenged her partner.

"I could be. I don't know," Eric replied, and then added, "No, I'm certainly not."

Julie thought no more about it but did conclude that Eric's mother was "awkward and frightening."

The following year, Julie was again pregnant and wanted to regularize her status. After searching for a bigger home, Eric bought a rundown three-bedroom house north of London. In March 1961, their second son, Nicholas, was born in south London although, unusually, his birth was only registered in June. That same June, Esther died and the chance of Eric's Jewish background being revealed in his lifetime receded. Three months later, on September 26, Jeanette obtained a divorce from Eric on the grounds of his adultery with "Julie Brett." On October 24, 1961, Eric and Julie were married at Caxton Hall in Westminster and celebrated with some friends at the Savoy. Although Julie registered her address as 28 Culross Street in central London, they had already moved to Barham Avenue, where Eric had opened a real-estate agency.

Amid the leafy suburbs, surrounded by dogs, Eric and Julie were determined to enjoy a happy marriage in a fun-loving atmosphere. Questions about their previous relationships were brushed aside. Julie's four children knew little about their parents' past. Humorous, gentle, and generous, Eric spoke only about his happy days as a major in India and never mentioned his childhood or first marriage. His two children with Jeanette were forbidden by their mother to meet Julie. Instead, they enjoyed excursions on Saturday afternoons to Battersea Fun Fair and holidays alone with their father, unaware of his new family.

Similarly, Simon Cowell was not told about his grandparents' past, his father's childhood and religion, or about his uncles, aunts, and cousins, all living nearby. Nor did his mother reveal much about Bertram Scrase, although both his sons, Michael and Tony, who had been living with their grandmother, moved into the house on Barham Avenue. Having lost contact with Bertram, Tony Scrase regarded

Eric as his father, but Michael resented his stepfather's discipline and after many arguments, left and broke all contact with his mother. He met his father only in 1971 after Bertram appeared on a television program. At the end of his life, Scrase was calling numbers in a bingo hall. Those details were either unknown or not mentioned in the Cowells' home.

Only much later did Simon Cowell realize that his parents were unmarried when he was born—his family never discussed the adulterous relationships. Eric and Julie saw no reason to disrupt happy childhoods. For them, nothing was more important than giving their family a secure home, which neither had provided in their previous relationships.

Soon after Nicholas Cowell's birth, Eric spotted Abbots Mead, an eight-bedroom ruin in Elstree. Since trading his own houses provided additional tax-free profits, he bought the run-down house with large grounds for ten thousand pounds, a considerable amount at the time. The renovation was completed just after Simon's second birthday and the family adopted a luxurious lifestyle.

In the postwar boom, Eric's business was expanding. To take advantage of rising property prices, he opened a new office in central London. In the mornings, he sped down the gravel drive in a convertible E-Type Jag smoking a Havana cigar, leaving behind a gardener, cook, and nanny to help care for the four children and their friends. Although Eric was never seriously wealthy, he had sufficient money to host large Sunday family lunches, where Julie, theatrical and charming, could be heard calling everyone "Darling" and approving of men who applied makeup to conceal blemishes. "Your personal appearance makes a big difference," Julie would say.

The large house was not only buzzing with children but the Cowells enjoyed an increasingly full social life thanks to a prized neighbor who was the head of Warner studios in Elstree. The mogul indulged Julie's showbiz passion by introducing her to Bette Davis, Trevor Howard, and Robert Mitchum.

After working twenty years in show business, Julie plunged into the semblance of a Hollywood lifestyle. She rarely appeared for breakfast in the morning without full makeup and would certainly never leave the house without perfecting her appearance. Always dressed elegantly, she was thrilled when Eric bought her her first mink stole. "Mummy looks like a poodle," was Simon Cowell's appreciative comment when Julie asked her four-year-old to admire her appearance before she left for another of her neighbor's parties. Cowell adored his mother's theatricality and vanity, which some would endearingly call "camp." Posing for effect and addressing people as "Darling" epitomized Julie's Gospel about the importance of charming people, creating no critics, and offering generous hospitality. Rudeness and aggression were unwelcome in the Cowell household and the universal response to visitors was warmth. Professionally, Julie Cowell had craved attention and she did the same socially. "The stars soon became our friends and neighbors," wrote Simon Cowell in 2003, in a grossly exaggerated account of those childhood events, "and whenever they were in town I got to rub shoulders with the cream of Hollywood, as long as I could squeeze my way past my mum. . . ." The highlight for Cowell was sitting on Bette Davis's lap. Theatricality was Julie's oxygen, and at an impressionable age it affected, even infected, her son. Life, he learned, was best when "one was noticed."

Among the famous neighbors was Stanley Kubrick, the film producer. Kubrick regularly pestered Eric to sell Abbots Mead and finally raised his offer to a price that Eric could not refuse. Since selling property was Eric's business, Julie reluctantly agreed, and in turn was thrilled by his new purchase, the Warren, in Radlett, four miles from Elstree. The house was smaller but had potential for expansion and for subsequent resale. Although they left Abbots Mead after just four years, they retained the relationships with several film personalities and would meet Roger Moore, Elizabeth Taylor, and Richard Burton, among others, at parties, although not over their neighbor's fence, as described in previous accounts.

The move to Radlett coincided with Simon and Nicholas leaving the local private prep school and starting at St. Columba's boys' school in St. Albans. The teachers were monks in their robes, decent men who were bewildered by the Cowells' indiscipline. At home Simon dressed up as the science-fiction hero Captain Scarlet, and at school he behaved as if he were a master of the universe, fashioning his personality as a self-assured youth whose criteria for success would be to fail exams, an attitude fed by Eric's encouragement of a relaxed atmosphere in the house. No member of his family had gone to university and none of his children were under pressure to read or excel at school. Success would not be judged by academic rigor but by having fun and making money.

Resistant to diligent study, Simon was disruptive in class, enjoyed playing pranks on other schoolchildren and the teachers, and, when reprimanded, challenging authority. To his teachers' fury, chastisement did not cause contrition but hilarious laughter. The troublemaker, they realized, was an unashamed attention seeker intent on disturbing the class. Punishment was administered by an assistant teacher who ordered Cowell to hang from the wall bars in the gymnasium. The process encouraged his rebellion at school, which was a continuation of mayhem at home.

Living in a permanently messy bedroom, Cowell's love of pranks was little short of anarchy. He once shaved the top of his younger brother's head so that his hair was styled in an inverted Mohawk; after finding a Father Christmas outfit hidden in the attic, he had set fire to the beard and left it smoldering, which nearly caused a huge catastrophe; and he held a toy pistol at a bus driver's head, ordering, "Take me to Watford," which ended in his temporary arrest after the terrified driver called the police. Nothing, however, equaled his reckless enjoyment of driving his father's cars down the drive and onto the road. Outraged by his poor behavior and lack of discipline, Julie frequently hit Simon. His nonchalant disregard, amounting to subversion, infuriated his mother. "It was a mental battle with a strong woman," said Cowell. "Always fractious."

"I was the dragoness," Julie later admitted. Her appeals to Eric to "do something" were greeted with a smile.

"I nagged him, 'Have you done something?'" Julie would complain, coping unsuccessfully with the strife, "but he usually didn't." At crisis moments, she would wait anxiously for Eric's return home, gave him a gin and tonic, and when he had "settled in" say, "The boys are playing up." "I'll take care of it," Eric would reply quietly and go upstairs. Invariably, his sons were listening to a Beatles LP.

"Tell your mother I gave you a jolly good rollicking," he'd say to his smiling children. Closing their bedroom door, he'd report sternly, "I read them the riot act," and, sipping his gin, he'd resume the *Daily Telegraph* crossword. Twenty years later he confessed to his ruse.

"I was," Simon Cowell would admit, "outspoken, obnoxious, cheeky, and bored very easily. A strong-willed little brat." Cowell was shaped by his teachers' universal criticism of his arrogance and inadequacies. "Giving lip" at school and at home was his revenge on humiliation by teachers' caustic put-downs. Trying to keep him in line, the teachers displayed a large repertoire of stares, threats, silences, contempt, ridicule, scoffs, mock disbelief, and jokes at his expense. Gradually, he absorbed their performance as a model for delivering his own snap judgments of friends.

His emotional survival depended upon cultivating a sense of superiority over those who mocked him. "I have an absolute hatred of losing," he later admitted. "Even losing at Monopoly as a kid. I just want to beat the competition." Aggravated by his imminent humiliation, he would tip over the Monopoly board the moment he saw defeat, rather than concede gracefully. Cowell would describe that behavior as "competitiveness"; others would say he was shamelessly spoiled.

Intelligent, he was frustrated by his academic failure and inability to find a remedy. Frequently, he avoided school by faking illness, sometimes placing a hot teapot on his forehead. Those who would later mock his "Mummy, look at me!" attention seeking could not pinpoint the characteristic underlying the son's relationship with his mother, except that her critical love gave him unusual, even unjustified, self-confidence.

New wealth allowed Eric to indulge his children. In the late 1960s, through contacts, he was appointed a director of EMI, the music corporation, with responsibility for its property portfolio, a task similar to the one he had undertaken for Barratts. After selling his real-estate agency, he flourished on a high salary and liberal expense account. His children were spoiled by regular excursions to fairs and historic sites and vacations in Spain, which were still unusual for English families. He bought a debenture on Box 60 at the Ascot Racecourse to entertain his friends and the family on Saturdays, and encouraged his sons to miss school for big races during Royal Ascot week.

While delighted by the constant improvement of her fortunes, Julie forbade Eric to give her sons an allowance. Accustomed to earning her living as a teenager, she insisted, "They should earn their own money." Regularly, Simon washed neighbors' cars and windows, looked after their children, and mowed their lawns. During vacations he worked the fields at a local farm and worked in a shop. Before he reached his teens, his sole ambition was "to get rich."

Although his sons could have progressed to the senior school at St. Colomba's, Eric decided to move. He had received a good offer for the house in Radlett and bought a house about thirty miles south, in Fulmer, near Maidenhead. Simon, aged twelve, and Nicholas, aged ten, were enrolled at the local Licensed Victualler's School, originally established for the children of bar owners.

"It's really bad," Simon told his parents in a rare observation about the quality of his education. His parents were unconcerned. Instead, they encouraged their sons to have fun. A self-contained flat within the new house was assigned to the two young boys and became the center of their school friends' social life to play records and, later, drink and smoke. Many attractive girls, including Paula Hamilton, a future model, drifted into the flat after school.

One year later, Eric realized his mistake and, on the recommendation of a friend, transferred Simon and Nicholas to Dover College, a traditional boarding school in the Channel port. Nicholas's messages to his parents were not encouraging. "It's dreadful. Awful," he wrote. Even his housemaster described the living conditions for his seventy-five boarders as "crushed like rats in small cages."

Forewarned by Nicholas, Simon arrived with a single ambition: to leave the oppressive environment as soon as possible. He joined no clubs, played no sports, and disliked the drab gray herringbone uniform. Having learned that the school motto, "Non recuso laborem," meant "I shun no work," the only Latin he perfected was the opposite, "Recuso semper laborem," "I always shun work."

"I couldn't bear the discipline and the boredom," Simon said. "I just wanted to get out and earn money." In a letter home he wrote,

"Dear Mum and Dad. I hope you're happy to finally have got rid of me. I also hope you're happy in your centrally heated warm house and you have a lot to eat. Because I am lying in a dormitory which has icicles on the inside, and there's nothing to eat. I'm freezing cold and hungry. I hope you're finally satisfied." In reply, he received two letters. A long one from his mother encouraged her son to study and remember his father's sacrifice to pay for school fees. A thinner letter from his father in an EMI envelope enclosed a fifty-pound note. This response urged Simon to send regular complaints and await the identical replies to finance his frequent forays to the local pub to drink and, particularly, to smoke.

By then, he had identified Mickie Most, an acerbic judge of a television talent competition called *New Faces,* as his hero. In the program, Most, a record producer who counted the Animals and Donovan among the successes on his own record label, joined other famous producers and singers to judge the performance of young artists auditioning in the studio. The contestants on *New Faces* relied on the panel's decisions, and Most ranked among the most acerbically judgmental. The judges' humiliation rather than the contestants' music excited Cowell. Pertinently, he was not particularly interested in the deluge of original songs produced in the 1960s and 1970s. Occasionally he went to concerts and he often played records, but his favorite preoccupation at the end of every school day was smoking with friends and on Sunday evenings expressing his dread of going back to school the following day. At sixteen, in the weeks before taking his "O" levels, the first public examinations that would determine his fate, he was never seen studying.

After taking the exams, Cowell's popularity and unauthorized presence in the pub prompted his suspension for the last two weeks of the summer term. "I did him a favor, I suppose," the housemaster later realized. "Sending him home was the opposite of punishment." Cowell passed just two out of nine exams at the lowest grades, ranking him as a failure. Content, he returned home, albeit to a new house.

Eric had completed another sale and repurchase. The family moved into a new mock-Edwardian house in nearby Pinkney's Green that had been abandoned in mid-development by a bankrupt builder. After the construction work was completed, Eric intended to resell the house. Cowell was enrolled at Windsor Technical College to re-take the exams he had previously failed and eventually obtain one more basic pass. His only achievement at the college was meeting Debbie Spears, his first serious girlfriend. At seventeen, he fell in love and during their eighteen-month relationship lost his virginity. The affair ended, he said, when he found her kissing a tutor at a party. The following day he telephoned her. "Can I have my crash helmet back?" he asked. The more serious challenge was for him to decide his career.

Regardless of his academic failure, Eric indulged his son. He was allowed to drive the family car with the promise of his own car in the near future, and he was given ample food and clothes and taken every weekend for a family lunch to a local Indian restaurant. Only occasionally did Eric mention to his son his grim career prospects. After disastrous employment as a waiter and at the local Brillo factory, Cowell spent his days at home in some despair. Isolated from regular routine, he became a loner spending his days reading *The Beano, The Hotspur,* and other boys' comics interspersed with a *Flashman* book, the adventure of a ruthless cad.

"With no qualifications and no talents," he admitted at the time, "my prospects are poor." Driven by Julie to get a job, he found menial work at a warehouse and invited home the boy who was driving the forklift truck. Over dinner they compared their family lives. "I never realized how lucky I am," Cowell admitted afterward. "I've taken a lot for granted." His next job was working at the counter of Laskys, a hi-fi shop. The only "buzz" he got from it, he later volunteered, was getting the paycheck at the end of the week: "I love getting money. I want to make money. Real money. Pocket money isn't enough. I want to be rich."

Good humoredly, Eric suggested his son become a quantity surveyor and follow him into the property business. With poor test scores, that was a forlorn suggestion. Next, Eric drove his son to a building site in Birmingham. After walking for two hours in rubble and mud, the seventeen-year-old exploded, "Are you completely mad?" and insisted they return to London. Eric next used his contacts to arrange interviews for his son as a management trainee at Tesco, a grocery chain, and as a civil servant. Both ended in disaster because of Cowell's refusal to consider working in a structured environment. He returned home defeated but still buoyant. Despite his plight, he used his sole talent, entertaining his friends, at parties, and with his charm and good looks he attracted girls. "I lost my virginity to Simon Cowell," Paula Hamilton admitted. "He was very, very protective of me and he was funny and rebellious."

Exasperated by her son's luxury-seeking lifestyle, Julie urged Eric to use his influence again. Finally, even Simon Cowell realized that the offer engineered by Eric of working in EMI's mailroom for twenty-five pounds per week could not be rejected. "I'll work my way up," he promised.

"Always be polite and charming to people," Julie urged on his first day, in 1976. "Manners maketh the man. They cost nothing. Courtesy is the hallmark of the civilized." Eric, by then his best friend, added his own wisdom: "Everyone you work with has an invisible sign on their head that says, 'Make me feel important.' Be polite to everyone."

Delivering the mail to offices occupied by energetic young men and women pursuing ambitions denied to himself was humiliating. His fleeting appearance was casually accepted and swiftly forgotten. At the bottom of the business food chain, he regularly pushed a cart from EMI's headquarters in Charing Cross Road to a subsidiary in Dean Street, Soho. During those turgid months, there was one memorable moment. After Cowell entered the building one day, a youth his own age made a denigratory comment about the "post boy pushing the trolley." Cowell was stung. The glib comment highlighted his failure. Protected from poverty and worthlessness by his parents' safety net, he was taught to conceal his feelings. The daily drudgery gave Cowell a moment of epiphany when he realized the consequences of his indiscipline. But now he silently pledged, "Right, I'll show you." In that cathartic moment he finally shed all traces of obnoxious behavior and overnight became ambitious. Noticeably, he changed his appearance and manner to assimilate EMI's culture.

Holding his cigarette at head height, he began addressing people as "darling," began wearing V-neck T-shirts cut to show more skin, and had his long hair permed. His vanity was no longer put to use only to attract girls but to become part of the music world. To tone his appearance, he bought a crude sunlamp and, frustrated by the slow progress to become tanned, remained in front of the light longer than recommended and without safety goggles. Soon he was screaming in agony. He was rushed to the hospital with burned eyes by his mother, who feared during the week his eyes were covered in bandages that his sight could be damaged. Vanity had triumphed where all the teachers' reprimands had failed.

Life outside the mailroom had improved. Nicholas Cowell, prospering as a junior in a real-estate agency, a job his father had arranged, had moved into an empty flat in Mayfair. Simon followed to enjoy evenings at Samantha's, a local club, and parties at the flat. His new skinny, elfin girlfriend was the victim when Paula Hamilton arrived in a jealous fit. "Paula's gorgeous but crazy," Cowell told his brother in the aftermath of a bitter argument.

Two weeks later, he returned to live with his parents. While supporting him financially, Eric became exasperated by his son's careless driving. Repeatedly the speed nut crashed Eric's cars. He once drove through the center median on a two-lane highway in Maidenhead—"Simon swerved and saved my life," Nicholas was ordered to say—and soon after, he took his father's new Rover and again crashed at top speed. To disguise his culpability, he positioned the car against the wall of the family's house to make it seem that Julie had forgotten to apply the hand brake. Without comment, he watched Eric admonish his bewildered wife. After more scrapes and dents, to protect his own car, Eric bought his son an old Citroën, followed soon after by a Lancia convertible. Like all of Cowell's cars, the floor was soon covered with discarded cigarette packets, beer bottles, and candy wrappers, reflecting his untidy existence.

After eighteen months at EMI, Cowell confidently applied for promotion to work for one of EMI's record labels. He was abruptly rejected. He lacked any knowledge about music, he was told, a judgment he could not deny. His personal record collection was limited to the Beatles, the Rolling Stones, and other mainstream groups, and he never visited gigs or concerts. Frustrated, he left EMI and with the help of his cousin, a production manager on a TV series being shot at Elstree, he was employed as a production assistant for fifteen pounds a week. "I was a slave to everyone," he said about following others to climb the ladder. "Whatever I was asked, I'd say 'yes' and did it." Once the production was completed, his cousin arranged his next job as a P.A. on Stanley Kubrick's *The Shining.* Days later, he was told that Kubrick didn't want P.A.s. Unemployed again, he asked Eric to intercede. His father telephoned Kubrick and reminded him about the house sale. "Why didn't you offer my son a job?" he asked. Kubrick relented, but just then another string pulled by Eric produced a better prospect.

Eric was friendly with Ron White, the head of EMI's music-publishing division. At the heart of the music business, the record companies maximized their income by licensing the copyright of popular songs and music to artists. White offered Cowell an opportunity to begin a solid career, but just when it seemed arranged, White disappeared to Australia and Cowell was once more sitting at home with no work.

Devoid of any ideas, Cowell was impressed by his brother's fate. Within two years, Nicholas was earning £250 per week, driving a company car, and had bought a flat. Reluctantly, Simon Cowell asked Eric to arrange a job in the property business. Once again, Eric drew on his contacts and his son was employed in the shops department of Hillier Parker, a leading firm of London real-estate agents. Within hours on his first day Cowell realized his mistake. "They're toffee-nosed public-school twits," he later told Nicholas. He had been dispatched to compose a list of all the shops along Oxford Street, and afterward he confessed his misery to his parents.

"I want to work in music," said Cowell.

"I know you're unhappy," said Julie, "but you must give it time and settle in." Cowell insisted on resigning immediately.

"I don't think that's a good idea, but you must be happy in what you do," said Eric, firmly establishing himself as the bigger influence. Unlike Julie, who was emotionally upset about her son's poor school record and directionless life, Eric offered solutions with uncomplicated advice. Cowell agreed to stay at the job for another three months, during which he continually confided in Eric about "my screwups." At the end of those months, Cowell was again unemployed, sitting in his family home considering his future. "He looks crestfallen," Julie told Eric.

2

RISE AND FALL

UNEMPLOYMENT DID NOT DENT COWELL'S ENJOYMENT OF CLUBS, dancing, and girls. On May 15, 1982, he went with Mel Medalie, a music producer, and others to Morton's, an expensive Mayfair club. Cowell was Medalie's unpaid runner, hoping for a paid job. Glancing across the room he spotted Jackie St. Clair, a stunning young woman, famous, he would later discover, for posing nude in top-shelf magazines.

Handsome, charming, and persistent, he persuaded Medalie to make an introduction and later persuaded St. Clair to come for dinner at Rags, a members-only club in Mayfair. Without money, he relied on his father to arrange for him to sign the bill as a member. The beautiful Miss Nude UK was unimpressed. Although she was "too expensive for me," as he told his brother Nicholas, there was finally a brief affair. St. Clair, however, preferred men who did not rely on their fathers to pay the account.

Pertinently, while Julie lamented her son's unemployment, he spent the weekends with his brother and a gang of friends drinking and picking up girls in London's cheaper clubs. Simon and Nicholas would be sent to "pull the girls" from the bar or the dance floor while the others ordered champagne and Amaretto for their table. "Young guys operating," was Nicholas's description of a group "working and playing hard." Afterward, they often headed at Nicholas's suggestion to lap-dancing clubs. To some, lap dancing was vulgar, but in Cowell's eyes it was fun wrapped up with a flash of showbiz, and his life's purpose was enjoyment.

Cowell's forlorn days at his parents' home temporarily ended after Ron White unexpectedly returned from Australia. At Eric's behest, White summoned Cowell for an interview. "It doesn't mean you'll get the job," warned Julie as her son, unusually dressed in a suit, returned home racked by nerves. "I'd give my right arm to get back into the music business," he admitted. At eight P.M., White called and said, "You've got the job." Eric Cowell's advice on the eve of Simon's first day of work was unexceptional: "Spot people who can teach you and stick to those you can learn from." Unexpectedly, his son would scrupulously follow that suggestion for the next thirty years.

Excitedly, Cowell returned to EMI. To his horror, he was greeted by silence. Everyone knew that Eric had fixed the appointment for his unqualified son. Undeterred by the hostility, Simon relied on Ellis Rich, his immediate supervisor, who bore no resentment, to explain his task. Search through the catalogues of music owned by EMI, he was told, and match suitable songs to popular singers. Then persuade their agents during personal visits to use EMI's music. Cowell finally discovered his undoubted talent. Personable and entertaining, he could ingratiate himself by following Eric's advice, "In business always make sure that you make the other person feel important. Always shake hands and say 'hello.'" Easy with conversation and charmingly polite, he formed solid relationships with agents but was irked by all the A&R—artists and repertoire—men who scoured pubs, basement gigs, and concerts across Britain for new talent. "The biggest arseholes in the music business," Cowell declared, identifying the gulf between himself and genuine music aficionados. Those pursuing art in music, he scoffed, were "snobs." Unaccustomed to diligent, methodical research and also to showmen's bravura, he disliked the A&R men's self-importance after signing new clients. The middle-class interloper felt alienated from the A&R men's drug-infested lifestyle. "I'm bored by them," he told friends about the combative clique, who brassily supervised their artists' careers by choosing producers, finding new songs, and overseeing recordings.

Unable to conform, Cowell was attracted after one year to Ellis Rich's suggestion that they leave EMI and set up their own music-publishing business to "make a lot of money." Without first securing a commitment from songwriters, they left EMI, rented an office in Soho Square, and began operating as E & S Music. "Within a day of moving into our new offices," Cowell admitted, "I realized I had made a big mistake. We didn't have the funding to do it properly. We couldn't get the business off the ground, and many of the fundamentals of running an independent business were foreign to us." Without telling Rich, Cowell asked Ron White whether he could return. "No," replied White. "I was going to groom you for the top but you've betrayed my trust."

Moaning that he had been misled, Cowell persisted over the following months with Ellis to develop the business in Britain and America. A doomed visit to Los Angeles incited Cowell to blame Rich for the disaster. Relations between the men deteriorated. "When you're young you're paranoid," he later reflected. "I was jumpy, insecure, and worried. It was not a good time." Their finances were going downhill. The upside was that he was tackling the steep learning curve in the music business. "It's amazing," he told Eric Cowell. "The bits of plastic cost fifty pence to make and you can sell them for eight pounds." Making and selling, he decided, was more lucrative than publishing. In 1983, after a year of arguments, he left Rich. Much later he conceded, "Ellis was right. Publishing is a long, slow business, which he understood. I would have earned millions, much more than I've got now, if I had stayed. The money was in music publishing and back catalogues. Ellis was disappointed that I didn't stick with him."

That was not quite the recollection of E & S Music's landlord at 46 South Molton Street, Iain Burton, the sharp and ambitious owner of Ferroway Ltd., a music-production company, whose own offices were in the same building. Ferroway was also the holding company that owned Fanfare. They had first met when Cowell, dressed in hot pants, had arrived on Rollerblades at Burton's West End office with Nicholas and Nicholas's close friend Mandy Perryment, an actress.

Although Burton was seven years older than Simon, he became part of the Cowell brothers' weekend gang. Nicholas was by then earning about two thousand pounds a month selling luxury properties in northwest London. Together, they toured the clubs, drinking and looking for girls. Eager to be known as "the Crazy Gang," the Cowell brothers liked impressing other clubbers, although the bill was often paid by Burton, who at the end of the night invited everyone back to his penthouse.

Burton watched as E & S Music floundered and he spent time with Cowell during his return to the wilderness searching for work. In that forlorn period, Burton became Cowell's inseparable best friend. "He was ultra confident, very funny, and super charming," was Burton's sentiment. Besides sharing an interest in pop music and girls, Burton recognized a kindred spirit in Cowell. "In those days," he recalled, "none of us had any problem with being a little camp." During one of the Cowells' Sunday lunches, he was persuaded by Eric to offer his son a job selling books published by Fanfare and to explore how he could develop Fanfare Records, Burton's fledgling music label.

Burton allocated a desk in his office to Cowell to work for about ten thousand pounds per annum to learn the business and find new artists. "An amazing break," gushed Cowell later, acknowledging his debt for being rescued from "the bottom of the heap." On reflection he acknowledged, "From the mailroom up, the first fifteen years in the entertainment industry was about learning. I always worked on the basis of being patient and if you work hard it will come to you." At twenty-six, he could finally afford to move out of his parents' home and rent a flat in Fulham. But he left reluctantly: "I liked my bedroom and I liked the house." He took with him a well-read copy of the *Guinness Book of British Hit Singles*.

Burton had already signed a license to sell Rondò Veneziano, a commercially successful Italian orchestra that played a fusion of contemporary and baroque music. On Burton's instruction, Cowell hired Nigel Wright, a young studio producer who was fast and imaginative, to supervise a remix of their recordings. "Get the music played on TV," Burton told Cowell, realizing how television promoted sales. Endlessly and unsuccessfully, Cowell harassed television producers to use Rondò's music. "Don't take 'no' for an answer," Burton told his disorganized employee. "Keep trying until you get it." In Burton's opinion, he was mentoring his best friend and junior. "Watch and listen to me," he told Cowell. "Sit opposite me and learn from what I do."

Eventually, Cowell heard that *Crossroads,* the TV soap, was to be set in Venice for one week. He successfully harassed the show's producer to use Rondò's album *Venezia 2000* as the theme music for that week. Over a hundred thousand copies were subsequently sold. Thereafter, Fanfare was always profitable. Only commercial music, Burton decided, was worth promoting.

In the quest for profits, in early 1982 Cowell visited Fairlight, a German laboratory specializing in manufacturing sounds. Among their products was a dog barking a song in tune. "I think I can make this a hit," said Cowell. Back in England, with help he turned the Fairlights' sound into "Snap the Wonder Dog" singing "Ruff Mix." To promote the single, he targeted the producers of BBC's *Top of the Pops,* television's most important pop-music program. The teaser, he explained, would feature a "singer" dressed in a dog's outfit miming "Snap's song." The producers fell for the novelty and the valuable slot was secured for early September. Gung-ho, Cowell arrived at the BBC studios to discover his "singer" slumped by several empty beer bottles. "I'm not doing it," the man slurred. To save the slot, Cowell drank a couple of beers to give himself courage, dressed as the dog, and told the producer, "I'll do the act."

"Walk onto the stage," he was told by the studio manager, "turn left, then turn right and walk past the camera to the middle and sit down." On cue, Cowell stumbled across the floor, fell over children in the audience, and unsteadily sat down by a table as the single was played. After a chaotic mime, he staggered off the studio floor and was told, "You're banned for life." Unfazed, he anticipated earning "a fortune" from the record and a TV series.

To boost sales, he had commissioned Hanna-Barbera, the animation studio, to draw a cartoon for the album's cover. Days after the record's release, Disney threatened legal proceedings because the album's cover was a copy of a Disney design. The successful launch was curtailed and the album was withdrawn, but Cowell's legacy in the music industry was fixed: He inhabited his own world. His weakness was his personal poverty. Unable to earn enough money, he still depended on his father.

To survive, most players in the music business drift to profiting from the current fashion, and at the time some of the best money was earned from subversive, violent rock music. Unlike the traditional A&R men racing between six gigs every night, Cowell could not nurture personal relationships with the opinionated, druggy rock groups performing in bars and clubs. Although he rebelled at school, he sympathized with his family's genteel society rather than the rockers' cultural resentment. Fanfare also lacked the financing to promote successors to the Beatles and the Stones. Stuck on the fringe, looking for a break to earn money rather than create art, his good fortune was an introduction by his brother. Sharing a flat in Chilton Street with a friend, Nicholas was dating a Welsh ballerina while his friend was going out with Sinitta, an aspiring dancer and the daughter of Michael "Miquel" Brown, a famous singer from Canada. During the relationship Sinitta had appeared as a dancer on TV and once in a West End musical. Occasionally she drank and danced at the clubs visited by the Cowell brothers and was invited to spend weekends at the Cowells' family home. In 1982, after Eric retired and moved with Julie to Majorca, Sinitta would travel as Nicholas's girlfriend to the island for holidays. Shortly after, not for the last time, Simon inherited Nick's castoffs. "It's their naughty face which attracts me," Cowell said about girls with dark skin.

In late 1984, after another family holiday in Spain, Sinitta suggested to Simon Cowell that he should listen to her recording of "So Macho." Excited by the music and with nothing else in prospect, Cowell offered Sinitta a contract. Soon afterward, however, Burton telephoned to announce that he was pulling out of Sinitta's record to invest his money in a new project. "I'm begging you," implored Cowell, "please don't close this down. Just give me some money and I'll make this record a hit." Burton, proud of his reputation of "nailing" his commercial adversaries "to the floor," relented and gave Cowell five thousand pounds. "But that's it. Final," warned Burton. By industry standards, it was a pitiful amount. The following day, Cowell started the weary routine of touring all the radio producers of music programs to get airtime for his new artist. Although Cowell was welcomed for his charm and humor, the record was universally rejected as falling outside mainstream pop. His only hope was to target gay men at a time when homosexuality was legal only between consenting adults meeting privately.

To understand the gay market and its twilight dance clubs, Cowell met with Ian Levine, an openly homosexual songwriter and producer whose successful career in disco music had soared after he left school in 1975 when he discovered and promoted Evelyn Thomas, a soul singer from Chicago. Thomas's first record, in 1976, had been a modest success. Next, Levine wrote and produced Miquel Brown's hit song "So Many Men, So Little Time," a song about a woman sleeping with countless men and waking in the morning unaware of the name of the person sharing her bed. Initially, Brown's record appealed uniquely to the gay community in North America and especially New York, and then spread to the gay dance clubs in the north of England. Levine's challenge was to persuade producers at Britain's dominant pop station, BBC's Radio 1 in London, to overcome their prejudice against gay music and the north-south divide. Real success, however, depended on "the Crossover"—when a record that was popular among gays but unknown to mainstream music fans was suddenly demanded by heterosexuals in the traditional record shops across the country. If those sales were sufficiently high, the record would rise in the commercial record charts and automatically be played on Radio 1. "So Many Men, So Little Time" achieved the Crossover and became a major hit.

Cowell needed to understand how Levine had scored the rare jackpot that eluded so many producers. He found the producer working at Record Shack in Soho. Levine's was a familiar story in the music business. At the height of his success in 1979, he had been crushed by catastrophic financial problems. Scarred, he worked behind a shop counter but on Saturday nights he was the principal DJ at Heaven, a gay club near Charing Cross station. Every weekend, more than two thousand men danced frantically until daybreak there. In that small community, Levine had become influential by importing ideas from the Sanctuary club in New York.

Cowell walked into Record Shack and introduced himself. Wearing a V-necked white T-shirt exposing his hairy chest and high-waisted red trousers, Cowell asked Levine to play Sinitta's "So Macho" at Heaven and to produce a record with Arlene Phillips and Hot Gossip singing "Break Me into Little Pieces." Sinitta, he added, should be included in the group. He expected Levine's help. Sinitta was Evelyn Thomas's daughter.

After one hour's rehearsal at a recording studio, Levine booked a lead singer with a voice like Marvin Gaye's. Cowell arrived to watch Levine mix the tracks at the Trident studios in Wardour Street. Normally Levine would need four hours for a mix but Cowell's interference prolonged the process. "That's fabulous, darling, but . . ." Cowell sighed, urging more drums, bass or vocals, each suggestion canceling the previous "improvement." "I'm pulling my hair out," screamed Levine as he reached for another Kool cigarette, an American menthol brand bought by his parents. As Cowell introduced himself to the brand—it was never clear whether the attraction was the taste or the name—he urged Levine, "Darling, can we have a bit more treble . . ." Fourteen hours later, the mix was completed, but despite Levine's efforts at Heaven, the record flopped.

Failure did not dent Cowell's self-confidence, nor his trust in Levine, whom he embraced as "hilarious, conceited, and very talented." On the next occasion, Cowell entered Record Shack with his chest shaved. "Don't you think it's more defined?" he asked. To Levine, Cowell appeared as "a camp, silly, indecisive record executive who was catty and judgmental," yet they often spent time together at a Japanese restaurant near Cowell's office. During those meals, Levine suggested that Cowell revive the black disco music popular in the 1970s featuring James and Susan Wells, an American brother and sister duo. "They're great," said Levine. "You sign them up, I'll make the records." Cowell arranged for the two to fly to London and during 1984 Levine recorded three records: "R.S.V.P.," "Mirror Image" and "No Care for Me." With Levine's help, all were successful in the gay clubs but none reached the charts. "Everything Levine's producing is hot," Cowell realized, "but we're not making any money."

Sitting in his office, gazing at a large mirror on the wall—a gift from Sinitta, who had adorned the top with an inscription: "Yes Simon darling, you look beautiful"—Cowell contemplated how to copy Levine's recent successful crossover launches. Sensitive to the taste of gay men at Heaven, Levine had noticed that dancers now wanted music with more beats per minute than normal disco music. In the underground, even the term "disco" had been ditched in favor of "Boytown." Levine had redefined the market focused on gays when he recorded Evelyn Thomas singing the up-tempo "High Energy." Played by DJs in gay clubs across the United States and Europe, the new release achieved the Crossover, hitting number 1 in Germany and selling more than five million copies across the world.

Evelyn Thomas's success coincided with another hit, "Whatever I Do," produced by Pete Waterman, a hugely talented but still unrecognized producer. Waterman's next record was "You Think You're a Man" sung by Divine, a drag queen with a huge following among gay and transvestite clubbers in America. Like Levine's, Waterman's formula matched Cowell's ambitions. "I'm aiming for the gay market," Waterman later told Cowell, "because we can't afford to go anywhere else." Without any money for promotion and occasionally not even for a pint of beer, Waterman told Cowell, "It's a market where money can still be made if a massive hit in the underground creeps into the mainstream in the bigger shops."

They had first met while Cowell, employed by EMI, visited Waterman's primitive studio in north London, and then, later, in Waterman's studio at the rear of the Marquee club in Soho. Waterman's skills, Cowell recognized, were not only, "like a DJ at a wedding, always knowing what music people wanted to dance to"; he with his two partners, Mike Stock and Matt Aitken, possessed all the talents required to produce pop music. Combined, in their company Stock Aitken Waterman, they could write songs, master the technical wizardry in the sound studio, and perfect promotion. By 1984, after Waterman had built a modern studio in south London, Cowell acknowledged him "as my point of contact. He knew what a song should sound like. We had a lot in common." Pop music, Waterman told his admirers, was difficult to write. "Either it's pure sugar or it's undercolor. And both are not liked."

Fascinated by Waterman's challenge to the A&R snobs and the major record labels, Cowell relished an antihero who was neither fashionable nor cared what people thought, an unusual combination in show business. Clutching Sinitta's twelve-inch vinyl, Cowell sought Waterman's opinion about the failure of "So Macho." "You've got a hit," said Waterman generously. "She can chirrup a tune."

"Would you do the follow-up?" asked Cowell.

"I'm too busy," replied Waterman.

"Doing what?" asked Cowell cheekily. Cowell's fate depended on making Sinitta a star. Remembering Iain Burton's mantra, "Never take no for an answer," he returned twice every week to Waterman's studios to watch the recording sessions, learn about the business, and meet his rivals. "I followed Waterman around like a dog," Cowell admitted. Rushing through his offices, Waterman saw a man who was "ambitious and great fun." He also described him as infatuated by Sinitta, and "the most stylized human I'd ever met. Always the same hair, wearing a T-shirt and carrying cigarettes. He was always the same." Behind the smile, Cowell was aggressively absorbing Waterman's promotion techniques. "Music is showbiz," Cowell was told. "People steal your lines. Do the same."

In early 1985, Cowell's frustrations grew. A second launch for "So Macho" had entered the charts at number 40, only to stall and crash. "Why aren't the kids interested?" he asked Waterman. "The market is not stupid," replied Waterman, delivering the scripture. "Gays like a particular type of music but don't want a badge put on it. You can't make a gay record and say it's gay. You must make a record for the market and be serious about it." Cowell nodded.

"He wants to be the most famous man in the universe," Waterman told an assistant. "But he's shambolic, indecisive, and not focused, except on fame. He doesn't know how to get there."

Aware of Waterman's criticism, Cowell pledged to prove him wrong by obeying another of Waterman's homilies: "You can hype a record if it's got legs. You can give it longer legs if it's stuck between 40 and 50 in the charts by remixing it to give it a boost. But then you need radio or TV play to get real sales." To improve Sinitta's record, Cowell spent the last pounds of Burton's budget on a third remix, commissioned a video for fifteen hundred pounds, a paltry sum compared with slick American videos costing a million dollars, and hired a plugger, to get the record played on Radio 1. Cowell and the plugger waited for an hour to see the Radio 1 producer. The record was placed on the turntable. Ten seconds later, the producer said "No" and bid the two men farewell.

"My records don't fit," Cowell lamented, wondering just how any record producer could get a play on Radio 1. Some believed American-style payola operated within the station, with DJs pocketing wads of cash. To reach the producers, Cowell began inviting their secretaries for lunch and to nightclubs, only to discover that British payola amounted to giving the producers dinner with good wine. "You had to play by the BBC's rules," he accepted, but since there was only one producer on *Top of the Pops* and one on each Radio 1 program, everyone was entertaining the same people and his "soft bribery" failed.

The irritation was watching others' success, in particular that of Tom Watkins, a brash gay record producer who had become the manager of the Pet Shop Boys during 1985. Later that year, Watkins negotiated the rerelease of "West End Girls," a high-energy record popular in gay clubs in America and Britain. By the end of the year, Watkins had achieved the Crossover and the record was number 1 across the world. Capitalizing on his new wealth, Watkins renovated a large house in Holland Park with a swimming pool, began hosting riotous parties for boys, and spoke about the "knack of the gay market." That was the elusive magic Cowell was seeking.

Having crisscrossed northern England and financed two remixes of "So Macho," Simon Cowell was "desperate." Burton had declared that Fanfare was unable to pay its bills, making the song a "life or death issue." Even getting "a play" at Heaven had become "critical" and, irritatingly, Cowell's relations with Levine had deteriorated after Cowell had succumbed to an irrepressible urge to humiliate the producer by what he called "a prank."

At MIDEM, the music industry's annual trade exhibition in Cannes, Cowell and a friend meddled with the stall at the entrance to the exhibition hall rented by Record Shack. Prior to the opening, Levine had adorned the stand with framed records—the industry's plaques testifying to his glowing record of hits. Early in the morning of the opening, the two entered the hall and rehung the records at extreme angles and upside down. "We've destroyed his stand," laughed Cowell, hiding to watch Levine's reaction. He was more distraught than they had anticipated. "Cowell," he screamed, instantly identifying the culprit, and began searching frantically for the delinquents, eventually finding them collapsed on the floor shedding tears of laughter.

Levine's revenge was brutal. He refused to play "So Macho" at Heaven.

"I won't," said Levine. "It's too naff. I've banned it."

"I've done you so many favors," retorted Cowell angrily, suspecting Levine's anger was fueled, he suspected, by an unexplained resentment linked to his relationship with Sinitta's mother. Determined to secure the play, Simon Cowell walked into Heaven with Sinitta and a copy of the record on a Saturday evening. Two thousand men, many stripped to the waist, were dancing.

"Play it," he ordered Levine.

"I won't," replied the DJ. "It's a pile of shit." After an angry exchange of curses, Simon Cowell pulled a record off the turntable and put on his twelve-inch vinyl. Puffing indignation, Levine in turn snatched the record and smashed it over Cowell's head. Amid the shower of pieces, the club fell into an eerie silence. "Mr. Piggy, you're a . . . ," screeched Sinitta, hurling abuse at the obese Levine.

Days later, the two men met accidentally at the Hippodrome in Leicester Square, which was owned by Peter Stringfellow. Four times a week, the Cowell brothers and their friends took two tables on the first floor. "Why didn't you play my record?" asked Cowell. As Sinitta watched, Levine gently slapped Cowell's face. In return, Cowell delivered a mighty punch to Levine's cheek.

Petulantly, Levine refused to retreat. His weapon was *The Street,* a weekly music magazine. In "Eurobeat Bitch Session," Levine's gossip column, he sniped about the encounter at MIDEM. "It was almost spoilt for me somewhat by the presence of the awfully camp Simon Cowell. . . . The reason for my anger at the dreadful little man is that I produced a track for Fanfare called 'No Cure for Me from Love's Insanity' for James and Susan Wells. Despite promising to release it, Simon has not as yet, and doesn't seem about to, as he still bears a bitter grudge against me for not playing his poxy Sinitta records." Levine continued, "I also hear that Cowell—who reminds me of the Wicked Queen in Snow White, in front of [Sinitta's] mirror all day— plans to use the track on a segued compilation LP . . . sandwiched between two Sinitta tracks [which] makes me feel nauseous, a feeling which is overpowered only by the queasiness I feel imagining Simon in front of his mirror every morning: 'Mirror, mirror on the wall who is the fairest of them all.' Not you, you vain old queen."

The following week, Fanfare released "So Macho" for the third time but only after Cowell masterminded a ruse. Instead of allowing PRT, the distributor, to supply copies of the record on demand to shops, he had arranged for PRT to take the orders but to withhold supplies for three months with the excuse, "Due to excessive demand it is out of stock." As the orders accumulated, Fanfare released the records in one go in March 1986. The surge of sales was officially acknowledged in the industry's regular Tuesday charts.

"So Macho" was in the top twenty. Cowell immediately called the BBC producers to announce the "breaker position," the break for play on Radio 1, and offer his inferior video. After three attempts, his ploy worked and with a play on Radio 1, Cowell had finally achieved the Crossover, selling nine hundred thousand copies and pushing the record to number 2. Fanfare's profits were heading toward half a million pounds.

Flush with triumph, Cowell replied to Levine's attack in *The Street*. Without considering the consequences, he compared his own "beautiful body" to Levine's overweight figure, which "vain people like myself find repulsive" but which guaranteed Levine victory in the "Mr. Barrage Balloon" competition. As a postscript, he added, "Which reminds me, do you want any more introductions to Escort Agencies? I know how much you enjoyed your last visit." Puzzled about Cowell's sexuality, Levine replied, "With all the time you spend looking at yourself in the mirror and shaving your chest, I doubt whether you get much chance to involve yourself in the music business, do you?" Levine's outburst reflected the gay community's antagonism toward Cowell's musical taste. "I hate you so much," Levine told Cowell. "You'd be as happy selling Andrex lavatory paper as records. Nothing is too crass for you." Cowell's camp mannerisms were somewhat puzzling to others—"he's light in his loafers," sniggered one music executive—but Levine lacked any evidence that Cowell was not completely heterosexual. Still, he could not resist putting in another column his recollection about "some very personal things" involving Cowell and sniping that "anyone who shaves his chest so regularly in order to look more hunky in a M&S singlet can hardly criticise anyone else."

Levine's misfortune was that Pete Waterman, whose company was by then being celebrated for producing in a short period nearly thirty number 1 hits for Donna Summer, Dead or Alive, and Bananarama, disagreed. London's leading studio was in the midst of producing a run of three hundred hit songs. Cowell knew his fate would be turned by persuading Waterman to hand him just one of those songs for Sinitta. His plan was partly undermined by Sinitta herself. Having won a part in *Mutiny!*, a West End stage show, she began an affair with David Essex, the star. The opportunity of a relationship with her childhood heartthrob, whose poster had been on her bedroom wall, was too good to miss.

"I've been dumped," Cowell told his brother, clearly distressed.

"He'd been playing around," replied Sinitta, "and when I said we should marry, he said 'No.'"

Cowell was also stymied by Waterman. "Will you help me?" Cowell pleaded.

"I'm too busy," Waterman snapped.

With no music to promote, Cowell was seconded to Burton's other businesses, selling primitive currency convertors and taped guides for museums, and visiting shops to promote Burton's latest business, "books-in-a-bag," a do-it-yourself kit to grow vegetables that included seeds. Pertinently, he also sold hi-fis and electronic equipment manufactured by Audio Fidelity, a public company that Burton had bought in 1986. Ferroway, which by then was earning about four million pounds a year, had been "reversed" by Burton into Audio Fidelity to cancel the public company's continuing losses. Burton praised his ownership of a ten-million-pound public company as "brilliant" and Cowell had no reason to doubt his friend's decision. He did not oppose the injection of his 25-percent stake in Fanfare into the public company.

"It's a great relationship," Burton would say about Cowell. "We're best of friends. I was very successful and we had a great time partying together." Gradually, the only absentee from their fesitivities was Burton's live-in girlfriend, Vanya Seager, an exotic Indonesian actress and topless model, born to Chinese parents, whom Cowell judged to be "the most beautiful girl in the world." Increasingly unhappy in her relationship with Burton, she remained at her home in Wimbledon. Cowell, observed Maurice Veronique, a friend who also worked at Fanfare, was "sniffing around Vanya." That was not, in Veronique's opinion, surprising: "Simon always went after his friends' ex-girlfriends because he wasn't good at picking girls up himself."

In early 1987, Cowell's relationship with Sinitta had resumed, although it had turned more professional than personal, as both wanted to capitalize on her fame. Waterman's help, Cowell knew, would be decisive but could only be triggered by an irresistible tease.

"Have you seen it?" asked Cowell excitedly. "Look at today's *News of the World* story about Sinitta going out with a young man who they've called a Toy Boy. Can you write a song for Sinitta called 'Toy Boy'?"

"You've pulled a clever stroke," Waterman told Cowell, convinced that he had contrived the feature. "You've made Sinitta look like Madonna."

Inspired by "a whim and a fancy," he threw off the idea to his partners. "Let's have a song called 'Toy Boy,'" he told Mike Stock; he asked Matt Aitken to write the music. Twenty-four hours later the song was written, but by then Waterman wanted the sixteen-year-old girlfriend of his friend, the Rolling Stone Bill Wyman, to be the singer.

"It's meant to be for Sinitta," Cowell pleaded.

"She's arrogant," replied Waterman. "She doesn't impress me and there's no pleasure working with her."

In the music business, Cowell had discovered, the intensity of success and failure on a grand scale depended so much on personal relationships. Under pressure, Waterman finally buckled. "Get Sinitta down here," he ordered. "She can sing 'Toy Boy' for one hour and then go away. I don't want you telling me what to do. Sit outside the studio."

Cowell's next priority was to hire Ron McCreight, a plugger and promoter who was universally liked and used by Waterman. Among McCreight's talents was persuading BBC producers to play records lacking any merit. Like rival pluggers, he knew the only payola was the BBC producers' enjoyment of a good meal, the best wine and, occasionally, a night at the greyhound races. By then, McCreight could not help knowing Cowell. At Waterman's frequent parties to celebrate another number 1 record, Cowell could always be seen circulating around the room in what appeared to McCreight as bordering on desperation, arousing suspicion as to why he put so much energy into networking.

"I'll get 'Toy Boy' a play," promised McCreight before its release in July 1987. Shortly after, he reported, "It's guaranteed on Radio 1. Happy days." That exposure made arranging Sinitta's appearance on *Top of the Pops* much easier. The record hit number 4 and stayed on the charts for more than three months. Cowell's lament was Radio 1's reluctance thereafter to continue playing Sinitta's songs, reflecting the producers' implacable hostility to pop music.

Finally, Cowell had established himself in the business, but the cost was a fractured relationship with Sinitta. Cowell was obsessed by details and image rather than the music, and both he ane Sinitta were opinionated about trivia, not least about the ideal clothes she should have worn on *Top of the Pops*. Their arguments grew and their relationship deteriorated as Sinitta's worldwide success influenced her behavior. Among those disenchanted by the singer was Waterman. "She's overconfident," he told Cowell. Nevertheless, Waterman included her in a forty-day tour of clubs, concert halls, and ballrooms across Britain. The tour was soon disrupted by what Waterman told Cowell was "a diva nightmare." In Dundee, Sinitta and a group of her friends kicked down a bathroom door, there were regular disputes in hotels, and finally she demanded her own bus. Knowing that what happened behind the curtains was often ugly, Cowell paid all the bills, relieved that the disruption remained unknown to the public, but the real cost was Waterman's refusal to assign another of his best songs to her. "All the best hits come from Pete," Cowell told Sinitta. "I feel physically sick when I hear Donna Summer because after 'Toy Boy' I can't get those songs for you. Only Pete and no one else can give you that quality of material."

Pete Waterman's veto sealed Sinitta's fate and Cowell casually began searching for new artists. Inevitably, he sought advice from Ron McCreight. "Getting pop played on Radio 1 is a nightmare," McCreight confessed, noting that even the popular Kylie Minogue "is ignored." The publicist's salvation was television shows. Frequently, McCreight accompanied Minogue, a young Australian singer, to TV studios and was bemused how often Cowell tagged along to meet the producers and used the opportunities to promote artists whose names would later elude him. Arranging one live act on Saturday-morning television featuring a boy and girl duo was fixed by McCreight after considerable effort. Carefully, Cowell choreographed their dance routine and dictated their clothes, including a hat for the boy. Watching the program at home, Cowell saw the hat fall off and the performance collapse into chaos.

"A fucking disaster," Cowell told McCreight.

"You chose what they should wear," replied McCreight. "Another punt that's gone wrong."

Cowell appeared untroubled. He was enjoying his moment in the sun, the universal dream of those involved in the music business. Fanfare had earned more than a million pounds from Sinitta, hardly enough to pay off its debts, but that was of little concern to Cowell. If there was cash he would spend it. "I thought I was Jack the lad," he later admitted. He borrowed money to buy a plush flat in Fulham and a second-hand used black Porsche 911 and paid for endless entertainment on his company credit card. Encouraged by Iain Burton and trusting his employer's acumen to compensate for his own commercial naïveté, he also bought shares in Audio Fidelity, Burton's manufacturer of hi-fi speakers. To pay for the shares, Cowell borrowed £250,000 from the Midland Bank. There seemed no reason not to trust Burton.

The only cloud was his dependence on Stock Aitken Waterman, by then established among the most successful production teams in music history. To some A&R veterans, Cowell was a sponge lacking originality but adept at regurgitating his mentors' insights. At that point in the music industry, Cowell ranked as an outsider among a community still boasting about its successful invasion of America during the 1970s in the wake of the Beatles and the Rolling Stones. Groups including 10cc and Genesis had signaled that Britain had cast off its colonial dependence on American music, but the independence was ending.

During the 1980s, many of the industry's heroes were self-destructing. Daily, messengers would arrive at London's music corporations to deliver packages of "champagne and flowers," a euphemism for cocaine, for the A&R men to take to that evening's gigs. Cocaine had become an essential and dangerous currency wrecking the industry's finances. Beyond the carnage and phony accounting stood Cowell, frequently spotted driving his Porsche convertible, wearing Ray-Bans, and with a voluptuous girl in the passenger seat. To Lucian Grainge, a rising star at PolyGram, Cowell was "not credible. He looked like he was in charge of Easter eggs and separate from the most fertile period of British music: Wham!, Eurythmics, Duran Duran, Spandau Ballet—a fantastic time, and all Cowell does is Sinitta and a few dodgy records." Later, Cowell could not disagree. "I wouldn't be able to spot a good rock band and I couldn't sign good commercial music."

Even in that genre, he suffered consistent failure. Sinitta was slipping into the past and, unable to find other hit artists, Cowell risked being ranked as a one-trick pony. Like a leech, he clung to Waterman for a break, signing groups with no prospects except as useful fodder to appear on Waterman's *The Hit Man and Her,* a TV music program that he hosted in Manchester on Saturday nights between midnight and two A.M. "It's the lowest end of the market," admitted Waterman, targeting people coming home drunk to watch live pop music interspersed by Waterman playing his own records to more than a thousand clubbers. To keep in touch, Cowell copied Waterman by acting as a DJ in gay nightclubs in northern towns presenting his own singles. None were hits and he foolishly rejected opportunities, including a request from Waterman. During a week in 1987, Waterman had asked Cowell to listen to Kylie Minogue singing "Locomotion," a hit in Australia.

"You'd be doing me a favor if you put it out," said Waterman.

"I quite like it," said Cowell, "but will you let us do the follow-up?"

"No," replied Waterman, concealing his agenda.

"Then there's no point," concluded Cowell.

The song would enter the charts at number 2, selling 440,000 copies in England, exposing Cowell's limited understanding even of pop music.

Minogue had arrived in England during the same week and, as ordered by her agent, had gone on Monday morning to Stock Aitken Waterman's studio in hopes of catching someone's eye. Throughout the week, she sat in the reception area, ignored by everyone. Late on Friday afternoon, Kylie still refused to move. As a throwaway gesture, Waterman told her to record "I Should Be So Lucky," another song just churned out by the newly dubbed "Hit Factory." As she headed for the recording studio, Waterman went home for the night.

Cowell, meanwhile, was fretting about the dearth of new talent. He placed some hope on Fanfare's Christmas party, the pinnacle of his year. He had invited about three hundred guests, including all the top personalities in the industry, to the Villa Cesari, a boat moored on the Thames, until midnight, and then for a second party after midnight he invited London's best-looking models. He scoured the agency catalogues, picking those models he liked and excluding those who were not his type. The cost, borne by Burton, was ignored. "I believed in spending money I didn't have," said Cowell. His agenda was undisguised. "The parties were good for business."

Buttering up Waterman was critical: "If Pete had a good night out we had a chance of a record, so he and Mike and Matt got the best tables. Anything you could prize out of him was good for your artists. I didn't want the crumbs. I wanted the cake. Everyone asked Pete for his best songs." An opportunity arose during the party. Waterman handed the DJ a record.

"I Should Be So Lucky," Kylie's new song, boomed across the boat. Cowell was thunderstruck. Waiting for a few minutes, he began searching for Waterman.

"How did that happen?" he asked. Waterman explained that after Kylie had been ignored all week, she was about to be tossed out of the studio. "Someone said to me 'That's unfair,' so as an act of charity I let her record 'I Should Be So Lucky,' which Mike wrote in forty minutes while she was waiting. Out of pity. But I've only just heard it. Same time as you."

"I'll offer two hundred and fifty thousand pounds for the Kylie contract," said Cowell.

"No," replied Waterman.

"Three hundred thousand?" offered Cowell.

"No," said Waterman. "We'll take the risk."

The record became a worldwide number 1 hit, but only number 28 in the United States.

In consolation, Waterman agreed that Cowell could have the song "Instant Replay" for Yell!, a boy duo he had created. The song reached number 8 on the charts. The duo's popularity then dipped and Cowell began beseeching Waterman to allow Fanfare to produce *The Hit Factory 2,* the second compilation album of Stock Aitken Waterman hits. Waterman agreed. The kudos for Cowell was that the record companies allowed their hit songs to be included on the album and therefore, by default, on Fanfare's label, so Cowell could claim to have Kylie, Donna Summer, and other stars under contract.

The only hiccup was a successful legal action by George Michael against Cowell for misusing his music in a mix.

Cowell was still scratching for crumbs. Among them was Waterman's success with Sonia, a lackluster artist singing "You'll Never Stop Me Loving You."

"How did you manage that?" Cowell asked Ron McCreight.

"TV's doing it," replied McCreight, showing Cowell a list of TV shows with music.

"I didn't realize there were so many TV shows," said Cowell, more than ever intrigued by the process. There was no graduate entry program to the music industry even for those who had studied marketing. Access for music producers to TV depended increasingly on fantasy statements like, "We've got a four-hundred-thousand-pound promotion budget for this record," which would prompt a producer to reply, "Wow, we'd better look at this." Cowell's problem was credibility. Fanfare could never afford an impressive budget and despite agreeing with Waterman to produce another "Hit Factory" album, he had failed to find a new star.

Like so many independent labels, Fanfare had hit the skids. It could no longer afford to buy any good music even from Waterman. Its only recent success, Yell!'s "Let's Go Round Again," had produced insufficient profits. Fanfare was struggling, sparking the deterioration of Cowell's relations with Burton.

"You should realize," Burton told a relative of Cowell's during one of his many visits to Cowell's family home, "that Simon would be useless without me." Over Sunday lunch, Burton told Julie Cowell, "Your son owes everything to me." Burton won her gratitude for that generosity without revealing that his business's borrowings had run out of control. All of Fanfare's capital was being diverted by Burton to sustain Audio Fidelity, a disastrous investment that was sliding toward insolvency. Burton needed cash, and the threat by a major shareholder at a board meeting in their new offices in St. John's Wood to pull out had caused Cowell new fears. Burton had literally locked the office door to prevent the shareholder from leaving. "We need the money and you can't leave without committing yourself," Burton said. After witnessing a ferocious argument, Cowell and others were astounded as the shareholder climbed out of a window and ran.

Maurice Veronique, a close friend of both Cowell brothers from Windsor College who was also employed at Fanfare, warned Cowell of the company's predicament. "Burton's greed driven," said Veronique. "It's all heading for collapse." In particular, Veronique was surprised by the public company's finances, which were beyond Cowell's understanding. "It's getting very messy," Veronique warned Cowell, whose financial acumen amounted to spending everything he earned. "Iain knows how to play all the games," added Veronique. "I'm getting out."

With £250,000 tied up in the company's worthless shares, Cowell had little option but to stay, although he would remain permanently baffled by Burton's financial engineering. His naïveté was secondary to his resentment toward Burton. Their relationship remained close but tinged with Cowell's anger that his employer's egoism was holding him back. As the face of Fanfare Records, he had been transformed from the humiliated loner into an A&R man commanding some acknowledgment. But now their predicament was aggravated, not least by a telephone call Sinitta made to Burton.

As Burton told it, Sinitta had argued with Cowell and decided on payback. "Something was really bugging her," Burton said.

She told Burton, "Simon's been having an affair with Vanya for at least a year."

"Don't be ridiculous," said Burton, who described himself as "simply dumbstruck and unable to breathe. It hit me like a thunderbolt." Although his relationship with Vanya had already come to a painful end, he did not imagine that his best friend, whom he loved, would get into his old bed. In Burton's melodramatic words, "Simon stabbed me in the back. In one go I lost the woman I loved and my best friend. They're the two people I love most in the world. It's so painful."

"Why did he do it?" Burton asked Sinitta.

"Don't you understand?" replied Sinitta. "He wants to be you."

As Burton's financial troubles increased, he did not dare mention his anger and hurt about Vanya to Cowell. Although the tension produced by working in the same office as Cowell was, in Burton's opinion, unbearable, he needed Cowell's support to survive. "It was the beginning of the end," said Burton. "Our relationship was irreparably damaged."

Dismissive of the financial meltdown, Cowell traveled to Acapulco for a vacation, ignoring Burton's pleas for support in a boardroom battle to save the company. Upon his return to London, he arranged a champagne party with crowds of attractive girls at Villa Cesari to celebrate the second "Hit Factory" album, released in time for Christmas 1989. Waterman had been amenable to the deal. The previous album had earned good profits and, as he left the party enjoying "all the froth," Waterman expected the same again.

Soon after the profits—at least £500,000—began to roll in, Burton lost his battle to save Audio Fidelity. "I didn't know what was happening," Cowell would tell Waterman. "It was a shock when it ended quickly." Although Burton had separated Fanfare from the risk of insolvency, Waterman's expected income from the album, about £250,000, disappeared into the debt-ridden public company.

More seriously, Cowell lost the same amount he had borrowed from the bank to buy Audio Fidelity shares; his flat and his Porsche had also been bought on credit. Overnight his glamorous lifestyle financed by credit cards had crashed. Unable to pay his mortgage, he suddenly lost his home and car, and could not repay the loan for the worthless shares. "Successful but broke" was Sinitta's verdict, bewildered by Burton's financial management.

"I've lost everything," the thirty-three-year-old told his father, "and I've lost my car." As an afterthought he added, "I've also lost my flat. I'll have to rent."

"We have a spare room here. Come and live with us," said Eric, who with Julie was renting a flat in a large house owned by Nicholas in the Swiss Cottage district of London. Nicholas and his family also lived in the house. Eric, who had retired five years earlier, had just returned to London after spending nearly five years in Majorca. He bought Simon a red Triumph TR6 for seven thousand pounds. "I'll never borrow money again," pledged Cowell.

The family safety net had once again saved Cowell from a life of poverty. With a loan from his father, he lived on about two hundred pounds a week, dating a beautiful brunette he had been introduced to by Kim Cowell, Nicholas's wife. A hostess on *Sale of the Century,* a TV quiz show, she went on vacation with Cowell and his parents to Thailand, but soon Cowell was complaining, "She's too clingy." He had enjoyed the chase and, having succeeded, became disinterested.

On his return, to resolve his £250,000 debt for the worthless shares, he negotiated with the Midland Bank to repay £60,000 over four years using a loan offered by NatWest against his father's guarantee. To everyone, Cowell appeared relaxed about his fate. "I feel almost a sense of release in a strange way," he told his father. "Like all these burdens have suddenly disappeared and I genuinely don't miss any of them." The façade concealed his real fear. "I haven't ever been more unhappy than now," he told a friend. "I've always been fairly jittery but this is bad." In turn, the pressure suffocated his girlfriend as well. "I've never believed this is going to last forever," he told her. Like other women, she would find that his generous gifts and endless attention counted for little once he decided the commitment was too onerous. After six months, she flew to Hong Kong, leaving behind a man unwilling to face the prospect of unemployment: "I literally had to start again with nothing," he said. "It was a pretty awful time."

Burton had extricated Fanfare from Audio Fidelity before the crash and hoped to continue in business with Cowell. Inevitably there were strains, partly because of Cowell's secret relationship with Vanya; a larger conflict, though, was Burton's reengagement with the record business, which had become Cowell's domain. Ignoring the simmering tension, the two men opened an office in Putney and planned to launch "Ritmo de la Noche," a Brazilian dance track. Fighting for his turf, Cowell resisted Burton's choice of the singers and dancers. "I've discovered this fabulous sexy Brazilian girl called Karen," enthused Cowell, "and she'll be brilliant." Burton agreed and invested fifty thousand pounds on promotion, including a stunning video of Karen leading the Mystic group in a song and dance routine. In reality, Karen was lip-synching to words sung by Maria, a Spanish vocalist. Eight TV appearances had been arranged and the two were thrilled by the market buzz. "We'll earn a million pounds from this," predicted Burton. "It'll be the summer hit. We'll be saved."

On a Sunday morning in the spring of 1990, on the eve of the launch, Cowell was roused from his sleep by a call from an investor in the project.

"Have you seen today's *News of the World*?" she raged.

"No," replied Cowell blearily.

"Well, your Karen is all over the front page. She's a hooker. She offered her services to a reporter and that's blown everything."

Now Cowell understood why Karen kept disappearing into the office corner to take calls on her cellphone. It was all over and he was to blame. Burton accused Cowell of having sacrificed his judgment because of a sexual relationship with the prostitute. "Not really," replied Cowell sheepishly. "It was just a K and a C"—a kiss and a cuddle.

That loss was compounded by Cowell trying to relaunch Sinitta with a song from Pete Waterman. Without faith in the project, Burton had agreed to press five thousand singles, but an invoice arrived for sixty thousand. Just why Cowell had wasted so much money in an inevitable flop was never explained. By then, Cowell had decided that "there were two birds in the nest and there wasn't room for both of us." The only solution, they agreed, was to sell Fanfare.

Offers were invited from PolyGram (which became Universal) and the German Bertelsmann Music Group (BMG), the fifth largest record company (after PolyGram, EMI, Sony [CBS], and Warner), led by John Preston, the chairman. To Cowell's irritation, PolyGram rejected the offer to buy Fanfare despite, in Cowell's opinion, "my great presentation." In revenge, Cowell refused their offer to accept the "Man of the Year" award at a music event in July 2004.

Burton began negotiations with John Preston, a levelheaded businessman appointed to reverse the music business's decade of cocaine use and financial profligacy. The counterrevolution, Preston decided, should include promoting pop and dance music beloved by white middle-class boys like Cowell and ignored by most of the independent companies. Cowell's friendships with television producers added to Preston's interest in a man with a reputation for a magnetic personality who habitually refused to take no for an answer. His strategy was decided while Cowell and Burton were pitching in his office for RCA, part of BMG, and their investment in Fanfare. Preston's telephone rang. "Is Simon there?" asked Pete Waterman. Pop music's God was telephoning for Cowell, thought Preston. His interest in Burton evaporated. In Preston's mind, the complexity of financing Fanfare had resolved itself.

For a different reason, Cowell's relations with Burton also finally cracked. Angry about becoming the victim of unsatisfactory financial management, Cowell was outraged that his employer intended to sell Fanfare without dividing the proceeds despite his original 25-percent stake. "If you don't give me my share," warned Cowell, "I'll go without you." Burton ignored the ultimatum.

To Burton's surprise, he arrived on Monday morning and discovered that Cowell had abandoned their office. "He's walked off without saying goodbye," fumed Burton. Throughout that week, Cowell ignored Burton's calls and, to avoid confrontation, ran away when Burton approached him in the street.

"Iain never thought I would leave," recalled Cowell, pleased to have taken the career-defining move.

"I can't blame Simon thinking about himself," Burton said years later. "The situation was messy and not of Simon's making. But he could have been loyal as a friend."

Cowell had already set up IQ Records, his own company, as a consultant A&R man for John Preston. Assigned to the RCA label for fifty thousand pounds per annum, he was guaranteed a 50-percent share of the profits in a joint venture if he delivered a number of records and sales over the following year. In Preston's view, "I fired Burton," but he was unaware of the unresolved disputes between Cowell and Burton.

"I never saw him again," said Burton. "He couldn't face me." On reflection, Burton was sore: "His priority was to be successful and in the limelight no matter what the cost or risk to the bottom line. And in the end, Simon exhibited an utterly ruthless streak and showed no sense of personal loyalty toward me." Cowell prefers not to reply to that accusation.

Cowell's comfort was Waterman's forgiveness over his own £250,000 loss. Cowell did not apologize and, in Waterman's opinion, "He didn't need to. He didn't do it on purpose. He was a mate. I've lost more and didn't care. I liked Simon and just moved on to make more hits and more money." Waterman's only comment was a homily to Cowell about his predicament: "If you're not at the top, you're going nowhere."

3

ENDLESS HUMILIATION

JOHN PRESTON HAD THROWN COWELL A LIFELINE, BUT COWELL SUF-
fered no illusions. In the music industry, success was exaggeratedly
worshiped and failure was punished by swift expulsion. "My job was
precarious because I was thirty-three and I hadn't signed 'the big
group,'" Cowell said. "I had failed because I wasn't good enough at
that time. I wasn't stupid about my situation." After setting up IQ
Records' office in George Street, Cowell tried to operate as RCA's consultant but his plight got worse.

Among the first visitors to his office was Nigel Martin-Smith, the
manager of Take That, a boy band that had started in 1989. Over the
previous two years, the group's songs had flopped. Among the critics was Waterman, who had damned the group on his TV show *Hit
Man and Her,* as "tacky." Martin-Smith needed a major record company to risk a million pounds to relaunch the group. Like all major
music corporations, RCA gambled its revenue from its back catalogue to nurture talent, accepting that bankrolling failure was a
necessary risk. Artists were cast off once they were no longer worth
the bet.

Cowell was faced with a dilemma. Risking a million pounds in the
first weeks of his consultancy on a group described as "pure gay porn"

was unnatural and, without Burton's guidance, Cowell's uncertainty exposed him as indecisive. Eventually, after listening again to two new songs, Cowell told Martin-Smith, "I don't like the lead singer; he's too fat, but I would be interested without him." "Over my dead body," replied Martin-Smith. Cowell was not disappointed. He didn't believe in the group. Soon after, Cowell moved into RCA's building. Walking around the office dressed in his normal uniform—a white T-shirt and high-waisted trousers—and lightly leading Harry, a bad-natured Yorkshire terrier belonging to Sinitta, he introduced himself and Vanya Seager, whom he had brought with him as his assistant. The former model had no office experience—she couldn't even type—but she needed an income. She would be loyal, Cowell reasoned and, he thought, according to friends, "handy" in the office. He had offered her the job after they had bumped into each other accidentally.

Entering Mr. Sing's, a Chinese restaurant in Earl's Court, he had been taken to a table where Vanya was waiting for "Mr. Cowell." To Cowell's surprise, she was waiting for his brother, whom she was also dating. The brothers enjoyed swapping girlfriends and Simon stepped in, restarting their relationship. Soon after he brought her on as his assistant, however, he complained to Denise Beighton, RCA's national sales manager, "She's too possessive. She's driving me nuts." He needed his personal space but resisted firing her. Seager covered for his unpunctuality, disorganized schedule, and endless loss of car keys, papers, CDs, and glasses. Before he left the office, she always made sure he was holding his cellphone, a packet of cigarettes, and pills to relieve his frequent migraines. Daily, she crossed the road to the local greasy spoon to buy a sausage in a roll for his lunch. In return, he bought her endless gifts.

"Could you tell Simon I'd like the bag that so-and-so has got in the magazine?" Vanya would tell Denise Beighton, referring to a celebrity star, and he usually obliged. In their fiery relationship, which provoked curiosity in the office, Seager tolerated her boyfriend/employer enjoying himself at lap-dancing clubs but complained bitterly when he bought a lap dancer a Gucci coat for three thousand pounds. "I hate him going off with other girls," she complained whenever they separated. His happiness with women regarded by others as sleazy irritated even a former topless model. "Can you find out who he went out with last night?" she frequently asked Beighton, who in turn would be asked a similar question by Cowell: "She's being so secretive. What did she do last night?"

The jealousy was bewildering even for Beighton, who was forging a close friendship with Cowell: "He was terribly camp and there was no sexiness about him," she said. To those who speculated to Beighton that "Simon's gay," she would reply, "He's not gay. He sleeps with girls." But she was puzzled by his "girliness"—when he visibly winced if a woman's period was mentioned, for instance. "Girls with a period," he told Beighton jokingly, "should be locked in a room with straw on the floor." Beighton concluded that her new friend was "complex" and "had an intimacy problem." After watching him for some months, she decided that he loved and chased beautiful women but disliked the details of their female lives.

His priority was to ingratiate himself with RCA's other A&R men, a competitive group. As at all music companies, the people he was working among commonly used recreational drugs—marijuana and cocaine. Some used amphetamines and acid. Despite Preston's ambitions in an era of diminishing scandal and rebellion, drugs and sex remained intertwined with the company's culture.

Preston expected RCA to sign between seven and ten artists a year, hoping that two cash cows would support the rest. To survive, Cowell needed to find one of the successes in an alien atmosphere.

RCA's head of A&R was Korda Marshall, a rock-music fundamentalist whose staff was told to "search for talent at gigs, pubs, rehearsals, sports centers, youth clubs, and at the end of the pier." During their weekly meetings, Marshall expected his six A&R men to discuss the charts and the opportunities for new signings. His handicap against giants like Warners, who had sixty million pounds to spend, was his limited budget—nine million pounds. In his cutthroat world, Marshall understood that his own survival depended on his A&R men's performance. Knowing that the casualty rate to justify the money at stake was high, Marshall did not warm to the new arrival who joked that while the "cool people" went to "two or three smelly gigs every night, I do my A&R watching TV at home." In Marshall's words, "Cowell doesn't go to clubs where his feet stick to the floor—he stands on glass for showbiz." Sensing the discord between Cowell and Marshall, Preston diverted Cowell in a new direction.

Cowell's arrival coincided with the decision to rejuvenate the Arista label as a platform for Clive Davis, the legendary New York producer, who had been dismissed as president of CBS Records amid accusations of fraud, to get back into the business. Famous for acts like the Grateful Dead, Dionne Warwick, Whitney Houston, and many others, Davis regarded the London operation as "my gateway into Europe to sell my records." Davis expected Diana Graham, Arista's new managing director in London, to also massage his ego and supply music that he could sell in the United States. If she failed to deliver within three years, she would be dismissed. The principal drawback was Arista's lack of artists, a problem that Cowell was expected to cure. His moment in the sun with Sinitta had passed, but Preston, trusting that Cowell possessed the relationships to promote pop music, urged Graham to rely on the maverick.

Initially, Cowell found Davis's backwater a welcome sanctuary. Pertinently, neither Preston nor Graham was aware of Cowell's financial plight. Concealing his emotions, Cowell lived by his parents' mantra of "get on with it" and smothered his bosses with charm. In the roller-coaster music world it was usual to be up one minute and down the next, and being penniless was not necessarily a stigma. Survival in the business depended, some insiders would say, on "woodshedding"—the accumulation of expertise. To rise from the bottom and survive, Cowell had listened to awful music until he had focused on a strand that he could justify as commercially viable. Next, he had forged connections and relationships with those he rated as trustworthy and talented. Others called it the "kiss up, kick down" technique. That was the "woodshedding" dynamic, which transformed indecisive men into those who were confident about their judgment. The only pitfall Cowell had not anticipated was that Preston, against Graham's wishes, would appoint Nigel Grainge and Chris Hill as Arista's A&R team for rock music.

Grainge and Hill had earned credibility in the business. Working at the cutting edge with Chris Blackwell and Island records, and later at Ensign Records, they had produced Eddy Grant, the Boomtown Rats, 10cc, the Waterboys, Sinéad O'Connor, and other successful artists. After selling Ensign to Chrysalis Records in 1986, Grainge felt that he "had a pretty hot reputation." Proudly, he was a harsh purist in the rock scene and disdained Arista. "It's got no culture," he announced. "It's got to be created by a new A&R team, which is me." Like most rock A&R men, Grainge would race between gigs every night and listen to demo tapes throughout the day.

Looking across the large open-plan office, Grainge noticed Cowell in "a cubby hole." Opinionated about music and placing his judgment above commercial profits, Grainge was dismissive of a man floating in a comfort zone without cultural credibility. Cowell was infamous for worshiping Frank Sinatra—a decidedly uncool affliction—and disparaging most modern music, which he hardly played. "I love Sinatra's music and his way of life, especially the drinking and smoking," admitted Cowell.

In an introductory conversation, Grainge gave an honest opinion about Cowell's past records. "Your stuff is shit," he declared loudly. "We're on different planets. We've had success and you haven't." The chance of an amicable relationship seeped away as Grainge kicked Cowell's credibility, leaving him struggling for breath.

First, Cowell tried once again to revive Sinitta. Although he was penniless, he paid three hundred pounds a month for hair extensions for her and would patiently listen to her frustrated tirades on the telephone, occasionally putting the receiver down to light a cigarette while she ranted. Then, ignoring their turbulent relationship, he hired Ian Levine to produce a recording of "Love Is the Only Solution" by Maxine Nightingale and watched Levine's mix at the Chiswick studios. "I love it," he declared. The following day, Vanya Seager reported, "He loves it so much that he's playing it all the time. He's been dancing around his office." Levine was thrilled. Cowell was notorious for stopping disagreeable records after seconds. Twenty-four hours later, Cowell changed his mind. The recording was abandoned and he released another song by Sinitta, which flopped.

Next, he signed Sonia, the twenty-year-old from Lancashire made famous in 1989 by Waterman's production of "You'll Never Stop Me Loving You." Although the song hit number 1 and there were other successes, Waterman and the singer parted in 1991. Cowell hired Nigel Wright to produce "Only Fools Never Fall in Love" for her. Signing a Waterman product, Cowell imagined, propelled him into a higher league, but he had ignored the reason for Waterman's decision to let her go. Sonia was short, looked dumpy on television, and rejected advice on what to wear. After she reached number 10 with Cowell, her career declined, despite appearing, like Sinitta, on TV. "I don't know what to do with her," Cowell told Beighton and cast her adrift.

His next hope was Allison Jordan, an attractive blonde whom he was also chasing romantically. He persuaded BBC TV's *That's Life!* to stage a talent show and Jordan became his favorite to win. Promoting her popularity and thus propelling her to victory in May 1992 singing "The Oldest Living Boy in New York" was not difficult, and in an extraordinary eight-minute plug, the BBC featured Cowell, among others, predicting a hit at number 5, or even number 1. "The record's cheap and nasty," Beighton told Cowell. "Those sort don't sell." Even Jordan spotted the tackiness. Holding the cover on television, she announced, "They've spelt my name wrong." Allison had been spelled with one "l." The record reached number 23 on the charts and disappeared. Sometime later, Cowell recalled, "We had a brief thing. She'd done her boobs."

In the midst of those forlorn productions, Cowell heard terrible news. Six months after he had rejected Take That, Korda Marshall was negotiating with Nigel Martin-Smith to sign the group for RCA and planning to invest over a million pounds. To avoid the potential embarrassment, Cowell called Martin-Smith and made an offer. "Fuck off," replied the manager. Days later he signed with RCA. Martin-Smith, Cowell realized, would make sure that Marshall knew about Cowell's rejection.

The backwash intensified Grainge's antagonism. Cowell was damned for massaging TV producers and newspaper journalists to promote forgettable pop. "Nothing seems fast enough for him," carped Grainge, a man proud of nurturing artistic genius. He had sympathizers in RCA, not least Korda Marshall. Cowell, Marshall agreed, was "unashamedly a pop tart with appalling taste and blatantly commercial." In an unusual burst of anger, Cowell snapped back, "Korda's so up his own ass." His anger was really with himself for rejecting Take That. "I'm feeling sick," Cowell confessed to his father. "I lost a good signing." His father, he hoped, could explain why things were going wrong, but even Eric, he realized, could not teach judgment. "I was bruised and frustrated," said Cowell later. "I had to toughen myself up."

To compensate for his mistake, Cowell began searching for another boy band. The idea was not new. Every decade, a new cycle of music producers scrutinized sexy young men flashing Ultra Brite smiles while they danced and sang pop to appeal to a new generation of teenage girls who disliked rock. The producers' trick was to find teenage boys blessed with delicate good looks who could be packaged to flatter the cult of youth. In the 1960s there had been the Beatles and the Monkees, the Osmonds and the Bay City Rollers in the 1970s, and in the 1980s, Wham! and the New Kids on the Block. In 1992, at a studio in Chertsey, Cowell began auditioning a group of black teenage dancers for a boy band to be called Chaos. Nigel Wright, the producer, looked forlorn. None could sing. "You're making a fool of yourself," Ian Levine told Cowell when asked for help. One hundred young black singers appeared for an audition organized by Levine.

"Crap, you're no good," cursed Levine, dispensing most applicants after less than a minute.

"You're heartless," gasped Cowell, standing in the background.

"I'm not going to waste my time," replied Levine. He chose a nine-year-old to lead the group of five and brought the singer-songwriter who replaced Smokey Robinson in the Miracles from America to add vocals to the new record. By the time the record was completed, Cowell was dejected.

Uncertain about his judgment, he decided on a whim to abandon Chaos.

"I just didn't get the feel for it," he explained. "There was no momentum. I was pushing uphill."

Chaos would be relaunched as Ultimate Kaos by another producer. Their modest hits embarrassed Cowell.

"Cowell's been fabulously unsuccessful," Levine chortled.

"I didn't know what I was doing," Cowell later admitted. "It's incredible how stupid I was through lack of experience."

His only consolation was that despite Korda Marshall spending a million pounds on Take That, commissioning two songs from Levine, the group still languished. Cowell was not disappointed when Preston fired Marshall. Desperate to rescue RCA from total disaster, Preston risked another million pounds on the group.

Regularly, BMG's German directors held three-day conferences for sixty A&R men summoned from America and Europe to a hotel to present their best recordings and receive either congratulations or a "run down" for bad offerings. At the Excelsior Hotel in Rome, Cowell presented his latest from Worlds Apart, a boy band that he had created. Minutes after hearing the track, his rivals renamed the group "Cheeks Apart." Cowell deflected the criticism by joking about "scary Germans" and was soon embraced by colleagues who found him entertaining. Unusually in the music business, his self-confidence was untainted by crushing arrogance. Back in London, Cowell spoke about "that ghastly convention which I despised" and was blasted by Grainge. "I can't stand your shit pop," he told Cowell. "Signing camp boy bands and worshipping remixes of Barry Manilow!" Arista's reputation was bad enough, he continued, and would fail to win respect "if we're contaminated by pop."

Cast as the Antichrist, Cowell let the hostility pass over his head. Only a fool, he knew, revealed his weakness to an enemy. His apparent helplessness was a source of strength. Grainge, he accepted, was "into serious music," and he laughed off a drunken accounts employee telling him loudly at the Christmas party, "Oh, you're that idiot who signs all that shit." But in the new year, his plight worsened.

Three singles by Worlds Apart released during 1993 only reached between 20 and 51 on the charts, reinvigorating Grainge's regular denunciations. "I'm not putting out any more of this shit," said

Grainge, a man who boasted about being "pretty strict" with his values and who enjoyed, as his own brother, the fellow music executive Lucian Grainge, revealed, "battle-scarring people."

By the end of his second year, as his boy bands failed to gel, the ridicule crushed Cowell. "I felt very alone," he said. "I was empty, desperate. If enough people tell you you're an idiot you start to believe it. It was typical in the A&R culture that if it's not a great time commercially you lose your self-confidence. It was a miserable time."

Looking over her domain, Diana Graham concluded, "Arista has become a full-scale battle. The atmosphere is foul." Graham was Cowell's only ally. "He's absolutely charming," said Graham of her employee. Although Cowell was not making profits, he was at least generating some turnover, unlike Grainge and Hill, who spoke a lot but had produced only losses. Her affection inflamed Hill's irritation about a man who habitually arrived late, driving "a flash car": "I can't understand his relationship with women. Cowell just schmoozes with them." Like others, Hill was puzzled that Cowell was dating beautiful women yet aroused speculation about his sexuality. Even Graham shared a bystander's observation about Cowell's aggression: "He can be a total bitch about people. He keeps saying a person is 'so ugly.' He wants everyone to be good looking," Graham said.

As news about the warfare leaked out beyond the confines of the company, Jonathan King, a music-industry grandee who published the influential *Tip Sheet* magazine, initiated peace talks over lunch. Grainge and Hill reluctantly arrived at a Chinese restaurant in Whiteleys, the shopping center on Queensway, to meet Cowell and King. "You are three people I really like," said King, "and I want you to get on." Cowell smiled approvingly. He was adept at dispelling hostility in a showbiz way and could charm anyone, including, momentarily, Grainge. By the end of the meal, the combination of King's salesmanship and Cowell's charisma appeared to reconcile the former enemies.

The peace was short-lived. Teamwork, Cowell cursed, was "a big lie to me." At the next weekly marketing meeting, he played another "Roland Rat" record. "Oh my God," spluttered Grainge. "You may laugh at this," continued Cowell, playing another record, this one of hillbilly music, "but I've got seven TV stations lined up this weekend." The following week he offered "Sound of the Universe," an African dance record. "I can sell some of these," he said. "You should be head of TV promotions," mocked Hill, irked that Cowell had even placed a record on BBC's six o'clock news. "Let's do this one by Nik Kershaw," suggested Cowell about the reissue of his 1980s hit "Wouldn't It Be Good." After fifteen seconds, Grainge turned off the machine and drew a zero on his flip chart.

"This isn't art," Grainge spat.

"Well, I don't know how you would promote what you've just played," countered Cowell. Broken for the day, he headed to Denise Beighton and Vanya Seager for comfort. "Why do these people hate me? What have I done to them?" At the next meeting, he resolved to secretly carry a tape recorder.

"I'm hard done by," Cowell complained to Diana Graham, but Graham was so frightened by Grainge that publicly she put Cowell down as well. Once she walked into Cowell's office as he was listening to a proposed song and said, smiling, "Simon, don't even think of signing that." The humiliation, Cowell felt, was total. "The records aren't selling the way I want," he complained. Arista's publicity machine could not promote pop music. Unlike other A&R men, Cowell attended every RCA marketing meeting to understand the business culture. Selling, he believed, was more important than art.

Repeatedly Cowell argued with Arista's lackluster publicists about their failure to place his music on radio or television. To prove his point, he once waited until they admitted that they hadn't been able to place Whitney Houston's "I Will Always Love You" on radio or TV. Then he arranged mass coverage for the new track in the media. Afterward, the embarrassed publicists were not allowed to forget that he had rescued them. In the music business, he knew, no one enjoyed someone else's success. Everyone shared the fate of an ungenerous career, which ended either on top or on the skids.

"You're not helping," Grainge snapped at Cowell, irritated that there was again no new rock record to offer Clive Davis on his next visit.

Davis's A&R conventions were a living hell. After ordering that the room temperature be reduced to near freezing to keep his staff awake—some brought blankets—Davis would play his latest R&B records and extol their virtues in excruciating detail. "They're hits," he would emphasize as an introduction, expressing dismay that Cowell's records did not "cross over" to Europe or America. He declared that a rockabilly album could never sell in America, and would not even be released in England because it was so bad. And he lambasted Grainge for failing to unearth a new group. The criticism hurt. "Arista is awful," Grainge complained. "It's lost its way." Cowell's continued presence made it worse. Grainge wanted Cowell out and Cowell's own conduct helped Grainge's campaign. "In the middle of a really tedious presentation at a weird off-site meeting," Cowell would admit, "I just lost it and started laughing. And I couldn't stop laughing. And a guy actually told me in front of about twenty people to leave the room. Like I was a six-year-old. And at that point I just thought, I can't do this. But I was fearful that if I didn't toe the line they would fire me." Waterman understood the ambivalence Cowell excited: "Simon can be offensive because he thinks it's funny." The renewed blistering arguments prompted Graham to appeal for help to John Preston. "Hold on and see what happens," Preston replied. The battles entrenched Cowell's attitudes against those "cynical and snobby people in the music business who I despise." Arista's office, he concluded, was "a space—physically and mentally—where everyone has become the enemy."

Cowell's strength was to conceal his emotions. He was rarely rude, even to his critics, and frequently generous. At the end of lunch in a neighboring PizzaExpress, he would pay for the table, sometimes for a dozen people, despite his financial plight. "I had a unique ability to ride lows," he explained. "When things went wrong I realized it was my fault and I had to repair it." Ever since his near bankruptcy, Cowell had accepted that "actually it's me that gets myself into a situation." The paradox of his struggle against adversity at Arista was, with Eric's support, the strengthening of his self-confidence. Relying on his father's advice did not end after he had moved out of his parents' flat and bought Coombe Kanata, a house on Kingston Hill in west London, for £800,000 with a big loan. In their frequent conversations, Eric encouraged his son to stick to his convictions. "Be patient," advised the permanent optimist. "Expect to cock things up and believe that you can work things out." His fault, Cowell realized, was "to believe my own hype, and while going through a sticky patch start blaming the world." Musically, he still loved Frank Sinatra and little else. Asked at a BMG group meeting how he discovered new music, he replied, to unanimous disdain, "I read *The Sun* to see what people want."

Although Cowell's successful competitors were earning high profits from what he called their obsession to sign new rock groups, he sat at home watching TV and asking, "How can I turn this into a record?" In spring 1992, he noticed that within one hour of the American World Wrestling Federation's announcing a show at Wembley Arena, sixty-two thousand tickets had been sold, two-thirds of the stadium's capacity. The Sky network's broadcast of the show attracted an audience of six hundred thousand. Cowell, impressed by the numbers, arranged breakfast in Holland Park with the show's manager. By the end of the meal he had come up with a new idea. Instead of arranging for a musician to appear on TV, he would use TV stars to make a record. The same afternoon, he called Vince McMahon, the WWF boss in Upstate New York. Ignoring the probability that none of the wrestlers could sing, he told McMahon that Arista wanted to make an album. "Come over to talk about it," agreed McMahon. At a regular A&R ideas meeting, Cowell announced his plan. "Fanatical kids watch the show and they'll buy the album," he said, enjoying Grainge's predictable outrage. "So long as one of the wrestlers can sing, we can do the rest." Even Diana Graham was aghast. "She went on her knees and begged me not to do it," he told Waterman as they flew to New York.

Waterman went for the ride because there was money to be earned and he sympathized with his friend's plight: "He was categorized as a novelty merchant. The industry had put him in a box, pushed him to one side, and thrown away the key. They hoped he could be buried. No one had time for Simon and he wasn't happy." Nor was Waterman happy after they entered the WWF's headquarters in Stamford, Connecticut. Greeted by seriously heavy characters exuding men-

ace, Cowell made a charming introduction and then, without warning, announced, "Pete will tell you about it. Over to you, Pete."
Flummoxed but never lost for words, Waterman spoke about his talents and success, fearing that any flaw risked an exit in a lead coffin
or his premature end in a concrete overcoat. "Okay," said McMahon.
"Done."

With the contract signed, the group's tracks were mixed by Mike
Stock in London. The single, released in September 1992, was a British number 3 hit. A subsequent album, released the following year,
was accompanied by a "Slam Jam Music Video" featuring wrestlers
dressed in garish clothes and dark glasses leaping or being thrown
from great heights onto a canvas ring accompanied by roaring music.
It would sell more than 1.3 million copies and reach number 4 on the
British charts, although it failed in America. His success at producing
profitable TV shows emboldened Cowell. He needed to escape
Grainge's outrage, get out of Arista, and get revenge. His target was
"people who have taken advantage of me in the past. I have a long
memory and I'm very patient. One day I'll get my revenge by being
more successful than them."

Diana Graham agreed. "He should join the boys," she said, and
suggested that Cowell should move across to his fun-loving contem-
poraries at RCA. His path was helped by Jonathan King. "You should
take on Simon," he urged the star executives at RCA. "He's good."
Cowell's priority, explained King, was commercial value rather than
"cool acts," and that inevitably meant the music was unworthy
and untrendy, but Cowell appealed to the silent majority who
bought two or three records a year. King's plea was transmitted to
John Preston.

"I can't bear this environment anymore," Cowell confirmed to
Preston. "If I've got to stay with the arty set and music snobs I'm leaving." Convinced that Cowell possessed unique qualities, BMG's
chairman decided to accommodate this mercurial character, who resisted housebreaking.

Finding a solution depended on RCA agreeing that they wanted
to work with Cowell. He had rejected Take That, which, after risking
a fortune, they had turned into a massive hit. The ideal test, they

agreed, would be their Easter skiing trip to Val d'Isère, France. Staying with Cowell in a small hotel, the RCA executives recognized that he was "bruised, desperate, and crestfallen." Cowell's wit gradually dissolved their doubts, while his limited skiing skills added to the hilarity.

Dressed in a Crombie coat, his interest was plainly in clothing rather than sport. Stiff-hipped, unwilling to bend his knees, and unable to carve the corners, he found difficulty even on the gentle runs and steered away from the more challenging trails. At the end of the vacation, the seven RCA employees held an Oscar ceremony that included an award for the week's most boring comment. Cowell won for describing the change of tires at Formula 1 races.

"You've passed the test," said a fellow producer at RCA. "Take six months off to get your mojo back. Come in when you've found what you want to do."

"I'm really going to fit in here," replied Cowell. "I never want to be that miserable again."

"I'm very grateful," Cowell would later tell Jonathan King. The experience hardened his resolve to surround himself in the future only with people who would nod and fall into line.

4

A HIT—AT LAST

ALTHOUGH COWELL HAD SUPPOSEDLY MOVED FROM HELL INTO SHOW-biz heaven, he remained the man who had rejected Take That.

At one of RCA's six monthly A&R conferences, he sat through Take That's new single "It Only Takes a Minute," which won applause, and was then asked to play Worlds Apart's latest track, "Together."

Diligently, he had arranged for the group to be taught to dance, launched on to the club circuit, fixed photo shoots for teen magazines, and charmed TV producers into booking them on Saturday-morning slots. His hype had predicted that Worlds Apart's record would rise to number 3. Instead, it reached number 88 on the British charts and disappeared. His record was beaten by Take That at number 1; "Around the World" by East 17, managed by his old rival Tom Watkins, was at number 2, selling three million copies. The Worlds Apart song was "a failure," Cowell admitted. "Sitting here is agony."

Equally excruciating, Ultimate Kaos's song "Some Girls" hit number 9 on the British charts. "Another very bad time," admitted Cowell. "After that, I dreaded the presentations at the annual marketing meetings because Take That would come up and make me feel sick." His attempts to compensate for his mistake compounded his error.

Insecure about his fate, he regularly asked Denise Beighton to walk with him from meetings to his office at the end of the corridor. "He hates being seen alone as he passes the secretaries," thought Beighton, sympathetic to his anxiety. "I love him to bits even though he's a laughingstock."

The cure, Cowell decided, was safety and success in his unique area of expertise: "manufactured pop" based on TV shows. No other A&R man sat watching children's television and relied on salesmen in retail shops. No other music producer would have enjoyed the *Mighty Morphin Power Rangers,* a new American program featuring teams of violent, costumed superheroes. His problem was not to persuade John Preston that an album could produce serious profits but that he could secure the rights. "Get on a plane and sign up the Power Rangers," Preston ordered. Cowell flew to Los Angeles fearing that failure could mean his dismissal from RCA.

"The deal's not going to happen," Cowell told himself thirty minutes after entering Saban Entertainment's headquarters. An executive employed by the billion-dollar children's entertainment empire had derided his offer and was, in Hollywood's brutal manner, forcefully bidding Cowell farewell. As the door opened, the executive's telephone rang. Haim Saban, the owner of the corporation, was asking in Hebrew who was in the room. "Go up and see him," Cowell was told.

"How much will you give?" Saban asked, referring to the rights.

"Not much," admitted Cowell, laughing, "but it would be a number one hit."

"What's the big deal about a number one?" asked Saban. "I've just earned half a million dollars by putting the Power Rangers on chewing gum paper, so why should I take your pennies?"

"Because you haven't got a gold record on your wall," replied Cowell.

"Okay," said Saban, laughing and offering his hand. "You've got a deal." Saban would do better than that—he later affixed a platinum record on his wall.

"Wherever there's a TV audience, I need to be there," Cowell recited. "Youth cult tie-ins" was his new buzz phrase. Television programs, he asserted, produced high sales by stoking emotions. With the production of the Power Rangers album under way, Cowell contracted an album for Zig and Zag, two furry puppets from the planet Zog featured in several different TV shows. "I felt that I was latching on to something unique," Cowell would write later, "that could potentially grow into a fantastic business. I would always say to people during this period, 'Laugh all you want. This is my target practice.'"

To conceal his frustrations, he gave a convincing impression of fearless unconcern about failure and disdain for the mockery while he dreamed of becoming a celebrity like Clive Davis or even Phil Spector. Darting in and out of the adjacent national sales office, he always asked the same question about rival colleagues: "How many records has he sold?"

"He's always angry about others' success," scoffed a skiing companion in France who had brought Kylie Minogue to RCA after she fell out with Waterman. "He's good at one-line put-downers of others after they've put in ten months' hard work. He's the biggest cuckoo in the building."

The competitiveness camouflaged his insecurity but he was delighted to chortle about "those imbeciles at Arista, most of whom are out of the business today." Grainge and Hill had been paid off, Diana Graham had also departed, and Arista in Britain was defunct. Yet despite the acrimonious contest, Cowell made unusually few enemies. By defining his own market, he had detached himself from the street fight among his competitors, seemingly heading toward a dead end. Self-confidently, at the beginning of that year's skiing trip, this one to Flims, Switzerland, Cowell moved out of the group's inferior rooms with pull-down bunks and took a bedroom in a nearby five-star hotel. He wanted comfort and style. All that eluded him was sufficient wealth to finance all his wishes.

Momentary success was followed by seeming permanent failure. Searching for another gimmick in 1995, Cowell signed Curiosity Killed the Cat, a four-man group whose unusual mix of jazzy and funky pop shot them to fame in 1986, with Andy Warhol appearing in the video of their hit "Misfit." Cowell was planning the group's

ill-conceived revival with "I Need Your Lovin'" when Denise Beighton walked into his office one Wednesday soon after he arrived at
eleven A.M. What she said changed Cowell's life.

"I watched *Soldier Soldier* last night, and it had me sobbing like a
baby," said Beighton, referring to an ITV television drama series
based on an army regiment languishing in the aftermath of the Cold
War. "If it can get to a hard bitch like me, you should take a look at it."

The hook, explained Beighton, was the two stars, Robson Green
and Jerome Flynn, singing "Unchained Melody," the 1955 hit revived by the Righteous Brothers in 1965 and again by *Ghost,* a Hollywood blockbuster, in 1990. "You should get them to make a
recording," suggested Beighton. "I'll make some calls," said Cowell.
At lunchtime he entered Beighton's office. "ITV doesn't want to co-
operate and the actors say they won't make a record. So that's it."

Two days later, Beighton returned. "Simon, you need to think
again," she said. "I could have sold a hundred thousand singles today.
The buyers for the high street shops haven't stopped asking whether
RCA could supply a recording by the two actors. The public wants it.
It'll be a definite number one." Beighton's prediction changed Cowell's attitude. His biggest dream, more than money and fame, was a
number 1 hit. Cowell's instant enthusiasm to produce a record by the
actors was dampened by Jeremy Marsh, RCA's chief executive, and
John Preston. Both doubted Cowell's prediction that a recording,
which would take months to release, could be successful. Prompted
by Beighton, Cowell ignored his superiors. Beighton's taste, he often
said, was typical of the average Briton, just the people he was targeting. "I only understood the real importance of TV after Robson and
Jerome were suggested to me," Cowell would say. Cowell was now
thirty-six; this was his decisive moment of transition from opportu-
nistic survival to a more considered strategy. The combination of experience and inspiration propelled him to bet everything on
Beighton's idea. His fate depended on getting a number 1 hit.

The skepticism within RCA was puny compared with Robson
Green's vehement rejection of Cowell's calls. Repeatedly, Cowell was
repelled by the actor and later by his agent, uttering threats of legal

action. Using the "never take 'no' for an answer" approach learned during his Fanfare era, Cowell switched his efforts to Green's mother until the actor finally telephoned to complain about harassment.

"Why won't you talk to me?" asked Cowell.

"Because I'm not interested."

"Why?"

"Because I don't want to appear on *Top of the Pops*," replied Green.

Cowell cut to the chase: "Listen to me. You both will get fifty thousand pounds for just two hours' work to record the song, even if it doesn't sell."

After a pause Green asked, "Are you prepared to put that in writing?"

On the eve of the two actors' arrival in Waterman's studio, Cowell was driving down the Westway spur toward Shepherd's Bush when he was inspired to add a twist. The media was in full cry about a free concert happening soon in Hyde Park to celebrate the fiftieth anniversary of VE Day. The star of the show would be Vera Lynn, the military's sweetheart during the Second World War, who rallied the troops in 1942 by singing "White Cliffs of Dover," among other songs. "We'll put that song on the B-side of a 'special,'" he decided.

"You're mad," Beighton told Cowell, who would need to persuade Robson Green and Jerome Flynn to record the second song as well.

Waterman, however, was impressed: "He never goes into a room thinking he knows the answers. He goes in with his ears open, fires a rocket, and sees who salutes it."

Soldier Soldier had been forgotten by the time Cowell arranged for his first meeting with the actors to sign the contracts.

"I don't know what Robson looks like," Cowell confessed to Beighton. "I've never watched the program." To avoid embarrassment, they agreed that she would greet Green first. In preparation, on the night before, Cowell also watched an England soccer match. Green, he knew, was a passionate supporter and he wanted material for a conversation. After a successful meeting, Cowell began plotting how to revive an old song into a number 1 hit.

Much depended on Mike Stock in Waterman's studios. He was

paid £180,000 to produce and mix the track to sound like a million-dollar Hollywood production. Stock ranked among the world's best producers and was dismissive of the A&R man—or the "Um and Ah" man, as he subsequently described Cowell—who didn't understand his art. So after delivering Robson and Jerome to Borough Road, Cowell did not stay for the recording. Two hours later, after the actors had left and the mixing began, Stock decided that a few vocals could be improved. As usual, he hired Des Dyer, the lead singer of the pop music group Jigsaw, as a session singer to "ghost" a few words, for which he was paid ten thousand pounds. Handing over the completed tape, Stock told Cowell, "You can make your fortune from this." Both laughed, although Cowell dreaded the skeptics within RCA eager for his failure: "I bet the houses on Robson and Jerome, but after Wrestlers and Power Rangers I knew what I was doing." The record was due to be released in November 1995, six months after the original TV program aired.

At nine A.M. every Monday morning, BMG's twenty managers met in the boardroom. As usual at the beginning of November, Beighton was present and "taking the flack for Simon, who never arrived before eleven A.M."

"How's our team of solicitors?" asked Preston, referring to Green and Flynn. "Denise, I really don't think we should release it."

"We should," insisted Beighton, infuriated by the sniggers and skepticism, "because it's going to be a number one." Cowell, she knew, had deliberately avoided the meeting to defend his own record because he was "paranoid and hated even thinking about people laughing about him." Preston's skepticism was supported by Clive Rich, BMG's business manager. "This guy's a liability," Rich told the meeting. "Simon's costing us too much." Rich's accounts showed that even Cowell's chart successes had been loss-makers. He spent so much in acquiring the artists and promoting the records that the profits disappeared. Now, Rich warned, Cowell was repeating his profligacy. Beighton ignored the doom mongers.

In the prelaunch marketing, Cowell called in every favor from his media friends to feature the actors on radio and television, including

Top of the Pops. His efforts failed. Both actors, unwilling to demean themselves as mere singers, rejected all appearances except on one program, Cilla Black's *Surprise, Surprise.*

Cowell had waged a blitz on newspapers and magazines and was roundly ignored by everyone except Piers Morgan, the pop columnist at the *Mirror,* who agreed to write a double-page plug for the record. Cowell also commissioned a slick video based on the film *A Brief Encounter.* In anticipation of some success, he even renegotiated his contract with BMG to remove the limit on his bonus. Preston agreed because he doubted that the public would buy the record.

Records in 1995 became hits if they sold about 150,000 copies during the first week. The independent shops, RCA's salesmen reported, were refusing to stock the record. Beighton, responsible for selling to the chain stores, called in favors and sold a hundred thousand records.

The night before the launch, twenty-two million people watched Robson and Jerome perform on *Surprise, Surprise.* Cowell's fate depended on whether the viewers' excitement of eight months earlier would be rekindled. The following morning, he nervously awaited the first day's sales. At lunchtime, he saw on the computer that RCA was shipping 350,000 copies and there were outstanding orders for nearly one million more. Overnight he had personally earned one million pounds.

"Oh, darling," Cowell gushed to Beighton, "I want to buy you something."

"My electric toothbrush broke this morning," replied his staunchest ally.

Cowell returned that afternoon with a Cartier watch and a Dunhill lighter.

That weekend, he went with his father to the local Currys electrical-appliance store in Swiss Cottage. "Unchained Melody" suddenly wafted from the store's speakers. "My son here made that," Eric told the sales assistant. Cowell protested his embarrassment, probably for the last time. As sales rose toward three million copies, he had won credibility among some, but criticism from the purists for "shameless commercialism and raw populism." The more perceptive realized that Cowell had "shifted the goal posts." Television, he proved, could produce stars as popular as those nurtured by the traditionalists, and they could earn as much money as "genuine artists" although they lacked credibility in the music world and would leave no legacy. In his euphoria, Cowell dismissed the carpers as "arty snobs." He craved fame but was satisfied with notoriety. Success was his revenge against his enemies. "I've become more than confident," he told a friend. "I don't care what everyone in the room is saying—if they're against me I tell them they're wrong." He spoke about enjoying every moment and taking nothing too seriously. "The thrill," he would say, "is not the money but the game."

The only shadow over his success with "Unchained Melody" was a dispute started by Des Dyer. After the song became a hit, the session singer asked Stock for a share of the unexpected bonanza, possibly 2 percent of the profits. The demand was laced with the threat of rumors that Dyer's voice rather than Green's was on the record. Session singers were a familiar noose around studios' necks. Instead of placating the angry Dyer, Stock resisted his demand. Undeterred, Dyer approached RCA. Initially, Preston ignored the allegation. After all, Nigel Wright, the producer of Robson and Jerome's first album, had reported, "Both can sing and I don't need session singers. Just a bit of tuning and editing." Cowell personally confronted Dyer. "I don't believe you," he said. But once the singer approached a tabloid newspaper in the week before Christmas to say "I'm the voice of Robson and Jerome," Cowell feared that a scandal would ruin his triumph. "This has become the worst week of my life," he told Stock melodramatically. "It's ridiculous to say Robson and Jerome can't sing. They sang on TV. I don't even believe you needed a session singer. You just brought up the backing during the mix."

Nevertheless he urged Preston to capitulate. Cowell's misfortune was the historic animosity between Stock and Preston. The producer had accused Preston, as head of the British Phonographic Industry (BPI), the music industry's trade organization, of having "rigged the market" to keep Stock Aitken's records out of the charts. Preston vehemently denied the allegation but acknowledged that other record companies had sent teams to buy their own records in the shops to push them up the charts, or had "bought up" space in the shops to exclude the independent labels. Even the Beatles' manager Brian Epstein admitted buying the chart place for the Beatles' first single back in 1962. BMG, insisted Preston, was innocent of that ruse and he had defeated Stock's litigation against the BPI. In that soured relationship, cooperation between Preston and Stock was impossible, even after they heard that the tabloid was about to publish Dyer's allegations. At his own expense, on December 20, Stock obtained an injunction against Dyer but Preston, at Cowell's behest, decided to buy peace. Since money was not a problem, he paid Dyer about £75,000 deducted from Stock's royalties.

With the problem squashed, Cowell focused on the follow-up to his big hit. After leading the eager Robson and Jerome back into the studio in early 1995 to record "I Believe," he persuaded the producer of BBC TV's National Lottery program, which had sixteen million viewers, to broadcast the duo singing their next new song, "Up on the Roof." The record went to number 1 with the sale of another million records; that was followed by "What Becomes of the Broken Hearted," another number 1 hit. To keep the tap flowing, in 1997, Cowell offered the duo three million pounds for another album. "Simon," replied Green, "you've made us a lot of money and we enjoyed it, but we're actors and this time we're going to say goodbye."

Green, the son of a miner, appeared to be bitter about the wealth Cowell had personally earned from his success and the estimated twenty million pounds in profits accumulated by RCA. Relations crumbled further after Cowell spotted Green and Vanya Seager kissing behind curtains on a TV set. He felt deceived and also feared a public backlash against the married actor.

"We're having an affair," Seager confessed to Beighton.

"You'll have to tell Simon the truth," Beighton urged.

One morning, Seager did not arrive for work. Unbeknownst to Cowell, she was pregnant and was planning to marry Green. Beighton watched Cowell's shocked reaction when he finally heard. "Simon, you've been very generous to Vanya and her daughter and you haven't been treated fairly," Beighton consoled her friend. His personal relationship with Green was terminated, but in consolation, he did at least possess enough tracks to produce a series of profitable "Robson and Jerome" compilation albums. He next met Green and Seager by coincidence in Mauritius on Christmas 2005 and they celebrated the new year together.

Nothing could now hinder a raft of new projects. With production-line creativity, Cowell began commissioning the casts of TV soaps to sing well-known pop songs. Millions of records had been sold when Cowell heard in 1997 that the BBC was selling the recording rights of *Teletubbies,* a popular children's program. RCA was quickly outbid by Telstar and Sony, prompting Cowell to show up at BBC's offices. "What's the highest bid so far?" he asked. "Three hundred and fifty thousand pounds," he was told. "Get all the lawyers in here," he told the bemused group. "I'm offering five hundred thousand, and I'll sign today." The public corporation could not refuse. "Some people will love these records," Cowell believed at the time, "others will loathe them. But as long as enough want to buy them, they serve their purpose." He personally visited the Woolworth's buyer and pre-sold half a million records to make another hit.

Cowell's pop and dance records, John Preston trilled, came out of "a brilliant strategy." RCA's market share had risen from 2 percent to 8 percent, prompting RCA's managers to claim credit for their inspired support of signing Green and Flynn, and rewrote Cowell's contract to increase his royalties, bonuses, and raises based on sales. The prospective sum, admitted RCA's manager, amounted to "a fantastic blue-sky package with the danger that he could earn more than Preston." With his new fortune, Cowell bought himself a black Jaguar XK8 and began looking for a house in Holland Park, one of London's most expensive districts.

To expand his niche and stymie rival labels and, in particular, Universal Music, Cowell next signed a million-pound agreement with Simon Jones, an executive with ITV who managed the business affairs of two major ITV companies, for RCA to buy the rights to any artists under contract by the broadcasters. Then he flew with Mike Stock to Hollywood. "We'll only do number ones now," Cowell declared as he sought the managers of Eddie Murphy, Antonio Banderas, and other TV stars. Every approach was rejected. He returned to London to hear that the "Singing Fireman," produced by Stock, had flopped, costing £100,000 and that Curiosity's latest record had also crashed. "A real donkey," said Korda Marshall, who was among many mocking the opinionated A&R man frequently seated at Mr. Chow's in Knightsbridge holding a Kool high in the air, as usual wearing trousers pulled high over his waist and exposing his hairy chest. "He always wants to come to the party but he's either not invited, or he comes and leaves early," said Marshall. His opinion was shared by Lucian Grainge, Cowell's rival at Universal. "Simon's not a credible A&R person. He's got a good name for concepts like *Teletubbies* and Zig and Zag, but he's a nebbish in the professional sense. Too clunky with artists and he can't talk to talent." In an industry employing at most five hundred people in key positions, somewhat like a private club, Cowell was flustered by his peers' continuing derision.

In desperation, he invited Ron McCreight for lunch. Expecting a good meal, McCreight found himself in a dingy café on the Putney Road with a cup of tea and a sandwich to hear Cowell's lament about a recent BMG international conference. As usual, Cowell explained, he had played an amusing prank—on that occasion surreptitiously taking out of the CD player a rival A&R man's track of a cool rock band and inserting "YMCA," which had won many laughs—but the bottom line was that BMG's German directors had not applauded his success. Seeking reassurance, he wanted an explanation. McCreight was genuinely flummoxed. Surely, said McCreight, he was appreciated in London and that was enough? Cowell demurred.

His consolers were the close-knit ski group. They were attractive to an inquisitive man who was happiest when surrounded by energetic people satisfying his short attention span. In their regular evening routine, visiting gigs at the Wembley Arena and the Hammersmith Apollo, followed by dinner at La Famiglia in Kensington and then Tramp or Annabel's, the Mayfair nightclubs, the group noticed how easily Cowell walked through those establishments. To his friends, he appeared as a handsome playboy rather than a sex symbol and, while enjoying banter with girls, he was easily bored. Marriage, they agreed, was unlikely for a man who dared to be different and attracted "no jealousy because he's lovable but too selfish."

Louise Payne, a well-built model who had been featured topless in *The Sun,* disturbed their preconceptions. In 1996, Cowell had spotted the blonde arriving at a music party. "I've got to meet that girl," Cowell told his friend Jackie St. Clair, who was accustomed to executing introductions on Cowell's behalf. When that operation failed, Cowell bribed Kim, his sister-in-law, with a ridiculously expensive handbag to bring Louise, a friend from the modeling world, to his home.

Volatile but not particularly intelligent, Payne didn't fit Cowell's usual taste for exotic, dark-skinned beauties. She was attractive, with the right figure, though not stunning. She was street smart, liked his type of fun, and fitted in with his friends. "I'm in love," he told Beighton and insisted that she meet Louise at a Chelsea hotel. Over the next weeks, he complained, "She's driving me nuts. She's playing me so well." Payne was refusing to have sex with Cowell. Eventually, on their second night at the Four Seasons Hotel during a trip to New York, she relented. In his excitement, he proposed marriage, buying her a large diamond ring, and she agreed to move into his house. A few weeks later, while "adoring her," he decided the commitment was too much and canceled the wedding. Payne moved out to live with her mother. Three weeks later Cowell telephoned from a holiday in Thailand. On reflection, he missed her. "I can't believe you have the nerve to call me," she said, but eventually agreed to resume the relationship.

Life together in Kingston Hill was filled with fun despite the constant presence of Sinitta and Jackie St. Clair. Payne found the ex-girlfriends "awkward" but accepted that Cowell needed their presence as companions for his self-confidence. "Simon's insecure," as Denis Ingoldsby, a record producer, told Payne. "He needs all the attention." Unusually, Cowell also appeared to have decided which woman he loved, although Payne's qualities, he would discover, were limited. When his parents were invited for tea to his house, Louise made an effort, despite Cowell's discouraging her, to arrange the cups and saucers, milk and cookies, and carry them into the living room on a tray. Cowell held his breath as his mother tilted the pot to pour. "You seem to have forgotten the water." Julie smiled, uncertain about her future daughter-in-law.

5

RESPECTABILITY

IN THE SMALL PARKING LOT IN WEST LONDON IN 1995, THE WHITE VAN outside the headquarters of Brilliant!, a new publicity agency, could easily have been ignored, but the rumors about the five girls inside had aroused Cowell's curiosity. Cowell had been visiting Nicki Chapman, a former promoter at RCA, who mentioned that the girls, members of a group called Spice, were exceptional. "Hi, girls," said Cowell, opening the van's door, and effortlessly persuaded them to play the tape of their new song. Within seconds of the start of "Wannabe," Cowell was electrified. "Thanks, 'bye," he said, racing back to his office.

Months earlier, at a regular A&R meeting, Cowell had asked Jeremy Marsh whether anyone had heard about Spice. The nervous looks terminated the conversation. Since then, he had heard nothing, so on his return to Fulham he called the girls' manager, Simon Fuller. The two Simons had first met about ten years earlier when Cowell had asked the musician Paul Hardcastle, a client of Fuller's, to write a track for Sinitta's album. Since then, they had met occasionally at music industry parties. "Have you had any offers for Spice?" Cowell asked. "Because we'll double whatever you've been offered." "I've already signed them to Virgin," replied Fuller. Cowell was irritated about a missed opportunity. Fuller's abrupt termination of the conversation was not surprising. They were neither friends nor kindred spirits.

Born in 1960 in Cyprus, Fuller had moved as a child to Africa, where his father managed schools, and then returned to Britain for his secondary education. Unlike Cowell, Fuller had used his school days in Hastings, Sussex, to become a businessman. First by booking groups to play at the school on weekends, and later acting as an agent for the groups, arranging performances in clubs along the Sussex coast and in London clubs. After leaving school, he became an A&R man at Chrysalis and then set up alone. His success, unlike Cowell's, had been swift.

In April 1985, while he was Fuller's client, Paul Hardcastle sold six million copies of "19," a song about the Vietnam War, worldwide. Fuller also took on Annie Lennox, whom he transformed into a global star. Rich and clearly exceptional, Fuller first heard about Spice from Marc Fox, a music publisher employed by BMG, in 1995.

Spice was the brainchild of Chris Herbert, whose career started by managing school friends keen to become professional musicians. After some success, his father, an accountant, suggested they jointly create Safe Management and, after various mishaps as managers, decided in 1993 to form a group. Scrutinizing the innumerable boy bands, Herbert made a radical choice: he would form a girl band. In the auditions, he was searching for characters with sex appeal to attract boys and "attitude" that would appeal to girls. Eventually he chose five young women and, at his own expense, drilled and rehearsed them for nearly a year in a rented house. The next stage, in November 1994, was to find a creative team by "showcasing" Spice to an audience of producers, songwriters, and music publishers. "Everyone's blown out," thought Herbert after the event, convinced that he would soon be offered a recording contract.

Unbeknownst to Herbert, his group was dissatisfied with his plans and was seeking a new manager. In what is known as "integrity," the five had identified their ideal music and image, and pinpointed Marc Fox, a music publisher at BMG, as an ally.

To advance his own career, Fox brought the group to meet his colleagues at RCA's office. As the ebullient visitors "nicked my drink, sat on my lap, danced across the room, and caused mayhem, the whole building came to a halt," Fox recalled later. By March 1995, at Herbert's expense, Spice had recorded "Wannabe," written by them with two professional songwriters, but Herbert suspected his relationship with the girls was fracturing. The bad news was delivered in a telephone call by two members of the group, Geri Halliwell and Melanie B, announcing his dismissal. "It's a kick in the teeth," said Herbert about the betrayal. "I've spent one year, day in, day out, creating them. I'm gutted." Herbert would find no sympathy in the industry for his loss. Loyalty was rare among artists, who selfishly pursued their own interests.

Ambitious to participate in the Group's career as their A&R man, Fox had by then introduced the singers to Simon Fuller at 19 Entertainment's office. Fox had two good reasons for selecting Fuller: his track record, not least with Annie Lennox, was widely acclaimed, and he was also contractually retained as a consultant by RCA, part of the BMG group.

"When I left the girls at 19," recalled Fox, "I thought BMG and RCA would have the rights to Spice, and also believed Fuller's promise that I would be the Group's A&R man." Fox's earlier introduction of Spice to Jeremy Marsh had prompted Marsh to arrange an audition of the group one mid-afternoon in February 1995 at his own house. Naturally he invited his friend and RCA's consultant Simon Fuller to accompany the performers. Sitting in Marsh's kitchen, Spice sang "Wannabe." At the end, Marsh's team immediately agreed to sign a contract with the group and they had every reason to expect a smooth process. Annie Lennox was an RCA artist, RCA's management of Take That was widely acclaimed, and Fuller, their friend, was contracted to RCA. BMG's chairman, John Preston, approved making an offer.

Negotiations began but after a short time, to Preston's and Marsh's surprise, the ground shifted. Fuller declared that he had become the group's manager and as manager he was no longer bound by his consultancy agreement with RCA, which specified his role as a "production company." As their manager, Fuller added, his demands for Spice were complicated. Although Fuller was demanding more money than any other unknown group in music history had received, Marsh believed that their friendship and the consultancy made an agreement inevitable. After all, the distinction between "manager" and "production company" was semantic. Fuller disabused him. As their "manager," said Fuller, he was expected to obtain the best deal, which was impossible if he were to act as their "production company." He could not be forced into a conflict of interest. The RCA team still did not anticipate any problems.

But as Fuller's costly demands increased and he mentioned that Virgin was eager to oblige, RCA smelled a lawyer's games. "Simon knows how to bend it," said an executive. "He's wriggling out of an obligation."

As the news percolated up to John Preston that Fuller was ignoring his consultancy contract, the chairman angrily insisted that RCA should use its personal relationship with Fuller to enforce the contract. "Fuller's cutthroat and ruthless," Preston complained. Everything depended upon Marsh. Waxing hot and cold, he eventually told Preston that although he felt betrayed by Fuller he did not believe that the consultancy contract could be legally enforced.

By then, Fuller was auditioning the group in Los Angeles. The reaction was positive, especially from John Ferriter, an agent who also persuaded Fuller to rename the group. "Spice, in America," said Ferriter, "means drugs, so why not call them Spice Girls?" Fuller returned to London, rejected RCA's offers, and signed with Virgin. Preston's suspicions about Marsh and his own staff grew. His unease was aggravated after "Wannabe" was released in 1996 and became America's most successful single that year. The Spice Girls' first album sold thirty million copies, making them the most successful girl group in history. Their triumph, reflected Preston, was helped by Nicki Chapman and another former RCA promotions executive lured by Fuller.

"I was very unhappy," Preston would later say. "I was pretty miffed. I couldn't know who I could rely on." "The whole building had a right to feel betrayed by Fuller," agreed Marc Fox. "I went to him at the beginning because of our mutual contractual relationship." "Scavenger" was among the more polite labels given to Simon Fuller by Chris Herbert's friends.

Cowell watched Fuller's glory with envy. A rival's success always gnawed at him, especially as Fuller's fame was global—including a trip with the Spice Girls in 1997 to meet Nelson Mandela. Cowell's only consolation, as the accolades accumulated, was the news that the group had decided, while Simon Fuller was recuperating from back surgery in Italy, to fire him. Some suspected that his alleged affair with Emma "Baby Spice" Bunton had contributed to the split. At that defining moment, devastated by the women's disloyalty, Fuller might have reflected on the sentiments of Chris Herbert, Marc Fox, and John Preston about his own conduct.

The dismissal by the Spice Girls encouraged Cowell to meet Fuller. The idea was that they should travel to the house Fuller had rented from Franco Zeffirelli in Positano. Cowell's jealousy of Fuller was not a barrier to brokering the first real meeting between two mavericks with complementary talents. Fuller was brave, a visionary who excelled at pragmatically molding an artist's ideas into stardom; Cowell was a big personality, even a show-off, who pursued his own understanding of the public's taste regardless of criticism. The bottom line remained that, unlike Fuller, he had not created a star, let alone a global phenomenon like the Spice Girls.

Over two days, the men discussed possible cooperation. Fuller had taken a year off to consider new ideas and artists and offered Cowell the chance to work with groups he was signing, including 21st Century Girls and S.O.A.P. Fuller also invited Cowell to invest in his latest Internet idea, Pop World. "I expect to earn about three hundred million pounds from it," predicted Fuller confidently, although, according to Cowell, he ended up losing about twelve million. At the end of the visit, neither the ideas nor the chemistry had particularly gelled. To put it bluntly, in Zeffirelli's magnificent house, Cowell felt inferior to Fuller. Not only had Fuller managed world-class artists while Cowell was merely a TV spin-off merchant, but Fuller was

much wealthier, and money counted for both men. Equally important, Fuller's sophisticated approach to business reflected his better
education. By coincidence, the two next met the following Christmas at the Royal Palm Hotel in Mauritius. Cowell was impressed that
he and Fuller were reading the same book. In Cowell's mind he could
imagine saying to Fuller, "I would be proud to walk onto the stage
and say you were a partner," but he resisted formalizing a relationship.

By then, Fuller was speaking about shedding his reliance on unpredictable artists, or anyone else. Instead, he was planning a multi-
media business that would include the pop group S Club, seven
young people on a TV adventure who break into a song. He planned
to sell a brand through a TV show, records, a tour, and memorabilia.
His offer to Cowell of an undefined job was again rejected. "I'm
happy at RCA," Cowell explained. By the time they next met in London, Fuller was planning to launch the website Pop World, with Bob
Sillerman, an American entertainment mogul. Over dinner, Fuller
again offered Cowell employment to launch records from the singers
starring on *Idol,* but Cowell, unconvinced about the stability of a
business based on the Internet, rejected the idea. He did not reveal
that he was immersed in a scheme to match the Spice Girls' success.

One year earlier a meeting was arranged between Chris Herbert,
still searching for salvation from the Spice Girls' betrayal, and Cowell. They agreed to create Five or 5ive, a new boy band. In the jargon,
the prospective group would "cross appeal" to boys and girls and
should sound, Cowell told Herbert, "Something like the Pepsi Max
commercial. Like urban sport, a sound for the boys." And he added,
"Don't show me anything until you're ready." Newspapers inspired
by Cowell reported auditions in spring 1997 to find the "Spice Boys."
Nearly three thousand hopefuls appeared. A few weeks later, Herbert
rented the Nomis Studios to reduce the best twelve to the final five for
Cowell to hear at the end of the day. "Great," Cowell pronounced,
instantly offering the group a recording contract with Herbert as
their manager. In his own mind, Cowell intended to finally establish
himself as a credible A&R man.

With that settled, Cowell went skiing with the RCA gang in La

Clusaz, France. On the second day, he raced on mini-skis in the night against two Italian air hostesses and crashed into a tree, tearing a knee ligament. Hobbling, he returned to London to hear that Herbert had rented a three-bedroom house in Camberley, Surrey, for the new group and was planning singing and dancing lessons for Five. "Forget that," said Cowell. "I've got an idea."

An A&R man's success, Cowell knew, depended on persuading songwriters to sell their best material, and Waterman had introduced Cowell to the Cheiron Studios in Stockholm. Known as the Hit House, the studios were famous as the haunt of Max Martin and Herbie Crichlow, who ranked among the world's best songwriters.

Herbie Crichlow flew to London to play Cowell a tape of "Clap Your Hands," his new composition. "I like the music but not the lyrics," Cowell told the writer. "Give me some other words." An hour later, Critchlow's new lyrics were "Slam Dunk (Da Funk)." Ecstatic, Cowell ordered Five to fly to Sweden for six months and begin recording. During regular visits, Cowell supervised the production and micromanaged their return to Britain to play in the "newcomer" slot of *Smash Hits* magazine's national tour. Scrupulously, Cowell watched every live performance and ordered improvements, building up to the fans' vote for the "best newcomer" at the end of the competition in the Dockland's Arena. Five won.

Heady with success, Cowell organized a massive launch party at five P.M. on November 5, 1997, on the fifth floor of Harvey Nichols, the Knightsbridge store. Arriving in the packed room with Louise, Cowell played his media contacts to secure widespread coverage, including a page in the *News of the World*. The results on the charts were less impressive. The record reached only number 10 in Britain and failed in America. Cowell became jittery.

The atmosphere in RCA's office was tense. Preston had not satisfied BMG's desperation for hits and the Spice Girls' fortunes fed Preston's suspicions about Marsh's ambition. The time had come, he believed, to leave, and BMG was not unwilling to let him go. Richard Griffiths, a British executive with mixed accomplishments in

America, was named as Preston's successor. In the days before the handover, Cowell nervously hoped that Preston, whom he regarded as his mentor, would speak positively about himself to Griffiths. He had reason for concern. Standing outside of Preston's office, Cowell had overheard the chairman snipe, "Everything which is shit in this building is caused by Simon Cowell." Some insiders would say that Preston, a corporate animal, misunderstood the maverick.

Griffiths was in no doubt that Preston's advice on the night before his departure was to dismiss Cowell. "He's an embarrassment" and "an impediment," Griffiths recalled Preston saying. Preston would deny that sentiment and assert that Griffiths was "bigging himself up" to present himself as Cowell's savior. However, Preston did recommend that Cowell's latest demand, for a new five-million-pound contract as a joint venture in a "label deal" was "too expensive." He told Griffiths, "I'm tightfisted and I'm not sure he's worth it." On that basis, Preston added, "Simon is expendable."

Jonathan King remembers calling Griffiths. "Simon's the one person you should keep on," said King. "Don't listen to John Preston." Griffiths was open-minded. With a background in rock, he had no taste for Cowell's pop music and little sympathy for his position in the music business, but he recognized that the sale of four million Robson and Jerome records and Five's debut had "changed Cowell's game plan."

On Griffiths's first morning, he walked into Cowell's office. "Have you got any hits?" he asked breezily. Cowell lifted a tape: "Five's new single and it's great." Charming and with impeccable manners, Cowell could not conceal his trepidation. "I know you're nervous about me," said Griffiths, "but I've made even worse records than you have. Let's hear what you've got." The sound was good. Cowell visibly relaxed. Griffiths gave Cowell the deal he demanded, a shared venture in S Records, Cowell's own music label, transforming him into a serious music executive.

Cowell had recorded Five's next record, "When the Lights Go Out." Success in America depended on Clive Davis's interest. Cowell flew to New York with Chris Herbert and Louise. Davis was keen. With his support, the group did an eight-day tour, appeared repeatedly on TV, performed in Times Square, hit the Top Ten, and scored more hits across the world. To celebrate, Cowell bought Louise an MG sports car but soon afterward decided the commitment was suffocating. Amid some recrimination, the relationship was again suspended. Unperturbed, Cowell was riding high and planning the next move for Five.

Davis, he discovered, had rejected Max Martin's latest song, ". . . Baby One More Time," on the orders of TLC, his group. "Can I hear it?" Cowell asked Davis. Cowell was electrified. Every year, he knew, the world's songwriters produced only three or four "exceptional" pop songs that would guarantee success for an artist. Martin's latest was one of those songs.

"I've now given it to a new girl called Britney Spears," said Martin.

"Never heard of her," said Cowell. "You're mad. No one can be successful with a name like that." Then he added, "I'll give you a new Merc 500SL if I can have that song. It costs ninety-five thousand pounds."

"No, it's contracted," replied Martin, convinced that Spears would make him much richer. Cowell was left with a problem. Five needed a Martin song. Fortunately, the writer agreed to work with them in New York.

"I don't want any complaints before I've finished," Martin stipulated.

"Absolutely," promised Cowell, setting aside time to deliver a stiff warning to the group. The song, written in Martin's "factory," was "Bye, Bye, Bye."

"What a bag of shit," said one of the Five as Martin played the tape. "Crap," agreed another, fueling a chorus of vitriol. Martin was outraged. After castigating the singers for their rudeness, Cowell asked Martin to forgive them. "No," snapped the writer. In early 2000 the song launched 'N Sync as a hit across the world. At the same time, Five began sliding in America. Beneath his smiling exterior, Cowell was incandescent with rage. He had fallen victim to the A&R man's familiar misfortune: he had created stars who had become ungrateful, self-deluded monsters suicidally convinced of their own genius. His only salvation would be their swift demise.

At that moment, Cowell was called by Louis Walsh, a genial manager from County Mayo in Ireland. For years, Walsh, the second-oldest son of a poor Catholic taxi driver with nine children, had struggled between football, drinking, and failed musical ventures until he created the group Boyzone in 1993. Ever since, the boy band was in the news, either because of successive hits or because the manager concocted colorful stories about them, including one saying that the group had crash-landed in the Australian bush. "I give the media stories and they use them," said Walsh. "They don't always have to be based on truth, but at least they're plausible. The one about the plane crash in Australia I made up, but who's going to know or check?"

In his search for Boyzone's original recording contract, Walsh had telephoned Cowell, but his calls had been ignored and he had ended up signing a recording contract with Lucian Grainge. Now he called Cowell again about Westlife, a new boy group he had created. "Simon was a hustler, ambitious, and the one to watch," Walsh would recall, "and unlike EMI and Virgin, who were snobby, RCA liked pop music." Again, Cowell repeatedly refused to take his calls. They finally met while Cowell was visiting Dublin on a Saturday evening with a group appearing on a TV program.

"Why don't you take my calls?" Walsh asked Cowell in the studio's greenroom. "You could have made millions with Boyzone."

"Darling," replied Cowell, waving his cigarette, "we'll work something out." Walsh was undeterred. Cowell's presence in Dublin proved his exceptional care for his artists. "I've got a new group you should see," continued Walsh. Six singers were waiting in a huge hotel suite for an audition. "I've called them Westlife," said Walsh, hoping that Cowell could provide the grooming and marketing, and a winning song.

Cowell agreed to meet the group at the hotel despite his new cynicism about boy bands. He had come to hate the vapid young men with plastic, virginal prettiness targeting young girls and gay men. "If you want to be a singer and can't play an instrument you join a boy band," he thought. "A lot of people are doing it just to be famous. There's nothing more nauseating than seeing a boy with a ghastly haircut and a fake smile singing an insincere song." Yet Take That, on its way to producing eight number 1 singles, was proving the contrary, that there was money to be made.

At the end of the audition Cowell was blunt. "Two of them have good voices but they all look terrible. I hate them. You need to recast the group." The lead singer, he added, should definitely be excluded. "No way," replied Walsh. Cowell returned to London convinced of his own judgment: "I was good at spotting who was in a different league in a group's early days."

Two months later, in June 1998, Walsh called again. "I've changed Westlife a lot," he said. "Come back to Dublin." The call came at the right moment. Five had failed to match either the Spice Girls or Take That and were causing trouble. The next day, Cowell returned to the Dublin hotel. After listening for thirty seconds, he called out, "Stop." Walsh feared the worst. "I'll sign them," said Cowell. "They'll be international stars." Walsh was astonished. "I've got the producers lined up," said Cowell. As he would later admit, after seventeen years of mixed fortunes, "I wanted to prove a point after the Spice Girls and Take That."

The group would be launched singing "Swear It Again," produced by Waterman. Meticulously, Cowell groomed the group and organized the promotion campaign. "You can't sell many records if they're rubbish," he often said. There was only one ingredient he could not fix—the luck of delivering the right sound at the opportune moment. The release was set for the second week of April 1999. Cowell's fate within RCA depended on the midweek charts published on Tuesday, April 20.

Two days earlier, Cowell flew to Boston for the annual BMG conference, anticipating the certainty of embarrassment listening to the latest Take That hit, the gut-wrenching egoism of Clive Davis offering his latest global hit, and the familiar scoffs about the *Teletubbies*. At least the detested grilling had been partially mitigated by Five's past success. But to the world he remained the promo guy who got lucky, lacking credibility as a serious player. Westlife, he hoped, would be his revenge against the doubters. Early on Tuesday morning, he called London. "It's at number one," he was told. Bubbling with excitement, he telephoned his parents, who were by then living in Brighton. "You'll never believe it . . . ," he started. Unusually, his mother's voice was strained. "Well done," she said. "I'll call you back." Mindful of Eric's homily "Let him enjoy his day," she resisted revealing the previous evening's events.

As usual, Eric had sat with his gin and tonic completing the *Daily Telegraph* crossword, a ritual he had followed for over fifty years. "Have you noticed these crosses in the crossword?" he asked Julie.

"I can't see anything," she replied.

"Yes, there is a pattern of four crosses."

"Yes," agreed Julie, unconvinced, "I can see them. I'll go and make dinner."

Minutes later, she found Eric slumped in the lavatory, dead after a heart attack. The following day, her son's call from Boston interrupted the gloom of the family gathered at her house. Unsure how to break the news, especially when her son was on a high three thousand miles away, she remained paralyzed and near silent.

After she replaced the receiver, the Reverend Martin Morgan, a family friend who was in the room, advised that Simon should be told. Nicholas Cowell made the call, catching his brother in his hotel room. Simon was devastated. Unable to conceal his despair, he went down to the hotel lobby in tears. After years of anguish, embarrassment, and failure, his consigliere and best friend had missed the moment of his triumph. Arrangements were made for him to fly to New York and travel on to London by Concorde. Infuriatingly, the supersonic jet had broken down, but after delays, Cowell finally reached Brighton. Tony, his half-brother, was arranging the funeral. Simon, he noticed, was distraught. He could not deal with his father's death, just as he had been unwilling during the previous two years to cope with his father's obvious decline. At a family lunch some months earlier, Eric had signaled that his heart problems were insuperable and he had given up hope, but Simon had ignored the reality. He had been unable to accept his father's mortality.

"Eric's death is an eye-opener that people don't live forever," Tony told Simon after Eric's funeral, held at a local church.

"I thought both my parents would live forever," replied Cowell.

Only in the following days were some of his father's secrets revealed. Namely, that he was Jewish and that he had been married more times than he had ever mentioned. At that moment there was much to ask, but the opportunity to hear answers was lost. No attempt was made by Eric's children to approach other members of his immediate family—his sister and his nephews and nieces—and his self-imposed isolation was preserved. Although he had introduced his children from both marriages to each other, they were estranged from his brothers and sister.

For Simon Cowell, the sadness was tempered by Westlife's success. Walsh joked that he had even ordered the group to sign agreements not to marry for five years, but on serious matters he deferred to Cowell. He had little choice. Whenever Walsh gave an opinion, Cowell walked away without a comment. "Yes, Simon," Walsh learned to say. Cowell had taken control and was listening to no one. After Waterman repeated a suggestion offered by Walsh, he was abruptly silenced. "You speak to nobody," Cowell said. "Only me. I decide. It's what I think that counts."

"Simon's become frighteningly focused," Waterman reported, bemused by Cowell's extremes. "He's totally absorbed. Totally wrapped up in it." Cowell had identified "Flying Without Wings" as the group's next song. "I badly needed it," he admitted later. "I felt total sickness, afraid I couldn't get it." Both writers were persuaded to come to his office to play the tape. Cowell locked the office door. "I had the bit between my teeth. Just the same focus as on Robson and Jerome." Two hours later they agreed to sell the song to Westlife. It was an instant number 1 hit.

Inevitably, success sparked obstinacy among the group. Previously, Cowell had been influenced by his artists but now he was intransigent, unwilling to allow any interference, especially about the choice of songs. Ferocious arguments erupted. "Get into the studio," Cowell ordered, exploiting the group's personal limitations: "My way or go to your lawyer and check your contract. You'll get a writ." Like lambs, they obeyed. The trick in the music business, Cowell had learned, was to get difficult people to do something they don't want to do. Resistance, he decided, should be crushed. Walsh, an affable Irishman, dodged the blows. He was not the sharpest manager but he understood better than most the internal politics of record companies. He had chosen Cowell and he stepped back as Rav Singh, the showbiz reporter, agreed to "expose" a member of the Boyzone group, Walsh's first success, as gay in the tabloids. Stars rarely "came out" and Cowell celebrated the scoop with Singh in a Mayfair nightclub. Walsh was uninvolved in that operation and similarly stood back as Cowell planned Westlife's first American tour.

Recent attempts by British groups to sell in America had not been encouraging. Unlike in the 1980s, when Irish groups including U2 and Sinéad O'Connor had stormed America, during the 1990s, British acts including Oasis and Five had withered. To compete with the Backstreet Boys and 'N Sync, Westlife needed a sharper edge with harder music. Only Cowell, Walsh knew, could fashion a high-cost promotional blitz. During the autumn of 1999, Walsh congratulated himself on choosing Cowell. The A&R man choreographed Westlife's release of "If I Let You Go" in America into a number 1 hit, and the group's next two singles also topped the charts. On his fortieth birthday, Cowell spoke about milestone birthdays as watersheds in his life.

The celebrations started with a lunch at San Lorenzo in Knightsbridge for the RCA crowd followed by go-carting. In the evening, Jackie St. Clair hosted a surprise party at Mirabelle in Mayfair. Forty guests arrived wearing wigs with their faces covered in foam and carrying bottles of Grecian Formula hair color as presents for Cowell. During the meal, a "monstergram"—a big-bosomed woman acting as an S&M strip artist—appeared and "assaulted" the birthday boy. Beside him sat Svetlana, a Russian beauty, dressed in a wedding veil. Finally, the same friends and family partied at Mr. Chow's. Cowell was on a roll, mixing with a collection of gossipy pop journalists, including Piers Morgan; music executives, including Lucian Grainge; and a clutch of former girlfriends, all supportive of a man who had finally established himself.

Westlife transformed RCA's fortunes overnight. The group dominated the Smash Hits tour and within three weeks Cowell delivered

"I Have a Dream," Westlife's Christmas record, which would beat Cliff Richard's "The Millennium Prayer" to number 1 and score the year's highest record sales. "He looks like the cat who got the cream," carped one of his RCA rivals. "I'm on a high," admitted Cowell. "So now it's confident Simon." Waterman, whose company had produced the records, was ebullient: "Simon is Mars and Venus. He's one man pulling all the strings and taken everyone to the cleaners. They now hate him because of his hits." Steve Redmond, the editor of *Music Week,* discarded his jaundiced opinion: "He's no longer the promo guy who got lucky. He's created new success. He's qualified to sit at BMG's table." Cowell's music, he believed, had made the rock A&R men look "old fashioned and pedestrian." Redmond was chairing the magazine's "Record of the Year" awards at the Grosvenor House in Park Lane in December 1999, the perfect venue to make a statement to the industry. Nearly a thousand music executives and artists would be packed in the ballroom.

As at a boxing match, the contenders and their contestants jousting to win the prestigious British award were bunched in the corners. At Universal's table, Lucian Grainge was expecting Ronan Keating of Boyzone to be the one called onto the stage. Instead, Westlife won. The applause was followed by Redmond blessing Cowell's success by naming him executive of the year and BMG as the corporation of the year. He anticipated a humorous, mixed reaction but was staggered by the outburst as the A&R geniuses screamed howls of derision because Cowell was regarded as an upstart promotor and he'd refused to flog around bars looking for talent. They liked to think they were a higher calling, what they called "art."

In the battle between art and business, Cowell had won. His triumph was a decisive turning point in his life. His only defeat later was inflicted by Naima Belkhiati, one of the group Honeyz. For weeks, Cowell had relentlessly pursued the beautiful woman. "I've got a big crush on you," he announced as he plied her with gifts of clothes and jewelry. Fearful of his pursuit, Belkhiati asked Denis Ingoldsby, her manager, to intercede. "Simon, please leave her alone," said Ingoldsby, who was critical of Cowell's treatment of Louise Payne. "She's very young and she doesn't fancy you."

"I can't," replied Cowell. "I'm obsessed by her." She resisted, he later concluded, because "she suspected that after I got her that would be it. And she wasn't wrong." There were compensations to her rejection.

Lucian Grainge made the first attempt to lure Cowell from BMG. The executive who would later become head of Universal Music in Los Angeles, the world's biggest record corporation, was cursing himself for having rejected Westlife when Walsh called to announce his latest creation. "Westlife? It's lowlife," Grainge had replied as he himself struggled to save Boyzone. Ronan Keating, Boyzone's lead singer, wanted to simultaneously manage Westlife, seemingly unbothered about whether or not his own group fell apart. In the midst of his battle against Keating, Grainge had watched Westlife "take off like a rocket," transforming Cowell, whom he had earlier regarded as "a nebbish," into someone serious.

Grainge invited Cowell for dinner at Julie's in Holland Park and offered "a sensational deal" as head of Mercury Records. The package, said Grainge, was worth between five million and seven million pounds, including the royalties that Cowell would receive on Westlife. Cowell's cool reaction reflected his new emotional maturity. He would use the offer to leverage a better deal from RCA. Grainge did not, however, anticipate Cowell's speed. The very next day, a senior BMG executive flew from Germany to meet Richard Griffiths and Tony Russell, Cowell's trusted lawyer and minder, at the bar at One Aldwych, a hotel near The Strand. Griffiths's hand was weak.

Cowell's importance to BMG's credibility had become more important than the profits. During the negotiations, Cowell waited impatiently. The details about royalties, rights, and incentives were less important to a man who sought cash in the bank. "He's looking for a simple equation," realized one of the RCA team. "A check in his hand to see what he's got, and he'll sulk if he doesn't get what he wants." "He's a big fish in a small pond," said the executive, trumping Grainge's offer, "and he stays in our pond." Cowell was finally flush with money.

Over the previous eleven months he had been living at Jackie St. Clair's house while his new home in Holland Park was renovated.

Originally he had moved in for "just six weeks," but his constant changes to the house's design had prolonged St. Clair's mayhem. During his twice-daily baths (to be "minty fresh and squeaky clean, using lots of gels") he allowed the water to run, innocently, but then he became angry because it wouldn't have happened if he had been allowed to use the bigger tub. The water poured through the ceiling. On top of that, he regularly threw away small silver spoons with his empty yogurt containers, burned the sofas with cigarette ash, started a fire in the living room, and destroyed an electric oven, filling the kitchen with smoke.

There were other strange habits. Before leaving for the office in the late morning, he regularly ate shepherd's pie and watched cartoons; occasionally, though, he remained bleary and once he even crashed his Ferrari into the neighbor's wall. "The eleven months felt like eleven years," St. Clair complained later, presenting "the visitor from hell" with a bill for over £100,000. Cowell's mother sought to have the final word. "As you grow older," Julie told her son, who smoked heavily and ate junk food, "you need to look after your appearance. You've only got one body." He ignored her advice and was similarly deaf to her pleas about his clothes. He bought only white and gray T-shirts, and black and gray sweaters. "I'm bored with your T-shirts," Julie told him. "I like it when you wear suits. You look nice in suits."

St. Clair sought to change her guest's appearance by introducing him to regular weekends at spas, a foray into cosmetic dentistry, and shopping trips for the best Savile Row suits, shoes, and even cologne. He would spare no expense to own the best of everything.

At forty, Cowell believed he was unbeatable and even untouchable. He was comparatively wealthy, enjoyed status in the music world, and played with one-night stands while maintaining an on-off relationship with Louise Payne. Foolishly smug, he was unknowingly heading toward a fall.

6

DOUBLE DISASTER

COWELL'S MOOD ON ARRIVAL IN MAURITIUS FOR A FAMILY CHRISTMAS holiday and the millennium celebrations was still troubled by Eric's death. There was no compensation for losing his best friend.

On the plane from London were his mother; brother Nicholas with his Russian girlfriend following his separation from his wife, Kim; Sinitta and a boyfriend; and Cowell's latest girlfriend, a blonde lap dancer, with her four-year-old son. "She's not a hooker," Cowell told startled guests at La Residence, a five-star hotel. "She's an erotic dancer." Jeremy Marsh, also staying at the hotel, watched Cowell become quickly irritated by his companion. First he told guests that the woman was "rubbish" in bed. Then he watched openmouthed as her son, dressed as Batman and waving a toy Keyblade, charged around the restaurant demanding sausages and chips. Finally, the woman committed the cardinal sin: she was boring.

"I've just heard," Cowell told her, "that I've got to fly today to New York for a business meeting." After dispatching the girl and her child on the next flight at his expense to London, he continued his holiday. The clear sunlight over the Indian Ocean on the eve of a new century reinforced Cowell's conviction that professionally everything was perfect. He had created a slew of new groups that, in combination with Westlife's four number 1 records and U.S. launch with a new album, suggested limitless opportunities.

Heading his new ventures was a new male duo called Mero, created during the spring of 1999 and launched that July as RCA's "biggest project in a decade." A song, "It Must Be Love," had been recorded in Los Angeles and a promotional video had been shot in Miami. During the autumn, Cowell had predicted that Mero would beat Wham! and the Spice Girls. "We had to fight off a lot of competition from the other labels," he told *The Sun*'s showbiz journalist, "because when a band like this comes along everybody gets wind of it." On his return to London he even spoke about Mero beating Westlife. "They will become our worldwide priority act," he puffed in anticipation of the record's release in March 2000.

"It's a disaster," Cowell moaned when the record flopped. "I wasn't involved enough," he later confessed. "I had no feeling for the band." His disengagement, he admitted, had grown as he focused on his ultimate challenge to Simon Fuller and the Spice Girls.

By 2000, the Spice Girls had sold over thirty-eight million albums, but their girly image had become tainted by torrid relationships and unexpected babies. Cowell's conviction that there was "a gap in the market," as he told Richard Griffiths, had been shared over the previous year by thirty-two rival A&R men who, like Cowell, calculated that the Spice Girls' "popularity was over" and had launched girl bands with the quip, "It's time for somebody new." The image Cowell sought to manufacture was again drawn from a Pepsi Max commercial featuring five women, embodying "girl power," excelling in various extreme sports. He relied again on Chris Herbert to produce the new stars. Both were motivated by revenge on Simon Fuller. Herbert blamed Fuller for his loss of the Spice Girls and Cowell because "beating Fuller had become a preoccupation." "Girl Thing was a cynical attempt to copy Spice Girls," admitted Cowell. "The dust had settled enough for us to do it without looking like we're bitter," said Herbert.

Five girls were recruited in auditions and began rehearsing together in a suburban house under Herbert's direction. In Herbert's vision, the new Five would not utter gimmicky girl-power slogans but deliver a "fresh, funky, bubble-gum rap" sound. Using the Pepsi advertisement as the blueprint, they hired the same songwriters for what Herbert hoped would be "the ultimate girl band." Despite Cowell's entrenched doubts about manufactured bands, he believed that while it was almost impossible to create an original group, Girl Thing could be, as he told Richard Griffiths, "the biggest ever. We'll overtake the Spice Girls." Impressed by Cowell's detailed scrutiny for the autumn campaign, Griffiths approved a £1.5-million budget. "I've got a great feeling about this," Cowell told the showbiz writer Rav Singh. Much of the budget was spent recording specially written songs, among them "Pure and Simple," but Cowell chose "Last One Standing" to launch the group. The only hiccup was the significant loss of Pete Waterman. "I've got to get off the gravy boat because success is drowning me," he told Cowell before disappearing.

The chief executive of the Deconstruction label within BMG was responsible for marketing the new group. He regularly refused Cowell's request for more money, especially for the promotion video. Shying away from confrontation, Cowell smiled and headed straight for Griffiths, who approved the extra amounts. Financial budgets were not an obstacle Cowell would tolerate. The chief executive, who had brought Kylie Minogue to RCA after her split with Waterman, was bemused. "Girl Thing is just Kylie by numbers," he said, laughing. The comparison did not deter Cowell. After all, Kylie had become a global sensation before Richard Griffiths had terminated her contract, wrongly believing that her best days had passed. Griffiths believed in Girl Thing and Cowell was more committed to them than to any previous group. In his endless prelaunch interviews, he presented himself as the brilliant producer of Five and Westlife who was challenging Fuller and the Spice Girls in cooperation with Chris Herbert, who was certain he could beat his original invention.

"The amount of hype is unprecedented," bubbled a *Smash Hits* editor excitedly. "There's a real buzz about them. They are five gorgeous girls and the song is great. People want something new and in-your-face and they definitely fit the bill." Few journalists could resist the story.

Drawing on every relationship he had, Cowell placed the group on nearly forty TV and radio shows before unveiling the climax of an unprecedented promotion campaign at the Eiffel Tower. About four hundred European and American music executives, journalists, and celebrities were invited, at RCA's expense, to travel to Paris.

By the time two hundred arrived on the Eurostar train from London, most were "well oiled," reported a promo executive. The girls' flamboyant live performance before lunch in the tower's second-floor restaurant was greeted rapturously by the journalists, who then traveled across the city to a five-star hotel for dinner and a party. Most felt obliged to write gushing prose. Cowell returned to London expecting an instant number 1 hit.

"Last One Standing" was released in July 2000. Two hundred thousand copies had been distributed to the shops. The factory was on stand-by to manufacture hundreds of thousands more. At ten A.M. on Tuesday—unusually early—Cowell arrived at his office, where the head of sales delivered the "Midweeks" sales sheet. Cowell's stomach churned as he looked down the list to find Girl Thing at number 8. "Complete disaster," he muttered in shock. "Black Tuesday," said Blackhurst, saddened by the blow.

Cowell dreaded Griffiths's call. Griffiths believed in only backing winners. "He could have destroyed me," admitted Cowell later. "He could have said, 'You fucking idiot, you've blown all this money, you're not as good as you think you are.'" Instead, Griffiths delivered a considered judgment. "All I will say to you, Simon, is that this is the best thing that will ever happen in your career." And he put down the phone. Cowell waited two hours before entering Griffiths's office.

"My ego is out of control, isn't it?"

"Yes, Simon," replied Griffiths.

"I've made a huge, huge mistake," groaned Cowell, retreating in depression.

Crushed by failure, Cowell knew that the music village and especially Fuller were thrilled about his humiliation. The self-styled genius feared being swept away by public exposure. He hated his enemies' describing him as mediocre. In the blame game, he first cursed "surrounding myself with 'yes men.'" Next he cursed Waterman's absence. Then, finally, he blamed "my own stupid mistakes." The group had also flopped in the U.S. It was, he conceded, "hard to settle down. Until then, my earlier failures could be blamed on others and I was quite retaliatory. But this time I couldn't blame anyone else. I had made the bad decisions. The Girl Thing song wasn't good enough. The cynical attempt to copy the Spice Girls had crashed because they were still doing so well and there wasn't a gap in the market. It was a very difficult few weeks to get my confidence back. I was responsible for an expensive flop. After Westlife I had believed my own hype."

The crisis of confidence was compounded by a realization that he had hit a plateau. Pop music had hit a buffer. Neither Waterman nor the Swedes were mass-producing new hit songs and Cowell could "no longer plan the next twenty years with confidence." Despite their phenomenal success, purists were even attacking Westlife. "A bunch of karaoke monkeys barely able to scratch their empty testicles," commented one newspaper. Cowell believed in hits rather than in artists, but he needed a twist in his career to find the stars.

The seeds were sown over dinner at the Ivy in Beverly Hills soon after the Girl Thing flop. Cowell and Griffiths were entertaining Stephen Ferrera, the producer of Shakespeare's Sister, an award-winning pop-rock band. Inevitably, the three men were dissecting their recent misfortune. "All you do is great and makes a lot of money," Griffiths told Cowell, "but if you want a legacy in the A&R world you need to sign artists who have credibility." Cowell disagreed. "To me the future of the music business is tied to TV, and TV in America has not been a platform to drive music like in Britain." He outlined his vision for a television program with music that Ferrera would later swear bore similarities to *American Idol:* "Nostradamus, because it was just as he said." On Cowell's return to London, he discussed his ideas with Jonathan King, whose influential *Tip Sheet* made him a prime candidate in November 2000 to become EMI's chief executive. Days later, King's career imploded. He was arrested for engaging in sexual activities with underaged boys. Among his calls from the police station seeking sureties to be released on bail was one to Cowell, who later denied knowing why King had been arrested.

"Right, I'll do it," promised Cowell instantly.

"Don't you want to know how much?" asked King.

"I said I'll do it, just tell me where I go," said Cowell, who would pledge fifty thousand pounds.

"It won't do you any good," said King apologetically.

"That's what friends are for," insisted Cowell.

"Simon's the last of the non-gay queens," King would later say.

To raise his spirits, Cowell decided to revive Girl Thing. On reflection, number 8 on the charts did not spell doom. All they needed was a brilliant follow-up. "We shouldn't have cloned the Spice Girls," said Herbert, constantly working with Cowell to re-craft the group's image during a lengthy tour of Britain. The fate of another girl band, Atomic Kitten, was encouraging. The hit group had just been on the verge of disbanding when a new song, "Whole Again," restored their fortunes. The same, Cowell and Herbert hoped, could happen for Girl Thing. Cowell's first thought was "Pure and Simple," a song written by a team created by Cowell and Herbert. RCA had spent a huge sum for hundreds of mixes to perfect the recording. As a test, the record was released in Asia but it flopped. "We'll try it here," Cowell sighed until Griffiths persuasively argued that the record would fail in Britain. Cowell dithered and during the following days the song slipped from his control into the hands of his rivals in a succession of events that would change many careers and television history.

Weeks earlier, Cowell had been invited to lunch by Nigel Lythgoe, a successful producer of TV entertainment programs. Cowell arrived with Denise Beighton. Lythgoe explained that his son, living in Australia, had sent a video of *Popstars,* a show aired by a local station, about the creation of a pop group. The Australians, continued Lythgoe, had copied a similar program in 1999 in New Zealand.

The program, itself based on *Opportunity Knocks,* ITV's blockbuster, which started in 1956, featured a panel of two men whittling down a group of five hundred contestants to find five girls to be fash-

ioned into a pop band. The show's magic was the auditions, the contestants' rags-to-riches stories and the climax, a recording contract
for the winners. TrueBliss, the winners in New Zealand, had scored
some success.

Now, Lythgoe explained, Claudia Rosencrantz of ITV had commissioned a British version of the program to be shown in two parts.
First, thousands of aspiring young singers would be auditioned and
reduced to a talented handful. The second part was a recorded documentary series featuring the chosen five rehearsing as a group for
their break into stardom with the launch of a single record. The new
group would be called Hear'Say. Coming to the point of the lunch,
Lythgoe said, "One of the three judges will be a record executive. It
could either be you or Lucian Grainge." Instantly, Cowell expressed
his interest.

But then, slowly, the tone began to change. Lythgoe boasted
about his achievements, the size of his office, and even the perks he
enjoyed. Cowell counter-boasted and soon Denise Beighton's mouth
dropped: "Two gladiators were fighting without a reason. It was
shocking." At the end of the meal, Cowell accepted the offer. His
only condition was that RCA would be given the recording rights for
the group. During their return to Fulham, his interest disappeared.

"I can't work with that man," he told Beighton; "he's an egoma-
niac, a nightmare."

"Simon, it was both of you. It was a clash of egos. I've never seen
you like that. You reacted badly."

"Well, I can't see it working."

"You'd be absolutely crazy not to do the program," replied Beighton, before adding, "In Australia the program made a number one
hit."

There was a long silence. Then, "Okay, I'll do it."

Cowell's acceptance triggered Simon Jones, an ITV business manager, to begin negotiations to formulate a contract. The two had
known each other since Cowell, on RCA/Arista's behalf, had bought
all the rights to Granada Television's music programs. As their discussions progressed, Cowell again equivocated. Indecisive at best, he
was racked by his uncertainty. Cowell imagined that the program

would be vaguely similar to the American MTV channel's *Making of the Band,* appealing to a fringe audience. "I don't see it," he told Waterman. "I can't see how it'll work." Privately, he also feared public humiliation. "I didn't want to fall on my face in front of millions in an uncertain format," he would admit. "I wouldn't be in control." Instead of explaining those fears, he called Jones with a reasoned excuse. "I don't think I can do it," said Cowell. "I've got a band splitting up and I've got to dedicate my time to that." He added that the music industry was a private world and, like magicians not revealing how someone was sawn in half, he needed to protect the secrets. "If you made baked beans, you wouldn't show the public the ingredients."

Jones was surprised by Cowell's somersault. He clearly had failed to grasp the potential to sell records. RCA, declared Jones, had automatically lost the record deal. "Cowell's galled by that loss," Jones later told Lythgoe. "He was angry and hurt. Tough. Tell Universal that it's their deal and their executive will be on the show." Grainge was delighted. On the eve of becoming Universal's deputy chairman, he refused the offer as inappropriate.

Two others were needed for the panel. The previous year, Lythgoe had suggested Jonathan King. "Over my dead body," replied Rosencrantz, "but what about you?" "Done," said Lythgoe, and put down the telephone. Lythgoe, Rosencrantz realized, was "obsessed with being famous and being watched by millions." He would be joined by Nicki Chapman, encouraged by Simon Fuller to be a judge. Soon after, Cowell met Fuller at an industry dinner. He could not understand Fuller's excitement about *Popstars,* but persuaded Fuller that Chris Herbert should become Hear'Say's manager.

Naturally, Herbert was eager for Hear'Say to have a winning song. Noting Cowell's decision to abandon "Pure and Simple," he secretly brokered the song's sale to Cowell's rival at Universal. In the nature of the industry's practices, RCA had not formally signed a contract for the "mechanical license" with the writers of "Pure and Simple" and Cowell was powerless to stop the deal. Normally, Cowell resisted confrontation and rarely lost his temper, but on that occasion his self-restraint disappeared. "We spent time, money, and energy on this song," he screamed at Herbert, "and now we don't have a single." Eventually, Herbert retreated: "I was his protégé and I abused my alliance with Simon." But by then, it was too late. As a fallback, Cowell chose "Girls on Top" for the group's relaunch in early 2001, to be followed by "So You Want to Have Sex." Cowell's anger with Herbert was aggravated by the buzz at RCA about *Popstars* and Universal's excitement about "Pure and Simple." Even before transmission, Cowell knew his Girl Thing errors were about to be compounded.

Cowell flew to St. Lucia for Christmas with his family and brought Mandy Perryment, who had been married to Iain Burton for five years and then, after their divorce, had a brief "fling" with Cowell in London and Miami. Also on the trip was Louise Payne, reunited once again with Cowell. "Simon has a healthy appetite for my women," Burton observed. "First he goes off with my live-in and then he's off with my ex-wife." Their conventional beach holiday in St. Lucia changed after a hotel refused him admission because he was wearing a T-shirt. Standing outside, he met Michael Winner, the film director and producer.

"You should come to Barbados," suggested Winner. "It's much better than St. Lucia and I've got six empty rooms at Royal Pavilion which you can use." The extra expense was untroubling. Cowell was spending on "a reward basis: I was buying everything I wanted but kept back enough for a bad day." Barbados was an introduction to a new way of life. "I like the people, the restaurants, and hotels," he declared.

Throughout his vacation he was tormented about hitting a plateau. Past glories had faded and he could not imagine his own and the industry's future. "The normal system has failed," he said. The only solo star of substance to have emerged in recent years, in Cowell's opinion, was Robbie Williams. Although he had been in Take That, a boy band of the kind Cowell was so adept at creating, Cowell struggled to imagine where he would find a similar artist. Pop music, he sensed, had reached the end of an era and he needed to change. How, he wondered, could he plan his future when he probably would not secure any of the million-plus-selling hit songs that would be written the following year? And how could he "ever get any leverage to avoid dependence on a mad businessman" just when insiders were gossiping about falling record sales?

The dilemma was compounded by Cowell's unease with singer-songwriters, over whom he could exercise little control. "I don't like to put myself in a position where I am dependent on one individual's creative talent to bring what we need to make this company profitable," he said. He preferred creating a star rather than nurturing someone who believed in their own creative talent. Cowell confided his fears first to a friend who was also in Barbados, staying at the exclusive Sandy Lane Hotel. Cowell also planned to outline his salvation to Louise. His on-again, off-again fiancée was eager to eat at the Crane resort, which had a traditional restaurant right on the beach.

"Okay," said Cowell, "so long as I can spend the evening describing my idea of *Pop Idol*." On his return to London he invited Simon Jones for lunch in Fulham. "I've got a great idea for a TV show," he said. "I'm changing jobs to Pearson TV," replied Jones. "Tell me after I get there."

Cowell's worst fears were soon realized. On January 10, 2001, he was staying with Louise at the Mandarin Oriental in Knightsbridge while his house was again being renovated. Both were watching the first episode of *Popstars*. Quickly he became agitated, not least because Louise, "with the attention span of a gnat," was engrossed by the program. Just before the end, he telephoned Waterman, at the time sharing a hotel room in Cheshire with two girls. He too was watching *Popstars*.

"I've made a huge mistake," moaned Cowell. "My stomach dropped. That was great TV. Universal's going to sell a ton of records." The program reached 7.6 million viewers who had been riveted by Lythgoe's brutal honesty about awful performers. "I'm sure there's a tune in there somewhere," carped the self-styled Nasty Nigel.

The excited chat about *Popstars* over the following days in BMG's building magnified Cowell's irritation. The so-called TV expert, hooted his rivals, had rejected his biggest break. Cowell was contrite. He confessed to Beighton that he had failed to understand TV's potency because his instinctive interest was in selling instant packages rather than in nurturing talent. To recover, he realized, he would need to launch his own TV program. "They've got it wrong," he later told Waterman. "It doesn't work. There's no pathos. There's no end. It's not real. It should be like real auditions. Bad and real. And it should be single singers, not groups. They should compete so there's a winner at the end. Are you in?"

His worries were aggravated by the fate of Girl Thing. Their new release bombed at number 25. "It's not the best of times," Cowell moaned. "We'll cut and run," agreed Griffiths. "It's better to accept defeat and move on to the next war. It's not all doom and gloom. Westlife is a success." Already murdered by the media, Cowell pulled the plug on Girl Thing. "We were dropped. It was awful," complained one member of the group. "When it went wrong, Simon just vanished in a puff of smoke. He melted away."

Cowell admitted his error: "I shouldn't have presented myself in public as a Svengali figure behind the band. I should have kept way in the background."

There was a more fundamental fault. Cowell's short attention span was not suited to the nurturing of artists. Although he paid enormous attention to detail, he was interested in artists' appearance, their songs, and the marketing rather than the development of their characters. Just as his turnover of women was fast and unpredictable, he had shown limited patience to engage with each girl in the group. His qualities were perfectly suited to television.

By then, Cowell had once again met with Simon Jones, who had moved to Pearson TV, later to become FremantleMedia. Over lunch, Jones heard Cowell's description of a talent competition that would become *Pop Idol*. "And I'm just off to see Simon Fuller because he's good at these things," said Cowell, acting on Richard Griffiths's advice. "The two of you should do some work together."

Over dinner with Fuller and Nicki Chapman, Cowell admitted, "I've made a mistake," and laid out in detail his notion of *Pop Idol* with himself as one of the judges to find a real star during a series of auditions. The idea, Fuller knew, was nearly as old as television itself, but he immediately offered Cowell a twist to the *Opportunity Knocks* format that he had been mulling over since 1998: "The audience should decide the winner by telephone voting."

"Brilliant," said Cowell.

The next stage, they agreed, was to interest a broadcaster. Their ideal was Claudia Rosencrantz but the likelihood of ITV's jettisoning *Popstars* for an untested show was remote. Nevertheless, after a conversation, Lythgoe agreed to mention to Rosencrantz the refined idea, which would have Lythgoe continuing as a judge. "Good news," Cowell told Jones. "ITV have agreed to consider *Pop Idol*. We can pitch to ITV through you. I'll see you tomorrow." To Jones's surprise, Cowell arrived with Fuller.

"This is not a crappy TV producers and talent show," said Cowell, dominating the discussion, "but this is how I will find my next Robbie Williams or Cliff Richard." Four judges, he explained, would hold real-time auditions and discuss the contestants' merits. The audience would be entertained not only by the contest but also by the music. "The public loves hearing their old, favorite songs," he said, emphasizing the importance of music for the show's success. "And then the audience will vote by telephone for the winners."

His motive, Cowell admitted, was to secure for BMG the worldwide rights to every record released by *Idol*'s victor. Jones's task would be to compose the detailed presentation to ITV. With Jones on board, Cowell needed Griffiths's approval. He arrived for a meeting accompanied by Jones. As the two Simons entered the office, Griffiths shouted, "I know your fucking game. You just want to be a TV star."

In the division of labor, Cowell would produce the records, Simon Fuller would manage the new star, and FremantleMedia would create the show. In the agreement drafted by Jones in early February 2001, the creators of the format and the owners of the show's format would receive 5 percent of the production budget as a fee. Since there were three owners—Cowell, Fuller, and FremantleMedia—Jones increased the fee to 6 percent to be divided equally. Fuller rejected that suggestion. He wanted the ownership to be divided between himself and Cowell. Jones's insistence on one-third each finally prevailed. Ten years later, Fuller would say, "I offered FremantleMedia one-third ownership for producing the show," and called it "the biggest Christmas present they'll ever have, ever, ever, ever." Neither Simon Jones nor Cowell recalled that interpretation of the discussion.

On Tuesday, February 13, 2001, Alan Boyd, an experienced producer of TV entertainment who would also later be employed by FremantleMedia, was asked by Jones to meet him and Cowell. To Boyd's surprise, Fuller also arrived. Dominating the presentation, Cowell explained, "We've done a sketch of what we want. Now we want you to build it up." The television professional was tasked with creating a bible describing the logistics for the studios, the videotaping facilities, the logistics of auditioning fifty thousand contestants, the installation of a telephone system for voting, the running order and, finally, an estimate of the cost.

"On that day," Boyd would say later, "I had no idea who created the idea." Boyd made an appointment with a BBC executive who was eager to compete with ITV's *Popstars* on Saturday nights. But before Boyd, Cowell, and Jones arrived at BBC's headquarters, Claudia Rosencrantz called.

"Come and see me before you go to the BBC," she said. Fearful that the BBC would get an advantage, she was excited by gossip that Hear'Say's recording of "Pure and Simple" had undoubtedly secured a huge audience for the new show. Her excitement was mirrored at BMG, although not by Griffiths, who had been summarily replaced.

At that moment, before pitching to the BBC or ITV, Cowell and Fuller sat down with their respective lawyers, Tony Russell and Andy Stinson. At the end they orally concluded two critical agreements. First, that income generated by the format of the program should be divided equally between Fuller and Cowell. Second, that Fuller's company, 19, would manage the winners' careers while Cowell and BMG would own the recording rights. Soon after that, Fuller called Cowell to propose a change.

"I've got an idea," said Fuller. "To make it simple, you take the record rights and I'll take the TV rights. And both the rights are for life." Cowell consulted Griffith's replacement at BMG, but crucially neither understood the value of the intellectual property rights of television programs, or had experience selling a TV format to foreign broadcasters. They only wanted to sell records and reproduce the phenomenal success of the *Popstars* final in February. Trusting Fuller, Cowell accepted his suggestion and did not consider that their arrangement should be immediately formalized in a signed contract. There was naïveté, Cowell would later admit, but also faith in his oral agreement with Fuller. In the frenzy, Cowell's only concern was to persuade Claudia Rosencrantz to accept the program, which had been outlined in a twenty-page proposal.

"We won't be relying on music to make the show successful," said Cowell, taking the lead while Fuller and Jones listened. "It will be a soap opera."

"I love it," said Rosencrantz, committing ITV before the BBC could make a counteroffer.

While finalizing the contracts, Fuller called Jones. "I've agreed with Simon[Cowell]," he said, "that I should have his third, so that means I have two-thirds." Surprised, Jones called Cowell, who confirmed his arrangement with Fuller. Accordingly, unbeknownst to Cowell, Stinson negotiated on Fuller's behalf with Jones a far-reaching contract between ITV, FremantleMedia, and 19, Fuller's company, to make *Pop Idol*.

In sharing the royalties or income from the intellectual property of the program across the world, FremantleMedia would own and be responsible in perpetuity for all *Pop Idol*'s production and distribution rights, and the merchandising of any products. In return, the company would give Fuller 50 percent of any income received in the United States and 10 percent from the rest of the world. In other words, if *Pop Idol* succeeded, Fuller would effortlessly earn millions of pounds. Fuller also insisted that if the program was sold in America, he would receive a credit as executive producer. In turn, Jones demanded the same. To increase his status further, Fuller stipulated on another single credit at end of show: "Created by Simon Fuller."

Ten years later, Fuller gave his version of those events to Richard Rushfield, the author of *American Idol*: "Simon [Cowell] has been a friend of mine forever. We both love music. We're both entrepreneurs. So when it came to me finessing this show, there were two things I needed. One was a record company, because I was a management company, to offer the prize and drive the show. Then also a kind of partner in crime, someone who could work with me, who knew artists, who could be on the panel."

Fuller claimed responsibility for choosing Cowell as the record executive and said that Cowell, on being offered the job by Fuller, replied, "Yes I want to do the exact kind of show. I've got my vision to have some artists on my record label."

Fuller continued, "He was on the same page. We were very much two peas in a pod. It was a perfect combination. He'd be on the panel and my idea would come to fruition, we'd go conquer the world."

Cowell was unaware of both the agreement between Fuller and FremantleMedia and Fuller's interpretation of events. In his version he was instead focused on developing the show with a team that included Nicki Chapman. Lythgoe was excluded due to legal complications, so Cowell suggested that Pete Waterman should be a judge.

"We're starting *Pop Idol* next Thursday at a conference center in Manchester," Cowell told his old mentor. "They'll pay you five hundred pounds for each program. Be there at nine o'clock." The fourth judge was Neil Fox, a radio DJ.

The show was revealed to the media on March 22, 2001. Prominent at the presentation was Nigel Lythgoe, who had been appointed executive producer. Talented and perceptive, Lythgoe was seething. He had adored the fame of "Nasty Nigel" and was furious about losing that role, especially to Cowell.

Two days after the program was unveiled, Cowell was shocked to hear that hours after its release, Hear'Say's "Pure and Simple" was a chart sensation, heading toward 1.5 million sales. "Have you seen these numbers?" Cowell asked Simon Jones, quoting the Midweeks. "They're incredible."

Daily, Cowell would stare at the statistics in disbelief, distressed that Hear'Say was outselling Westlife's new single by ten to one. The music industry's battlelines for the next decade were being drawn. The first blow was delivered soon after, at the industry's prestigious Brits awards in a Park Lane hotel.

"Oh, Lucifer," Cowell sniped at Lucian Grainge backstage. Grainge had just been declared the victor with Hear'Say and Cowell had booed the loudest. "Our success has killed you," joked Grainge, chortling over the way he had successfully lobbied the votes in Universal's favor against BMG.

"Okay, let's move on to the next thing," Cowell said the following morning, seeking to reassert his status: "I've sold twenty-five million albums and scored fifteen number one singles over the past ten years. There's more to come."

The hectic pace to produce a television show finally ended his relationship with Louise. "You're going to die a very lonely man," were her parting words. "I probably won't," Cowell replied, appearing unconcerned. He did not like commitment, he wanted an unhindered choice of women, he did not want children, he wanted fun, and he did not want to retire at sixty-five, sitting bored on a beach with "someone I wouldn't be speaking to."

A few days later, his mood changed. Payne's warning "hit home." "I could die lonely," he admitted to himself. "I need to fill the gap by building a career for myself."

7

MOMENT OF TRUTH

"WE MUST GO TO AMERICA," COWELL TOLD SIMON JONES IN MARCH 2001. Even before the first auditions of *Pop Idol* were taped, Cowell wanted the format sold to an American network as a vehicle to sell records, and Fuller agreed. Jones booked three business-class tickets to Los Angeles and reserved rooms at the Four Seasons. "I'm flying first," said Fuller.

Cowell was flummoxed. BMG refused to pay for an upgrade, so, to avoid humiliation, Cowell personally paid the difference to fly first as well. The day after arriving, the three Simons were due to meet network producers. "I'm staying by the pool," announced Fuller. Neither Cowell nor Simon Jones was suspicious. Instead both set off enthusiastically to pitch *Pop Idol* to NBC, ABC, CBS, and Fox. All four networks were looking for formats to reverse sliding ratings. Cowell's pitch was that a talent show with live auditions and the public's vote offered viewers the chance to share in the American Dream.

"And what exactly do you think we're supposed to be doing for you?" asked a "lippy" female executive dismissively at the end of Cowell's speech.

"Well actually, sweetheart," Cowell replied, "it's more a question of what I could be doing for you."

The next meeting ended with the terminal "Well, we'll get back to you." At the third, Cowell was stopped in mid-flow. "No," said the executive. "Why not?" asked Cowell. "Because it's a music show." Every music program in America had flopped. In 2000, ABC's *Making the Band*—about creating a boy band—had failed to win a wider audience beyond young girls, and another network had dropped *Popstars*—about the creation of an all-girl group—blaming low audiences. The consistent failure persuaded Mike Darnell, the producer of Fox's alternative entertainment, to dispatch an underling to meet Cowell. "It's not for us," announced his "wishy-washy" mouthpiece.

Sitting on the curb of Pico Boulevard outside Fox's 20th Century complex, angry because he had forgotten to order a car to return to the hotel, Cowell lit a cigarette and tearfully moaned, "That was the worst meeting I've ever been to." Back at the hotel, Fuller appeared unconcerned, an odd stance, Cowell would later reflect, for a man who would claim to have invented and owned the format. Together they flew back to Britain to film the first auditions in Manchester.

Amid inevitable disorganization, the judges met for breakfast with the program hosts Ant & Dec, who had been lined up as the hosts who would introduce the show and provide continuity links. The producers had supplied just one camera for the audition, directed initially at the contestant. When he or she had finished singing and left the room, the camera would swing to record the judges' discussion. Then the contestant would be recalled to be told the result. Cowell had agreed on that format with Lythgoe and Richard Holloway, an experienced producer of talent competitions, including *Opportunity Knocks*. At the last moment, Claire Horton, the producer, installed a glass desk in front of the judges. Beyond that, despite Boyd's twenty-page proposal, the detail of the program's content was as flexible as Cowell's original pitch. Cowell's only certainty was relying on the right mix of people to find a new star for S, his music label.

The first day was chaotic, with the hesitant procession of contestants followed by the judges' ponderous opinions, and then the meeting with the contestants to politely reveal the results. By lunchtime, Cowell had had enough: "I'm dying here. We have to be ourselves and tell them the truth like in a real-life audition."

"It's purgatory," Waterman agreed. "We would never listen to these kids. We would throw them out before they've finished."

"Why would you want to interrupt?" asked Lythgoe indignantly.

"Because they're crap," said Waterman. "We have to tell the performers to their faces what we think. They've come for a laugh. They're not being serious. We've just got to tell these boys and girls the truth. They're rubbish."

"And we need two cameras," added Cowell. "One on the judges."

Extra cameras were quickly installed and the contestants were asked to repeat their performances. Led by Waterman, the judges spoke unpleasant truths. Cruelty was good television, Cowell realized, soaking up Waterman's performance like a sponge. "Simon only turned nasty," Waterman would say, "when he saw how much fan mail I was getting after the first *Pop Idol.*"

To craft "Nasty Simon" Cowell adapted the deadly one-liners familiar in the music business. Waterman was as bemused by Cowell's swift reinvention of himself as he was by Lythgoe's frustration. "You're being bombastic," Lythgoe complained. "You shouldn't tell contestants to 'piss off.' You should be reasonable."

"Nigel," said Waterman, "You want to script us? We've done this routine for fifteen years. Telling people they're complete assholes is usual in the business."

"Wrap," Holloway called at three A.M.

"It's working better," Cowell told Waterman self-interestedly. "We're making it work."

That first day shaped the demarcation that would permanently disfigure reality television in Britain and America over the next decade. Namely, who devised the detailed format of *Pop Idol*? Those who opposed Cowell moved with Lythgoe onto Fuller's side. Cowell's supporters were Claudia Rosencrantz, Waterman, and Claire Horton.

Pertinently, Simon Fuller had not traveled to Manchester and was unaware of the show's evolution. "Just as well," thought Waterman. "There's a clash of personalities." A beast was conceived that was neither one person's creation nor under one person's control. Nevertheless, ten years later Fuller would say, "I was so fast off the mark because

I'd already had it worked out . . . It's not so rare that I was ahead of the curve, but I was ready to go."

Despite his invisibility at the critical moments of *Pop Idol*'s conception and execution in Manchester, Fuller's lawyers were hyperactive. During the program's production but before transmission, Cowell's lawyer, Tony Russell, called Cowell with alarming news. When BMG had started negotiating the recording rights with Andy Stinson, said Russell, the lawyer replied that Fuller owned all the rights, including the recording rights, in perpetuity.

"You've blown it," said Russell. "Do you want to go on or pull out?"

Cowell gulped. He had assumed that Fuller would honor their verbal agreement to divide the income fifty-fifty and to split the TV and record rights between them, but with the absence of a written contract, he was paralyzed. "We're really fucked here," Cowell said to himself. "I'd look like the biggest mug in the world if I pulled out," he told Russell.

His priority was to sell records. He had even agreed to appear on the show without a fee because he knew that Universal would jump in if he withdrew. Other news from the BMG negotiator compounded his concern. One member of Fuller's team was heard to say, "We're going to punish Simon Cowell," reflecting Fuller's depiction of Cowell as the junior partner who should be grateful for any participation in the deal.

"That was a moment of truth," Cowell would later say. Reflecting on the previous months, he wondered whether he should have been suspicious about Fuller's lack of any enthusiasm after Rosencrantz had approved the program. "There were no high-fives from Simon. I was screwed right from the beginning," he concluded.

The best tactic, he decided, was to ignore Fuller's threats and allow the negotiations to continue while he immersed himself in the show. His teacher, Claudia Rosencrantz, was emphatic after viewing the first rushes: "TV is an intimate medium and the viewer needs to empathize with the presenter. Be genuine and never let the viewer down, because you're in their homes. Panels thrive on dynamics. Know your characters and stick to them. Neil Fox is the professional,

Nicki is the warm and kind mum, Pete's the madman, and you're the gladiator." Lythgoe, the executive producer, added his advice: "You've got to take control of this show. Be the judge."

Listening and watching carefully, Cowell fashioned himself on Mickie Most and Tony Hatch, famous during the 1970s for terrorizing hopefuls on ITV's *New Faces* talent search. In the creation of a new soap opera, he offered himself as "Sarcastic Simon," whose withering criticism dashed dreams. To perfect his performance, he sat uncomplaining through intensive all-night editing sessions to learn the craft from those making the programs. Scrutinizing his performance, he noticed how the pose of his head, the squeeze of his mouth, and a blink of an eye was magnified into a special meaning. To excel in television's drama, he needed to produce a flawless act, milking every moment, aware that acting is the art of perfecting the lie. That feat, he hoped, would also conceal his personal insecurity from his critics' scrutiny.

The media launch for the show was arranged at the Hard Rock Cafe in Park Lane. Before the fifteen-minute promotion tape was shown, Cowell sat smoking in a corner, ignored while the other judges were besieged. After the tape was shown and the ecstatic applause ended, Cowell was mobbed. Noting the square jaw, perfect teeth, blow-dried hair, and toned muscles, the journalists discovered a "star" delighted by instant celebrity whose brutality in the program contrasted sharply with his personal courtesy.

"Fame will not change me," Cowell told Rosencrantz after a summons to her office. "I've never really hungered to be in front of the camera," he continued, but in truth he luxuriated in realizing an attention seeker's dream.

Celebrity is a drug that can only be satisfied by nurturing relations with the media. A mutual addiction feeds the celebrity's hunger for recognition and the need to increase sales for newspaper and magazines. A publicist had been hired by Simon Fuller to place interviews and glowing profiles of himself in several newspapers. His brief was to position Fuller as a successful, magnetic, and enigmatic personality who shirked publicity.

"Fame has its price," Rosencrantz warned Cowell, introducing what she called "my standard lecture." "It's a double-edged sword. After you've been seen by fifteen million people, I will read about whatever skeletons you've got in the cupboard in next week's *News of the World*. So think about it." In the lucrative kiss-and-tell era, tabloids sold extra copies by exposing celebrities' sex lives. There would be women, Cowell knew, eager to cash in on their freewheeling encounters with him. He decided to hire Max Clifford, an infamous publicist, to manage his reputation. To many, Clifford was an unattractive operator, known for his confessions as a serial adulterer. He was admired, though, for protecting his clients and offering what Cowell would describe as "realistic advice."

Clifford's work began hours after *Pop Idol* was launched, on October 5, 2001. Cowell was no longer the unknown bachelor but was promoted as the superstar stud. Every aspect of his life was to be amplified in the tabloid newspapers, including descriptions of his regular visits to lap-dancing clubs.

For months, Cowell had been a regular visitor to Stringfellows with his friends, including Rav Singh. He enjoyed being "swamped" by lap dancers, whom he treated affectionately, rewarded with generous tips, and occasionally took home at the end of the evening. The girls' attractions were their looks, their fun, their uninhibited nudity, the convenience and the lack of commitment. Some tabloid writers drew a different picture, hinting that his trips to Stringfellows were a smoke screen for his alleged homosexuality.

Amid the wave of initial publicity, the *Mirror* published on the front page a photograph of Cowell scantily dressed in woman's clothes, including frilly undies, with his arm around a man. The implication was that Cowell was gay. Cowell telephoned his mother. "When the *Mirror* journalist came for an interview, did you give him the family photograph album?"

"Yes dear, he was so nice and promised to send it back."

His next call was to Piers Morgan, the *Mirror*'s editor. "Do you know who the man next to me was?" "Yes," replied Morgan. "It was your brother. We seem to have forgotten to mention that."

"Did I come across as camp?" Cowell asked Beighton hours after transmission of the first program.

"You came across just as you are," she replied diplomatically.

His mother was less polite. Regularly while shopping in Brighton, she was attacked by neighbors for her son's insolence on air. Even Nicholas Cowell called to describe his torment in a dentist's waiting room, fearing he would be criticized for his brother's behavior.

"I've made the biggest mistake of my life," he told Beighton over lunch at their local PizzaExpress. "My mother's been attacked. I shouldn't have done it."

As the ratings rose, his fears disappeared. Britain was becoming excited by Cowell's snap brutality: "You sound like Mickey Mouse on helium"; "What if I told you you couldn't sing?"; "I'm afraid to say that really hurt my ears"; and "I don't believe you're a star. If you win I'll believe we have failed." The tabloids described the program as "brilliant TV" and blessed his and Waterman's performances as "brilliant" for encouraging contestants to degrade themselves and for "weeding out the freaks, the geeks, the Bolsheviks, the trade unionists, people with funny shaped heads and all the other fruit bats that make this show so enjoyable." Even Lythgoe joined the chorus: "Cowell is really cruel. I mean, this guy was thrown out of the Gestapo for cruelty."

The controversy about his rudeness—or replicating the music business's honesty—fuelled the publicity. "Having a tough time for two minutes on camera," he retorted. "So what? If you don't want that, go to another talent show."

Cowell's vitriol was not limited to the contestants. Although he had tried since his school days to avoid confrontation, his competitive instincts spotted the benefit of provoking rivalry against two of the panelists during the show. He disliked Nicki Chapman, whom he dismissed as a cipher planted by Fuller and ridiculed the fourth: "Foxy, all you do is play bands' records on the radio while I actually create these bands for the likes of you. Your remarks are unfair. Once you've created a band and made them into a multimillion success, then you can criticize me. . . . Unless you have something constructive to say, don't. You're boring me." In retaliation, Fox raged about Cowell's "poisonous" put-downs, calling him "a pantomime dame." Enjoying the gulf he had created, Cowell recalled, "He really went for me. I was shocked. He called me a prat and I've never seen him like that before. He lost it."

Cowell's brashness was fed by his possession of "real money," guaranteeing freedom. Ever since his childhood chores for pocket money, Cowell had longed to be rich. "Money. I want as much money as I can get my hands on," he unashamedly told *Rolling Stone* magazine when asked for his biggest wish. His regret, he added, was not to have been the Beatles' A&R man in the 1960s. Not for the music but for the royalties.

Finally, he could afford the best homes and cars. He flew by helicopter to Blenheim Palace with Jackie St. Clair to collect a new Aston Martin DB7 to support the manufacturer's publicity stunt.

One of the perils of fame was the hate mail and crank calls. "You've fucking had it. I hate your fucking guts," was the pattern of abuse. "I just try to be honest with people," he told *The Sun,* the newspaper he had identified as his favorite mouthpiece. "Rejection is hard for some."

By the end of November 2001, "Sarcastic Simon" was hailed "as the most outspoken dasher of dreams, reducing young hopefuls to tears with his blunt assessments of their talents." The image he preferred was the fun-loving good guy who adored his mother, cared for his friends, enjoyed his Aston Martin, and flashed his white teeth, which he confessed "are not my own."

"Women Fans Fall for Mr. Nasty" was the *Sunday People*'s headline. "It's certainly come as a surprise," Cowell said with a smile. "I thought that by being outspoken it would create a lot of animosity but it has had the opposite effect." His camp behavior, failure to marry, and his interviews encouraged speculation about his sexuality. Cowell had the reputation of enjoying an easy, flirtatious relationship with women, especially his coterie of old girlfriends. But women who worked closely with him, even those who regarded themselves as his friends, spoke discreetly about how his narcissism prevented him from truly falling in love with anyone. Their suspicions gained credibility by an interview he gave the *Mirror:* "I've never had a girlfriend. I chased Naima from Honeyz for years but she always turned me down. She is my dream woman."

Such a self-deprecating, inaccurate answer was unusual for a star, but by then Cowell had mastered the chemistry of media manipulation. Understatement, teasing, and a smoke screen combined with a sprinkling of stardust were crafting his persona into a mystery. While nurturing his stardom, he was simultaneously creating an enduring veil to guard his privacy.

The strategy instantly worked. Rival tabloids portrayed the celebrity in contradictory guises. Some described him as a sad single man living alone in Holland Park hiring escort girls, wearing the same clothes, and fearful of his mother's wrath for saying "bollocks" to Waterman. Others gleefully described his arrival at Spearmint Rhino at three in the morning chain-smoking and drinking iced Amaretto, while a stream of naked, busty girls "bumped" into him.

Soon, Georgina Law, a twenty-three-year-old lap dancer with whom he had spent the previous Christmas in Mauritius, was, with Clifford's help, identified as Cowell's favorite. "She's a great girl," Cowell declared honestly, "but she'll never be a pop idol. If you've heard her sing in the shower you'll know what I mean. But she has tremendous talents in other areas. She's got a great body and the moment I saw her I thought Wow! She was a magnet for me—that's why I spend a lot of time in Spearmint Rhino." Then he added, "When we're with each other we don't think of anyone else."

Within a day, more was discovered about Law's past. As a regular presenter on Playboy TV's Adult Channel, she was well known as the girl-on-girl queen in porn films who had once said, "I don't do men" and had featured in *Star Whores,* a lesbian romp. "There's no point denying the truth," advised Clifford.

Cowell was unabashed. "She loves giving happiness wherever she can," he commented about the new revelations. "She has certainly been giving me a lot and I hope there's plenty more to come in 2002." The following day, the *People* newspaper revealed that Law worked for the London Paris Escort service as a prostitute called Linda, charging two thousand pounds a day anywhere in the world so long as she flew first class. She had also, asserted the newspaper, featured in "vile lesbian porn films" where she "writhed in bondage and licked chocolate off other women and more." Again, Cowell appeared unfazed:

"I have no problem with her blue movies. At least no men were involved in them—that I know of. Of course I have forgiven her. She is a great girl and I think the world of her."

The antics of Mr. Nasty in Mauritius encouraged more women to sell their stories for the tabloids' assessment of Cowell's sexual prowess. "Is he a Bonk Idol or Flop Star?" the *News of the World* asked three women. The most memorable comment for Cowell was that of Debbie Corrigan, his first girlfriend. "Making love to Simon," she recalled, "is like going on a cross-Channel ferry. He rolls on. He rolls off. And frankly I felt sick throughout. . . . In words Simon will understand, he's not good enough. He's not a bedroom idol." Asked to rate him between one and ten, she replied, "I wouldn't even give him one." "She's bitter that I haven't called her," was Cowell's best retort.

Once the tabloids had finished, Clifford urged his client to be interviewed by *The Guardian.* Posing as "invincible, defiantly laddish, and magnificently queenly," Cowell explained how *Pop Idol* had been devised by himself and Simon Fuller over dinner. Asked "What makes you most happy?" the man who openly admitted getting easily bored and dissatisfied with women, work, and life replied, "God, not a lot. I am quite miserable because I'm never satisfied with what I've got. You're always looking for the next high and that is what I define as happiness. I go through mood swings and the highs don't last very long." Celebrity, he knew, was an insatiable quick-fix drug: "When you're hot, you're hot."

The return after Christmas for the *Pop Idol* finale in February should have been a roller coaster to glory. Cowell had identified Gareth Gates, a stuttering seventeen-year-old music student from Yorkshire as the winner and disparaged the other favorite, Will Young, a twenty-two-year-old student of musical theater. A third contestant, Darius Danesh, who wore a goatee and a ponytail, was cast as the wild card. The astutely edited competition, boosted by the tabloids' exposure of the contestants' private lives, was attracting growing audiences as the show headed for "live" programs to choose the last ten contestants at the Criterion Theatre in the West End. The "hook," ITV discovered, was to catch viewers' interest to decide the contestants' fate.

"That's the end of the judges," Nigel Lythgoe told Cowell before the finale.

"What do you mean?"

"It was never assumed you would judge this until the end. Now we just use the audience votes."

"Of course it was," snapped Cowell, outraged about any prospect of being excluded from the live shows. His relationship with Lythgoe, theatrical at best, had never recovered from Lythgoe's disappointment about disappearing from the screen. Like Tom and Jerry, they could be good friends who enjoyed dinners "winding each other up," but Lythgoe's abrupt declaration, Cowell suspected, was personal revenge.

"He's been put in an awkward situation by Simon," Cowell told Waterman, referring to Fuller. "Simon's taking our publicity personally. His ego is one hundred times bigger than mine. I don't crave publicity." Although skeptical about Cowell's professions of modesty, Waterman agreed they were heading for a showdown. "He's definitely jacking up the ante," warned Waterman.

"I've sent the judges off on holiday," Lythgoe told Claudia Rosencrantz. "I beg your pardon?" Rosencrantz exploded. "The fun of the show is whether the public agree with the judges. They must be in the studio. I'm calling them now. No judges and I'll pull the show." Lythgoe retreated but the atmosphere was poisoned. "What should have finally been a good time has become awful," complained Cowell. His simmering argument with Fuller had escalated to a call for "battle stations."

"Please come to my office now," Cowell asked Simon Jones in an agitated tone. "I can't believe it. Simon's trying to take the record rights off me. I need your help on this." Cowell was racked by fear. His hopes of an amicable settlement had been dashed. Fuller, reported Cowell, had told BMG's lawyers that their corporation lacked any written contract for the record rights to the *Pop Idol* winner and he also denied any verbal agreement with Cowell. Now, continued Cowell, there was gossip that Lucian Grainge—Fuller's neighbor in Richmond, who had recently signed Fuller's group, the S Club—was negotiating for Universal to sign the record deal for the *Pop Idol* winner. Although Cowell would say that Grainge "is my best friend in the music business," the two were continually competing. Both marked every personal success by erecting a promotional advertisement for their winning album outside the other's office. More seriously, Grainge was attempting to poach Sonny Takhar, Cowell's key music executive. Cowell had called Grainge from his bath: "I've got to tell you, I respect competition but you've crossed the line. Our friendship is at stake."

"That's the way it is," replied Grainge.

"Bastard," snapped Cowell, who eventually talked Takhar out of leaving by offering a lot of money.

Although Grainge would deny discussing a deal with Fuller, Cowell was fearful of Universal's repeating the Hear'Say bonanza.

Simon Jones was surprised by Cowell's news. Not only about relations between "the two Simons" breaking down but also by Cowell's failure to sign a contract with Fuller. To broker a reconciliation, Jones called Fuller. "Simon thinks he's the creative genius behind the show," said Fuller, "but he isn't. You can never believe what Simon says." Relations, Jones realized, were indeed fractured. Advised by Stinson, Fuller's challenge—"Don't fuck with me. We had a deal"— was delivered in a precise undertone. The skilled poker player had outwitted Cowell. "I've been double-crossed," Cowell claimed.

The argument rapidly infected the production staff. "Backstabbing and paranoia," gasped Claire Horton as she emerged from Cowell's office. Horton, Rosencrantz, and others watched as Cowell, alternating between sulks and excitement about the program, became aggravated by Fuller "dragging out" the negotiations as the contest between Young and Gates gripped the nation in the week before the final show.

By the end of January, ten million Britons, 48 percent of the TV audience, were watching and ninety thousand tickets had been sold in two days for the final contest at Wembley Arena. Gates was tipped to be the victor after winning 62 percent of the 1.3 million telephone votes in the semifinals.

On screen, Cowell appeared unaffected by Fuller's tactics. He even smiled as Ant and Dec appeared on the set wearing trousers up to their nipples to mock his characteristic style. "It does look ridiculous," Cowell admitted and thereafter wore his T-shirt over his trousers. There were no other laughs during the final week. A record audience was expected to vote and, Cowell heard, "preorders for the winner have gone through the roof." Sales of over a million records were expected. Both Gates and Young had recorded a double A-side single of "Evergreen" and "Anything Is Possible" to be ready for a rush release. The loser's version would be jettisoned in an incinerator. Fuller's intransigence jeopardized Cowell's windfall.

"The show is on fire and everything is at risk," Cowell told a meeting at BMG, by then part of Sony Music. The corporation's choice, advised the lawyers, was stark. Either sue for the 50-percent share of the show's income on the basis that a court would believe Cowell's version of his oral agreement with Fuller, or accept Fuller's offer of a four-year record deal for the winner and nothing else. Compared with Fuller's deal that all the finalists give 19 Management a 20-percent cut of their earnings for the following twelve years, BMG's and Cowell's profits would be limited.

On the morning of the finale, February 9, 2002, nothing had been agreed. Arriving at the Fountain studios in Wembley, Claudia Rosencrantz sensed "a horrible atmosphere. You could cut it with a knife." Others spoke of witnessing "a Shakespearean betrayal" as Lythgoe tore into Cowell, and Cowell attacked Nicki Chapman for supporting, on Fuller's instructions, Will Young rather than Gates. Horton spoke about "the most exciting day ever."

The bookies' favorite was Gates, who Cowell hoped would win to become the "new" David Cassidy or Cliff Richard and reap the same profits as Hear'Say. Just before nineteen million viewers, 59 percent of the total TV audience, tuned in for a national TV experience, Cowell capitulated and accepted Fuller's offer of a four-year exclusive recording deal to release the winner's song on S records, his label.

Fuller's request to include a credit—"Created by Simon Fuller"—at the end of the program was forgotten. "I haven't seen him at a production meeting or single show," scoffed Horton.

Across the country, people gathered in pubs, clubs, and private parties to celebrate the birth of a star. The telephone network crashed as 8.7 million votes were cast. "Bad news," said Cowell with undisguised fury when the votes were in, "Will has won." Young had secured 53.1 percent of the vote.

Cowell headed for his dressing room to plan the promotion of Young's record. "The whole night was horrific," he complained. "It was a miserable time. I felt sick to my stomach because I realized I'd made a mistake." From down below, he could hear Claudia Rosencrantz and the two hundred members of the production team wildly celebrating with champagne.

Will Young's "Evergreen" sold over a million records in the first week and then a further eight hundred thousand. Cowell did not conceal his antagonism toward Young, indiscreetly ignoring the winner. "Will is a great singer but Gareth is a pop idol," he said curtly.

The national excitement about Will Young did, however, alter Cowell's understanding of the show. Initially, he had focused on *Pop Idol* creating a star. After the final, he recognized the value of his own stardom.

"I've got to maximize what I've got," he said. Using his new fame, Cowell railed against the "snobs": that "awful" congregation who attended the hateful Brit awards. "Same people, same outfits, same gossip," he said. He was equally dismissive of the artists: "Our pop stars today have lost their sense of mystery. I think it's because they are too accessible. There is no frenzy over bands these days. Fans are not going crazy and fainting. It's all so boring."

His success and jeers stirred the "snobs" animosity. Watching poor performers humiliate themselves for the audience's gratification and then for Cowell's staged vilification evoked accusations of exploitation and manipulation.

The anger was not misplaced. Lythgoe confessed to "choreographing" the results. Producing the program, he said, "allowed me to screw around with emotions and manipulate. They say I'm a master manipulator. I love that. It's fun and we screwed around with people. But if you come on the show you know that you're going to get that. Every time someone knew which trick I'd used, I'd switch the trick."

Established stars turned their hatred of *Pop Idol*'s manipulation against the star himself, Cowell. Their protests were championed by Elton John and Robbie Williams. "Cruel television," said Williams, "is fucking with people's lives for entertainment." Their disapproval was supported by EMI's president, who was excluded from all the TV spin-offs. "I'd rather develop artists who cross borders and produce catalogues for the future," he said. "Reality TV does neither." The professional criticism of Cowell was supplemented by personal attacks. His glory, his critics prayed, would be short-lived.

Fame aggravated Cowell's occasional despair. In his professional career, Cowell would say, he rarely felt joy about something that had happened. He was more excited about future challenges. But twenty years in the music industry had taught him the cost of transient fame. Pop stars rarely prospered for more than two years and only a handful of artists, like his beloved Frank Sinatra, survived forever. Lacking sympathy for fading stars he faced the same peril.

Unsure how long his own fame would last, he withdrew, living increasingly within his own world. Limiting his social life to trusted friends, he became sensitive about personal relationships and gossip. His reticence amplified the mystery.

The fact that he had retained Max Clifford, and his unusual candor about Georgina Law and other lap dancers, had aroused suspicion that Cowell was concealing his homosexuality. The evidence was complete conjecture. He was forty-two, unmarried, close to his mother, had provided security for Jonathan King's bail, and behaved in a flamboyant manner. His vanity, appearance, and manner drowned for some the evidence of his serial heterosexual relationships. So while not a single man had approached a tabloid to sell a kiss-and-tell story about even a suggestive approach from Cowell, detractors like Ian Levine continued to gossip despite the absence of any facts. The speculation grew in March when Will Young unexpectedly came out to Rav Singh, Cowell's friend at the *News of the World*.

At that moment, Louis Theroux, the TV documentary director, was filming a profile about Max Clifford. Cowell's provocative explanation for hiring the publicist as "protection" raised obvious questions which Theroux tested in early 2002. Referring to Cowell, Theroux asked Clifford, "Is he gay?"

"No," replied Clifford.

"Would you tell me if he were?"

"No, I wouldn't if it was something that we were going to keep quiet."

Cowell had agreed to participate in Clifford's vanity exercise and appeared to be surprised as he walked into the shot and was asked by Theroux, "Word on the street is that you're gay." Cowell laughed and, as Theroux added, "I had always assumed you were gay," looked into the camera, annoyed, and said, "I deny it."

"That was very embarrassing," Cowell told Clifford later. "Music is a gay-friendly business and if I was gay there would be no reason to hide it. But I'm not." After a few moments Cowell added, "The film has made us all look stupid." At the preview arranged by Theroux, Cowell exploded and asked for changes. "No way," replied Theroux, who had already obtained Cowell's signed consent. "That wasn't the smartest thing I ever did," conceded Cowell, angry about Clifford's self-defeating love for publicity.

His denial incensed people in the gay community. At the next London Music Radio Conference, Elton John was allowed to ask Cowell, who was sitting in the audience, "When are you going to come out and admit you're gay?" Cowell looked flabbergasted by Elton John's "childish game." "If it means I end up with you, Elton, then never." Later he would say he was joking: "I didn't think much about it. A lot of my friends are gay. I work with gays." Thereafter, he avoided the singer whenever possible, even when they became neighbors in Beverly Hills. "I can't stand being with Elton," he would say. "It's too heavy."

In particular, Cowell disliked the slurs from Elton John's crowd, who cast homosexuality and cocaine use as chic. In his opinion, gays dominated the music industry, but Elton John and his group had not sufficiently opposed the degenerate industry bosses who exploited the insecurity, frustrations, and desolation of young artists who injured or killed themselves with overdoses. Equally, while John openly denigrated *The X Factor* and paraded his gifts to charity, Cowell offered an open challenge: "Why don't you give money to starving musicians?" In self-justification, Elton John issued a long statement, but in Cowell's opinion, the singer forgot how he had booed Waterman in 1996 when he won his third Ivor Novello award for the best song of the year. John's anger, in Cowell's opinion, was jealousy, pure and simple.

The damage to Cowell's reputation among John's sympathizers was irreversible. Mention of Cowell's name often produced an automatic response that he was gay. Clumsily, Clifford sought to mitigate the injury by arranging for Georgina Law to "reveal" to a tabloid that Cowell had "licked champagne from her body" during a "forty-eight hour non-stop sex session." Clifford's ruse boomeranged after Spearmint Rhino, where Law performed, was revealed to be another of Clifford's clients. The only beneficiaries from the saga were the publicist, pocketing fees from Cowell, the club, and Theroux himself.

"I was angry about it all," said Cowell, not least because the spat was a distraction from his real battle with Fuller.

"Fuller's playing a different game of poker," Pete Waterman warned, but Cowell misunderstood the message. Naïve about business, he was still blind about Fuller's claim to the format's ownership.

He did, however, understand that *Pop Idol* was challenging the music industry to behave like other entertainment businesses. Money was the priority. The "snobs" were often uncommercial. Instead of agonizing over whether to invest a million pounds to nurture rock-and-roll artists singing about protest and rebellion, *Pop Idol* rewarded record companies who manufactured actors like Hear'Say and offered popular schmaltz with a synergy between product placement, advertisers and musicians. He was unashamed to lead the pop business against art but his real battle, he would discover, was against Fuller.

8

GLOBAL STAR

PLEASED BY HIS CONTRACTUAL VICTORY IN BRITAIN, SIMON FULLER reassessed his commercial opportunities in America.

Unlike before, when Simon Cowell was pitching a concept to the American networks, Fuller now possessed a tape recording of a format that had scored exceptional audience ratings. His agent in Los Angeles sent the tapes featuring Cowell's success to reengage the network bosses in a new reality series. To her surprise, the three major networks repeated their objections to music formats, so finally she and Fuller returned to Mike Darnell at Fox.

With the success of *24,* starring Keifer Sutherland, Fox was established as the fourth network, but its fortunes depended on finding other hit shows. Its search was hindered by the turbulent aftermath of the 9/11 attacks on New York and Washington. Uncertain about the public's mood, the network needed appropriate programs for the summer.

Just five feet two inches in Cuban heeled boots, dressed like a child cowboy and often behaving like a jester, Mike Darnell spoke frequently about his hunt for "visceral emotions." The result was a succession of eccentric reality shows including *Temptation Island* and *Who Wants to Marry a Multi-millionaire?;* and rejected plans for a beauty show in a women's jail and a quiz featuring adopted children picking out their biological fathers from a lineup. His hits had outweighed the failures.

The faddish producer was converted by the tapes of Cowell's caustic performance. *Idol* was worth trying but only if compatible with the network's financial poverty. To secure the commission, explained Darnell, Fuller would need to waive his license fee and also find sponsors to fund the production. Advertisers, both knew, were shying away from cable channels because viewers were using TIVO to fast-forward over the commercials. Coca-Cola and Ford were possible backers but others would be needed. While Fuller negotiated with the sponsors, Rupert Murdoch heard from Elisabeth Murdoch, his daughter, about *Pop Idol*'s success in Britain.

"What's going on with this show *Pop Idol*?" Murdoch asked Peter Chernin, his deputy at News Corp. "I spoke to Liz. It's a big hit in England and she says it's great."

"We're still looking at it," replied Chernin.

"Don't look at it, buy it," Murdoch ordered, "Right now."

Rather than wait for sponsors to finance eight episodes, Chernin ordered his staff to commission fifteen episodes financed by Fox. "Just close the deal," Chernin said.

An essential part of the deal, Fuller was told, was Cowell's appearing as a judge. Lythgoe made the approach. His telephone call caught Cowell by surprise. Firstly, because Fuller's success exposed his own failure the previous year in Los Angeles; secondly, because Fuller had sold the format as his own; and thirdly, because he was being offered an extraordinary opportunity. Every British star hankered for glory in Hollywood. As usual, Cowell dithered. Over dinner, Fuller was dismissive of Cowell's hesitation and fear of humiliation in America. "Don't be such a drama queen," Fuller told Cowell. "You've loved every second of it. The records are going to be big hits—America will love you."

Unable to decide, Cowell flew to Germany to discuss the offer with Rolf Schmidt-Holtz, BMG's chairman. "We're putting no pressure for you to go to the U.S.," said Schmidt-Holtz, a former television producer. "It's your decision, but don't bother if you don't want to." The German's lukewarm response was echoed by RCA's president in New York. He was outright skeptical about the attraction of a television "lark or game show" for the music business and the artists. The "push back" to this advice was orchestrated by Clive Davis, Cowell's champion. "It's an opportunity to showcase our musical heritage," said Davis, attacking RCA's blindness to the opportunity of introducing a new generation to classic rock songs, which would encourage reissues by new artists—called cover songs—and generate copyright fees. The friction propelled Schmidt-Holtz's sudden enthusiasm for the idea. If Cowell accepted, said Schmidt-Holtz, Sony would require a four-year license for the winners' records. But the corporation—unconvinced that the show would be a hit—refused to invest an extra million dollars in the production in exchange for a share of the advertising revenue, and consequently ended up losing huge additional profits.

"Nasty Simon" making gullible people cry appealed to Darnell's appetite for shock and sensation, but he was resistant to adopting more of the British production, especially allowing the judges to perform without an agreed-upon script. Spontaneity was judged too risky.

"Here's what I want to do," he told Murdoch.

"You don't change a thing," interrupted Murdoch, suspicious about Darnell's commitment. "This show works in England. And you're going to make the same show they made in England. The problem with you Hollywood people is you always want to change things and you ruin everything."

The program would be called *American Idol* and, at Fuller's suggestion, would be produced by Lythgoe and Ken Warwick, the producer of *Pop Idol*. Casting for three judges and one host, Darnell hired Randy Jackson, a former bass player and successful A&R man for Columbia Records, and Paula Abdul, an outstanding choreographer and singer and America's sweetheart, whose trophies included four number 1 singles, including the 1980s hit "Opposites Attract," and sales of twelve million copies of "Forever Your Girl," her first album.

Darnell chose Brian Dunkleman, a stand-up comic and minor

actor, as the host. After making that appointment he was inundated by telephone calls from the agent John Ferriter.

"Mike, you've got to use Ryan Seacrest as a host too," Ferriter implored, promoting an unknown DJ from Georgia with frosted hair. "You just can't rely on one host. If there are technical problems you'll need the same act as Ant and Dec."

"No way," said Darnell, putting the telephone down and leaving for lunch. Two hours later he returned and found Ferriter in his office. The agent was dedicated to Seacrest's stardom. After one hour, Darnell was persuaded to employ the attractive twenty-seven-year-old.

The final uncertainty was Cowell's attitude. Fox, he knew, was urging Fuller to secure his irreversible commitment. That alone was an incentive for Cowell to express more doubts, but not to Fuller.

After agreeing to a one-year contract for just $150,000 per show negotiated by the Creative Artists Agency (CAA), Cowell called Nigel Lythgoe and Kevin Warwick and announced he was pulling out. His fear of failure was camouflaged by misgivings about American TV executives. Their habitual interference, he told Warwick, would sterilize his performance.

"I'll look after you," promised Warwick. "It'll be just like England. You won't have to compromise what you do. You can be yourself."

"What if the show isn't a hit? After two weeks, they'll pull it."

"They've promised to stick with the show because it could take a few weeks," Warwick replied. Cowell was unpersuaded.

"Get me out of it," Cowell told Tony Russell, his lawyer. "I don't want to do it." Next he called Nicole Hill, a friend whose advice he trusted. "I'm pulling out," he announced.

"Hang on," exclaimed Hill. "Either way, if it fails or succeeds, you'll regret it. If the show is a hit without you, you're going to think you could have been part of that. And if it isn't a hit, you're going to think you could have made the difference." As so often, Cowell was influenced by those he trusted and her advice swung his decision:

"Right, I'll take the risk. But no option for a second series. I want my freedom."

"I'm not sure about this show of yours," the real-estate agent told Cowell as they walked around the house Fox had rented for him in Beverly Hills. "I wouldn't hold out too much hope."

"Why?" asked Cowell.

"Because Fox has built in a month's break in the lease."

Cowell's fears, he realized, were shared by Fox. No one anticipated that a British show with an unknown British music executive would attract a respectable audience even as a summer filler.

At stake was Fox's money and Cowell's pride. He had already clashed with the number two executive at Fox.

"Aren't you lucky that Simon Fuller chose you to be a judge?" she said, smiling, during lunch at a restaurant.

"I beg your pardon," spluttered Cowell, putting down his soup spoon.

"Well, you know, he could have chosen anyone else to be on the show," she continued, bursting into a viper's nest.

"You need to check your facts," said Cowell, abandoning his meal and walking out of the restaurant.

Now, with hindsight, he understood what Fuller was saying to him when they had been reunited in Los Angeles. "Don't contradict any description of myself as the sole inventor of *Pop Idol*," Fuller had told Cowell. "I invented it, I own it and you're just a performer."

Ever since that frosty welcome to Los Angeles, Cowell had noticed Fuller's endless self-promotion in the media as the great unchallenged power broker. In an interview for *The Sun,* a journalist had written, "Fuller is the supremo for *Pop Idol*—forget Cowell, Waterman and Nicki Chapman. Simon Fuller invented, controls and owns *Pop Idol* and has just sold rights to Fox and will start broadcasting in June." The defiance was incendiary. "Crazed," was Cowell's reaction. "I've decided I've got to start my own show," he told friends in London.

The advance publicity for *American Idol* was calculated to shock. "We are going to tell people who can't sing and have no talent that they have no talent," promised Cowell. "We're going to show the audition process as it really is. You're going to look through the keyhole at something people aren't normally allowed to see. Lots of useless people are going to be told that they're useless. I'm warning you now, you are about to enter the audition from hell."

No one had warned Paula Abdul, the only famous personality among the four American presenters, what to expect. Like most Hollywood stars, her personal life had been rocky. Two marriages had failed, other relationships were messy, and, following an airplane crash and repeated surgery, she had become dependent on painkillers and other medicinal drugs. Her introduction to Cowell at the first audition at the Millennium Hotel in Manhattan was, in that familiar showbiz style, gushing. He was attracted to her—an unpredictable, temperamental, petite woman—and assumed that she would soon succumb to a sexual relationship. On reflection he decided to resist. "It's the daytime test. We would have had to have a conversation afterwards," he explained, "and I don't know what we would have said." Abdul's observation about Cowell was more sardonic: "He's a flirt but his hands usually end up on his own chest."

The chance of seducing Abdul evaporated soon after the auditions began. Attracted by the slogan "Thousands sing, millions vote, one wins," none of the ten thousand people attracted to the auditions in seven cities had expected that their bid for stardom in Hollywood would be cruelly mocked by a vain English performer. Nor did Abdul.

At the end of the first contestant's song, Randy Jackson and Abdul uttered polite comments.

"This singer is just awful," Cowell lashed out. "Not only do you look terrible but you sound terrible."

"You can't talk to people like that," Abdul exclaimed as the tearful contestant left the room.

"Yes I can," Cowell replied. "In fact, I just did."

"But this is America," snapped Abdul.

"Yes, and?"

"And he's just a kid."

"A kid who happens to sing terribly," thumped Cowell, terminating the discussion.

Pioneering such crushing honesty was brave and to many viewers mesmerizing. It was also addictive.

"You're a loser," Cowell told the next contestant. "That was terrible, seriously terrible." At lunchtime, Cowell found Abdul tearful, threatening self-dramatically to quit. "The purpose of the show is to be honest," Cowell explained, "Like in the real world." Abdul's distress was not assuaged. "I think Paula is going to walk," Cowell told Lythgoe. "I don't think she's going to want to continue." To broker peace, Lythgoe sent Abdul away for a brief rest while Cowell and Randy Jackson continued without her.

"The tension," Cowell would later say, "was unbelievable. The bad feeling was so strong. I really thought the entire show was in jeopardy." The mood on the following day's flight to Atlanta, Cowell admitted, was "horrific," but he refused to relent. The talented few contestants were rewarded by the chorus "You're going to Hollywood," but whenever Abdul soulfully encouraged a hopeless contestant, Cowell exploded. "Why do you have to be so rude?" Abdul spat and the television producers smiled over their viewing prize. Regularly, Lythgoe placated Abdul, often by disparaging Cowell.

By the audition in the third city, Abdul had reluctantly acknowledged that the program was about "the truth." She agreed to continue the auditions but refused to fly on the same plane or sit in the same car as Cowell. The star himself was unperturbed. "She's a diva," he thought, "and she fancies me. I think she's in love with me, but the feelings are not mutual." To generate publicity, he told a journalist that a Las Vegas beauty had offered to have sex with him in exchange for advancing to the next round. "I would have accepted," smirked Cowell, "but my producer said no." Once the auditions were completed, Cowell returned to London to plan the second season of *Pop Idol*.

Fox broadcast the first recorded show on June 11, 2002. At three the following afternoon, Cowell was called by a Fox producer in Los Angeles.

"Simon, this is amazing. It's a hit."

"What are you talking about?" asked Cowell, caught unaware. "What's a hit?"

"*American Idol*. We opened last night and the ratings are going through the roof."

The first episode had been watched by 9,900,000 people, the highest number for American television that night.

The results program the following day, reporting the votes from the different time zones across the country and the consequent elimination of contestants, was watched by eleven million people. Fox executives, excited by the unexpected success, explained the growth of the audience as the "watercooler factor." Tuesday night's viewers had spoken about the program during the following day and encouraged more people to watch on that Wednesday night. Overnight, Fox TV was no longer the underdog. *Idol*'s audience was 40 percent higher than that of its rivals. Dozens of American journalists called Cowell for interviews.

By the end of the week, newspapers and magazines across America were featuring Cowell and the other judges on their front covers. On his return to Hollywood for the live shows to decide the winner from the nine finalists, Cowell was mobbed on the streets. He was a Hollywood star. His quips were being repeated like Shakespearean couplets. The criticism of himself as "genuinely loathsome," "arrogant," "smug," "snide," "smarmy," "obnoxious," "rude," "vain," "mean" and "prancing" increased his fame, matching his dream. "Anyone who has experienced recognition is a liar if they say they don't enjoy celebrity," he volunteered. "It's easy to pick up girls, it's easy to book restaurants." Every detail of his life was scrutinized— even his sharp exchange with John McEnroe at the London Mandarin Oriental, whom he told in the elevator to "stop being rude to staff." As they stepped into the lobby, they came close to a fistfight.

Returning to his house on Roxbury Drive in Beverly Hills, he took a telephone call from Terri Seymour, a British twenty-eight-year-old underwear model introduced to him eleven years earlier by Paula Hamilton. "Call me if you come to Los Angeles," he had said casually when they had last kissed at Mayfair, a Kensington nightclub. Seymour, a former cohost of ITV's *Wheel of Fortune,* had been dating Cowell's brother Nicholas before she had flown to Los Angeles for a commercial. She telephoned Cowell for a drink, unaware of his new fame. One week later, instead of returning to London, she moved into his house, hoping that the relationship would lead to marriage and children. She had not heard Cowell's outburst to Denise Beighton earlier in the month when he read that Paul McCartney was to marry Heather Mills. "Why on earth does he want to marry her?" he had exploded. "He can have sex and blow jobs from her and buy her presents, but you don't marry her." Beighton had been unsurprised. Mills seemed to be like so many of Cowell's girlfriends. "Terri's not like some of the others," Beighton told Cowell soon after, adding, "Not a hungry gold digger."

"Yes, she's sweet," replied Cowell, suggesting to Beighton a brother-and-sister relationship. Normally, Beighton observed, he said "gorgeous" for women he was chasing.

"*American Idol* is everywhere; it's taken over the country," Cowell kept repeating to himself. Wherever he went, people called his name and grasped his hand, eager to meet the English lord who dashed the dreams of American lasses. To his amazement, he had become a national personality. Among his new fans was the executive editor of the television show *Extra.*

"Everything's great," he volunteered, "but my fee is way too low."

A few days later, the executive editor telephoned Cowell: "Watch the show tomorrow and see what happens."

The next day a report on *Extra* featured New Yorkers saying they loved *Idol,* mostly because of Cowell. In the wrap-up, the reporter confidently asserted that Cowell's success had prompted rival networks to offer him contracts. The following morning, a Fox executive called Cowell with good news: "We're planning to renegotiate your contract and offer you more money." Cowell's total joy disappeared soon after, when the show went live.

Until then, Cowell had apparently never watched the recorded programs to the very finish. But sitting in the CBS studio in West Hollywood until the conclusion of the first live show, Cowell froze as the production credits ended. The last caption read, "Created by Simon Fuller."

Furious, Simon Cowell turned away. "That was a knife in my stomach when I saw that for the first time." Fuller had failed to get that credit on British television because Claudia Rosencrantz and other producers had disagreed with his assertion. But after his agreement with Cowell about his ownership of the format, Fuller's contention was legally irrefutable. Cowell discovered the result in the green room after the show in Los Angeles.

"So when were you hired to be on the show?" a junior producer asked, clearly expecting Cowell to express his gratitude to Fuller. The final aggravation was Fuller's successful sales blitz of the show to foreign broadcasters. He refused to extend the music rights to Sony beyond *American Idol* as broadcast in America. Instead, the music rights in the *Idol* programs to the rest of the world were sold to Universal.

Abdul noticed Cowell's "agony." Despite their fractious relationship, she resolved to "talk to him over the credits because I knew it wasn't easy." Behind the rictus smile, Cowell plotted his reprisals. "I'm never happy about a competitor's success," he said later. "I despise it when somebody who isn't working with me is successful on their own—it really upsets me. And I wish for their demise." At the same time, though, Cowell admitted that Fuller "has a lot of strengths I do not have," an assertion proven by Fuller's securing the Fox contract for *Idol*. Despite his anger, Cowell regarded Fuller's career as a model to follow to advance from a music producer and cartoon villain into a global television executive. First, he wanted the cash to buy the best lifestyle in Los Angeles.

Cowell's biggest asset was a half share in S Records, the joint venture he established in 2000 with BMG. Rolf Schmidt-Holtz, BMG's chairman, agreed to pay just over twelve million pounds for Cowell's share of all the income from the records linked to *American Idol*. To provoke Fuller, a newspaper was encouraged to speculate that Cowell received a "rumoured £25 million." Assured of cash to renovate his homes in Los Angeles and London, and to finance his new ventures, his critical commitment was to disprove Fuller's authorship of *Idol* and "determine my own destiny, my own future." Fox had reportedly paid Fuller $35 million to license *American Idol* for the second series. Cowell began thinking about creating a rival to *Idol* with similar income from format sales, telephone voting, and sponsorship deals.

"I'd be insane not to take advantage of my position," he told Schmidt-Holtz.

"One good idea," advised Schmidt-Holtz sympathetically, "will pay for your next ten years, so there's no need to rush out a project. You just need to sit back and look at the market and try to do something the public wants." Cowell's first idea, sold to ITV and ABC, was *Cupid,* a program following dating couples. "Workmanlike" was the kindest description of inconsequential pilots amid Cowell's battle with Fuller.

During the last weeks of *American Idol* in Los Angeles, Kelly Clarkson, a Texas cocktail waitress, emerged as the obvious winner. She was not only a talented singer and songwriter but her "journey" was the stuff of dreams. After appearing in school musicals she headed for Hollywood but returned home, dejected, to mixed fortunes, rehearsing in an empty room accompanied by a piano until she applied for the *American Idol* auditions. Anticipating huge sales for her first record after she won the finale, Clarkson was sent to the Westlake Studios in West Hollywood to record the record for Sony. Acting on Cowell's orders, Stephen Ferrera, the producer, began recording "A Moment Like This" until Fuller arrived.

"Why are you doing this?" he asked Ferrera. "She should be recording 'Before Your Love.' That's what I told you." Cowell's orders, insisted her putative manager, should be ignored.

Ferrera was caught in a seesaw squabble replayed several times. With neither willing to concede, the compromise was a double A-side record. "A match made in hell," concluded eyewitnesses. Some blamed egotism, while others spoke of Cowell's creativity competing against Fuller's strategic commercialism. In the midst of that argument, Fox offered Cowell a contract for a second season. "I'm helping the devil, Simon Fuller," Cowell told Tony Russell, but nevertheless accepted. On his behalf, his agent asked for $250,000 per episode. "Are you out of your mind?" Fox's head of entertainment replied. He offered $40,000 to $50,000 for each show—about one million dollars for the season—which Cowell accepted to start filming in January 2003; he refused, though, to agree to an option for a third season.

With his rival Cowell committed, Fuller had little reason to placate him, especially on the night of the finale in September 2002. Cowell and Paula Abdul arrived together at the Kodak Theatre. Both searched for their familiar position behind a desk opposite the stage. "Not here, up there," ordered Lythgoe, pointing at a box in the highest balcony without microphones.

"What are we doing up here?" asked Abdul.

"We've been set up by Fuller," said Cowell, seething. "They're humiliating us and letting Seacrest run the show."

Lythgoe had obeyed Fuller, thought Cowell, and forgotten the £250,000 he had just borrowed from Cowell. "Nigel works for Nigel," a consoling voice told Cowell. "He's a bitch," another voice volunteered. The only consolation was Lythgoe's last minute choice of "A Moment Like This" for Clarkson to sing in a thrilling show watched by 22.8 million people.

Without further comment, Cowell celebrated that night with Fuller and, after a long discussion at Fuller's house about commercializing their successful discovery of a real star, the two flew to New York to lobby Clive Davis for help. Although Clarkson's record was heading straight to number 1, Davis's skill was to "validate TV artists" by making the prize of a recording contract meaningful. In Cowell's words, "Clive would give Kelly Clarkson credibility as a legitimate artist." Davis regarded his two visitors as "apples and oranges." He respected Fuller as an entrepreneur while Cowell was "smart for coming out of A&R ranks and a wise, shrewd observer of the contemporary music scene." Davis gave both men the necessary assurances: "I'm getting the best writers in the world for her album. I don't want music that has fallen off the airwaves. I want to secure lasting territory, not bubble-gum sounds."

As Clarkson's agent, Fuller spearheaded the operation to turn the TV victor into a national star and dispatched Clarkson with the other contestants for a forty-city concert tour to promote the DVD of a two-hour TV program. Adroitly, Fuller also arranged for Clarkson to sing the American national anthem to President George W. Bush at a public ceremony. Appropriately, Fuller stood in the spotlight next to his new client.

Cowell watched the skillful refinement of Fuller's image. The "publicity shy" manager offered himself in interviews to the British and American tabloids as the genius who was crafting Kelly Clarkson with the same skills he used for the Spice Girls. "I'm about empower-ing people and making their dreams come true," he expounded. "Kelly will last longer than most reality pop stars because she's an amazing talent," he continued at a party at the Avenue, adding, "I'm thrilled by what's going on now." Fuller's publicist had massaged the journalist who had reciprocated by describing Fuller as trusted by "hopefuls" because he is "bright, amusing, and appears to be disarm-ingly vulnerable." That sentiment was endorsed by Fuller's self-deprecation: "Critics probably don't like me because I'm so nice. I'm incredibly articulate, thoughtful, and moral and think about what I do. I want to be known for doing something good. I'm not fucked up enough to want to be famous for doing bad things." He continued, "My business is creating fame and celebrity, and I'm one of the best in the world. I know it to the finest detail. I reflect what's out there, and if there's a demand for something I recognize it. I don't think I'm crass. I stand by everything I do."

Fuller's swagger reflected some concern about his image since S Club and the Spice Girls had ended on a sour note. His attempt to launch a TV program called *World Idol* had failed because the sixteen judges, including Cowell and Pete Waterman, divided by language and politics, appeared to be auditioning themselves for appearances on the British and American shows. "This is a farce," scoffed Cowell. "Morons from Poland and idiots from Australia. It's disgusting. As wretched as you can make a show." "A joke," agreed Waterman.

Fuller blamed Cowell for the flop. "You could have made it work," he said, believing that Cowell lacked his usual enthusiasm. Another failure was Fuller's *American Juniors,* a series about "youth culture" for six- to twelve-year-olds. Cowell enjoyed Fuller's setbacks although they mirrored his own. *Cupid* was canceled by CBS and ITV after one season. "It performed well and got an average audience of ten million in America and peaked at seven million in Britain," complained Cowell. "It could have been improved. We had the wrong producers and production skills. I learned a lot from the experience."

With women screaming his name around Hollywood, demand-ing his autograph, and even passing him slips of paper with their telephone numbers on them, there was a disarming aspect to Cowell's self-promotion. "Girls get fed up with me," he told a journalist, describing how "scary Hollywood women" were bored by him. He had been chatting up a girl at a bar, he said, when she leaned over and whispered slowly in his ear, "You must have a very, very small dick." He continued, "I almost choked on my drink. I think I looked down at my crotch, felt very small, then left."

Some were surprised that he offered that anecdote to a journalist, but he saw it as "amusing evidence of my humility." Others suspected a tease—but could not decide whether the target was men or women, or simply a love of reading more about himself the following day.

Cowell enjoyed the celebrity but needed a more secure home to protect his privacy. He rented a badly designed house on Loma Vista in Beverly Hills to share with Terri Seymour.

For the moment, she was The One, although, fazed by her flat chest, he urged her to have "a boob job." She resisted. "It would be a nice little treat for you," urged Cowell. "Life with him is amazing," Seymour told friends. "He's generous, energetic, charming, and funny." But there was a cost. He demanded her constant presence to discuss his work and needs, or, as she explained, "life is full-time hard work to keep up with him." His moods changed. Fearful of failure and humiliation, he needed constant reassurance. Usually ebullient and self-confident, on other occasions he became bored and fractious, even with Seymour. "A minefield," one friend concluded, unconvinced that Cowell was faithful to Seymour.

Cowell was reassessing his personal relationships. Fame and his absence from London had limited his friendship with some of his closest friends in the music industry. Inevitably, his regular Sunday lunches with his mother had ended and he spoke less to his brother. He spoke more often with agents, lawyers, and television executives. Most important of all were his women friends, especially Jackie St. Clair in London, and casual relationships he had picked up in clubs and elsewhere.

Juggling his work, his family, and his friends was complicated by his requirement for "my space." Personal responsibilities were eschewed by a man who made little pretense that he could remain faithful to one woman for long. His only commitment was to remain loyal so long as he was happy, but he insisted on the freedom to change if he preferred another woman. "When the buzz has gone and it fizzles out," he said, "then it's time to move on." A failed marriage would cost half of his assets and risking his money was "verging on insanity." There would be no obstacles to his freedom, either children or marriage. He was too old, he insisted, for both. Like Peter Pan, his happiness depended on remaining at the center of the universe and enjoying his fixed, fussy routine and never aging.

Serving his habits began the minute he awoke, late in the morning. Breakfast had become a hallowed ritual, perfected by Roxana Reyna, his housekeeper. In an agreed order, breakfast was served on a tray while he remained in bed. First oatmeal, then a smoothie, papaya, tea, and toast. Regularly the tray collapsed onto the bed and Marmite was smeared over the sheets.

Unashamedly hypochondriac, he swallowed a succession of vitamins and minerals before heading to his sizable bathroom. Depending on his mood, after a long bath, he might turn off his telephone and get a massage before applying a succession of creams, especially antiaging concoctions recommended by experts, newspapers, and friends. Next, he agonized about what to wear, albeit that the selection was deliberately limited. Looking perfect had become a professional necessity.

In that self-centered world, Seymour found no space for her own cosmetics in the bathroom. "I'm using yours," she told him. So long as everything looked perfect, especially his image, he was satisfied. In the house, every painting was straightened, every object was squared, and every surface was sparkling. Cleanliness was an obsession. Outside the house, his big cars gleamed with twelve coats of polish. If a hub was slightly scuffed while he drove carelessly fast, a replacement was procured immediately.

A Smart car he had ordered for delivery in London had been instantly rejected. "Take it away," Cowell told the salesman, fearing that its presence on the drive next to his Range Rover, Rolls-Royce, and Porsche was bad for his image. "They want to photograph me with the car," he scoffed.

Paradoxically, he believed that gratuitous rudeness about contestants enhanced his reputation. "I'm conscious I can get away with rudeness," he once said, smiling. Others lacked his charm; Jennifer Lopez was criticized by Cowell as "a joke" for arriving at *Top of the Pops* with an entourage of seventy. "I've never met her but I can't stand her," Cowell said.

To promote himself, he agreed that his maternal half brother Tony Cowell, who had changed his surname from Scrase in 1996, should ghostwrite his autobiography, to be called *I Don't Mean to Be Rude, But*... His approved story was the life of a self-confessed, rich "eternal egoist" blessed by the same talent, self-confidence, and star power as Frank Sinatra and Madonna. Surprisingly, he inserted into the book confessions of repeated propositions from beautiful nude women and even a middle-aged man offering "the most despised man in America" $100,000 to insult him while he made love to his wife. Unmentioned was his fear of failure, but he did approve a "confession" about Fuller: "Simon went on to create the format for *Pop Idol*." The sentence was allegedly included on Fuller's insistence, and over the following years he would aggressively threaten litigation if Cowell dared to hint that *Pop Idol* was not completely Fuller's idea. "I regret saying that," Cowell admitted eight years later. It wasn't true, he complained. Occasionally he forgave Fuller, but he never forgot the humiliation. As his life crossed a new threshold, his anger fueled his lust for revenge.

9

SABOTAGE

WITH GUARANTEES THAT HE WOULD EARN AT LEAST FIVE MILLION pounds in 2003, Cowell jetted off to Barbados, mixing with some of Europe's richest businessmen, including Philip Green, a fifty-year-old billionaire retailer who had just sealed his reputation by successively acquiring about half of Britain's high-street clothing chains.

Cowell had first met Green while visiting Monaco for the Grand Prix. In Barbados, listening to Green and other businessmen, Cowell began to understand the limit of his horizon. Beyond selling records and appearing on TV, there was a range of untapped commercial opportunities that he barely understood.

He returned enthusiastically to Los Angeles for the second season of *American Idol* beginning on January 21, 2003. Over seventy thousand people had been auditioned and the producers, after filming endless interviews and examining the contestants' backstories for their life's "journey," had decided the likely winners. Gradually, the producers were also relying on talent scouts to scour clubs and bars to find potential stars. An average of twenty-one million people watched the recorded programs, edited to tilt the viewers toward the contestants favored by the producers, who were regularly helped by Darnell's injection of a scandalous item into the media's gossip columns.

Vanessa Olivarez, a self-declared lesbian, enthusiastically followed the producers' script to humiliate Ryan Seacrest and was then publicly ejected; Fox's publicists leaked that strippers had threatened violence against Cowell; another week's seemingly manufactured shock was the revelation that Frenchie Davis, a potential winner, had been dropped after the "discovery" of her appearance on Daddy's Little Girls, a porn website. As Cowell's fame grew, Darnell contrived a poll asking, "Is Cowell sexy or does he suck?" "Suck" won, 58 percent to 42 percent.

The producers were unconcerned about charges of manipulation. "I hate rules. I absolutely despise them," said Darnell to the glee of Cowell, who feared the risk of the show becoming "a little too safe and boring." Darnell's cure was to "drop a bomb on everything." After the U.S. invasion of Iraq, Darnell's hunt for popularity prompted the release of a single record featuring the contestants singing "God Bless America." It went to number 1. Encouraged to go to extremes, Cowell called a white contestant a monkey.

Randy Jackson was outraged: "Week after week you've been insulting people. You can't call people monkeys."

"I can call people whatever I like," replied Cowell.

"I have a problem," said Jackson. "This is America. You don't do that to people. You don't insult them like that."

"Can we discuss this later?" asked Cowell.

The argument climaxed with Jackson standing up and challenging, "You want to take this outside? Come on."

Although such exchanges made for compelling television, it was apparently impossible to use "monkey," so the argument was restaged, with the men replacing "monkey" with "loser." As that argument waned, a new one erupted after a contestant alleged that he had enjoyed a secret sexual relationship with Paula Abdul during the competition. The story was energetically promoted by the ABC network and the evidence seemed initially credible, but Fox's casual investigation dismissed the allegation as unproven. Cowell drew the lesson to resist any temptation for an easy affair with the endless number of attractive and available females appearing on the show.

There were no doubts about the acerbic relationship between Cowell and Abdul. "You're a jerk," was one of her more flattering comments directed at Cowell during a program. "Paula's a brat," Cowell told confidants. "She's got a combination of arrogance and insecurity. She even sits on four cushions to be the same height as me." Feeble attempts were made to conceal their refusal to travel together. "Paula's totally insincere and stuck-up," Cowell continued. "I can't stand her. She thinks she's royalty and has an entourage of eleven people. She hired a scriptwriter to try and get me back last time—but it was awful and she kept saying things that didn't make sense. . . . She gives contestants false hopes. But when I challenge her to give up her time to help them she won't." To exploit their arguments, they were filmed enjoying a cozy dinner in Cowell's house. Unexpectedly, they bonded, eventually forming a close friendship. "A lot of artists are difficult," he said afterward, "but she became loyal and interesting."

Media fascination about their arguments pushed the ratings up to twenty-six million viewers. Cowell was acclaimed as "the frank, villainous Brit . . . without whom the series would most likely have been on a voyage to the bottom of the Nielsons." The praise encouraged Cowell's vitriol. "The biggest insult of my career in music," he told a contestant, "is that you even thought I would consider you to be a pop idol. Get out of here." After hearing another contestant sing "It's Raining Men," Cowell commented, "I thought you did Ryan Seacrest's favorite song justice."

To attract even more viewers, Seacrest was encouraged the following night to ridicule Cowell's personality, clothes, and sexuality live on air.

"What is Simon's favorite song?" Seacrest was asked.

"I don't know," he replied, "but his favorite club is called Manhole, where they are listening to 'YMCA.'"

Seacrest's barb was picked up by Howard Stern, a shock jock on American radio, with Graham Norton, a gay British comedian, claiming it was proof that Cowell was "one of us."

Being outed as gay was no longer a novelty and Cowell's denial sounded weary: "I've never fantasized about being with a man," he told a newspaper. Both stars were reprimanded by Fox's Standards and Practices department but too late to halt the ceaseless gossip that the two men were sexually involved. "If our gayness is the big secret," quipped Cowell, "then why would we joke about it in front of thirty million people?" To silence the gossip, he addressed his alleged homosexuality in his ghosted autobiography. He had "a more feminine side than most men," he admitted and added, "If I was gay why wouldn't I admit it? It wouldn't harm me . . . and my mother wouldn't freak out." Unmentioned still was the pertinent fact that not a single man had offered any newspaper evidence about an advance by Cowell, despite the promise of enormous financial reward.

The gossip about a possible scandal attracted 33.7 million Americans to watch the final *Idol* contest on May 20 and 21 between Clay Aiken and Ruben Studdard. Twenty-four million votes were registered and just 130,000 votes decided Studdard as the winner. To avoid another argument between Cowell and Fuller about the winner's song, the task was assigned to Clive Davis, working from a bungalow at the Beverly Hilton. He would, he conceded, be producing a celebrity rather than artist or a star. Singles by both men were hits, selling over a million copies, but there was to be no artistic legacy. There was no disappointment either. *American Idol,* gushed Peter Chernin, had been responsible for "the single most dramatic turnaround in Fox's history." After a contrived flip expression of disinterest about renewing his contract, Fox offered Cowell eight million dollars a year for a new three-year contract, which he accepted.

Secure in America, Cowell told Claudia Rosencrantz, "I definitely don't want to do a second series of *Pop Idol.*"

"You've got to consolidate," Rosencrantz countered. "We will work around your American commitments but if you want to establish yourself against your rivals, you'd be mistaken not to keep going in Britain." The unmentioned rival was Fuller. Rosencrantz's advice, Cowell decided, was right. She promised a power base to cement his popularity.

Claudia Rosencrantz's motive to lure Cowell back was not entirely altruistic. To fill the eighteen-month gap before *Pop Idol*'s return, she had commissioned *Popstars: The Rivals* featuring Pete Waterman and Louis Walsh, Westline's originator, creating rival girl bands.

Walsh had won the competition by creating Girls Aloud, starring Cheryl Tweedy, but had clashed with Nigel Lythgoe, the executive producer. "Nigel's an ambitious fucker who will do anything to anybody to win," thought Walsh bitterly, who was equally dismissive of Fuller as "small, well groomed, polite, and nice." On reflection he added, "Simon Cowell's got better teeth, better cars, and better women." Walsh urged Cowell to return to *Pop Idol* for another season, "if only to get rid of Nigel."

Cowell had just bought a new house in Holland Park for £5.6 million and commissioned a renovation. One more season, he decided, would not be fatal. He employed a former Royalty Protection officer as his bodyguard and driver.

In March 2003, the contracts were signed and Cowell began commuting between Los Angeles and London. Rosencrantz was relieved by the certainty of huge ratings while Fuller was delighted by the extra revenue for the use of the *Idol* format. The two men were doubly committed. For part of the week, Cowell was filming the *American Idol* auditions, and then, after jetting to Britain, recording the *Pop Idol* auditions for airing at the end of the summer.

To promote the return of *Pop Idol,* ITV featured Cowell on billboards across the country and sold T-shirts with the slogan, "Simon says what I think." Newspapers reported that the "nastiest" waxwork had been installed at Madame Tussauds. Cowell's only stipulation had been that the shirt on his effigy should hang over his trousers to avoid any ridicule of high waists. Visitors were encouraged to sing and trigger Cowell's taped judgments, like, "That was my favorite song of all time. Not anymore."

Finally, ITV staged a *This Is Your Life* program for Cowell, the very last of the series, to promote their star. In a weak production, there were many noticeable absentees from Cowell's life, including Iain Burton, Simon Fuller, and any executive from the music industry, especially from RCA. Pete Waterman appeared with some glib praise and resisted repeating his off-air skepticism: "*Pop Idol* didn't make Gareth Gates and Will Young, it made Simon Cowell."

Cowell returned to London seemingly committed to *Pop Idol*. Twenty thousand aspirants had been auditioned for fifty places in the final. "I only like two so far," he said ominously. True to form, he told a young man, "There are five hundred contestants left, so how come the chances of you winning are a million to one?" Other contestants heard, "I don't think anyone in London is as bad as you—and London is a big city" and, "The bad news is this is a singing contest." Away from recording the program, in a drab hotel conference room, Cowell targeted his venom against Nicki Chapman and Fuller. No one could ignore the arguments. Despite constant winking, Cowell's anger, aggravated by the eleven-hour trans-Atlantic commute, soured the atmosphere.

"It's terrible," said Rosencrantz.

"There's real animosity between Fuller and Cowell," agreed Claire Horton.

"Simon's dumping on *Pop Idol* to prove his power to Fuller," snapped Waterman. "They're at each other's throats."

The focus of the "unhappy ship" was Cowell's brazen championship of Michelle McManus for the winner. "You're pushing a girl who started the show at two hundred eighty pounds and is now heading toward three hundred ten pounds," Waterman told Cowell angrily, "and you're excluding real talent." To Waterman's bewilderment, Cowell kept saying with a wink, "Trust me, I've got it covered. It's all sorted."

At first, Waterman only spoke about being "so frustrated because the first series was such fun." Next, he accused Cowell of being "incredibly patronizing to the British public." Finally, he was puzzled that ITV would willfully abandon its biggest show. "Simon's sabotaging *Pop Idol*," he told his confidants, "because he resents Fuller's success. He's pushing for Michelle to kill the show."

The headquarters of the revolt was Cowell's dressing room. "*Idol* was my idea," said Cowell to his guests, including Jackie St. Clair, Terri Seymour, Vanya Seager, and Sonny Takhar, the manager of his record interests. Fuller's credit as the creator at the end of *Pop Idol* inflamed the mood.

Soon after Waterman arrived at the Fountain Studios on December 20, 2003 for the finale, he was seething. On air, Cowell was encouraging fourteen million viewers to vote for an overweight woman wearing an ill-fitting red dress. "You're mad," Waterman told Cowell during a commercial break. Not only was Cowell killing *Pop Idol* but he was also undermining Fuller's chance of promoting a good client. "He's killing it stone dead," thought Waterman, "saying to his enemies: 'You think you're clever, now see this. It's dead.'"

Five minutes before the results of 10.26 million voters were announced, Waterman stormed out of the studio, telling journalists, "I've had enough of this farce. It's a bad show for freaks and geeks." He left behind producers celebrating at a party without any stars. Fuller had disappeared and Cowell was fuming in his dressing room. The two Simons, Rosencrantz realized, were irreconcilable.

No fans were waiting for Cowell in the rain outside the studio. Stepping into his Rolls, he was content. His battle against Fuller was unknown to the media and the public's enthusiasm remained high. The sporadic accusations the following day about his sabotage were denied. McManus, he said, was "the only one with decent voice and a personality, and there was no real talent this year." It was, he insisted, "a series without passion and an anticlimax." The more substantial criticism was led by Billy Connolly, the comedian. Lashing out at Cowell's theater of cruelty, he charged, "He's so typical of the slime that's in control of rock and roll. . . . I think he's repulsive and I hate what he does. I want to slap him. I'd like to give him a big bitch slap." Cowell felt unscathed. Attacks by politically correct mouthpieces in the music industry were repulsed by a simple truth: *Pop Idol* existed to discover talent and then sell records. Money wasn't being spent to please those seeking universal admiration for dreadful singers. Billy Connolly, he added, had never spent any of his money to support young people.

To complete the housekeeping, Cowell relied on Peter Fincham, a FremantleMedia executive, to confirm that there had been no sabotage. Votes could not be bought and, regardless of talent, Scotland always voted en masse for a Scottish contestant and thus McManus won. In the event, Waterman's skepticism would be justified. Michelle McManus's single "All This Time" sold only 118,000 copies and, after suffering miserable isolation in London, she faded away.

Cowell rarely cared about a failed artist's fate. Bumblers, whether singers or executives, received no pity. Music was a business for sharks. In his ego-driven world, talent was second to self-promotion. But even Cowell, during the aftermath of the *Pop Idol* debacle, was caught breathless by Simon Fuller's next interview. The businessman had persuaded a journalist to write about him: "In the mid-1990's, he came across a struggling group called Spice that had spent eighteen months dismally chasing success. . . . He tweaked the name to Spice Girls . . . after noticing the trend called 'girl power.'" Chris Herbert, Cowell realized, had been airbrushed out of history just as Cowell had been. Once again the "publicity shy" executive whose publicist permanently intoned that his client refused to meet journalists, had given an interview in return for his description as, "the most brilliant entrepreneur in the British music industry. . . . Simon Fuller is to music what McDonalds is to fillet steak. He doesn't worry about obstacles or problems. He goes for it one hundred percent." The profile contained a blow-back. Fuller's skills, it said, included "the packaging of synthetic stars" like S Club 7. The group was suing him, alleging that while he earned fifty million pounds from their performances, he paid them just two thousand pounds per week. He was unapologetic. "I could put cardboard cutouts of you on the stage," he told them, "and it wouldn't make any difference." Like *Pop Idol* winners, his proteges' careers were short-lived. Even the exception, Posh Spice (alias Victoria Beckham) had been photographed the previous week shivering in Fuller's parking lot, humiliated, as he arrived one hour late for their meeting.

That treatment precisely mirrored Cowell's suspicion about his own relationship with Fuller. *American Idol*'s third season was due to start in January 2004. Eight million dollars had secured Cowell's appearance, but his dissatisfaction had increased. Flying to Barbados for Christmas with Terri Seymour, he resolved once again to exact his revenge.

A kind of Carribbean "Surrey on Sea," Barbados suited Cowell's simple tastes. Surrounded by serious tycoons and celebrities at the Sandy Lane resort, he liked the plain food at the Lone Star restaurant and the absence of nightclubs. Combined with the sun and blue sea his holiday should have been idyllic. Instead, he seethed about Fuller's credit on *American Idol*. "I can do better than this," he told Seymour daily while pondering his strategy.

Fuller, he suspected, was threatening to squeeze him out of TV. As flavor of the year, every new format Fuller suggested to the networks was instantly accepted. "He can sell anything," said Cowell, irritated that Fuller had sold *American Idol Junior* to Fox and excluded Cowell from any income from the records.

Angered by Fuller's aggrandizement, he had accepted an invitation to be interviewed on a New York TV program to criticize Fuller's show. Hours later, Cowell received a phone call in his hotel. "We heard what you said," screamed a Fox executive, "and it was disgraceful. You're no longer part of the Fox family." Cowell flew to London convinced that he was about to be dismissed. Instead, Rupert Murdoch had directed that his executives reassure Cowell that his contract would be renewed. Unwilling to be exposed again to Fox's caprice, Cowell thought hard: "I need some leverage," he realized. Eventually his ideas were formalized.

When not plotting his revenge, Cowell was being begged by Seymour to eat at the Cliff, the island's best restaurant. Cowell had resisted—the food, he griped, was pretentious and the ambiance was disagreeable—but he finally agreed on one condition: "We'll speak about general matters for the first five minutes and the rest of the time we'll speak about me." Cowell's conditions were not unusual. Seymour's life was always about Simon. These were the rules if you wanted to play with him. Over dinner, he outlined his idea for a new program called *Star Wars*. The conversation helped Cowell articulate his plan.

Later that night he called two *Pop Idol* producers, Nigel Hall and his wife, Siobhan "Shu" Greene, in England. "I want the judges to play a bigger role," explained Cowell, repeatedly mentioning that the judges would be looking for the X factor. Over the following days, the three developed his idea, renamed *The Greatest.* On his return to London, he swiftly sold his idea to Sony executives. Escaping from Fuller would be good news and, with Cowell and Sony choosing all the songs for the program, their profits would increase.

The next stage was to visit Claudia Rosencrantz. "There's good news and bad news," said Cowell, smiling with more winks than usual. "I'm not going to do *Pop Idol* again. However, I've got a new idea." Cowell's description of his new format raised a problem. Although there were differences with *Pop Idol*—groups could compete as well as individuals, the age range would be wider and, most pertinently, the three (not four) judges would wrestle against each other as partisan mentors of the contestants to sensationalize the offstage activities—Rosencrantz silently recognized the similarities with *Pop Idol.* Her dilemma was palpable. If she failed to accept his idea, her star would move to BBC's welcoming embrace. Her only choice was to jettison Fuller, clinch Cowell, and ignore the similarities between Cowell's idea and *Pop Idol.* After all, she reasoned, *Pop Idol* drew heavily on the Australian format originally delivered by Nigel Lythgoe (fortunately the Australian owners, after protests, had settled their copyright claim against ITV on modest terms, without any payment, after two days of arbitration). There was no reason to believe that Fuller's case to protect a format developing into *The Greatest* would be any stronger.

In any event, since Rosencrantz was determined to keep Cowell, Fuller's interests were secondary. "We love, love the idea," she exclaimed on the spot. The deal with ITV was done but would remain a secret until Cowell had overcome the next hurdle: persuading FremantleMedia, the producers who owned 50 percent of *Pop Idol* and *American Idol,* to also abandon Fuller. The program's title remained uncertain, but Cowell needed to return to America.

In Los Angeles, the production of *American Idol*'s third season had reached new records. Eighty thousand had been auditioned and the producers had improved the show's appearance. Twenty-nine million people watched the opening contest on January 19, the highest ever. Cowell's reaction was petulant: "This is the worst day I've ever seen in judging this competition. A disgrace. I didn't want to come in today."

In late February, Cowell returned briefly to London to present a dilemma to Tony Cohen, FremantleMedia's chief executive. "I don't want to do the show anymore," Cowell told Cohen, "but I've brought a proposal for a new program which ITV has bought. After much agonizing, I've decided to call it *The X Factor*." He proffered a carefully crafted document. Cohen's predicament was greater than Rosencrantz's. *Pop Idol* had become a global brand bought by over thirty countries. His choice was to either embrace Simon Cowell and confront Fuller or lose the ITV slot in Britain. The money argument, Cohen gambled, was in Cowell's favor. The new master of leverage did not anticipate Fuller's reaction.

Outraged and perplexed by the news, Fuller repeatedly called Cohen from his office in Battersea. "What are you doing?" Fuller asked, urging that FremantleMedia comply with its contractual obligations to 19 and take legal action against ITV and Cowell. "We must litigate. We must protect ourselves. Everyone is against us." Cohen repeated that *The X Factor* was different from *Pop Idol*. "You're our partners," said Fuller without raising his voice. "You're switching horses in the race. It shouldn't happen. If ITV choose Cowell, then sell *Pop Idol* to another British broadcaster."

Cohen refused.

"In that case, I expect you to sue yourselves," said Fuller, conscious that he would be losing not only the license fee but also the income for managing *The X Factor*'s winner and the record royalties. The argument about money became part of the undertone.

Another contest now erupted: Who was richer? Fuller or Cowell? The comparison became a clash of egos similar to those of football coaches. Before a match, they shook hands to signal their symbolic respect and then commenced a titanic battle. Previously mutual friends had portrayed "The two Simons" as wary but friendly toward each other. The raw emotions sparked by the television executives' decisions splintered that illusion.

In Los Angeles, Fox's senior executives feared Cowell's strategy. "If

X Factor is a flop," the network's chief told Cowell in a telephone conversation, "everyone will assume that *Idol*'s success has nothing to do with you. And if it's a success, you'll want to bring it to the U.S. and that will annoy us at Fox." Cowell ignored the warning.

The process was transforming Cowell. He was no longer the puppet but the putative executive of a show he would personally edit. Regularly, he sat with Claire Horton, Nigel Hall, Shu Greene, and Richard Holloway to develop the format and choose the panel. The Irishman Louis Walsh was an easy choice. "Wouldn't it be great if Sharon Osbourne would do it?" someone asked as they sat in Cowell's garden. Osbourne had recently come to public attention when she, her husband, Ozzy Osbourne, and their family appeared as stars of a reality show about them. "Yes, but she won't want to," replied another. "Well, I've got her telephone number," said Simon Jones, "so I'll call her in Los Angeles now." Osbourne immediately agreed. Four days later the deal was concluded.

Cowell had never met Sharon Osbourne but appreciated her achievements. The fifty-one-year-old daughter of a self-styled gangster, Osbourne was a loud and vulgar entertainer whose confessions about life amid music, violence, drugs, alcohol, adultery, and cancer commanded affection from women, despite her habit of sending excrement in a Tiffany box to special enemies. Her autobiography had sold more than two million copies. Cowell's first meeting with his new star at the Ivy in Los Angeles was complicated by an off-the-cuff comment he had made in December 2003. When told that Ozzy Osbourne had had an accident, Cowell had quipped, "He's probably done that to push his record to number one." Later he heard that the musician was in a coma. Since Sharon Osbourne wanted the job on *The X Factor,* she ignored the gibe and by the end of the meal declared, "We love each other."

The switch from star to executive producer triggered a change in Cowell's character. Fuller's commercial success, he realized, was born out of regimented organization, the antithesis of Cowell's own chaos and dithering. To organize a television show he needed to discard the ill-disciplined lifestyle of a careless record executive and emulate Fuller's methodical systems. The man who rarely scrutinized documents and found it difficult, even as a schoolboy, to focus on detail began repeatedly making lists and forcing himself to write "reminder notes." Suddenly he became appalled by the mess he inhabited. The detritus in his car—the empty cigarette packets, bottles, and papers— disappeared; he cut down his junk food and followed a nutrionist's menu; his dirty clothes were no longer dumped on a chair in his bedroom, but were fastidiously cleaned and stored in wardrobes. And while he did not curtail frequent shopping visits to Armani, he recruited a stylist to present him with a series of clothes and bought between five and ten identical shirts, suits, jeans, and T-shirts.

At the house on Loma Vista, the dressing room was transformed into a citadel of orderliness as he gradually filled the wardrobes with fifty pairs of identical trousers, nearly two hundred T-shirts, thirty suits, and twenty white shirts. Discipline had entered his life.

In March 2004, the British team met at Cowell's house in Los Angeles to finalize *The X Factor*'s set, music, lighting, themes, and structure. Cowell drove the debate to tweak, unpick, and rebuild the format. Always listening and thinking, his expectations and the budget grew. After twenty hours of discussions, the team returned to London while Cowell prepared for the finale of *American Idol* on May 26.

Watched by 31.4 million viewers, Cowell told Fantasia Barrino, a black teenage single mother from South Carolina, the winner after sixty-five million votes had been registered, "I think you are, without question, the best contestant we've had on any competition." Hyperbole came naturally to Cowell. Her single "I Believe" went straight to number 1, but while her career proved wrong those who argued that most victors of the talent shows disappeared, she did not live up to Cowell's hype. Eventually, another wannabe hit the dust, the fate of most artists. In contrast, Cowell's star was rising. *American Idol*'s ratings had risen by 13 percent and the rate for a thirty-second advertisement slot was heading toward $400,000. "The show's a cultural institution," pronounced Rupert Murdoch, unaware that his star had fled Los Angeles to supervise the first *X Factor* auditions in London.

As *The X Factor*'s debut approached, Cowell became nervous about his appearance. Although the forty-four-year-old smoked and drank regularly, he persuaded himself that exercise and vitamins were enough to counteract any risks to his health. The source of this convenient wisdom was newspaper reports and conversations with equally health-focused friends. The inevitable conclusion was that to preserve his looks, he should increase his vitamin intake.

On a friend's recommendation, he consulted Dr. Jean-Louis Sebagh, a French doctor in Wimpole Street. "We can do something better than that," said Sebagh. "When it comes to the skin, gravity is against us." He recommended regular vitamin injections and Botox injections twice a year. After the first course of treatment, Cowell examined himself endlessly in the mirror and praised his transformation as "a miracle."

He was less enthusiastic about the *X Factor* auditions. ITV's set designers had presented a scale model of the stage, but after listening to their description, Cowell began pulling at bits of cardboard, systematically destroying their work in front of their eyes. "I'm demolishing it because I hate it," he declared. "It looks cheap. Dreadful." The limited budget paid for little more, complained Cowell, than "audition rooms which look like wood shacks."

At least Shu Greene had selected contestants who played to his instincts. The characters were, she assured him, "twinkly, quirky, passionate, fun people with a light shining out of them." Despite his middle-class London roots, he loved the raw and uncontrived sense of humor popular in the north of England. The bad news followed quickly. Watching the edited version of the first two episodes, Cowell feared that the chemistry between himself, Walsh, and Osbourne had failed to ignite the contestants. Editing, he hoped, would remove the weaknesses and magnify the drama. He desperately needed a polished show.

His consolation was hearing of Fuller's frequent telephone calls to Tony Cohen at FremantleMedia.

"What does *X Factor* look like?" asked Fuller.

"It's not like *Idol,*" replied Cohen, fearful that because the same FremantleMedia team had been responsible for *Pop Idol* he was vulnerable to litigation.

"Let me see it," demanded Fuller.

"No, I can't," replied Cohen. The recorded auditions, introduced by Kate Thornton, a friend of many pop stars, started on Saturday, September 4, 2004.

"Literally anyone can win this show," said Cowell. Every debt and favor was called in to place stories on the front pages. Nothing, he decided, would be left to chance in his quest for revenge.

10

SIMON V. SIMON

COWELL WAS IN HIS BATH IN LOS ANGELES AT LUNCHTIME ON SUNDAY when Peter Powell, his agent, called. The ratings for the first episode, reported Powell, were not good. Only five million had watched the show, just 26 percent of the audience. Ten million had watched its BBC rival, *Strictly Come Dancing.* Compared to the ten million who had watched the first *Pop Idol,* continued Powell, it was a bad beginning. "I felt really awful," Cowell recalled.

Worse news arrived on Monday morning. Fuller served a writ on ITV, BMG, and FremantleMedia alleging unauthorized exploitation of the show he had created. Cowell was "stunned. I never have been so angry in my life. I was absolutely so mad with Simon Fuller. The timing was horrific. His motive was to destabilize the show. My concern was how it would affect ratings."

"When there's a hit there's a writ," sang industry insiders. Although Cowell's lawyers were certain that "Fuller doesn't have a cat in hell's chance or a prayer of succeeding," Cowell was "paralyzed by shock." Even "Sarcastic Simon" was careful about his safety. Fuller's audacity was unexpected, not least because he was litigating against FremantleMedia, his partner across the globe. His full aggression included even tipping off the media in advance, especially *The Guardian.* "He believes in reinterpreting his contractual position," was the opaque explanation by a Fuller insider.

"It's the worst week of my life," Cowell lamented. The first show, he knew, was poor, but the next two recorded episodes were better. Everything depended on promotion to improve the ratings the following week. The risk was huge. On the following Sunday, he was vacationing in Mexico with Terri Seymour. He called Nigel and Shu Greene, who were both shopping in Oxford Street.

"The figures are up by half a million—thirty-four percent of the audience," Cowell was told. Smiling with relief, Cowell celebrated the failure of Fuller's torpedo. Their relationship was broken, albeit that Cowell was in the midst of filming the auditions for the *American Idol*'s fourth season.

Over the following weeks, *The X Factor*'s ratings steadily rose. Each week the show engaged an increasing audience in the "storytelling business" hooked to the conviction that their votes would decide the universal dream and also attracted by Cowell's unpredictability. With a slight pause and movement of his head, he uttered spontaneous comments damned by some as breathtakingly rude but loved by others for their disarming charm. To shine, he suggested lines off-camera for Louis Walsh to use and then crushed him for talking "rubbish!" To create the same media interest as in America, he encouraged Walsh to attack him.

"I don't want to be like Cowell," Walsh told *The Sun.* "I don't dye my hair black. I don't do sun beds. I've had no Botox and I don't wear high waistbands."

Cowell adored the publicity.

"Louis's the strangest man I've ever met," he countered.

"The show has drained me emotionally," smiled Walsh, "and I'll need one month to recover."

"What's the talent like?" Lionel Richie, a guest on the program, asked Cowell after four weeks.

"It's not about them," replied Cowell. "It's about us." That was the defining difference between *The X Factor* and *American Idol.* Cowell's focus was on nasty competition between the judges, and the brutal truth toward the contestants, while *Idol*'s judges were soft and reassuring.

In London, the favorites had emerged within five weeks, provoking *The Sun* to accuse Cowell of rigging the vote. "Get *The Sun* on board," Alan Boyd told Cowell.

One month after Fuller's writ was served, in the midst of Cowell's commute between Los Angeles and London, the affidavits on which Fuller relied were delivered. He had three principal witnesses: Nigel Lythgoe, Nicki Chapman, and Fuller's lawyer Andy Stinson. Cowell took issue with Nicki Chapman's denial that she, Fuller, and Cowell had ever met at the Conran restaurant to discuss the idea that became *Pop Idol*. Cowell's recollection was very different. Fuller also mentioned a historic document proving his sole authorship of *Pop Idol*. The document was never seen by Cowell.

In affidavits sworn on Cowell's behalf by Waterman, Claire Horton, Simon Jones, and other producers, including those employed by FremantleMedia, all testified that *Pop Idol* had been developed from Cowell's and not Fuller's ideas. None could recall seeing Fuller's historic document. Pertinently, after his writ was delivered Fuller did not call those siding with Cowell.

One week later, Fuller telephoned Cowell. "Can we find a way to settle this?" he asked. Cowell was uncertain whether his adversary was belligerent or fearful. Knowing that Fuller was a better poker player than he, Cowell was suspicious and felt vulnerable. If his gamble failed, Cowell knew, his image in America would be dented. In any case, he reasoned, his television days were numbered because "people are going to be sick of me soon." On the other hand, he felt emboldened. "Fuller," he calculated, "is clearly freaked out that I might bring *X Factor* to America."

To supplement his income, Cowell had launched other ventures with mixed results. A new TV show called *Mogul* had been rejected; a high-cost "Rat Pack" album had lost money; and after two years of fraught work, he had finally formed Il Divo, an opera boy band.

"I'd like you to listen to them before anyone else," Cowell had beseeched a producer in New York.

"They'll never be successful," the producer responded curtly.

Cowell fumed. "I thought, I'm never going to put my life in the hands of an idiot like that again," he said.

He had assumed that fame would terminate such patronizing snubs. Instead, he also felt that he had been betrayed by a partner. "I am not happy about it," Cowell bristled, uncertain of Il Divo's fate. "Everything could crash." Suddenly his destiny seemed precarious. "None of this makes sense," he concluded about Fuller's extension of the olive branch. Toying between revenge and a settlement, he needed advice.

Lucian Grainge, who had stayed friends with both Cowell and Fuller, seemed an ideal consigliere. Cowell flew to the South of France to meet Grainge. "Find a commercial solution to litigation and not a legal solution," said Grainge, suggesting that they meet with Philip Green. "Come and stay with me on my boat for two days," offered Green the following day. During his visit, Cowell described his conflict with Fuller over *The X Factor*'s ownership. "Come up to the bridge," said Green. Climbing to the top of *Lionheart,* his 206-foot yacht, Green waved his arm over his gin palace nestling among other billionaires' overbearing trophies: "I didn't buy this yacht with a principle. I did it with a check. I've never gone to court. Is it worth going to court? You're an outsider on a massive learning curve. It's exciting. Fantastic. Can you work with Fuller? Move on." Green outlined a compromise for BMG and Tony Russell to offer Fuller but by then, the battleground had shifted.

The *X Factor* audience was rising and with the program's success Fox feared that Cowell might leave *Idol* and launch *The X Factor* in America. Peter Chernin called Cowell. "Is there anything I can do to help end the row?" Chernin's self-interest was shared by Fuller. Fearing the arrival of *The X Factor* and its impact on *Idol,* Fuller decided to sell 19 and the *Idol* franchise to protect his investment. "I've got leverage for once," Cowell said, smiling. "That was the gamble of the *X Factor* launch."

The publicity in the run-up to the British *X Factor* finale on December 11, 2004, predicted that Steve Brookstein, a thirty-six-year-old amateur singer, would win. There were, Cowell now realized, two

*X Factor*s: the one on the screen and the one featured in the tabloid newspapers. Carping criticism and a crisis generated front pages in the tabloid newspapers, and audiences rose. Stirring the pot increased the ratings.

"Steve's full of crap and people need to know that," said Sharon Osbourne, playing the game. "He's even fooled Simon. He's a fake. I don't like people playing the victim." Brookstein responded angrily to Osbourne and was equally incensed by Walsh's comparison of him to a mass murderer. The argument hooked 6.7 million viewers. Although 8.6 million had watched BBC's *Strictly Come Dancing,* Cowell had earned over two million pounds from the record sales and the show was gaining ground.

Brookstein, Cowell was sure, was another celebrity rather than a star. His critics, championing genuine artists, would undoubtedly carp about the damage to music he caused, but no one complained that Hollywood was damaged by the production of bad films. *The X Factor* had given Brookstein a chance denied by the industry but at a price. Walsh's take was that "they're all disloyal monsters. They get angry about failure and they never appreciate success. People think we're using them but in truth they're using us." Beyond the cameras, the contestants' family and friends were worse. They attached themselves to the red carpet and expected drinks and drugs. "We're looking for stars," Walsh told Cowell, "and all we're getting is competition winners with contrived stories. They want fame but don't want to work hard." Cowell was gliding above the fray. "Louis doesn't get it," thought Cowell, but his real anger was toward Sharon Osbourne. Her aggression had become intolerable. "I don't know if I can continue with Sharon," he told Rosencrantz. Her rowdiness, he explained, discomforted him. "I think she should go."

"But she's good telly," said Rosencrantz. "Go to Barbados, relax there, and we'll sort it out when you get back."

Days later, Cowell flew to the Caribbean and was joined at the Sandy Lane by Nigel Lythgoe, who impressively arrived with Jerry Hall and Ryan Seacrest. Cowell was doubly impressed after Jerry Hall was replaced by Raquel Welch, the actress whose poster had been stuck on his bedroom wall when he was a teenager in Maidstone.

Welch, Cowell persuaded himself, was being flirtatious, but she was soon being ignored as an argument erupted between himself and Seacrest over another girl Cowell was chasing.

Cowell's friendship with Seacrest, including trips together with Randy Jackson to Las Vegas, Miami, and Cabo in Mexico, reinforced his conviction that Seacrest was the buck intending to challenge the stag. "Your Highness," Seacrest chided Cowell, putting his arm around Terri the moment he spotted photographers as they walked out of the Ivy. Trumping Seacrest's publicity-seeking move, Cowell dived to pat a passerby's dog. To Seacrest's irritation, the photographers turned to snap the better picture. Seacrest followed, snatched the lead, and pulled the dog toward himself. The tomfoolery was part of Cowell's new friendship and part of Hollywood's unique lifestyle.

Keen to boost their clients' profiles, frequently agents called to announce, "I have a client who would like to meet you." If Cowell agreed, a good-looking woman appeared. On one occasion, the actress Denise Richards arrived—eight months pregnant and accompanied by a chihuahua. Some months later, she returned to watch *American Idol* at Cowell's house. In a similar arrangement, Amanda Holden, the host of *Britain's Got Talent*, was introduced only to announce as she entered, "I have a car arriving at eleven P.M."

The sybaritic life that Cowell lived was oddly contrasted by a passion for dogs. Before leaving Barbados, Cowell had visited the Hope Foundation, a charity caring for abandoned dogs. Cradling the animals set off what he admitted were his "odd" emotional relationships. As a patron of the Battersea Dogs & Cats Home, Cowell was known for walking dogs at night in London and for making appeals for animal charities including the World Society for the Protection of Animals. After two hours in the Barbados sanctuary, he had left a check for ten thousand pounds.

Cowell returned to Los Angeles for the fourth season of *American Idol* with foreboding. "I'm ignoring it," he would say unconvincingly about the litigation. He was certainly avoiding Fuller, who had been ungracious about *The X Factor* in an interview. "ITV in their wisdom backed the talent," he had said. "But if they had been smart and worked out a way of keeping Simon and I together with *Pop Idol,* it would have been to their advantage. What they have lost is a global franchise. Instead they have a poor man's copy with the rest of the world getting the real deal." *American Idol,* he enthused, had "become definitive." Thirty-second advertisement slots were selling for $395,000. Kelly Clarkson had sold five million copies of her *Breakaway* album in the United States, and twelve million worldwide, the third biggest sale in 2005. Irritated by Fuller's assertion that viewers were watching *American Idol* rather than himself, Cowell's interest in the program plummeted. Frequently, he arrived hours late for meetings and during the taping of a poor contestant, he turned away from the stage to gossip with Paula Abdul, who was by then under attack by Fox for her erratic behavior.

Surrounded by a constantly changing entourage, Abdul was attracting the wrong headlines. She had failed to stop after a minor motor accident, was occasionally reluctant to leave her dressing room for the studio, and appeared to be drunk during television interviews, although she insisted she was suffering from the effects of painkillers. Her publicized misfortunes increased the numbers watching, not least to see her caustic relationship with Cowell. On the sidelines, Cowell watched with occasional sympathy as an unpredictable and self-destructive star grappled with her demons.

As all that was going on, Cowell had spotted among the contestants Carrie Underwood, a twenty-one-year-old farmer's daughter from Oklahoma whose backstory was about frustrated attempts as a teenager to become a professional singer. "I resented that I'd have no investment in her development, so I said nothing about her being a probable star," he explained after she won. The reward belonged to Fuller when Underwood attracted nearly thirty million viewers to the finale on May 25, 2005. Fox's competition was no longer the opposing networks, whose midweek audiences had evaporated, but simply persuading people to stay at home and watch the show rather than go out.

Carrie Underwood's fame as a country singer was a sideshow to the litigation with Fuller, but her popularity reenergized his negotiations to sell 19. At forty-five, Fuller feared that twenty years' hard work could abruptly end without any residual value, just as it had with the Spice Girls. Often he referred to the unexpected demise of *Who Wants to Be a Millionaire?* Overnight the hit show had crashed from meteoric ratings to insignificance. However much he derided *The X Factor,* Fuller could not be certain in a "bubbly market" that *American Idol* would survive five more years. Repeatedly he asked his expanding staff, "What's the next big thing?" but none provided a significant pitch. Instead of risking his life's achievement, he negotiated to sell 19, including the *Idol* franchise and the management of the *Idol* winners, to Bob Sillerman, the New York media billionaire and owner of the entertainment company CKX. Sillerman had never watched *American Idol* but his eleven-year-old daughter and her friends raved about the show. That was not the only reason he was interested in Fuller's offer. He spotted a risk and smelled a bargain.

Originally, Fuller envisaged pocketing a billion dollars for 19, but *Idol's* continuity in America was threatened by *The X Factor,* and 19's last annual operating profits were only £10 million out of a £48 million turnover.

Playing poker, Sillerman paid $158.3 million for 19 in March 2005. Fuller also received a six-year contract plus a percentage of the annual net profits and an annual consultancy fee. In the erratic entertainment world, Sillerman judged Fuller's wish to cash in to be "smart."

To his confidants, Fuller spoke about building an empire of "bigger things" by combining Sillerman's wealth with his talents. He mentioned "a match made in heaven" and "a world beater" of TV production houses. Talking about "content is king," his genius would be to "unlock the brand value of famous names" including Elton John's music catalogue and exploiting the estates of Elvis Presley, Marilyn Monroe, and Mohammed Ali. Sealing the deal depended on settling the litigation, and the advance publicity for the new *X Factor* season raised the stakes.

Seventy-five thousand people had turned up for the British *X Factor* auditions, three times more than the previous year. Trumpeting the program's idiosyncratic identity, Cowell said, "The show's kind of a snapshot of this country: funny and sad in parts." He did not parry those asking whether the show reflected madness or was exploiting it. "Maybe a bit of both," he said with deliberate uncertainty. "It's looking at reality through a keyhole. Why sanitize it? I like to see the good, the fantastic, and the terrible." He had learned lessons from Brookstein's sale of only 250,000 albums. "Last year," explained Cowell, "it was a bit of a freak show. There were so many odd people there."

"There isn't one single endearing trait in his entire body," agreed Walsh about Brookstein, noting that the record by G4, the band that came in second in the competition, had scored a double platinum. Brookstein had been dumped ostensibly because of disagreements about his next album but in reality for commercial reasons.

Brookstein disappeared, complaining that Cowell was "very greedy." Like all artists, Brookstein discovered that his contract allowed the record company to charge all his expenses against his income and royalties. The "star" earned comparatively little. Few viewers had realized that the owners of *The X Factor* were earning 35 pence on each telephone vote; some telephone companies, like Virgin Mobile, were charging 85 pence for each call. In addition, Cowell and his partners were earning a share of ITV's advertising revenue, the music rights for the performance of each song, and the opportunity to promote their own artists, like Westlife. Not surprisingly, Cowell responded vaguely to questions about his income. In reply to those confused by the focus on himself rather than on the singing, he volunteered that he and the other judges were to blame for "letting our egos get in the way of the contestants." In reality, to increase the entertainment, the crazy mix was refined for the second season.

Among the freakish contestants chosen by the producers was a male stripper, a porn artist, and a crazed crooner who, after screaming rather than singing, was told by Cowell, "It's your weird smiles I don't like," and was then escorted off the stage by security. The friction between the judges also intensified. Sharon Osbourne fought with Cowell and then threw a glass of soda over Walsh. Later, she encouraged the audience to boo Walsh for favoring four Irish sisters against her favorites. "It's the Irish mafia," Osbourne stormed. "He says he's followed his heart but he's followed his passport." In retaliation, Walsh called Osbourne "a manipulative bitch" and, to Cowell's glee, the Irish president, Mary McAleese, entered the fray, asserting that "everyone in Ireland" was supporting Walsh.

To keep the promotional bandwagon rolling, Walsh confessed that Cowell's and Osbourne's ridicule had caused him "sleepless nights." Inquiring journalists were told by Walsh, "I'm actually taking sleeping pills to get some rest." Mischievously, Cowell offered himself to ITV's *This Morning* show to describe Walsh as "stupid" and to "reveal" Walsh's possible demise: "The real problem is finding somebody bland enough to replace Louis. Where do you start? It's hard being stupid. It's definitely not as easy as it looks. But Louis does it brilliantly." Later that day, Cowell added fuel by telling a newspaper, "Louis is an idiot, he has been tremendously stupid. He came into this competition bragging he had a winner—that he had the show all sewn up. But with the wrong song choices and wrong management Louis has managed to muck it all up." Pleased with his performance, Cowell flew to New York to settle the litigation with Fuller.

Cowell's appetite for a court hearing had diminished after he assessed his risk. The costs would be at least $10 million and Claudia Rosencrantz added a further twist.

"I'm on neither side," said the commissioning editor, whom he regarded as a friend. "My affidavit tells the truth, although I favored *X Factor* because ITV needed you." Both sides, she said, could draw some comfort from her statement. Then she delivered the sting: "Just think of the image of two hugely rich men arguing and it will be you who will be more harmed because you're in the public eye." Waterman also advised Cowell against "going into court and showing the public your bag of marbles." Combined with Philip Green's similar advice, Cowell agreed to Fox's brokering a settlement. But to devalue Fuller's stake, Cowell told *The New York Times* that he might not sign on again for *American Idol* because he no longer would have the record rights. He hinted that negotiations with ABC and NBC to broadcast *The X Factor* in America had started.

The countdown for the settlement involved what Cowell called "rather stressful hard bargaining." In exchange for Cowell's not selling *The X Factor* in America for five years, Fox offered Cowell a contract to star in *American Idol* for five seasons starting in January 2006 at twenty million dollars per year plus an escalating bonus based on ratings and additional payments if the production or programs were extended. Sony would own the music rights for the artists in America. Cowell received none of the profits from *American Idol,* while Fuller obtained nothing if *The X Factor* was ever shown in America but did retain his 25-percent share of *The X Factor*'s license fee in Britain. The negotiations were finalized at the Regency Hotel in New York on November 26.

In the midst of that hiatus Cowell was advised to sell his personal 50-percent stake in the TV programs including *The X Factor* to Sony for about sixty million pounds. Cowell understood the reason: "We've got no business plan, no strategy, no structure and no purpose. We're winging it." His focus remained on records, not the sale of TV formats. Critically, no one had explained to Cowell the value of merchandising the *X Factor* brand. He agreed that Sony should become the sole owner of the distribution rights of *The X Factor* and any other programs he invented, while FremantleMedia owned in perpetuity all the worldwide franchise rights. Simco, Cowell's trading company, would thereafter receive only a percentage of the profits, including income from the sale of records.

In the final hours after the agreement was concluded but before Fox's executives had signed the mountain of documents, Tony Russell called Cowell. "Keep your name out of the media for a few days," he urged. One hour later, Cowell was told by a journalist that Louis Walsh, upset by Cowell's ridicule, had resigned from *The X Factor.* "He didn't realize how sensitive I am," Walsh had complained. "I might be a clown on TV but I'm also a manager and he affected my credibility." "He can't judge a hamster competition," scoffed Cowell and replaced the receiver. To Cowell, Walsh was a loyal guy, "like a spaniel or red setter—always wagging his tail." If he sent a mildly critical text to Walsh, he could be certain that his insecurity would provoke an immediate telephone call. He also needed him on the show. But on this occasion, Walsh ignored Cowell's calls. Walsh was inconsolable. "I think Simon's very vain," he told journalists as he flew home to Dublin. "He wears platform shoes, has spray tans, wears makeup, and dyes his hair. I've resigned. It's the straw that broke the camel's back." Suspecting that Cowell was reeling, Walsh gleefully started a running commentary to the media: "Simon has so far sent five groveling text messages begging me to come back to the show." Eventually, Cowell groveled sufficiently and Walsh withdrew his resignation, but the respite was short-lived.

At nine P.M. on the same day that Walsh withdrew his resignation, Cowell's publicist, Max Clifford, called him. The front page of that night's *Sun,* he reported, featured a fat, topless stripper spanking Cowell. The source of the photograph, taken at his fortieth birthday party, was a disgruntled relative of a Girl Thing singer. "God, this is so embarrassing," said Cowell, fearing that Fox would be repelled by his seedy image. "We've got to stop it." Clifford immediately called an executive at *The Sun.* "If you run that snap you'll have no job tomorrow," he warned to no effect. Next, Cowell called and repeated the same threat. The presses were rolling and the editors at the paper's Wapping headquarters appeared unbowed. Unable to reach the editor, Cowell called Rupert Murdoch in New York. "I'm pulling out of the Fox deal," said Cowell. "What's up?" asked Murdoch, alarmed.

"How many are printed?" Murdoch asked his executive at Wapping. "Stop the presses," he ordered. Rapidly, a new front page was composed and the offending newspapers were pulped. In the trade between the tabloids and celebrities, Cowell had called in a favor and knew that if the photo had been more compromising his request would have been resisted. But he was satisfied. The tabloid journalists, accustomed to his frequent calls to their personal cellphones, depended on him for stories. In return he expected loyalty.

His influence was extended by granting his favorites admission to his dressing room. Although he complained that too many people entered his small, windowless "office, which drives me mad and I hate it," he still welcomed his retinue, including his mother—whom he treated like the queen despite her criticisms—and, recently, Philip Green and his daughter.

A love affair was developing between the billionaire and the star. "I'm cheap," Green replied to Cowell's expression of thanks for his advice. "I charge no fee." He was among the three hundred invited to Julie Cowell's surprise eightieth birthday party at the Savoy to be entertained by the cast of The Rat Pack. "Simon's always seeking his mother's approval," some guests observed warmly, adding that money was clearly no longer an issue. He finally signed the five-year deal he had been offered to appear on *American Idol*.

Although he privately claimed a 75/25 victory in the litigation with Fuller, Cowell issued a graceful statement: "Simon and I have shown just how well we work together in recent years. We have remained friends throughout this dispute and I think it was this friendship that allowed us to settle our differences." Asked about his ambitions, Cowell replied, "More money. If it could pour on me every day like a shower, I would lie in that shower for hours. I just love it." Those reading the sentiments recognized the reason for Cowell's elation. Until then, he was always in a bad mood, even sick, when newspapers' "rich lists" were published showing Simon Fuller's superior position. Now there was a chance to get even, or go ahead. "First he wanted to be a millionaire," observed Jeremy Marsh, "then he wanted ten million pounds, and next a hundred million pounds. Now he's dreaming of being a billionaire."

"That's true," agreed Cowell.

Fuller too had good reason to be bullish. After paying off a 25-percent shareholder, he was walking away with about $120 million to fund XIX, his new corporation, and to build a new empire in collaboration with Sillerman. He won universal praise for securing a "calling card for bragging rights." The new season of *American Idol*, starting on January 17, 2006, starring Cowell with Paula Abdul and Randy Jackson, promised to be more successful than the previous four. Another record was set when 35.5 million people watched the first episode, which combined awful singing, fame for the talented, and spats among the judges. Reigniting hostilities, Fuller's fateful summary was damning: "*American Idol* is the powerhouse, not *X Factor*."

In Britain, *The X Factor* dominated the front pages. No other television show generated regular reports about infighting, scheming, and tawdriness. The bitching between Sharon Osbourne and Walsh thrilled Cowell. "I encourage them to behave like brats," he admitted. "They're argumentative, spoiled, demanding but lovable." Thankfully Osbourne provided stories for the tabloids in the countdown to *The X Factor*'s finale on December 17. First, about her recent "breast job" because "my nipples were looking down at the floor"; and then about Kelly, her daughter: "She's not alcoholic. . . . She's just been finding her feet and experimenting with drugs. She's just been trying to find herself and get comfortable in her own skin."

Beyond the studio and the sound bites, a new maturity had transformed Cowell. Meetings to comprehensively discuss every aspect of *The X Factor*—the music, the production, and the commercial relationships—were conducted with unyielding resolution. There was a steely focus to every comment, order, and question he asked. The television producers, music executives, and professional advisors summoned to meetings were left under no illusion about Cowell's intransigence based on bitter experience. Technically he had unrivaled mastery of television and music production. No small detail about lighting, camera movements, sound quality, set design, costumes, song choices, or even an artist's makeup escaped his attention. Postmortem meetings ended with lengthy notes about future changes. His micro-detailed critique delivered in clipped sentences—not a word was wasted—was foreign to those accustomed only to TV's "Sarcastic Simon." Triumph could only be won, he knew, by challenging every employee to scrutinize exhaustively every detail. No one attending ever doubted that for Cowell, showbiz was a serious business.

The reward was the 9.2 million viewers who watched Shayne Ward, the twenty-one-year-old son of Irish travelers, beat Andy Abraham, an ex-garbageman, in the final. BBC's *Strictly Come Dancing* had pulled in 10.4 million viewers. "The other show's repetitious," said *Strictly*'s host, who declined to watch his competitor. The number of votes, over ten million, was double that of the previous year. Shayne Ward's record, "That's My Goal," sold 732,000 copies in its first three days, winning the Christmas number one spot. The shock factor had certainly influenced the producers' original selection of contestants. Revelations that Ward's father had just been jailed for eight years for raping a retiree; that two uncles and a cousin had been convicted for murder and gang rape; and that his older brother had been arrested for the murder of a pregnant mother but was subsequently cleared ensured that the publicity continued long after the finale.

Another winner was Walsh, who became Ward's manager and propelled him to a successful career. However, Walsh was irritated that he was paid half of Osbourne's £250,000 fee per season and much less than Cowell. "I had to point out how much they need me," said Walsh, who was rewarded with an extra £100,000 for the third season.

The biggest winner was Cowell. "I create the hype but don't ever believe it," he said. For over twenty years he had relied on his own judgment and never underestimated the public's taste for trivial drama to increase ratings. "When you do this kind of job," he continued, "the one thing you can't do is guess what other people would like. You have to do things that you like." He lacked any pretension about changing the world or leaving an artistic legacy. Just as he proudly asked for fish and chips in a top-rated French restaurant, the man who disliked "cultural snobbery" and spoke about "my very populist, incredibly juvenile tastes" adopted a plain manner to assert his supremacy over his staff, the network controllers, and his rivals. Guaranteed to earn at least $300 million over the next five years, his ambition to defeat Fuller in America would be launched from Britain.

"I don't want to end my TV career and grow old on *American Idol*," he said with a wink.

Slipstream, the nearly 200-foot yacht, Cowell's favorite holiday location (above), was a magnet for his friends, including Lauren Silverman and Kelly Bergantz (left), and in 2010, Mezhgan Hussainy (below), his fiancée at the time. © *Lauren Silverman*

Andrew Silverman (far left), Sinitta (third from left), Simon Cowell (center), Lauren Silverman (top right), and Mezhgan Hussainy (second from right). © *Lauren Silverman*

Simon Cowell's unusually close relationship with his father, Eric, sustained him throughout years of failure. © *Julie Cowell. Reproduced with kind permission.*

Cowell (left) and his younger
brother, Nick, enjoyed a
comfortable childhood in a
very close family. © *Julie Cowell.
Reproduced with kind permission.*

(from left): Tony Cowell, John Cowell, Simon
Cowell, Julie Cowell, Nicholas Cowell, and
Eric Cowell. © *Julie Cowell. Reproduced with
kind permission.*

Initially his relationship
with his mother was
volatile. Now she is a
critical supporter.
© *Lauren Silverman*

After years of frustration, Cowell scored his first hit—Sinitta singing "So Macho" in 1986. © *Alpha*

Cowell owed his break into the music business in 1983 to Iain Burton, a friend of both Cowell brothers, who often partied with Jackie St. Clair. (Top row, from right: Simon Cowell, Iain Burton, Nicholas Cowell. Bottom row, right: Jackie St. Clair.) © *Jackie St. Clair*

Cowell credited his success to Stock Aitken Waterman, London's best songwriters and producers. In 1988, Pete Waterman turned against Sinitta, and Cowell's relationship with the singer became temporarily strained. (Left to right: Matt Aitken, Pete Waterman, Sinitta, and Mike Stock.) © *Alpha*

Simon Fuller, the Spice Girls' manager, was Cowell's rival and then partner until a commercial dispute about *Pop Idol* in 2001 turned them into enemies. Ever since, Cowell pledged to get his revenge. © *Redferns/ Getty Images*

Fuller's success with the Spice Girls fired Cowell's ambitions. © *Getty Images*

Westlife, created by Louis Walsh (center), was Cowell's outstanding hit in 1999.
© *Haydn West/PA Archive/Press Association Images*

Girl Thing, created by Cowell in 2000 to copy the Spice Girls, flopped.
© *Getty Images*

Cowell was attracted to a certain type of girl, especially those appearing topless or scantily dressed. (clockwise): Vanya Seager, Louise Payne (his first fiancée), Jackie St. Clair, Georgina Law, and Terri Seymour. © *Mirrorpix,* © *TeamCamera/Rex Features,* © *TeamCamera/Rex Features,* © *Yui Mok/PA Archive/Press Association Images, and* © *Fiona Hanson/PA Archive/ Press Association Images*

Cowell's appearance on *Pop Idol* in 2001 launched his sensational television career, but fractured his relationship with Simon Fuller and even with Pete Waterman (second from left). © *Getty Images*

Starring with Randy Jackson and Paula Abdul on *American Idol*, Cowell became an American megastar. © *20th Century Fox*

Produced by Nigel Lythgoe (right), *American Idol*'s ratings soared but Cowell's relationship with Lythgoe soured. © *Alex Tehrani/Corbis Outline*

Kelly Clarkson, *American Idol*'s first winner, became a global star, making the show a TV phenomenon. © *LUCY NICHOLSON/AP/Press Association Images*

Cowell shared the global
fame of his shows' creations,
most notably Leona Lewis
(left), the *X Factor* victor
in 2006, and Susan Boyle
(below), the 2009 sensation
on *Britain's Got Talent*.
© *FremantleMedia Limited/
Simco Limited*

Bitter arguments among *X Factor*'s panel—Louis Walsh, Sharon Osbourne, Dannii Minogue, and Cowell—generated huge audiences. © *FremantleMedia Limited/Simco Limited*

This photograph of Cowell holding Dannii Minogue's hand in 2008 sparked speculation about an affair.

After a falling out with Cowell, Sharon Osbourne was featured only on *America's Got Talent*, NBC's number one show bought from Cowell, also starring controversial journalist Piers Morgan. © *NBCUPHOTOBANK/Rex Features*

Cowell and Ryan Seacrest, the host of *American Idol*, were good friends until an incendiary photo was taken of them exiting Stringfellow's strip club together, causing a rift between the two men. © *Copetti/Photofab/Rex Features*

Philip Green became the architect of Cowell's business empire and a peace broker among *X Factor*'s feuding producers. (From left: Andrew Silverman, Paul McKenna, Steve Wynn, Simon Cowell, and Philip Green.) © *Lauren Silverman*

Cowell's love for Mezhgan Hussainy, his former fiancée, cooled in 2011 after experiencing her intolerance of his relentless work ethic. Despite the broken engagement, he still felt affection for her. © *Lauren Silverman*

To some, Cowell seemed happiest when surrounded by dogs. © *Julie Cowell. Reproduced with kind permission.*

Cowell's inclusion among Hollywood's royalty at Oprah Winfrey's farewell extravaganza in 2011 confirmed his stardom, yet he appeared uneasy throughout the evening. © *John Gress/Corbis*

After fighting hard to include Paula Abdul and Cheryl Cole in *X Factor*'s American show, Cowell tried unsuccessfully after the first auditions in Los Angeles to persuade Cole to return to the British show. © *Startraks Photo/Rex Features*

The American *X Factor* in 2011 was a mixed success. Cowell blessed L.A. Reid (far left) as a triumph, but by the final night, won by Melanie Amaro (far right), he became less enthusiastic about Nicole Scherzinger and even Paula Abdul. Neither was rehired. © *Startraks Photo/Rex Features*

Slipstream is Cowell's perfect office. © *Lauren Silverman*

In 2011, Cowell once again found happiness on *Slipstream* during a summer Mediterranean cruise. To wind up the paparazzi in St. Barts in 2012, he posed with a banana held to his ear, alongside Kelly Bergantz (with hat), Zeta Graff (center), and Sinitta (far right). © *ELIOT PRESS/bauergriffinonline.com*

11

SUPREMACY

THERE WAS A LOT ON SIMON COWELL'S MIND WHEN HE MET DENISE Beighton and her business partner for lunch at the usual pizza restaurant in Fulham. He had received about two million pounds for selling *American Inventor,* a TV program, to ABC; he had lost ITV's commission for *Star Duets* after the BBC started a similar idea—"It was galling," he said with some suspicion; and fortunately, after arranging for Il Divo to perform on *The Oprah Winfrey Show,* five million copies of their album had been sold. Flush with money, Cowell paid six million dollars for his first home in Los Angeles—the house on Cole Place, on top of one of the hills in Beverly Hills, a newly built five-thousand-square-foot paradise overlooking the city. He employed a housekeeper and a cook to care for him. To finance the reconstruction and his new lifestyle, he was plotting a bigger TV show so, as he put it, "I'll earn money while I sleep."

To Beighton's surprise, after speaking about the shows and music, Cowell switched the conversation to sex.

Every day the tabloids published the most trivial reports about his life, sometimes real, occasionally fabricated, but always, in Max Clifford's judgment, beneficial to his client's image. "Anything Simon puts his name to is bound to generate huge interest," Clifford told *The Daily Telegraph,* in relation to an offer to launch his own line of cosmetics. A recent *Sun* opinion poll had placed Cowell second after the actor Daniel Craig as women's fantasy while making love. The Dream Man reacted unsurprised: "I would expect to be near the top, as I'm obviously extremely attractive. I am interested to know where Louis Walsh came. Was he even in the top hundred thousand, or didn't they include the over-seventies?"

Cowell's attitude toward women always puzzled Beighton. While she was convinced he remained unmarried because of his inability to commit himself to a relationship, Simon Jones, her business partner and a homosexual, was one of those who speculated that Cowell was gay. Both, however, were puzzled by Cowell's description during the meal of his new fantasy: "A girl," he said, "coming to my house dressed only in a fur coat and stockings." Beighton, who had witnessed so much of Cowell's sex life, asked later, "I wonder why he told us that?"

Shortly after, Richard Wallace, the editor of the *Daily Mirror,* received a series of explicit photos taken by a photographer hidden outside Cowell's west London home. They showed Jasmine Lennard, a twenty-one-year-old woman, dressed in a fur coat, arriving at nine P.M. Unusually for London, the temperature that summer day was 81 degrees. The photographer claimed to have overheard Cowell, while lying clasped with Jasmine on a hammock in the garden, speaking on the telephone to Terri Seymour in Los Angeles. The implication was that he had also heard sexual activity. Later, the photographer's flash caught Cowell's head peering around the front door as Lennard departed at three A.M. Naturally, Wallace wanted a comment from Cowell, not least because Lennard's father was known as the owner of a shoe chain and her mother had appeared in a James Bond film.

Clifford anticipated the editor's call. His client had already described his introduction to Lennard while eating at Cipriani with Sharon Osbourne. "I was set up," he would complain, asking Clifford to minimize the damage by keeping the story out of the newspaper.

"Can we stop this?" Clifford asked Wallace. The *Mirror,* he knew, was less malleable than other newspapers because Cowell had a commercial relationship with its archrival, *The Sun,* owned, like Fox, by Rupert Murdoch's News Corporation.

"Why?" replied Wallace. "I owe you nothing."

In a world of smoke and mirrors where editors cursed a publicist who would sell his own mother, the two agreed that the newspaper would quote "Cowell's spokesman" explaining that the photograph merely recorded "a meeting to discuss TV projects."

The following day, after Cowell and the rest of the world had gazed at the front page embarrassment, and Walsh was quoted saying how much he had "laughed" about the photo, Cowell called Wallace.

"I can't control you, can I? When I have a problem with News International I call Peter Chernin at Fox and say, 'Do you want a problem with your number one star?' What can I say to you?"

"Not much," said Wallace, who agreed to meet Cowell for lunch. The story, he suspected, had further to run.

Terri Seymour, his "permanent" girlfriend in Los Angeles, was humiliated. She had earlier suspected that Cowell was unfaithful but, after confrontations, finally accepted his denials. At least that had remained private. Now she could not resist flying to London. Her noisy departure encouraged photographers to stalk Cowell, who, fearing Terri's wrath, headed for Heathrow in his Rolls-Royce. As she emerged, Cowell shepherded his girlfriend away from the crowds to a Starbucks to seal her lips.

For twenty-four hours Terri was placated by his denials and expressions of affection, but then she read the tabloids and exploded. Cowell shuddered about the tears and tantrums from the woman whom his mother regarded as a daughter.

"I was set up," pleaded the bachelor. "I hate you asking questions. Nothing happened."

"Life," retorted Seymour, "is all about you, Simon. We never have a conversation about marriage."

She wanted his commitment despite Julie Cowell's warning, "You're pushing too hard for marriage and kids. He won't." His unfaithfulness, Terri feared, spelled the end of their relationship.

"I have heard brilliant things about you," said Cowell flatteringly when he met Richard Wallace. The editor was unmoved. He knew the deals Cowell made with his rivals. He was close to News International, cool with the *Daily Mail,* and had done a deal with the Express group, owned by a discredited publisher of pornography. The *Daily Express* was notorious for waging vendettas in pursuit of its proprietor's interests.

"We aren't going to have a problem about Simon, are we?" Philip Green had asked the publisher, a friend on the social circuit.

"No," he replied, "so long as he comes to my charity dinners."

To insure himself, Cowell had sat with him at that year's annual dinner for Norwood, an organization caring for sick children. Wallace refused to give similar undertakings. Soon after their meeting, Cowell had called Wallace at eleven P.M. one night: "Richard, you've been a naughty boy again. I'm just getting on a plane at L.A. and you're doing an *X Factor* story which is not helpful."

"I don't know what you're talking about," replied Wallace. "It's a five-part story of no consequence."

"It's a critical time for me," insisted Cowell. "Well, it's not for me," replied Wallace, who resented Cowell's passion for controlling people, even when he did it not by forceful cajolery but by charm and generosity.

On his return to Los Angeles, Cowell resumed his life with Terri Seymour, whom he showered with gifts.

To those who were suspicious, Cowell explained, "I don't want to ever seem stingy. My father was generous too." Just like his generosity of habitually picking up the tab at restaurants, he would not allow disgruntled girls to sell "kiss-and-tell" stories and jeopardize the burial of his past humiliations, especially just as he was enjoying his breakthrough in America. He only admitted the truth about the Lennard relationship two years later when, amid her tears, his relationship with Terri ended.

In 2003, Cowell had bored himself watching *Fame Academy,* a BBC program similar to *The X Factor.* "I'd prefer to watch a dog performing than that," he told Shu Greene. Hours later, he called Greene again. Dancing dogs, said the dog lover, would be a great program.

After brainstorming for two days, Cowell pitched to Claudia Rosen-crantz a talent show with three judges for all ages of amateur enter-tainers, including singers, dancers, and comedians. The resulting pilot was called *Paul O'Grady's Got Talent*.

"It's unwatchable," moaned Cowell. "It's so bad." He disliked O'Grady, an actor and comedian, and the program lacked a live audi-ence. Rosencrantz disagreed. "It's the funniest show I've ever seen," she said. "A no-brainer smash hit." A change of ITV's management ended the project. Three times Fox also rejected the idea. Then, in 2005, "out of the blue," Cowell would say, an NBC producer asked to see the *O'Grady* pilot. To improve the show, Cowell had edited the ninety minutes down to a sizzling seven minutes. At the end of Cow-ell's presentation at his home, the producer bought seven to nine episodes "on the spot" as a filler for the 2006 summer season. "It'll only work if you have sixteen episodes," insisted Cowell. His plea was rejected. Nine episodes of *America's Got Talent* were commissioned, starting with a two-hour show on June 21, 2006. Cowell chose the singer Brandy Norwood, the ex-*Baywatch* actor David Hasselhoff, and Piers Morgan as the judges. Morgan had good reason to be grate-ful to Cowell.

Ever since Morgan had helped Cowell launch Robson Green and Jerome Flynn, they had remained friends. In normal circumstances, that relationship could have been tested by a succession of scandals entangling Morgan's career as the *Mirror*'s editor. Notoriously shame-less, Morgan was suspected of involvement in a criminal share-tipping conspiracy, for which two of his own journalists were convicted and jailed for secretly buying shares before they advised readers to invest, and, to enhance his campaign against the invasion of Iraq, he had published fabricated photographs of British soldiers assaulting Iraqi civilians. Since his newspaper's circulation was also in free fall, the newspaper's chairman ordered that he should be frog-marched from his office into the street. Even his best-selling diaries had been exposed as unreliable, as were the questionable circum-stances of his stories about celebrities. Untroubled by Morgan's mis-conduct, Cowell had invited him for lunch soon after his dismissal, first to commiserate and second to discuss the future. Ever since he had been interviewed by Morgan for *Tabloid Tales,* a TV program about the stories behind the headlines, Cowell had marked the charming aspiring celebrity as perfect for delivering poisonous comments in his shows. Morgan would be ideal, he decided, for the first series of *America's Got Talent.*

Twelve million watched the first episode, which featured jugglers, acrobats, finger snappists, ventriloquists, and singers. Morgan proved to be an inspired choice. The cheeky entertainer shaped his humiliation techniques on Cowell's model, reducing contestants to tears. "Should he live or should he die?" he appealed to the audience like a Roman consul in the Coliseum.

An ever-increasing audience watched Bianca Ryan, an eleven-year-old singer from Philadelphia, win a million dollars in the finals on August 17 in Los Angeles. With that success, Cowell returned to ITV. *"Britain's Got Talent* is a no-brainer," Cowell told Paul Jackson, ITV's director of entertainment. Eventually the deal was agreed on. The winner would receive a cash prize and perform in front of the queen at the annual Royal Variety Performance. Cowell insisted that Piers Morgan's success in America made him a natural choice to perform in Britain.

The knave's resurrection was not universally welcomed. "Piers Morgan, what an easy person to hate," wrote the television personality Graham Norton about the brash self-promoter. "The Penis on Legs," commented the actress Maureen Lipman, describing a man horribly pleased with himself despite his dishonesty. Morgan's notoriety encouraged Cowell's excitement.

Cowell's position in British television appeared unassailable. As ITV's audiences declined and advertising revenue fell by 9.6 percent, ITV, Cowell was told, wanted a 10 percent cut in the budget. But Cowell was the network's lifeboat. In response to Jackson's demand for reductions, Cowell countered, "We need bigger sets, better lighting, and a bigger budget." At meetings with his staff, Cowell regularly cast aside the product of two months' work or demanded "twenty dancers" even though the budget was for six dancers. "And I want a helicopter shot," he insisted. His restless demands for constant change were challenged only by Claire Horton, protecting Fremantle Media's budget. The rest of his staff sat in silent acquiescence. "It's rare that he doesn't get his way," Horton complained. "Everyone is being treated as a facilitator of what he wants. It's too ridiculous. Everyone's failing to bring him back to reality." Confident of his authority to edit his show and even dictate where it should appear in ITV's schedule, Cowell refused to attend meetings at ITV's offices in south London and expected the executives to drive to his west London office at his convenience.

Cowell's twenty-million-pound contract in 2006 was for forty hours of broadcast TV (*The X Factor* and *Britain's Got Talent*) spread over two years, with a pro rata automatic pay increase for each additional hour. This provoked a bitter argument about his personal income between Cowell and ITV. "The devil is in the details," said Paul Jackson during a dispute about Cowell's demand for "overage"—extra payments for any work beyond the contracted hours—versus Jackson's interest in protecting the shareholders' funds. After bluff and counter-bluff, Simon Shaps, ITV's director of television, succumbed, and the company increased Cowell's fees and also the budget by 10 percent. The repeated retreats did not signal weakness but reality. Cowell's genteel vulgarity was delivering record audiences.

In *The X Factor: Battle of the Stars,* a celebrity show starring James Hewitt, a former army officer who had enjoyed a secret affair with Princess Diana, and Rebecca Loos, famous for a recent affair with David Beckham, the footballer, while he played for Real Madrid, the producers introduced mention of bisexuality and masturbating a pig. To stir the vulgarity, Sharon Osbourne goaded Loos after she tried to sing, asking, "Was there something stuck in the back of your throat?" As Loos's face fell, Osbourne added, "And put some knickers on to warm your voice." To everyone's glee, Loos screamingly beseeched Walsh during the commercial break, "Please stop Sharon doing this to me—only you can help." Instead, Osbourne, vowing a vendetta against the Beckhams, stormed off the set because Cowell refused to back her vote against Loos. Looking "bored," Cowell encouraged the battle but the following day called Peter Powell, his agent. "Get me off this show," he insisted. "We're all turning into prostitutes here."

Battles were always welcome. In the next British *X Factor* season—this time a hundred thousand people had applied for the auditions—Cowell was thrilled as a rejected female contestant advanced toward Walsh with a glass of water. "I saw her coming," said Walsh, wiping his shirt, "so I threw water at her first. She was the type who wasn't going to take 'no' for an answer." The tabloid hissiness of the show guaranteed that audiences would grow, but Cowell's attention had switched. Walsh, he decided, was dispensable. Cowell wanted change and Walsh was not only the weakness but also the eyewitness to Cowell's failures as a music producer. Cowell wanted the past expunged and his humiliations revenged, yet Walsh harped on those vulnerabilities, unwilling to appreciate Cowell's progression from the A&R era.

Their antagonism had not eased since the argument over Shayne Ward, the *X Factor* victor in 2005. Walsh still enjoyed telling the world that Ward had been his candidate and was opposed by Cowell. "Ever since then," Walsh complained to the tabloids, "Simon has been trying to make my life hell." The "hell" was their continuing competition over the contestants' fate for the 2006 competition. "Simon, you know nothing about guitars and real music, and everyone knows it," snapped Walsh in one broadcast. "He's petty and vindictive," retorted Cowell. "Simon," Walsh hit back in front of millions of viewers, "this song is dedicated to you. It's called 'Does Your Mother Know?'" As the episode ended, Cowell's bodyguard, fearing violence, separated the two men. Cowell retreated to his dressing room and refused to leave.

"I want a quiet word with Louis," Cowell told an assistant. "I'll give him a reality check."

"You've gone too far," seethed Walsh soon after, angered over some embarrassing criticisms Cowell had made to journalists. "What Simon did," Walsh retorted to the same writers, "was absolutely disgraceful. Childish and silly. He has run off to nurse his bruised ego."

The newspaper reports of their tiff helped generate 11.3 million viewers the following week.

Enjoying the argument and irritated by her exclusion from the publicity, Sharon Osbourne grabbed the spotlight during the next program by licking Cowell's face and rubbing his nipples. "Ooh, Simon loves a big haggis," she gushed in what some viewers thought were the "horrible" antics of a drunk. Cowell was furious. Revolt was intolerable unless he benefited. He wanted obedience. Instead, Walsh was carelessly digging his own grave by telling a newspaper, "Simon's obnoxious, smug and really loves himself but underneath that, he's a really great guy." After more backstage fights, Cowell and Walsh stayed at different hotels in Cardiff during the program's auditions. The Irishman, Cowell concluded, was "boring." In Cowell's lexicon, the adjective was fatal, particularly as, during the show, he had spotted a genuine star.

Although Leona Lewis, a twenty-two-year-old from Hackney in east London, was described as "a receptionist," her father had spent eighty thousand pounds on his child's education at musical and drama schools. After he "sacrificed everything," Leona Lewis had, at her own expense, recorded several songs before entering the *X Factor* competition. Long before she reached the finals, Stephen Ferrera, a Sony record producer in New York, had called Cowell. "She's dynamite," Ferrera said after watching Lewis on YouTube. "She's clean cut and wholesome with international appeal. She should do an album with Clive."

At the end of the second live program, the show's guest performer, Rod Stewart, told Cowell, "That girl's a star." Shortly after, Clive Davis called Cowell. "You may have a Whitney Houston on your hands. I will sign this girl whatever happens." Long before the final, Ferrera was researching hundreds of songs as possibilities for her first album.

By mid-November, Lewis's irrefutable superiority was forcing Cowell to deny that the competition was fixed in her favor. "I've bet a thousand pounds Ben will win," he said about Ben Mills, another contestant. "I genuinely think Ben will win," he insisted about a man who would be eliminated before the final showdown. Some believed

Cowell was dissimulating to conceal the producers' manipulation, while others questioned Cowell's judgment. Either way, he loved the publicity.

Some tabloids reported Lewis allegedly enjoying "sex romps" with an ex-boyfriend; others found an uncle who was a convicted robber and a cousin who had been raped; all reported her parents' separation; and to stir the spice, Lewis denied that she would sleep with Cowell to win the show. Consistent with their relationship, Walsh parodied Lewis as "dull and shy with no personality." He hoped, he said, that Lewis would lose so "I can see if Simon's face falls apart. He'd be gutted."

In a three-hour show on December 16, watched by 12.6 million viewers, Lewis won the final over Ray Quinn. She sang the specially commissioned "A Moment Like This." Eight million viewers voted, earning the four stakeholders—Simco, ITV, FremantleMedia, and the telephone corporations—about £2.8 million altogether. There was additional revenue from special merchandise, including video games, T-shirts, mugs, an *X Factor* karaoke machine, and a special Christmas record, which was downloaded over fifty thousand times within the first three minutes of its release. To Green's surprise, Cowell did not develop the merchandise business.

The X Factor had delivered a genuine international star. Clive Davis welcomed Lewis to Los Angeles to be "broken into the star-making machine." The producer arranged the same showcase as he had for Whitney Houston. "I invited top songwriters to watch Leona perform. I wanted to encourage them to write for her. I got 'Bleeding Love' and 'Better in Time'; both were number one hits." Producing the album with original material would take one year. Davis planned the launch of her debut album at "my annual Grammy awards party"—the hottest ticket in town—and on eighteen TV shows, on radio, and on a theaters "tour." The album, called *Spirit* in Europe and *Forgive Me* in America, was destined to go to number 1. By 2008, Lewis was the world's highest paid singer. A star had been born—or at least manufactured by the best producers. In turn, Cowell had become America's and Britain's highest paid TV star.

Another victor was Richard Griffiths, Cowell's former boss, who had established a management company for singers. His agency was struggling until Cowell called. "It's anarchy," said Cowell. "The judges are fighting to become the artists' managers. I want you to become the manager for all *X Factor*'s artists, so it's a level playing field." With Leona Lewis, Griffiths gratefully leapfrogged to success.

After a Christmas break in Barbados where he socialized with Nigel Lythgoe and Philip Green, Cowell returned to Los Angeles for the start of *American Idol* on January 16, 2007. The prospect filled him with horror. "I feel I'm in a prison," Cowell said to himself. "I've got to get out." Lythgoe, he decided, was becoming unpleasant, made worse by the hectic schedule and the program's success despite poor contestants. Over thirty million viewers would be watching what the advanced publicity promised to be a "meaner" show, but the meager highlights were Cowell being attacked by one contestant with a tub of hair gel, apologizing to another for saying that she looked like a giraffe, and making amends to a third for calling him "a bush baby." This was all profitable television for Fox but was boring for him.

His irritation sparked a spate of arguments about *American Idol*'s content with Lythgoe who, Cowell decided, was unnecessarily harassing him. After one public quarrel, Cowell told an eyewitness, "I'm quite comfortable having a bust-up with people to their face. It kind of clears the air." "Simon blew Nigel out of the water," sniggered Ryan Seacrest. The stalemate needed resolution.

Cowell was belligerent when *The X Factor*'s senior producers arrived in Los Angeles from London to discuss the new series for 2007. Meeting in Cowell's home, they discovered a restless star impressed by Darnell's mantra of constant renewal. Unlike other British TV producers, who looked for new shows rather than improving existing winners, Cowell spoke as a perfectionist about "raising the bar" and "refreshing the show" to prevent *The X Factor*'s becoming stale and withering. His shopping list was exhaustive.

First, he wanted a bigger budget to improve the show's appearance. Inevitably, the ITV producer refused, but Claire Horton agreed to see whether his expectations "to push the envelope," to tinker with endless technical details, could be met. "I also want major changes," Cowell told his visitors. "Louis," said Cowell, "is exhausted. People I trust tell me he's become pointless." Kate Thornton, the host, he added, was unimpressive. Both, he decided, should be fired. Some around the table were unconvinced, but sensing the mood, Shu Greene agreed. "I think Louis should be replaced by Brian Friedman," she suggested, referring to the choreographer who was directing a pilot called *Grease Is the Word*, a TV singing competition for couples to win a place in a West End production of *Grease*. Although Friedman's charms lacked universal appeal, Green's instincts commanded respect and Cowell confirmed Friedman's selection.

Responsibility for delivering the dismissals was assigned to Richard Holloway, a genial producer capable of delivering graceful executions. Everyone also agreed to Cowell's suggestion of the extra judge. He wanted Dannii Minogue, the thirty-five-year-old star of *Australia's Got Talent* and the sister of the hit singer. She had recently blamed her broken marriage, friendships and engagement on "my hectic work schedules." Female vulnerabilities attracted Cowell.

"I have bad news for you," Holloway told Walsh, who was standing in a hotel room in Stockholm. One week earlier, after a meeting with Cowell in Los Angeles, he had been sent to Sweden to find new songs. "I feel like I'm stabbed in the back," Walsh stuttered as Holloway revealed his fate. "I'm really shocked." Minutes later, Cowell was called by a journalist to comment on Walsh's dismissal. Startled, he assumed that the staff at ITV or FremantleMedia was paid by tabloid journalists for tips.

"It was ITV's decision," declared Cowell.

"I wasn't sacked," Walsh told the first journalist to call. "I made the decision to leave by myself." But after more leaks from the producers, Walsh admitted, "It seems I've been fired by Simon." Then he added, "I don't know where this rubbish about me being boring or dull has come from—it is completely untrue."

Hearing that Walsh was distraught, Cowell called. "It's nothing personal," he said.

"I'm devastated," admitted Walsh, looking at himself in the mirror. "Am I too old? I know I haven't looked after myself properly. My teeth, my hair, my skin . . . they all need fixing."

As he gabbled about his lack of self-confidence, Cowell assured him, "It's just ITV's decision."

By then, Holloway had personally visited Kate Thornton's home. In tears, the fired presenter recalled how another producer had mentioned her "bad teeth and bingo wings." Now, she told Holloway, she felt doubly humiliated because Cowell had "assured me privately and publicly that my job was safe." She refused to take Cowell's telephone call.

The reaction in London stung Cowell. Both casualties attracted widespread sympathy. He hated being portrayed as disloyal. The parting, he told each journalist who telephoned, had been amicable, and he went further: "I didn't fire Walsh or Kate. It was ITV. . . . It was not my decision." He had pleaded, he said, to keep Walsh and Thornton.

Walsh was incensed after the publication of Cowell's sentiments. "I have been completely shafted by Simon," he told the *News of the World,* adding that Cowell and not ITV controlled everything. "He has told me bare-faced lies about my future and, worst of all, he didn't have the balls to tell me personally that I was going." Kate Thornton, he added, "is very upset and feels really humiliated. She wants to speak to Simon but he hasn't even called her to wish her well." Thornton in turn blamed the "political cesspit at ITV."

The ITV executives Paul Jackson and Simon Shaps were prepared to take the blame. To Shaps it seemed that Cowell regarded Walsh's dismissal as part of a "guessing game of the panel's identity to generate media interest while the program was off the air." Cowell, he knew, enjoyed uncertainty.

To keep the story boiling and in reply to Sharon Osbourne's accusation that he was "a coward," Cowell summoned a *Sun* journalist to fly to Los Angeles. "I should have told Louis myself he was sacked," he explained. "What he should know is that there was only one person defending him and that was me." He added that he had nine new shows in development and in eighteen months hoped to have fifteen shows in production in the United States and United Kingdom. Walsh was unimpressed. "I'll never work with him again," he told *The Sun,* sobbing about his "heartless" firing. "He never even called me." No one, it appeared, could unearth the truth and Cowell had moved on.

The speculation about Walsh's replacement fueled more welcome publicity. Agents pushed their clients' names into the spotlight and Max Clifford stirred the pot. "Donny Osmond is definitely in the frame," said the publicist, "but I'm not sure Simon would be keen on choosing someone younger and better looking than him to be on the panel, so we'll see." Even Sinitta threw herself into contention. "I'm the rightful new judge because I've been groomed for the job," she said, grateful for Cowell's support during her marriage in 2002, a failed pregnancy using a surrogate mother, and the adoption of two babies. In early April, Brian Friedman and Dannii Minogue were confirmed. Cowell had taken pleasure from the hiatus. Control over his own kingdom was so much more fun than appearing on *Idol,* especially during 2007's lackluster competition.

On May 23, Cowell arrived at the Kodak Theatre in Los Angeles for *Idol's* finale. He was amused only by Paula Abdul, who had recently broken her nose apparently by falling while avoiding Tulip, her dog. "How's the dog?" he asked mischievously, knowing her fate on *Idol* was uncertain.

During early 2006, the media had reported Abdul's late, tearful arrival at the Fox studios and her involvement in some brawls around Los Angeles. She blamed her painkillers but Fox's producers questioned whether she was worth her $1.8 million annual fee and began considering replacements. The controversy had resurfaced during 2007. She had again called Cowell "a jerk" and "an asshole" after he covered his ears and mockingly told a man, "You should be singing in a dress and stilettos." Then she tried to slap him. And finally, she appeared on a Seattle TV show jerking her head, with slurred speech and glazed eyes.

Like Cowell, she was disillusioned by the inadequate contestants. Although in 2006, 63.4 million votes had been registered for Taylor Hicks, a twenty-nine-year-old from Alabama, Cowell had derided the winner as "a drunken father singing at a wedding." As Cowell expected, although Hicks's first record, "Do I Make You Proud," was a number 1 hit, he was dropped in 2007 by Arista. The 2007 competition was even worse. Melinda Doolittle, consistently winning most votes, was voted off the week before the finals after a negative campaign organized by votefortheworst.com, making Jordin Sparks, a dull seventeen-year-old from Arizona, the probable winner.

The season's only highlight had been Idol Gives Back, a humanitarian campaign featuring a trip by the judges to Nairobi to raise sixty million dollars for charities. Cowell spent three days in the Kenyan capital's biggest slum. "The toughest three days of my life," he told a friend. "I couldn't believe the extent of the poverty." Nevertheless, to make it palatable to the American public, he determined that 50 percent of the money raised would be given to American charities.

The worst moment during the season had been a cutaway during a live show of Cowell rolling his eyes while others were mentioning the massacre of thirty-two students and faculty at Virginia Tech. The public furor threatened permanent damage to his reputation. "It was damning," admitted Cowell. "An awful twenty-four hours and very frustrating because the Fox producers told me it had blown over and I should say nothing." Cowell demanded the chance to explain that he had been speaking to Abdul unaware of the discussion of the killings. "I may not be the nicest person in the world," he explained in a transmitted interview, "but I would never ever, ever disrespect those families or those victims, and I felt it was important to set the record straight."

Looking bored on the finals' night, his head resting on his arm, Cowell amused himself by reminding Abdul how before a previous show he had told her, "Ask me to tell the story about the moth and the melon." When she obeyed he had replied caustically, "I don't know what you're talking about," as the camera cut to Abdul's incredulous face. Abdul grimaced as Cowell glanced at the stage and noticed Sir Trevor McDonald, the distinguished British TV presenter. Acting puzzled, Cowell watched McDonald progress across the stage toward him holding a large red book. "Simon Cowell, this is your life," said McDonald as the audience roared. "Is this a windup?" asked Cowell. "I'm actually really embarrassed." The show would be taped in London after Sparks won, watched by 25 million Americans, compared with 36.3 million viewers in 2006. Sparks would sell about three million albums before her career declined.

Cowell was apprehensive about *This Is Your Life*. The same program four years earlier "wasn't great," he had admitted. "It felt too early. I never watched it afterwards or read the book. Ally Ross had written in *The Sun* that it was hilarious watching Cowell with no friends. This time I hoped it would be better." Inevitably he knew in advance about ITV's plan to give an old format just one more chance, and had played the surprise perfectly.

Cowell was introduced as "one of the most famous people on the planet . . . one of the most obnoxious men on TV, the Antichrist of the pop world." The first guest was Louis Walsh. In the contrived drama that Walsh later called "Laurel and Hardy," Cowell said as Walsh walked toward the leather sofa, "This is going to get very uncomfortable." "Not for me," snapped Walsh, who nevertheless gushed about their past collaboration.

"I humbly offer a groveling apology, Louis," laughed Cowell.

"All is forgiven but not forgotten," replied Walsh. Amid applause and clapping, Cowell said, "And we'll do some other shows together."

"I'm not sure about that," replied Walsh.

"Nor am I," said Cowell after a delay.

There were tributes from Ant & Dec, Pete Waterman, and the author Ben Elton, whose amusing monologue included the comment, "To Simon Cowell, masturbation isn't about self-abuse, it's about fidelity." Then, after his family and Andrew Lloyd Webber praised the hero, Ryan Seacrest and the *American Idol* judges stepped through the doors. "Simon's the only person who calls out his own name during sex . . . ," said Abdul, and got more laughs adding, "Looking at himself in the mirror is what Simon thinks is foreplay." When Trevor McDonald mentioned a "girlfriend," Cowell jokingly said "Linda . . . ," knowing that Terri would walk in. She smiled, unaware of the barb. The show ended with Cowell standing aside from his guests, pushing the red book toward the camera with his name spelled in gold. He was pleased that the program was better than the previous one: "I made bloody sure this time that there would be more friends."

After pocketing over thirty million dollars plus his share of the royalties on Jordin Sparks's records for *American Idol,* Cowell began intensive editing of *Britain's Got Talent.* The first series would start on June 9 and run daily for one week. Simultaneously he was editing *America's Got Talent,* to be introduced by Jerry Springer with Sharon Osbourne as a judge, starting on June 5. "Each edit," Cowell told himself, "improves the drama, music, and presentation of the contestants." His daily routine had changed too. Waking at noon, he worked seven days a week, sometimes until five A.M., with a nap in between. His restlessness had become relentless.

On the day the first of the recorded *Britain's Got Talent* episodes was transmitted, Cowell arrived at the Emirates Stadium in north London, the new home of the Arsenal football club. Eight thousand people had arrived for the first auditions of *The X Factor,* an unexpectedly high number. Cowell sat down with Sharon Osbourne, Dannii Minogue, and Brian Friedman to hear the first contestant. Ten minutes later he stopped and summoned the producer. "It's not working without Louis," said Cowell. The producer was surprised. "I miss Louis," Cowell told Claire Horton a few minutes later. "Brian was a mistake." After a brief attempt to start the auditions again, Cowell called another halt and went to his dressing room, a corporate box overlooking the football pitch. He telephoned Paul Jackson: "I've got to have Louis back." Shocked, Jackson urged, "Can you at least finish today's auditions and I'll drive out to the stadium to meet you." Cowell, he later discovered, had not continued the auditions but instead had locked himself in the dressing room, confirming his own problem. "Without Louis," Cowell explained, "there's no one to feed the lines for me to make my sort of jokes."

Even Osbourne was struggling. Cowell had stumbled on a truth that as the contestants became weaker, the show depended on the judges: "I need Louis. He's fun. He's a court jester." Cowell did not admit another reason. When they had worked together, Walsh had regularly uttered excellent lines that Cowell repeated. In the editing, Walsh's original version was dropped, and by selecting the best shots of himself, Cowell perfected his own appearance. He needed Walsh's return as a sparring partner. Another reason was Walsh's threat to transfer Westlife from Sony to Universal, and the group was destined to sell more than forty million albums.

This was the stuff of madness, thought Jackson. Eight thousand contestants and over a hundred crew members were standing idle while Cowell was pleading for the man he had fired. Cowell's financial wastefulness had reached new extremes. "Your career is on the line," said Jackson to Cowell. "You're going down. You've lost the plot. The Walsh situation is causing chaos."

"The show," Cowell replied, "is more important than the contestants."

"You're destroying the credibility of the show and you're making us all look stupid. The press will jump all over us for not knowing what we're doing," concluded Jackson.

Cowell was unfazed. Recording was abandoned and he agreed to meet Simon Shaps. "ITV think it's all doom and gloom," thought Cowell. "I can't understand why everyone is so scared about admitting a mistake." To Jackson's and Shaps's surprise, Cowell seemed to enjoy the crisis. Unusually, he traveled to ITV's headquarters.

"I'll take the responsibility in the press that we made a mistake," Cowell told Shaps.

"Simon likes to portray Walsh's firing and rehiring as drama, mischief," thought Shaps. Jackson was included in a conference call.

"Why do we want Louis back?" asked Jackson. "Is he the only option?"

"I've given you my reason," said Cowell ending the discussion. Shaps reluctantly agreed.

The same afternoon, Cowell telephoned Walsh: "There's a chance you could come back."

"My bags are packed," replied Walsh.

"Don't say a word or it won't happen," warned Cowell, knowing that the next problem was to fire Brian Friedman, who was already injured by Cowell's decision, announced during a press conference to abandon *Grease Is the Word.* "Simon's smothering my creativity," complained Friedman flamboyantly. "I haven't signed a new contract yet. I need six months to clear my head."

Within hours the news had leaked. Cowell, reported *The Sun,* had begged Walsh to return, offering a million pounds, but Walsh had refused. Cowell was paralyzed. "The tabloids," he acknowledged, "help you more than they harm you. They are promoting you, your shows and your artists. . . . When I've had a bad time with the press I've normally deserved it." *The X Factor*'s salvation would wait while he rescued *Britain's Got Talent.*

The reviews of the first episode of *Britain's Got Talent,* watched by 5.2 million people, 22 percent of the viewing audience, were poor. Cowell's publicist deflected the criticism by feeding trivia to TV reporters: Cowell had sat on two cushions because Piers Morgan was taller; Terri Seymour "revealed" that Cowell did three hundred push-ups a day to appear fit in his T-shirts, even when flying; and Amanda Holden was scripted to divulge her cure to Cowell's and Morgan's "squabbling." She behaved like their mother: "Neither has any social skills when it comes to saying something difficult without being rude."

Five days later the mood turned. The audience grew and the critics spoke about a "renaissance" as TV's Saturday night graveyard was transformed by a new "golden age" by reminding the audience of the English's eccentricity. The emerging hero was Paul Potts, a thirty-seven-year-old cellphone salesman from South Wales who had paid twelve thousand pounds for coaching lessons. On the final Saturday night, 11.45 million viewers, 48 percent of the audience, watched him win the vote singing "Nessun dorma" from Puccini's *Turandot.* "Oh God, not opera," sighed Cowell.

Just as Potts gloried in the spotlight, Brian Friedman faced his eclipse. Cowell, he complained, had caused a personal crisis, a sentiment echoed by Dannii Minogue. "I am at the end of my nerves," she told the producers. "I'm waking up thinking, 'Am I next?'"

Cowell was unaffected by their flutters. His success depended on exercising total control over his shows, the network controllers, and his producers in two continents. Any weakness was intolerable.

Walsh's mixed fortunes did not scratch the Cowell brand. Turning his mistake into a soap opera was welcome publicity. Max Clifford provided the tabloids with "color" to cover their front pages with praise for the hapless Irishman's resurrection. On June 22, Cowell and Walsh were photographed spending the day together racing at Ascot. The week's races were Cowell's comfort zone. Only his closest friends were invited to his box, and a different ex-girlfriend arrived every day. For Terri Seymour, Cowell's unusually close relationship with his former girlfriends was part of life. In return for his generosity and affection, they became trusted confidants happy to endure a celebrity's introspective monologues. The only man prepared to offer similar therapy was Louis Walsh, whom Cowell occasionally spoke of as "my best male friend." Like the other guests at Ascot, Walsh was unconditionally grateful to his host. Thanks to Cowell, his life would certainly improve.

To cover Walsh's return to *The X Factor,* Jackson and Cowell agreed to stage a scene of Cowell being filmed saying to Sharon Osbourne, "Something's wrong and I can't put my finger on it," to which Osbourne would reply, "We miss Louis." After the exchange had been refilmed several times, everyone declared themselves satisfied, except Jackson. Aspects of the staged discussion made him "cross." Holloway refused to consider his objections: "Simon has approved this, so if you want to change anything, you'll have to speak to him." After a "heavily charged" conversation with Cowell, Jackson ordered two seconds to be removed.

Considering Cowell's anger with those searching for evidence that *The X Factor* was rigged—and he hated the tabloids' use of the word "fix"—staging the scene was a strange decision. He always fumed over complaints about the voting that triggered official investigations by Ofcom, the British communications regulator. Although no complaint was ever justified, few doubted that the recorded programs were distortions. Purists could moan but "reality" television was by nature unreal.

The irrefutable reality was Cowell's ambition for supremacy. His success depended upon inspired producers unconditionally sympathizing with his whims. Those failing the test automatically became less useful. The casualty of the summer's turmoil was Paul Jackson. His unease about Cowell's play with Walsh reduced his value. Cowell, Jackson suspected, enjoyed the excitement of casting a judge off the program to give his show an additional boost. Public dismissals, the skeptic mused, could even become Cowell's trademark. Those heretical thoughts ended Cowell's complete trust in Jackson. Cowell disliked being second-guessed. And he disliked Jackson's unwillingness to recognize his emergence as a global star. If the protestor could not adjust, he was best edged out of the inner circle. Jackson would no longer be invited for Sunday breakfast in Holland Park or enjoy bantering in Cowell's dressing room. Cowell believed that he had drawn the best out of Jackson, and that his input had become irritating.

12

TOYS

"THEY'RE MY TOYS," THOUGHT SIMON COWELL, SITTING IN THE MEDI-terranean sunshine. He loved playing with women, especially those starring as judges on *Idol* and *X Factor.* Dannii Minogue added to his fun. "She'll be the new toy in the show and everyone will enjoy play-ing with her," he said.

In July 2007, Cowell had rented the appropriately named Villa SC near St. Tropez, with staff and a Ferrari Spider thrown in. Exhausted by the eleven-hour commute between Los Angeles and London, the frequent flights across the United States, and producing and appear-ing on two shows, he collapsed with Paul McKenna and Sinitta, his loyal friends, and was joined by Kelly Bergantz and others employed by Sony. Terri Seymour was not invited.

One year earlier, Cowell had tired of Terri. As he explained to a confidant, "I told her, 'I don't want to sleep with you anymore, but I want you as a friend.'" Tearfully she accepted the inevitable and, de-spite the split, agreed to pretend their relationship was continuing.

"I felt liberated," said Cowell, but he was "embarrassed" after the news inevitably leaked. "For the first time," he grumbled, "I've had to put out a press release to announce the end of a relationship." The statement was delayed until he arrived in France. To cushion her embarrassment Cowell volunteered, "Terri dumped me in a text message." He wanted neither marriage nor children, he said. "I treat my shows as my babies." Terri Seymour was suffering greater stress. Four years earlier, she had said, "I am pretty secure. He's never given me a moment's worry. Simon has said he has been faithful because there would be no point continuing the relationship if he were not." After his denials, she had ignored the Jasmine Lennard awkwardness but was distressed by his refusal to commit. "I said I want a baby," Seymour explained, "and Simon told me to buy a terrapin." His most romantic gesture, she said, "was to buy me a toothbrush." Less romantic were the repeated arguments caused by his boredom, demand for "space," and her accurate suspicions of unfaithfulness. After four years together, she sensed he was enjoying an affair in Los Angeles, possibly in an apartment he had recently bought nearer the city.

"The split is amicable," Max Clifford announced. Seymour's pride was protected by providing an apt quote from her: "Now I can use the mirror. He used to take forever in the mornings." The pain was mitigated by financial help. Cowell bought Seymour a Bentley, a Range Rover, and a house for $4.6 million in Beverly Hills and provided the renovation and maintenance costs. Through Cowell, Seymour also landed a contract as a reporter on *Extra,* a syndicated celebrity show broadcast out of Los Angeles.

Cowell's generosity, it appeared, had bought Seymour's discretion. Indeed, she never sold a kiss-and-tell story about their relationship. Nor, pertinently, did she reveal details about their sexual relationship. As Denise Beighton had observed, Seymour's figure did not match Cowell's fantasy, yet they were good friends. Moreover, Terri and her mother were close to Julie Cowell, and that was important for Cowell. Without any other real friends in Los Angeles, he knew he could rely on her.

On cue, Sinitta stepped forward to quash the new rumors about Cowell's sexuality and the reason for his generosity to ex-girlfriends. "Sex is so important to Simon," said Sinitta. "That's his trouble. It clouds his judgment. But I know what he really wants. Someone to be his companion, his buddy, his mentor, but someone who can put up with his work ethic as well. I'm going to find him his perfect woman. He does have this problem, though. It's called a roving eye."

Among those friends he met in St. Tropez was Philip Green, anchored off the coast on *Lionheart*. Cowell used the opportunity to discuss his sale of 50 percent of Simco to Sony two years earlier.

"Why did you do that?" asked Green.

"It was an advisor's idea to raise cash," replied Cowell.

Green shook his head. "A mistake. You're not thinking about merchandising. That's where you'll make your money," he said, mapping out a sketch of a media empire.

"He's been one of my biggest mentors and is one of my closest friends," Cowell said of Green after several conversations. He was grateful for one final suggestion: "Get a yacht for your next summer holidays. It's more private and you can move around."

America's Got Talent had been extended to twelve two-hour episodes running from June until August with Sharon Osbourne, Piers Morgan, and David Hasselhoff as the judges and Jerry Springer as the host. The competition, which was won by Terry Fator, a ventriloquist, was consistently the summer's number one show, helping sales of the format to other countries. At the same time, Cowell was preparing for the *X Factor* auditions in Britain. A hundred and fifty thousand hopefuls had applied and recordings would begin in mid-August just after *American Idol*'s auditions began in San Diego. Crisscrossing the Atlantic, he couldn't resist casting the fly: "I'm working on a secret project. Bigger than *American Idol*." That was guaranteed to wind up Fuller.

By mid-August, playing with his toys on *The X Factor* was providing more fun than he anticipated. "Dannii Minogue and Sharon Osbourne are at loggerheads," he rejoiced. "When I sit next to one, the other sulks. I have to try to give each one equal attention." To generate more tension, he slanted toward Minogue and described Osbourne as the "queen bee," who disliked the Australian "strutting around as if she owns the place." The closer he sat next to Minogue, the more Osbourne and Walsh suspected their employer's motives.

Playing with the two women fed his appetite to enjoy similar games with the contestants. The producers had gathered a collection of freaks. One seventy-year-old woman was dressed in Jacko-style clothes with sunglasses and a cap to conceal her face and poor teeth. "You're like something out of a horror movie," observed Cowell. "I urgently need dentistry," she admitted, adding, "I'm standing here like someone who actually has the X factor." "Yes, but not on planet Earth, darling," cut in Cowell. Other put-downs were similarly original: "If you sang like this two thousand years ago people would have stoned you." And, "If your lifeguard duties were as good as your singing, a lot of people would be drowning." Some thought the climax of his games was the crucifixion of an unemployed drug addict: "You're lazy, deluded, and talentless." In reply, she screamed, "Kiss my arse . . . the way you lot live your lives you're all fucking shits." She was then ejected from the studio by Cowell's bodyguard. She was "the worst contestant I have ever met," Cowell chortled to *The Sun,* encouraging the viewers to watch that night "the amazing rant" of a woman revealed to be "a sixty-pound-a-time hooker in a massage parlor."

Others marked the humiliation of a hugely overweight girl filmed with her similarly oversized family—mother, father, sister, and grandmother—as a highlight of Cowell's playfulness: "That dress is all wrong and you sang out of tune, and you sounded like a baby." Tearfully, the heavy girl left the audition and was filmed telling her family that the dress was "so good," followed by the family entering the room to complain to Cowell.

"Take a good look at yourselves," replied Cowell robustly. "You are the reason why this girl is disappointed. You have given her false hope." Critics would say Cowell and his producers had given the "false hope" but he was unbowed. Another contestant made it to the next stage only to subsequently be told that she had been excluded. "You're pregnant," Cowell said. "It's crazy because you'll give birth during finals."

No one was disappointed as she raged and her fiancé threatened to smash the camera. By the third episode, over ten million were watching, a massive 48.9 percent of the total TV audience. And playing with his toys was keeping the audience high.

To Cowell's glee, Sharon Osbourne threatened in early September to resign. Tired by the weekly commute between Britain and America for *The X Factor* and *America's Got Talent,* she had become emotionally drained by disclosures her brother made to the *News of the World.* A convicted criminal, he told the newspaper that his sister hated Cowell, was jealous of Dannii Minogue, and was trying to sabotage *The X Factor.* Grabbing the priceless publicity, Cowell encouraged Osbourne to defend herself. "My brother," she said, "has lived off me for years, taking millions, but after I stopped the checks he became bitter."

She quickly withdrew her resignation, but her suspicions about Cowell and Minogue were revived when she and Walsh, sitting in their private plane on the tarmac, spotted the two getting into their own bigger jet. "They're having it off," she told Walsh, peering through the window. Cowell denied her allegation but subsequently confessed to a discreet affair.

"I had a crush on her. It was Dannii's hair, the sexy clothes and the tits. I was like a schoolboy. She was foxy. She was a real man's girl. Very feminine." He loved the conquest of a star who was fun on the program. Secrecy, he knew, was vital. Even after he was photographed holding Minogue's hand in the back of a limousine as they left the BBC studios, most speculated that the clasp was posed for another headline, although Cowell would admit, "It was genuine love." But there were limits. To his surprise, he found Minogue gloomy, "and after Terri, I wasn't ready for another relationship."

Sharon Osbourne's suspicions entrenched her jealousy of Minogue. Just why Osbourne cared about the secret relationship was hard for Cowell to understand but, amused by the screams in a mid-Atlantic twang from her cosmetically enhanced face, he gladly stoked the fire by backstabbing and spreading rumors about Osbourne's dubious family and large entourage. Provoked into retaliation, Osbourne burst into dramatic spoilers during the program. "Fix," she regularly screamed, which satisfied Cowell's critics. "That's great TV," agreed Cowell, "but it's creating a daily drama for people management."

Regularly, Richard Holloway hastened to Osbourne's dressing room to "douse the fire" and urge the distraught woman to "calm down." "You tell her it's not good enough," Cowell said. "It's all fixed, so who the fuck cares," cursed Osbourne, whose public-relations man spoke about Cowell's employing a call center in India to get winning votes. To Cowell, this was great sport. Playing with Minogue, he knew, incited Osbourne. "I often ogle Dannii's bum," he told *The Sun,* knowing that Osbourne was irritated by Minogue's flirtatious and frequent visits to Cowell's dressing room.

In October, Osbourne arrived for a live episode angling for a showdown. A journalist had tipped her off about Minogue's scoffs that Osbourne used plastic surgery to conceal her age. Shortly before the show started, Osbourne entered Minogue's dressing room. Not coincidentally, she chose Minogue's birthday for the confrontation. "Happy birthday," she seethed and began to rant. Within seconds, the Australian was crying. As her makeup disintegrated, Holloway intervened. "Fuck off," screamed Osbourne. Five minutes before airtime, Claire Horton rushed into the room. "I'm quitting," screamed Osbourne. Nearby, Cowell sat in his room. "I wasn't happy about it, but I didn't come out because I didn't want to get involved," he said. With moments to go, Osbourne was shepherded into the studio, Minogue's makeup was repaired, and Cowell emerged with a smile. "I find girls fighting very amusing," he said. "The competition adds spice to the show, and the show is about the judges, not the contestants. Everyone is enjoying playing with the new toy."

After the program, watched by a record audience, Osbourne justified her outburst to a newspaper: "I've had it up to here. . . . It's like a bloody circus. It's a pantomime with the pyro, feathers, girls dancing and wiggling. . . . But I've made a mistake. I don't know if they want me back." The following day, she phoned Cowell to apologize. They met the following night. "Stop fighting, stop flouncing . . . and stop getting on my nerves," Cowell ordered sternly, anticipating a new peak in the ratings. Meekly, Osbourne complied.

In Cowell's world, success deserved a prize. The battle between the two women justified a reward for himself, and nothing was more appropriate than a new dressing room in Wembley's shabby studios. On a higher floor were some dirty rooms. Cowell spent twenty thousand pounds renovating them for himself, tripling the size of his

suite. The walls were covered in slate-colored leather tiles and enormous mirrors. The furniture was also leather, and a bathroom was
built with Spanish marble in a separate room. From then on, one
hour before the program, while mayhem and screams raged beneath
him, Cowell would be soaking in a large hot bath watching *Strictly
Come Dancing* "to wind me up to do better." Louis Walsh was suitably
impressed. "The funniest moment," he observed, "is watching Simon
doing his hair in the dressing room before every show. He loves looking in the mirror." The conversion of the dressing rooms was a trifle.
Cowell had also bought a Bugatti Veyron, the world's most expensive
car, for £750,000 and paid $400,000 for a Rolls-Royce Phantom Drop-
head Coupé with a cream leather interior. The bigger trophy would
be a second house in Beverly Hills. Pressed for time, Cowell needed a
friend to undertake the search. Naturally he turned to Terri Seymour
who, with gentle coaching, had recovered from the split and became
another trusted "ex."

Louis Walsh had sided with Osbourne in the Minogue battle, so,
to generate publicity, Cowell encouraged Dannii to complain to a
newspaper that "Louis keeps grabbing my bum at work and I am like,
that is wrong . . . please get off me." Walsh denied the accusation and
at the next opportunity during a show, criticized Minogue's comments about a singer: "How would you know? You've never had a
hit." As the show ended, Minogue rushed tearfully to Cowell's dressing room. Like an errant schoolboy, Walsh was summoned by Cowell. "I'm in trouble," Walsh thought as he entered the room and saw
Minogue sobbing.

"You can't say that sort of thing to Dannii on live TV," said Cowell. "It's bullying."

"But I did," replied Walsh, believing that Cowell had loved the
snub and was merely acting to please his lover. Controlling women
gave him great pleasure.

"Well, it mustn't happen again," said Cowell, smiling as he got
up. His hair needed a quick wash and while his visitors remained, he
blow-dried his hair in front of the mirror. "He tilts his head just like a
woman," thought Walsh. "Anyway, it's all for show. We love slagging
each other off and we try to out-bitch one another." The bust-ups

raised the tension for the finale on Saturday, December 15. "Sharon's an old witch," said Minogue in a loud whisper overheard by the studio audience during a break in the final show. "That was wonderful," Cowell decided. "Better than the singing."

As planned, Sharon Osbourne was tipping toward an explosion. The speculation about the "relationship" had been refuelled by Minogue's "revelation" in the press that while "desperate for love" she preferred "a man's man." Although she flirted with Cowell, she said, "that man could flirt with a book, a wall, anything, and I don't fancy him."

An invitation was arranged for Osbourne to appear on the *Graham Norton Show*. Asked about Minogue's "contribution to the music industry," Osbourne spat that Minogue was only on the show "because of her looks" and because she and Cowell "are close." Getting up, she turned her back to the camera, patted her backside, and compared her ample behind with Minogue's Botox face. "She's younger, She's better looking, Simon wants her and he doesn't want me . . . thank God." Minogue, Osbourne would add later, was cursed by "appalling" plastic surgery and only stayed on *The X Factor* because she wanted sex with Cowell.

"A loose cannon," said Cowell.

"A car crash," agreed Walsh about a woman he adored.

While the "toys played," Cowell had no qualms about show business's cruelty. Up one day and out the next. Nor was he bothered either by his critics' prediction about a contestant's demise, or by others' moaning about *The X Factor*'s dismal influence on the music industry. The show was never conceived as a charity but as popular television to enrich Cowell and Sony by reducing the cost of finding and marketing stars and securing high sales of their music.

The multimillion album sales in 2007 were by Snow Patrol, Kaiser Chiefs, Razorlight, Keane, and Franz Ferdinand, proving that *The X Factor* did not kill original music. The show provided a different platform of instant success to those lacking sufficient experience to complete the stiff ascent. While most fizzled out, unable to sustain a career, some succeeded. Paul Potts sold three million albums that year and reached number 1 in seventeen countries; Will Young, the

Pop Idol victor in 2002, remained successful; Leona Lewis was on the eve of international stardom; and Kelly Clarkson was also selling millions of albums.

The nature of stardom had changed. The aura, mystique, and mythology which had enthralled fans for years had been ripped apart by mass exposure. The isolation and idolization of most stars was being replaced by stars being in thrall—even grateful—to fans. Despite the marketing budgets, some *Idol* and *X Factor* victors would eventually entertain passengers on cruise liners or turn on the Christmas lights in unknown villages. That was show business—"A lot of people want you to fail," sighed Cowell—and even he lived with the fear of his own humiliation, although not in the immediate future. His American career was entering a new chapter. The end of his five-year contract with Fox was in sight. The success of *The X Factor* and *America's Got Talent* had altered all his relationships.

Cowell was more irritable than usual on his return to Los Angeles for the start of the seventh season of *American Idol* on January 15, 2008. His relations with Fuller during their occasional conversations about the show remained coolly stable, but his dealings with Nigel Lythgoe had become intolerable. The auditions had again not thrown up a potential star and Cowell was frustrated by his lack of influence. The hook to keep the audience, he believed, was to contrive arguments among the judges or to focus on characters among the contestants. *Idol*'s talent scouts and producers were charged with finding not only great singers but colorful backstories. In Cowell's words, he wanted "oddballs because they're entertaining."

During February, Cowell pinpointed Kyle Ensley, a computer nerd among the potential contestants, as the "geeky antihero" to satisfy his requirements.

"I can't let you have him," said Lythgoe.

"I want him," insisted Cowell. "I want someone I can pick on."

"No geeks this year," replied Lythgoe, unconvincingly opposed to manipulating a "victim." *Idol,* said Lythgoe, was about the contestants, not the judges. Cowell was equally adamant that slick entertainment required high production values. During their heated argument, Ensley's role as a curiosity became academic.

Asserting his authority, Lythgoe loudly criticized Cowell's intention to "wreck" the show's credibility and condemned Cowell's "verbal assault" upon himself. "The argument went on for a long, long time," Cowell recalled. "And I couldn't shake it off when we were filming." Appalled by Lythgoe's petulance, Cowell cornered Darnell.

"What's the problem?" he asked.

"Everyone has voted against it," explained Darnell. Not only Abdul and Jackson, but also Cécile Frot-Coutaz, FremantleMedia's purposeful chief executive for North America, was opposed to Ensley remaining. Cowell backed off, telling Ensley in front of more than twenty-five million viewers that his expulsion was regrettable.

Cowell suspected that Lythgoe's victory reflected Fuller's influence. Still fuming about the litigation and irritated by Cowell's growing success, Cowell assumed that Fuller had rekindled Lythgoe's resentment, festering since 2002, about Cowell's fame. "This has all left a sour taste," Cowell told Darnell. "This is a decisive moment. I'm absolutely furious." His revenge would now be directed against two people.

Just as Les Moonves, the chief executive of CBS, was damning *Idol* in an interview as "a monster" and urging, "Please kill that show," Darnell saw the results of all the arguments on the screen: Cowell was openly bored and the ratings were falling. The salvation, Darnell decided, was Lythgoe's dismissal from the next season. Mortified, Lythgoe had no doubts that Cowell had demanded his removal as one condition for extending his contract in 2010. Cowell denied the accusation: "I wasn't bothered. I had no part in Nigel's dismissal. I have zero contractual influence." Lythgoe determined on revenge at the very moment Cowell intensified his bid to break out of "prison."

During his weekly commute from Los Angeles to London, Cowell switched into conquering mode. The next season of *The X Factor* had been increased by five slots to twenty-seven episodes, some staged in the giant O2 Centre and Wembley Arena. The new season of *America's Got Talent* promised to be another winner while *Britain's Got Talent* had been praised by the press. Instead of appearing daily for one week, Cowell had persuaded ITV to run fourteen *Got Talent* episodes over seven weeks. In his search for poignant performances, Cowell had jetted around the country listening to ten hours of auditions every day. Among the "finds" was Andrew Johnson, a thirteen-year-old choirboy from an impoverished north England council estate who spoke about repeated bullying at school. His rendition of "Pie Jesu" had moistened the eyes of everyone in the room. In reality, Johnson did not live in poverty and the "bullying" had been a single incident years earlier. But "sob stories" were good television that drew viewers and so appealed to Cowell and his producers.

Cowell returned to Los Angeles for the *Idol* final and watched the lackluster David Cook win in front of a declining audience. He jetted straight back to London to work on the *Britain's Got Talent* finale on May 31. His effort attracted 14.4 million viewers, about 54 percent of that night's TV audience, the highest for an entertainment program in that decade. George Sampson, a fourteen-year-old dancer, won, and Andrew Johnson came third.

The success of *Britain's Got Talent* and *The X Factor* had transformed Cowell from a performer into a major producer. His contracts with Fox and ITV would expire in 2010 and thereafter, he hoped, he would open a new chapter of his life. Cowell was on a roll, and among those he expected to suffer were Lythgoe and Fuller. To his surprise, Fuller offered a peace treaty.

Bob Sillerman, the owner of *American Idol,* had earned "hundreds of millions of dollars" from his $158.3 million purchase of the program and the company from Fuller in 2005. His sole concern in 2007, when he reduced his stake in CKX to 20 percent, was securing Fox's extension of the contract for *American Idol* so "it lasts forever."

Sillerman had first met Cowell the previous year during a rare visit to CBS's studios in Los Angeles. The stage on Beverly Boulevard was used for *Idol*'s live shows. Sillerman recognized Cowell as "a genius" and feared *The X Factor*'s success in Britain. When Cowell's contract with Fox expired in 2010, he suspected, Cowell would be tempted to abandon *American Idol* and introduce *The X Factor* to America. The danger had been confirmed when Fox paid Cowell fifty million dollars for a five-year agreement for the first option to stage *The X Factor* in America. Sillerman's strategy had been explained to CKX's board of directors: "I want to combine Fuller's and Cowell's expertise.

They're competitors but also friends. I want Cowell in the CKX family, bringing *X Factor,* the *Talent* programs, and the recording rights to develop the business long term and build an entertainment empire."

Getting Fuller's· support was effortless. Fuller was concerned about *American Idol*'s future and Cowell's threat of upstaging him. To anticipate Cowell's shift in 2010, Sillerman, with Fuller's support, made in 2007 a seemingly irresistible offer.

"I'm offering you three hundred million dollars to come in with us—a full buyout in perpetuity," Sillerman told Cowell on his next visit to Los Angeles. "That's a ridiculous amount of money," thought Cowell. During early 2008, Sillerman and Fuller sat for hours in Cowell's home in Los Angeles and his trailer at the studio lot discussing a merger. In Sillerman's opinion, "it wasn't 'if' but 'when' and 'how.'" To finalize the deal, Cowell entrusted the negotiations to Tony Russell.

Certain that he would soon be worth over $500 million and his future would be in America, Cowell urged Terri Seymour, his closest friend in Los Angeles, to look harder for a bigger second home. Money, he assumed, was unlimited—he had even been offered a million pounds to advertise Viagra, an offer he rejected. The ideal house, Seymour reported, was owned by Jennifer Lopez and was for sale. Unfortunately, Lopez had promised the new building to Gwen Stefani. "Who designed this?" asked Cowell after a tour. "Jennifer Post," replied the agent.

Seymour finally found a suitable house on North Palm Drive in Beverly Hills; Cowell bought it for eight million dollars and Terri Seymour agreed to supervise the renovation. After searching through *Architectural Digest* for an interior designer to transform the twelve-thousand-square-foot traditional house into a modern extravaganza, she persuaded Cowell that Jennifer Post was ideal. Eccentric but well respected, Post suggested that Brian Biglin, a local architect, should be hired to "transform the house into an open and flowing stylized project," retaining the privacy at the front but "opening up the garden at the back to let the light in."

Cowell had very specific tastes about everything: the rooms' design; the surface materials of wood, marble, and stone; the colors (especially black and other dark colors); the lighting (concealed); his bathroom (vast); the cabinets (plentiful); the kitchen (functional); and the cinema room (comfortable). Only the design of the grounds remained uncertain. As the first plans were offered, Cowell began to have doubts.

"Close your eyes," Post ordered Cowell and Biglin. "Now open them." On the table they saw a black toy model of a Maybach car. "This is your house," said Post. Cowell was puzzled. Shortly after, he encountered Post again in the house. "Your T-shirt," she said pointing at his usual gray top pulled down over his waist, "That's your house."

Sometimes, even Post was confused about the similes. "This is project Bentley," she would tell Cowell, referring to the standards she expected. "Like the car, you've got to put all the wood, metal, and leather together to make it look seamless." The ultimate in luxury would be cashmere couches, walls covered in Ultrasuede, and exterior flooring of black basalt stone—"the most solid, purest black stone God introduced to the earth," Post told Cowell. "I always used the word 'Jacometti' in my designs," she told him, "but you don't seem to recognize the name." Nor, it was said beyond Post's hearing, did anyone else. In Post's opinion, New York design was a hundred years ahead of London's, so she embarked on educating her client. "He didn't know what a fine piece of wood looked like," Post would say after their relationship crumbled. "When I said, 'We're not going to put Picasso in this house,' he asked, 'Who's Picasso?' He thought only Frank Sinatra was famous. I told him, 'I can't believe it.'" Cowell would later explain that he was mischievously teasing Post.

For the initial $3.5-million building budget, Cowell accepted Post's proposals: the floors would be covered in "super slabs" of Greek white Thasso marble lowered into position by cranes; "elegant but functional" custom-made cupboards throughout the house and kitchen would be supplied by Poliform in Italy; Fenestra windows imported from Italy would provide a perfect sealant from the heat; and the lighting would be centrally controlled from the master bedroom by phone. There would be a cinema room with a fourteen-foot convex screen and a sound system engineered to focus the sound at a "sweet spot where Simon will sit." The centerpiece of the design would be Cowell's bedroom and a "spa bathroom allowing water to become a feature." A special custom-made British tub was ordered from Zuma measuring two meters by one and a half meters, shaped to allow Cowell to relax on special backing. The water could cascade into the tub from special taps in the ceiling. Built adjoining the bath was a marble chair for a friend to keep Cowell company while he bathed and watched cartoons.

Adjoining the bathroom with radiant-heated marble floors was a shower and steam bath. In the ample cabinet space for his creams, pastes, ointments, sprays, pills, and gels there was no space for "her" creams, but "she" would be welcome to use his. Altogether, it created an atmosphere suggesting a temple of self-obsession, the worship of Cowell's vanity.

The room assigned as the dressing area was sufficiently spacious for two people to "chat while preparing to go out without feeling cramped." Downstairs, the kitchen, filled with Miele appliances, was a chef's dream. At the back of the yard there would be two separate houses: a gym with a treatment room, a big steam shower, and an area suitable for a photo shoot, and a guesthouse called Vietnam by Post. It would be "one large room designed in contemporary architecture like a nice hotel suite," according to Brian Biglin.

Reconstructing the house on North Palm Drive encouraged Cowell to rebuild his house in Holland Park as well. His incessant demand for change not only applied to his homes but to his shows, including the new season of *X Factor*. The highest number of people ever, 182,000, had applied for the auditions.

Sharon Osbourne and her antics were already forgotten. After the final show in 2007, she had issued an ultimatum: she would leave unless Cowell fired Dannii Minogue. Cowell refused. He had already lined up Cheryl Cole, the star of Girls Aloud, the group created in 2002 by *Popstars: The Rivals,* to take Osbourne's place. Cole led Britain's most successful girl group with eighteen consecutive Top Ten singles under Louis Walsh's delegated management.

Cole was born Cheryl Tweedy in 1983 on a council estate in Newcastle. Her family included one brother who had appeared in court over fifty times for theft and vandalism. She too had been convicted—for punching a black female bathroom attendant at a nightclub—and given 120 hours of community service. In 2006 she had married Ashley Cole, a star soccer player with the Chelsea team, in a ceremony paid for and featured in *OK!* magazine. Months later, a twenty-two-year-old hairdresser had sold her story to a tabloid describing her recent one-night stand with Ashley Cole. To Cheryl Cole's distress, that confession provoked other women to sell their stories of sexual experiences with her new husband. But in 2008, when Cheryl Cole was revealed as Sharon Osbourne's successor, Cheryl and her husband appeared to be reconciled.

Cowell had first met Cheryl Cole as she waited for him in the cold outside the Wembley studios in 2007 to raise money for the Comic Relief charity as part of the TV series *Celebrity Apprentice.* Cowell was particularly struck that the singer had waited without a film crew, showing her dedication to raising money. "She's cute," thought Cowell and wrote a check for £25,000. Weeks later, she accepted his offer to become a judge on *Britain's Got Talent.* Three days before the show started she pulled out. Explaining that she was "uncomfortable," he concluded she lacked the self-confidence needed to criticize other artists. Her place was taken by Amanda Holden.

On the rebound from her refusal, Cole told Cowell, "I made a mistake." "Don't worry," replied Cowell. "You'll be on *X Factor.*" Again she declined, admitting her unease about criticizing others, but finally she agreed, joining for £600,000 compared to Dannii Minogue's £500,000. "Now we've got two toys on the panel," thought Cowell. His affair with Minogue was over—"There were a few bonks and then it petered out while I was in America," he told a friend—and he was tempted, if the opportunity arose, to enjoy one with Cheryl Cole. At the same time, he looked forward to playing games with Cole and Minogue. The omens were good. At the reception in a Mayfair hotel to introduce the panel to the media, all the attention was focused on Cole while Minogue was ignored. "A bitchy battle of the babes," thought one of Cowell's aides, watching Minogue, who was clearly frazzled by Cherylmania. "That's what the public wants," agreed Cowell. The media were encouraged to believe that just as Minogue had not spoken to Osbourne, she had no contact with Cole.

Cheryl Cole arrived for the first auditions in mid-June 2008 looking thin after a make-or-break holiday with her husband. Five minutes into the program, Cowell whispered to his producer, "A star is born." By the end of July, Cowell was congratulating himself. Eliza Doolittle from the council estate was perfect casting. Cole cried during the auditions because, she said, the contestants' hard-luck stories reminded her of her tough youth. "I wish I could bring someone home to the family," she said memorably. Increasingly, Cowell included shots of the two together, especially with his arm across her shoulders, and he repeatedly mentioned her in newspaper interviews. Cole's light knowledge about music—"she doesn't even know Elton John's 'Crocodile Rock,'" Walsh told Cowell—was glossed over with Cowell's help.

"Do you fancy him?" Walsh asked the woman who ceaselessly flirted with Cowell.

"I look at Simon as an uncle," she replied. Her detachment inflamed Cowell's interest. Unlike Walsh, who went to Cowell's home after each show to watch a recording along with the entourage—Sinitta and Jackie St. Clair competing over who should sit on the sofa next to Simon—Cole returned home "to look after my dog." Surprisingly, Minogue showed no jealousy about the teacher's new pet. She simply ensured that her clothes outshone Cole's.

By the end of the auditions, Cowell spoke about "the strongest season ever." The tearful stories about poverty, struggle, expulsion from school, marital betrayal, and relations dying of cancer were mixed with his barbs and admiration: "You've got great legs," he told a transsexual drag queen; and, "That's one of the best bodies I've ever seen in my life," he praised a model who said she typically posed nude. His empathy was also edited into a spell-binding exchange with a sobbing twenty-three-year-old describing the traumatic abandonment by his parents and sexual abuse by a family friend. His story proved to be untrue but the subsequent confession—"I didn't mean to lie"—was great television. In the trailer, Cowell vowed that judges were nastier than ever: "We're going to hell and I'll be driving the bus."

Before leaving for summer vacation, in the week that ITV's profits and ratings dropped to a seven-year low, Cowell started a critical fight with the channel's managers. He wanted the network to broadcast the results in a second live show on Sunday nights. Paul Jackson, ITV's head of entertainment, was torn. To save money, some suggested that the results show should be recorded after Saturday's episode. Jackson disagreed and insisted that the show be live but was worried about the content and the cost. Cowell's insistence was destabilizing.

Jackson's position was precarious. Opposition to Cowell, he knew, usually curtailed careers, but he could no longer tolerate Cowell's "lunatic level" of self-promotion and interference in ITV's management of the schedules and even the appointment of senior managers. Unwilling to tolerate critics or those who displeased him, Cowell unhesitatingly expressed his dissatisfaction to ITV's Peter Fincham, the supreme director. "Simon's lost the plot," Jackson, who had decided to leave, told Fincham. Free to offer his opinion, he added that there were neither the producers nor the money to make yet another show of uncertain quality. "The network is too much in hock to Simon. It'll damage ITV because our business is too enmeshed and reliant on him. This is getting out of hand." In a final warning, Jackson told ITV's executives, "The deeper we get into the water with Simon, the further we have got to swim back." On that basis, Jackson rejected Cowell's latest proposal for a new dance program.

In Cowell's opinion, Jackson similarly suffered from losing the plot. ITV's salvation, he believed, depended on exploiting the successes he offered. He called Jackson to repitch the dance program.

"Can we stop talking about this bloody show?" snapped Jackson. "We said we don't want it."

"I don't like the tone of your voice," said Cowell calmly. Jackson apologized.

Cowell's whole lifestyle seemed to confirm his new status, including his summer vacation plans.

On Philip Green's advice, he had chartered *Xanadu,* a sixty-meter yacht that could sleep twelve, for a month. Sailing in the Mediterranean with Paul McKenna, Sinitta, Kelly Bergantz, and the Silvermans from New York, he met Green, Steve Wynn, and other billionaires sailing on considerably bigger yachts. By all, he was welcomed as a star.

Britain's political leaders were also competing for his affections. There was an invitation from Gordon Brown, the prime minister, to Downing Street for drinks and, later, he and Piers Morgan enjoyed dinner at Number Ten. With unusual charm, Brown converted Cowell, a natural Conservative, to consider helping the Labour government.

Soon after, he was introduced to David Cameron, the Conservative Party leader, by a member of the Murdoch family while they were dining in Mayfair. Cameron's easy manner and grasp of Cowell's career secured the star's sympathy. "He's a regular bloke," Cowell told his host. "I like him." Weeks later, Cowell attended a Conservative ball to raise funds and recruited *Britain's Got Talent* finalists to attend a party hosted by Cameron. Gordon Brown was agitated. Downing Street was determined to secure the star's endorsement. The statistics showed that Cowell's show faced no rival.

The X Factor's first episode was watched by 10.2 million Britons in 2008, 54 percent of the viewing audience. The launch of the season—the biggest in ITV's history—beat *Strictly Come Dancing.* The star was Cheryl Cole, elevated by the public to the role of champion of abused women struggling, after betrayal by a cheating lover, through their crisis. "Just being around Simon and his ego has taught me quite a lot," sighed Cole. "He's actually made me a lot more confident and a lot more comfortable. The fact that he respects me means a great deal." All the ingredients existed, Cowell believed, to launch *The X Factor* in America and challenge *American Idol's* dominance. His armory was enhanced, Cowell believed, because he had found another star.

Alexandra Burke, a twenty-year-old girl of Jamaican and Irish parentage—with the style of looks that appealed to Cowell—had reached the last group of twenty-one contestants in 2005's competition but had withdrawn before the finals. The public was told that she had withdrawn before entering the finals because she was too young, but in reality she had been pregnant. Three years later, after professional coaching, she had shone during the auditions. To promote Cole, Cowell had assigned the singer to be Alexandra Burke's mentor. But Cole would not be allowed to reach the finals with her contestant without Cowell "playing" with his new toy to create some headlines. Inclined to treachery, he provoked those whom he had created.

"You're doing my head in," Cheryl Cole snapped at Cowell for disputing her judgment and encouraging an argument with Walsh.

"And you know nothing about girl bands," Cole accused her manager, the same Louis Walsh. To spark more arguments, Cowell probed Minogue's insecurities. First about her choice of music and then by giving Cole more airtime in the edited versions.

"What's your problem?" Minogue asked Cowell during a break.

"I haven't got one," he replied.

"You have," she insisted. And then, to Cowell's delight, Walsh reduced Minogue to tears during an argument, allowing Cowell to order Walsh and Minogue to "kiss and make up" live on air.

As the audience increased, Sony promoted its artists. Will Young, Take That, Beyoncé, Il Divo, and Leona Lewis appeared on *The X Factor* and were joined by Mariah Carey, a Cowell favorite, and Cole singing with Girls Aloud. "That's when I realized Cheryl's a big star," Cowell said. The biggest trophy he attracted to appear on *The X Factor* was Britney Spears.

The soap opera of Britney Spears's rise, fall, and slow resurrection amid addictions, abuse, and hyped relationships had been followed across the globe. In the pop industry, the fineness of the thread separating genius from insanity had destroyed many fame seekers, but few thrived on attention like Spears.

Cowell appreciated celebrity madness. Those artists who could transcend a decade qualified, in Cowell's opinion, to become superstars. "I like artists who take charge of their careers," he repeated. "Game changers are those prepared to die while trying." Spears had gone closer to the edge than most.

"She's a plain Jane," Cowell had said after Spears's disastrous appearance in September 2007 on MTV's Video Music Awards. His insult was ignored when, in November 2008, the singer searched for slots to promote her latest single in Europe and Cowell wanted to boost his ratings. But he had not anticipated her antics.

"There'll be no rehearsal," Cowell was told in the chaos following Spears's arrival at the *X Factor* studios in Wembley. "She's on medication. The studio must be in lockdown." Having demanded two Winnebago luxury trailers—every star is normally assigned just one—she took Cowell's old dressing room and refused to meet her host. "She's frosty and I haven't got a clue why and I don't care," said Cowell. "I love all this stuff." But even Cowell had not anticipated that Spears would also ignore the contestants and mime "Womanizer," her new single, for three minutes during the live show. "She forgets her lines," an aide explained. When Cowell finally entered the diva's dressing room, he recalled, "She was just staring at me. I said, 'Have you ever watched the show?' 'No' she said. And I said, 'Touch me, I'm human,' and I think that broke the ice." One minute later, Cowell walked out of the room. Her freakish visit pushed the audience to 12.8 million, another record.

Under pressure to increase the audience further, the publicists picked a new angle every week. At the end of November, they coerced Rachel Hylton, a failed contestant, to curse Walsh as "a vile old buzzard" and to attack Dannii Minogue with vitriol. "It's a black thing," she exclaimed, outraged that "they were intentionally trying to take the piss out of me" to please "white middle-class viewers" because Hylton, a former drug addict and the mother of five children (with three in foster care), had been exposed as having posed in a photograph with a gangsta gun gesture. "That's how we express ourselves," she spat. "I'm from the 'hood."

As that sensation waned, an attractive contestant expressed her "shock" that Cowell wanted to spend a night with her: "He's not really my type." Once that headline was used, Walsh reduced

Minogue to tears again by calling her an actress. The following day's newspapers reported his apology and then his breathlessly quick retraction "because she *is* an actress." Finally, in the countdown to the climax on December 13, Downing Street announced Gordon Brown's personal letter to all twelve finalists advising them not to take Cowell's comments to heart.

Not for the first time, the prime minister misjudged the nation's real concern. The series had been about Cheryl Cole: her dignified retort to her unfaithful husband, her uncontrolled sobbing of "real tears," and her rehabilitation: "Our Geordie princess as the nation's sweetheart." Featured on *Vogue*'s cover, the waif had become a fragile fashion icon. She appeared as a serene and beautiful national treasure. Her publicist had persuaded millions of besotted viewers that despite Cole's being "under an enormous amount of pressure during the ten weeks of *X Factor,* she has worked herself up to get Alexandra Burke ready for the final." Even Cowell was glorified for allowing Cole to snatch his popularity. To add grist to the mill, Cowell was simultaneously damned by Minogue as "the biggest diva on the show," overshadowing even Mariah Carey's demands for rooms, flowers, and candles. Playing with his toys, Cowell caricatured Minogue as tortured by jealousy. Eleven years younger and more beautiful than she, Cole was permanently seated next to Cowell. "He moved me away from him," sighed Minogue, "and now he sits next to Cheryl and is in her ear all the time. It is a snub but I'm fine." Cowell knew she was not fine and that was intentional.

In all the emotion, some might have forgotten the contestants. During the finals, Burke, the favorite, sang Leonard Cohen's "Hallelujah." "That was incredible," said Cowell. "You've got to win." Minutes later, Sony released the recording as a digital download, and it became the fastest selling song of all time. To maintain the momentum, three days later viewers read that Burke's mother risked missing the show because she required four hours of dialysis every day to prevent a fatal kidney failure. "Alex will be heartbroken if I don't make it," said her mother, "so I'll try my very best." That night, joined by Beyoncé on a stage covered with candles, Burke sang "Silent Night" in an uplifting voice, provoking Cole to tearfully sigh, "Love you,

love you, love you," and Cowell to pronounce, "A star has been born."
He hoped that his hunt for a global star, another Robbie Williams,
had been achieved.

A record fifteen million watched the finale and voted for Burke as
the winner. Cowell's bonus was that three other contests, including
the boy band JLS, were also signed up for Sony labels. Like other winners, Burke's prize was a million pounds, but she could expect at
most £150,000. The remainder would be used for her expenses. In
the aftermath, Cowell could not resist feeding speculation that the
model Kate Moss, who had often sat in his dressing room with Philip
Green, might replace Dannii Minogue. "Yes, possibly," he said, winking at the journalist who asked.

13

MEDIA MOGUL

IN EARLY 2009, TOMMY MOTTOLA, THE FORMER HEAD OF SONY MUSIC Entertainment and ex-husband of Mariah Carey, telephoned Cowell out of the blue.

"I'm in London," said Mottola, whom Cowell had never met. "I wanted to come over and say hi and see if we could do something together." In the course of a ninety-minute conversation, Cowell trusted his visitor enough to unburden himself about his predicament: "I'm tired, fed up, there are lots of bills, and I'm not sure where this is leading." His two contracts, he continued, with Fox for *American Idol* and with ITV for *The X Factor,* would expire in 2010. He did not want to continue with *American Idol,* and because *The X Factor* was so successful in Britain, an American offer was certain. If Fox refused to bid, then NBC, thrilled with *America's Got Talent,* would certainly be interested.

Over the past year, said Cowell, everything had become complicated. Since 2008, Tony Russell had been negotiating on his behalf with Rolf Schmidt-Holtz, Sony Music's chairman, and Bob Sillerman. Both offers, Cowell continued, were unsatisfactory. All he had received was an emotional two-page letter from Schmidt-Holtz pleading that Russell should "not stand between us. You should speak for yourself."

Now, Cowell felt that possibly he had treated Sony badly. Unmentioned was his niggling suspicion that Sillerman's $300-million offer to forge a partnership with CKX and Simon Fuller might have been his "trying to pull a fast one." Why would Fuller, he thought, want to "make up and cooperate?" Only recently, Fuller had irritated Cowell by telling a journalist, "I'm worth more than Cowell. He's in a different league." By which he meant a lower league.

Aggravating his own discontent, Cowell admitted to Mottola, was monotony: "I am bored. I easily get bored and I'm hot and cold about the program." Mottola's instant analysis crystallized Cowell's thoughts: "You're not thinking it through. You should own your own rights and be making new shows as the exec-producer and owner." Cowell understood. He needed once again to redefine himself and should start by recovering the ownership of the rights to *The X Factor* and the *Got Talent* programs, which he had sold to Sony in 2005.

After some thought, Cowell called Philip Green, who was by then a close friend. "Help me, I'm overloaded," pleaded Cowell. "I can't understand what's happening." Green drove over to Cowell's office and read through the correspondence between Russell, Sony and Sillerman. "I can't run a business like Lucian Grainge," said Cowell, referring to another of the Barbados "mafia." "I'm hopeless."

"I'll help," offered Green, recognizing Cowell as a kindred spirit who "needed help." Cowell, he decided, was "an honest, hardworking man who woke up in the morning loving his work. I can look after his back because otherwise he'll get hurt." The added bonus was Green's attraction to showbiz. Particular celebrities intrigued the entrepreneur, especially those who could benefit from his skills.

Green was unconvinced by Tony Russell's efforts and by what he felt was his meager achievement in the current discussions. Pertinently, Sillerman felt the same. Russell, thought Sillerman, was "smart but inflexible." He could conduct the single-issue negotiations for his clients but he was lost trying to grapple with the big deals. Sillerman was not surprised to hear about the strained telephone conversation when Green terminated Russell's twenty-year relationship with Cowell.

"You twiddle the knobs and I'll do the deal," Green told Cowell.

Green's next call was to Howard Stringer, Sony's global chairman, based in New York and Tokyo. "You've nearly lost Simon to Bob Sillerman. Do you want to be part of the deal? So if you want to do business about the future of *X Factor* and *Britain's Got Talent,* let's talk in London." Green's warning that Sony Music risked losing its most important profit maker compelled Stringer to arrive in London shortly after, on May 1, 2009.

Showbiz contracts and intellectual property rights among celebrities were foreign to Green. So were their lawyers' and agents' methods of negotiation. Having honed a negotiating style that suited the clothing and property market, Green's blunt approach was, said an early victim, "like a bull crashing around a china shop." Nevertheless, Stringer's lengthy visit to Green's office in Marylebone with his Sony executives quickly got to the heart of the matter.

"Simon wants to be the owner, not an employee," Green told Stringer. By the end of the session, Green had established the outlines of a deal for Cowell to recover total ownership of *The X Factor* and *Britain's Got Talent* and also receive a financial windfall. Green was understandably pleased with the result:

"You'll get a hundred percent of the TV programs from Sony in return for Sony getting a perpetual music license. I've also persuaded Sony to consider buying back a part of the new company owning the TV rights which they've just given to you for nothing!"

"You should be paid for your work," said Cowell, thrilled—an offer Green dismissed.

On May 3, 2009, Green flew to New York to meet Sillerman. "My job," announced Green, "is to get all of this cleaned up and tidied." Sillerman was pleased by the chance of progress. In contrast, Fuller felt uneasy that Cowell, for the first time, was represented by an accomplished businessman. During their conversation, Green disentangled Sillerman's proposals to discover a noncompletion clause empowering Sillerman, if he wished, to exclude Cowell from appearing on any TV program. In effect, Cowell could be paid not to work.

The following week, Green flew to meet Cowell in Los Angeles. "They could park you in the wilderness in a lockout," explained Green. "Perhaps Simon wants me off the air," Cowell told Green, suspicious that the unusual clause could have been Fuller's brainchild. "This isn't going to happen," declared Green, sharing Cowell's suspicions. Both were possibly mistaken. The clause had been inserted, Sillerman later said, at Russell's request, obeying Cowell's instructions. "I don't know if I always want to appear on television," Cowell had said. "I want the right to refuse."

Since Sillerman's sole interest was to capture Cowell, he had agreed without scrutinizing the words—or so he told Green when Cowell's suspicions threatened their relationship.

"Cowell was right to be suspicious," Sillerman would say. "He knew Fuller better than me, and he hardly knew me. And I don't understand the business. So Green was protecting Cowell and I only realized after Green left New York how complicated it was."

In public, the arguments were unknown. Cowell was performing to perfection on *American Idol,* telling one contestant, "You should be a hooker"; to another, "That sounded like you were drunk and not on one or two bottles—a whole crate"; and to a third, "It was really boring and I hate what you're wearing." He also joked on *The Tonight Show* with Jay Leno that he had rejected an invitation to meet President Obama because "I wasn't available." In Britain, the tabloid headlines featured his confession "I'd like to kiss Cheryl." His focus was on the third season of *Britain's Got Talent.* ITV's audiences were still falling and their half-year losses had escalated to £105 million. Without Cowell, though, the network risked collapse, and so the *X Factor* budget was increased by £5 million to £19 million in 2009.

"Will you take over *all* the negotiations with Sillerman and Sony?" Cowell asked Philip Green. "He's trusted me with his life," thought Green, and he drove across Los Angeles to visit Lucian Grainge to "sniff out" Cowell's market price. Grainge volunteered that it was more than Sillerman's offer of $300 million, but to extract the higher value Green would need to simultaneously negotiate with Sony, FremantleMedia, Fox, and ITV. That played to Green's strengths, but Grainge didn't envy those navigating through the inevitable bombast. At least the survivors would discover Green's talent for creating perfect contractual structures.

Green next telephoned Peter Chernin, the chairman of Fox, and described himself as Cowell's representative. Fox, said Green, had paid to keep *The X Factor* off the air for five years and the time had come to negotiate something new. Chernin had already announced his departure from News Corp. and decided not to engage with Green, unexpectedly introducing him to Hollywood's charming ritual of stabbing irritants in the face.

Fighting was natural to Green. In the midst of his negotiations, he suggested to Cowell that he fly to Las Vegas to watch Joe Calzaghe, a Welsh light heavyweight, box against Bernard Hopkins. At the end of a good fight, the two had dinner with Sylvester Stallone, and Green began playing roulette at the Bellagio. In the early hours, he won $650,000, but the dealer insisted that the bet had been placed after the wheel began spinning. Outraged, Green demanded to watch the video. The evidence favored Green and in the middle of the night the casino's owner telephoned and agreed to pay the money. Impressed, Cowell became fully committed to entrust his commercial future to the businessman.

On his return to London, Green invited Peter Powell, Cowell's agent and a former DJ, to meet at the Dorchester.

"What's your job?" asked Green.

"I'm on call twenty-four–seven," Powell explained. "I am his eyes and ears."

"How come I've never heard of you?" murmured Green, examining the sheet of paper listing Powell's earnings. "We're not going to need you."

Another of the old guard had been erased. Cowell expressed no regrets. Green was firmly responsible for Cowell's commercial fate. Cowell's search for a new father figure had been fulfilled. "I want you to meet Karren Brady," said Green, introducing the managing director of the Birmingham Football Club. "She understands organization, planning, and structures." Brady's self-introduction as she walked into Cowell's office was blunt: "You look knackered. You need help." Some would later interpret those weeks as the passing of the torch.

"Refresh" was Cowell's new mantra. At the outset of the year, he had tried to improve *Britain's Got Talent* by adding Kelly Brook, a model, as the fourth judge in the hope of sparking a new catfight with Amanda Holden. Chosen just twenty-four hours before the program started, Brook asked Ant and Dec after their introduction, "What do you do?"

"Have you ever seen the show?" asked Dec.

"Yeah, bits," she replied.

"She's out of her comfort zone," agreed Cowell at the end of the night. His gut instinct had been wrong. After three days she was dismissed, but she kept the hundred-thousand-pound fee. "I wasn't sad," admitted Holden. "I do like being the only girl."

To bury the bad publicity, Holden was encouraged to confide, "I have a crush on Simon. He has this charisma and charm you can't fight." On cue, Cowell reciprocated: "Amanda is filthy . . . cute . . . and with a glint in her eye, but unfortunately she is married." And since in the cause of publicity nothing was too vulgar, he encouraged *The Sun* to report that he had been "blown away by a professional farter—all the way through Blue Danube." "You're a disgusting creature," Cowell told the contestant after approving his inclusion in the program. "The show," Cowell admitted, "is like watching a train wreck. Britain's talent is for rubbish." He was next seen with Holden cheering at the Ascot races.

Cowell's sideswipe concealed his excitement about a discovery. Watching the edited version of an audition, he noticed that a forty-seven-year-old unemployed spinster looked better on screen than in the flesh. Curiously, his producers had not alerted him to anything special, yet by careful crafting they had polished an average performance by an overweight and frumpy middle-aged woman with unruly hair and a stodgy dress. She lived in a council house in West Lothian. The backstory was magical. Afflicted by a lack of oxygen at birth, learning difficulties, and bullying at school, the pudgy woman had been urged by her mother until her death in 2007 to audition on

ITV. Since then, said the youngest of nine children, she had suffered permanent depression. Despite her illness, she had made her way through the audition process, starting in Glasgow.

"This is a strong story," said Cowell after rewatching Susan Boyle's appearance. "She says she's never been kissed and loves her cats. All's good." But even he could not anticipate the public's reaction on April 11, 2009. Sniggers from the audience could be heard as Boyle stepped forward to sing "I Dreamed a Dream" from *Les Miserables*. Before she had finished, the audience erupted with affection. The wild cheering did not surprise Cowell, but ten million would watch the program, and within three days more than thirty million would watch her audition clip on YouTube. Two weeks later, 120 million had clicked on and she had been besieged by America's talk shows.

"Is Susan Boyle ITV's savior?" asked a newspaper. "She's a little tiger," said Cowell. "Get yourself together, sweetheart, for the big one—the semifinal. Shut the door, dye your hair, choose the right song, and come back as you are, not who you want to be." The only public warning about a person who some were describing as "a pitiful middle-aged frump with a good voice" came from those who had tracked down Michelle McManus, the winner of *Pop Idol* in 2003. She had just switched on the Christmas lights in Cumnock, East Ayrshire. Not much of a gig.

Cowell heard the warning about Boyle too late. The pressure, he was told privately, was "destroying" her. Two days before the finals, he invited Boyle and her female friend to his dressing room. "Do you want to back out?" he asked. Both declined. "I want to go on," replied Boyle. Convinced that she would win, not least because of the block Scottish vote and her popularity among the over-forties, Cowell was thrilled. His winning streak seemed unstoppable.

With Boyle tipped to win, 19.2 million people were watching the final show. Their excited voting added millions to Cowell's profits. The announcement at the end of the singing that Diversity had won with Boyle second stunned Cowell. "Horrendous," he said as he watched Boyle's face crumble. After quickly congratulating the winners, he sped across the stage to the distraught woman. "We'll still give you a recording contract," he whispered in what he would call "an embarrassing situation." As usual, the producers headed from Wembley to the Bar at the Dorchester hotel to celebrate a remarkable series. Cowell arrived, he said later, "anxious." "I had a weird feeling and went home early." At two A.M. he was called. Boyle, he was told, had been taken to the Priory, a private hospital for mental illnesses, after suffering a breakdown.

The following day, Cowell was accused by newspapers of failing in his duty of care by allowing a sick woman to remain on the show. The irony that the same media accusers had dispatched over fifty camera crews and journalists to camp outside the Priory to snatch a photograph of the patient was ignored by everyone, including Cowell. Controlling his image had always been Cowell's strength, so he instantly began telephoning all the tabloid editors. "We're paying Boyle's bill at the Priory," he said. "She's got emotional problems. But have we done something wrong?" he asked. None, he believed, had said that "I was entirely to blame" but there was criticism that she had been exploited as a freak. He did not disagree. Unnervingly, she called him "sir" and "boss" and expressed her fears of being abandoned by Cowell. In his defense, Cowell described the misery of her solitary life before the show. Youths had thrown stones at her house, she was tossed into a ditch full of nettles, was permanently depressed, and, although vulnerable, she had always wanted to be a singer. The best thing, he consoled himself, was that no one accused him personally of being responsible. That was questionable. There was a resignation from FremantleMedia about the treatment of a disturbed woman and there were complaints at ITV.

Cowell rebutted the critics. "I made sure she had a good manager," he would say. Yet her first manager's tenure was short-lived, and Richard Griffiths refused to take up the offer. "It wouldn't be a pleasurable experience," he explained. "She would need too much personal attention." Griffiths had not anticipated Boyle's continuing success among her middle-aged fan base in middle America, many attracted to a star who said, "My Catholic faith is the backbone of my life." Even on *China's Got Talent* in 2011 she would be watched on TV by an estimated 510 million viewers while singing in an arena filled with sixty thousand fans.

Blessed by the controversy, Susan Boyle's global stardom ratch-eted up Cowell's bargaining power over the networks in Los Angeles. He returned to the United States brimming with confidence. His first stop was to see his house on Palm Drive. As he entered, the building site was spotless. Although over eighty craftsmen were working on the site, there was hardly a speck of dust.

That was the only source of satisfaction. His relationship with Jennifer Post was proving difficult. She was resisting his demand for a circular staircase to the second floor, insisting that a loft-style stair-case was perfect. One completed staircase had been rejected by him and a second had just been assembled. On entering the house, his first glimpse evoked anger.

"Pull it down," he ordered. "I want a circular one."

"No way," Post shouted back. Then, as he walked through the painted building, his mood darkened: "I don't want any more fuck-ing white in the house." Every wall and wooden surface was white. Entering the garden, he was blinded by the shine. The surface was white concrete. "This is like an asylum," he moaned. Post offered al-ternative dark colors but it was too late and he wanted to move in. "Build a circular staircase," he demanded. In the meantime, he lived at nearby Cole Place, in a house he had rebuilt for two million dollars into an ultrachic hilltop refuge.

Cowell's principal task in Los Angeles was to notch up his nego-tiations for *The X Factor* with Fox. With Chernin's imminent depar-ture, he needed to introduce himself to Peter Rice, Chernin's British-born successor. Rice, formerly a senior executive film pro-ducer at Twentieth Century Fox, was still basking in congratulations about his adroit purchase of the completed film *Slumdog Millionaire* when he arrived for dinner at Cecconi's in Beverly Hills. In Holly-wood, Rice knew, executives in TV were regarded as second rate be-cause the best stayed in the movie business.

"I've decided to leave *American Idol* in 2010," Cowell said, "and launch *X Factor* in America." Rice's face, partly covered by horn-rimmed glasses, gave nothing away. Clearly, he was thinking about the risk to the estimated $850 million that Fox had earned during the *Idol* season in 2009 from advertising revenue. "My departure will be good for the program," Cowell continued with his tongue in his cheek. "You'll get new stars and new energy. And you'll be pleased to see me go. I'm always so late nowadays." Eventually, Rice replied that he wanted Cowell to remain. "When my contract runs out, that's it," repeated Cowell. "I'm going to launch *X Factor.*" The question, thought Cowell, was whether Rice understood the difference between *American Idol* and *The X Factor.* The new program would include younger and older contestants and feature the intense competition between the judges in the mentoring of the contestants. Rice, Cowell realized by the end of the meal, "did not trust me completely."

Hours later, James Murdoch, the head of News Corp in Britain, telephoned Cowell and urged him to stay. "I've done it for ten years," Cowell replied. "I've made you a lot of money and now I want to do something new." No one at Fox took Cowell's threat seriously. Negotiations always started at the extreme.

Soon after, at a party at the London home of Elisabeth Murdoch, Rupert's daughter, Philip Green approached the senior Murdoch. "You and me will do a deal for Simon," said Green. What followed has been hotly disputed. Green's critics suggest that Murdoch recoiled from any discussion. Cowell recalled the opposite. Green reported the next day, "I had a great conversation with Rupert." Either interpretation placed Green at the center of the negotiations at two P.M. on June 3 when he welcomed the Sony board to his office in Marylebone. By the end of the meeting, Sony had agreed to return 100 percent of the TV and record rights for *The X Factor, Britain's Got Talent,* and any other program he made back to Cowell and agreed on increased percentages for all the recording rights—in exchange for absolutely nothing except participation in the new joint venture. Green had built the first block of Cowell's new business.

Gossip about Cowell's plans reached Ryan Seacrest. His contract as the host of *American Idol* was expiring and he decided on a ruse involving a date with Cowell in London. Seacrest's arrival on June 11 was controversial. John Ferriter, his agent, who had masterminded his transformation from a Georgia DJ earning $30,000 a year in 2000 into a $3.5-million-a-year host, was comatose in a Los Angeles hospital. As Ferriter would later complain, "Ryan didn't drive one mile to visit me but he flew five thousand miles to meet Simon." Somewhere across the Atlantic, Seacrest dumped his agent.

The trip was frantic. Within forty-eight hours, Seacrest would be expected at the Gillette Stadium in Boston for the first *Idol* auditions. But eager to play a game, Seacrest entered Green's office with an advisor. "I want to work with you guys on *X Factor,*" said Seacrest.

"You've got a contract with *Idol,*" replied Green. "It's only for one more week and I've told them I'm not turning up," retorted Seacrest.

"It's a bad idea not to turn up," Green told Seacrest and later, during dinner, he telephoned Darnell. After explaining the situation, Green asked, "Can I help you? In any case I'll make sure Ryan turns up tomorrow." After the meal, Seacrest suggested to Cowell that they go to Stringfellows. By then, Cowell thought he had persuaded his friend to use Green as his financial advisor. "He's sorted me out. He would do the same for you." Seacrest seemed persuaded.

At five A.M., the bleached-blond star emerged with Cowell from the club covered in lipstick from lusty lap dancers. Camera flashes burst through the darkness. The following day, the photographs were published in the London tabloids. "It's a riot," Sillerman told Fuller.

As Seacrest had anticipated, the images sparked Fuller's fear that *Idol*'s host intended to abandon the ship. The next day Sillerman called Green.

"What are you doing with Ryan?" he asked.

"Monkey business," replied Green.

Cowell was fuming. He had been used by Seacrest and the image was damaging. The malicious rumors about Seacrest's sexuality matched those about himself. On the Internet, the spiteful gossiped that any association Seacrest enjoyed with a woman was a smoke screen.

The following week, June 19, Sillerman arrived in Monaco for a dinner on Green's yacht. Although CKX's directors opposed his $300 million offer to Cowell as too expensive, Sillerman thought there was a chance to do a deal and use that success to repurchase control of his company from the other shareholders.

Though Green didn't know it, the visit was make or break for Sillerman. If he failed, the corporation would be sold. Over six hours, he increased his price by pledging "a piece of *American Idol* for a piece of *X Factor.*" The atmosphere was nevertheless uncomfortable. Jews celebrating the Friday night Shabbat on a giant yacht appeared incongruous to the Jewish visitor, and despite "falling for Tina," Green's wife, Sillerman hated the positioning by everyone around the table. "You know the old saying about the half-filled glass," he told his host. "The optimist says it's half full, the pessimist says its half empty, and the realist says the glass is too big." That night the glass was not big enough. "I realized I was part of the problem," Sillerman would say. "I was the only man on the planet who liked both Cowell and Fuller. It was like sitting on the electric chair and being asked, 'Do you want AC or DC?'"

While Sillerman was flying back to New York, Green was telephoned by Seacrest. "I've got a new deal for *Idol,*" he said. "They're paying me forty-five million dollars over three years. Up by eighty percent. Most from Fox but also some from Fuller and Sillerman." Soon after Sillerman landed, there was a telephone call from Green.

"Is there something you forgot to tell me?" he asked.

"I don't think so, Phil."

"What about the little matter of paying Ryan forty-five million? Did you forget to tell me that during our six-hour dinner?"

"Well, I promised Ryan not to say anything."

Green was exasperated. The symbolism of Friday's dinner was abused by Sillerman's deception. "I can understand Philip's anger," Sillerman would later say. Pertinently, Cowell was sympathetic to Sillerman's tactics and could not understand Green's anger.

The last stage of the divorce was Fuller's arrival soon after in Green's office.

"Look, I'm really confused," said Green. "I'm trying to do business, so why pay Ryan forty-five million dollars?"

"You don't understand," replied Fuller. "Things have happened between me and Simon in the past. The deal is done. The train has left the station."

"We can't deal with you if you don't trust us," Green scoffed. Soon after, Green read critical comments about himself, Sony and Fox in the media. He telephoned Fuller's publicist. "He yelled at me," complained the publicist unconvincingly, "and I don't know why." Cowell called Sillerman: "The deal's not going to work but let's stay friends." One day, Cowell hoped, Sillerman would pay a fortune for his empire.

Cowell had reached another Rubicon. Liberated from Fuller's shadow, he had the energy and inspiration to realize his dream and simultaneously wreak his revenge on Fuller. "He's the shrinking violet who just got married," said one of Cowell's aides about his rival. Cowell had not been invited to Fuller's wedding in San Francisco. Instead, he was preparing to finally move into the Palm Drive house. Except that there was nothing for him to do. Banned by Jennifer Post from the property for two weeks so that she could complete her "full turn-key service," he entered his new home to find everything unpacked, the fridge full, the fire burning, and not a box in sight. The cupboards were filled with Egyptian cotton sheets, Christofle dinner and tea sets, a sterling silver tea set, a Dunhill cigar box, nine period decanters, and black monogrammed linen table napkins. Black-and-white photographs of Frank Sinatra covered the walls, including a signed copy of Terry O'Neill's famous shot of Sinatra arriving with his bodyguards on Miami Beach in 1968. To compensate for Cowell's dislike of white, Post had even introduced black lavatory paper. Dotted around were sealed packets of Kool cigarettes. Cowell had become accustomed to smoking cigarettes only from newly opened packets, to enjoy only fresh tobacco.

Perfection had been delivered for an additional $6 million, making an estimated total cost for the house of $22 million. Except that within weeks Cowell was niggling, thinking about change. The paint finish, he decided, was unsatisfactory, the rooms were badly designed, and he wanted more open-air living space at the back. Brian Biglin was summoned and told to submit plans adding another four thousand square feet of living space to transform the grounds into a new "living area." The initial budget was $2.5 million. "Simon makes things better," said Biglin.

"Harry Benson is booked to fly to Los Angeles," Jennifer Post told

Cowell, "to shoot the cover for *Architectural Digest.* He'll need three days."

"You're not going to photograph the house," replied Cowell.

"You can't turn Harry down," wailed Post, who discovered she had been replaced by Jiin Kim Inoue, a designer based with Finchatton in London. Between regular flights to Los Angeles, Inoue was told to communicate her plans and progress to Biglin and Cowell using 3D pictures. But there were to be no photographs of her work. "I want my privacy," said Cowell.

His privacy was also protected by increasing his staff. Beside Reyna, the head housekeeper, there was Zoe, the estate manager, who had an assistant; two groundsmen to look after the yard and maintenance and provide security; a chef; and four housekeepers. (His house in London was looked after by two housekeepers.) Chauffeurs were hired through an agency. His working staff included three personal assistants, an assistant dedicated exclusively to the care of his property and hiring the staff, and another dedicated to supervising construction work.

The excitement of owning two iconic houses in Beverly Hills—he had decided to use one as a home and the other as an office—and the collapse of negotiations with Fuller inspired Cowell to jettison past ambitions. He would no longer be content to only produce the best TV shows; now he envisaged creating an entertainment empire. Green, the manager of a retail empire, bestowed credibility on his ambition.

In a public statement, Green announced that he and Cowell had established a joint business to "build a company bigger than Disney." Syco, the new holding company, would own Cowell's interest in all TV programs, talent management, and merchandising. Green would be responsible for the multibillion-dollar conglomerate's finance, global strategy, and sale of branded products like T-shirts and drinks. The entertainment world was introduced to potentially the world's richest TV mogul. "You must have a share of the new company," said Cowell. "I'll take five percent," replied Green, "and nothing in writing." "Twenty percent," insisted Cowell. Green anticipated that once

Cowell cashed in, his share would be worth a fortune. In anticipation that Cowell would one day be earning in excess of $100 million a year but "only spending a fraction of what I earn," Green arranged for a weekly summary of Cowell's cash position and encouraged him to write a will. "I'm giving my money to animals and kids," he said. He liked both but wanted responsibility for neither. Thinking about the fortune that the charities would receive after his death, he sighed, "I had more fun making money when I earned much less."

The announcement of Syco's creation sparked a reshuffle among the other players. In July, Sony presented an outline offer which Green judged "very good." Next, a summit was called in Los Angeles. The chiefs of FremantleMedia, Sony, and Fox—Rupert Murdoch in person—met Cowell and his agent, Bryan Lourd. On Tony Cohen's insistence, Green was not invited. The chief executive of Fremantle-Media claimed that during one argument about Syco sharing in the ancillaries' profits—including the two million pounds earned from voters' telephone calls—Green became irritated by Cohen's refusal to listen. Green allegedly lost his temper and jokingly threatened to throw Cohen off a cliff. Green strenuously denied the accusation. The only relevant truth was that all the players had a positive response to Green's orchestration of Cowell's fate.

Murdoch and the Fox executives arrived at the meeting to offer Cowell $130 million to stay on *Idol* until 2012, and launch *The X Factor* in 2013. "That's not enough," said Cowell. Jeff Zucker of NBC, he explained, had just offered $300 million for *The X Factor* and *America's Got Talent*. "I won't read or entertain your offer," he had told Zucker, "because I don't want Fox to think I'm using you as leverage." After revealing the offer, Cowell looked at Murdoch: "It's personal, not financial. I'm attached to Fox. Your people had been very kind, but I want to start *The X Factor*." Nevertheless, by the end of the meeting Cowell agreed to a transition period—Cowell would appear on *American Idol* for two years and then launch *The X Factor*. The finances were to be finalized by Lourd and Green. FremantleMedia agreed to reduce its interest in *The X Factor* from eighty-twenty in its favor to fifty-fifty, and Sony suggested a more complicated division of ownership, the income to reflect that 70 percent of Sony music revenue in Britain was generated by artists contracted by Syco.

Green assumed that the negotiations were completed until Rolf Schmidt-Holtz arrived in his office with a group of Sony executives. "This is my final offer," said the Sony chairman. Sony's accountants, it transpired, had protested that handing Cowell 100-percent ownership of the TV rights followed by Sony paying Cowell for a share of Syco, the new company, was too disadvantageous.

"It's crazy giving this up for free," exclaimed Schmidt-Holtz.

"It was agreed," spluttered Green, who was shocked next by Schmidt-Holtz's legal but controversial treatment of past income. In particular, he was furious that Sony described Fox's $50-million payment for the *X Factor* option as a profit rather than an exceptional item.

"This is my new offer," said Schmidt-Holtz, offering a document showing a fifty-fifty split of Syco, substantially less than the 100 percent he had previously agreed on.

"No," said Green, after reading through Sony's proposed contract. "This is not what we agreed."

"Yes, but this is my final offer," Schmidt-Holtz repeated.

"This is outrageous," said Green excitedly. "It's not correct. You're a bagel *gonif.*" Schmidt-Holtz did not understand the Yiddish name for the man who steals the hole in the bagel but he could not ignore Green's anger.

Upset, Schmidt-Holtz drove from Green's office to Cowell's home. The German, Cowell noticed, was in an emotional state.

"I won't negotiate with Green," he said. "This is my offer and you must sign it whatever Green says. It's fair. We've stood by you. You owe me more."

Cowell agreed to Sony's offer of a fifty-fifty split, a decision he could live with despite Green's understandable fury.

By then, news of the tortured negotiations had reached Dan Sabbagh, the media editor of the London *Times*. On September 2, Sabbagh wrote a report that Green was due to fly to New York to negotiate with Fox about the introduction of *The X Factor* to America, and that

NBC was an alternative network should those discussions fail. Sabbagh highlighted that Green's negotiations with Peter Rice had become "fraught amid a series of differences." Despite Sabbagh's efforts, Fox had refused to comment, even though the network and the newspaper were both part of Murdoch's empire. Injudiciously, Sabbagh decided at nine P.M., as the newspaper's first edition was about to be printed, to fill an unexpected gap on his page with his report. The absence of Fox's comment, he knew, was risky. Minutes after the story appeared in the online edition, Peter Rice became available. Hysterical and aggressive, Rice told Sabbagh that "fraught" misdescribed the negotiations.

"That's untrue," Rice screamed. During the night, successive editions of the newspaper changed "fraught" to "fruitful." Sabbagh left the newspaper soon after, saying, "I felt I was right." Neither the *Times*'s report nor Rice's overreaction influenced the outcome.

The final deal was that Cowell and Sony would unite in a new fifty-fifty joint venture within Syco. Sony would contribute its assets—*The X Factor* and the *Got Talent* shows—while Cowell contributed his exclusive services as the creator of all content and contracted his services as executive producer for five years. Sony advanced fifty million dollars to Cowell to be set against the income from the programs and records. Syco, however, did not receive the income from all of Cowell's personal appearance fees on *The X Factor,* the *Got Talent*s, or from advertisements. That money was deposited in Cowell's private companies in America and Britain, subject to Syco receiving a small fee. The deal, it was colorfully asserted, would earn Cowell a billion dollars over the following six years. On Piers Morgan's recommendation, Cowell appointed Ellis Watson, formerly at the newspaper publisher Trinity Mirror and the transportation operator FirstGroup, as Syco Entertainment's chief executive.

Cowell's agreement, spurred by personal sentiment, was a relief for Murdoch and the Fox producers, but the mood soon soured. On the road with Paula Abdul, Randy Jackson, and Ryan Seacrest, Cowell was feeling wearier than he had anticipated. The contestants were not potential megastars like Kelly Clarkson, and the winners' records were no longer amazing hits. Lythgoe's absence had sapped energy from the show and sniping with the other judges was no longer fun. In the aftermath of Seacrest's twenty-four-hour dash to London, Cowell's relationship with him was near poisonous. "He's like a young deer at a party," Cowell told Abdul. "Young, ambitious, and very competitive. He's just signed his new contract and I just want it to end." Seacrest's fifteen million dollars a year enraged Abdul, who was enmeshed in another personal crisis.

Over the previous weeks, a failed contestant had stalked her and just days earlier had committed suicide in front of her home. Distressed, Abdul complained that Darnell offered her little sympathy. Now came the gossip that the Fox executives were considering paying Cowell over $300 million while her annual fee was just $1.9 million. Worse, her request for a new contract was being brusquely ignored by Darnell and Rice. "It's unnecessarily hurtful and certainly rude," complained her agent. In the customary horror of corporate life, the victim was the last to hear the fateful news. In late July, Abdul was waiting for her luggage at Kennedy Airport in New York and switched on her cellphone to listen to the messages. Ken Warwick, Lythgoe's replacement, flippantly mentioned that there would be a fourth judge on the show. Shocked, Abdul called Warwick.

"This is not good news," she said, feeling "really crappy." "What's his name?"

"He's a she," replied Warwick, "and you won't know her."

"If she's a songwriter," snapped Abdul, "it's Kara DioGuardi." There was a long silence from Los Angeles.

"How do you know?" asked Warwick.

"I started her career," said Abdul. "I picked her off the street in New York, moved her into my home, and with my help she got a number one hit. Then off she goes and I don't hear from her for four years. Do you mean she didn't tell you?"

"No."

"How do you think I feel to be the last to know about this? And about someone no one has ever heard of? Even the lighting man probably knew before me."

Warwick was contrite. "It was Simon Fuller's idea," he said. Abdul was shocked. She couldn't quite remember how many times she had ever spoken to Fuller but she knew it could be counted on the fingers of one hand. Nor could she understand why Cécile Frot-Coutaz and Mike Darnell, probably encouraged by Lythgoe, had treated her so poorly except that by creating insecurity they hoped to make her feel paranoid.

Kara DioGuardi, she knew, would be hopeless, and as for Ellen DeGeneres, another name that had been floated as a prospective replacement, no one, said Abdul, was mentioning her recent marriage to her girlfriend, Portia de Rossi.

Kara DioGuardi joined the auditions and, as Abdul predicted, her performance was poor. Backstage, their mutual dislike climaxed in a physical fight outside Abdul's dressing room. Darnell's purpose, Abdul raged, was calculated to depress her demand for an increased fee. She had originally asked for $10 million and Fox offered $3 million for one season. Eventually she reduced her demand to $5 million and Fox offered $4.5 million. Now, Fox refused to compromise even for such a small amount, and on August 5, Abdul announced her immediate departure. Fuller, Abdul assumed, was delighted. "Creatively," said Cécile Frot-Coutaz enigmatically, "no one wanted Paula to leave *American Idol*." Victoria Beckham, alias Posh Spice, who was also Fuller's client, was inserted as her replacement. Cowell's apparent enthusiasm was contradicted by an overnight media report that he had found her "wooden." The following day, Posh arrived incensed and refused to accept Cowell's insistence that the report was fictitious. The chemistry of the panel had failed to materialize.

Cowell immediately telephoned Abdul. She spoke about life in the wilderness and "the end of my career." "Don't worry," said Cowell. "Just hang on. Things are happening and you'll be back with me."

The X Factor's prospective launch in America in 2013 spurred Cowell to keep the show at the heart of Britain's national conversation in the new season. Boosted by the success of Leona Lewis and JLS, the increased budget had changed the program. For the first time, the contestants auditioned in front of an audience rather than in a soulless room, and Cowell arranged for Ashley Cole, the cheating husband, to sit in the front row to witness Cowell's barbs with the "wronged woman" loved by millions of Britons. "Footballers' wives," Cheryl Cole had written in 2006, "are just as bad as benefit scroungers—it's just a higher class of scrounger." Playing with emotions gave the show edginess. "Cheryl Cole and Walsh Mock Cowell's Judgement" was a *Sun* headline Cowell had encouraged. "I like the show in the press," said Cowell.

Taking his cue, Louis Walsh picked an opportunity to make a confession in a newspaper interview. Cowell, he explained, had told the fifty-seven-year-old, "Darling, we should get the eyes and teeth done. Do some cosmetic maintenance." The result was surgery on Walsh's eye bags and gleaming porcelain caps in his mouth.

"What's the difference between God and Simon Cowell?" asked Walsh during a newspaper interview. "God doesn't walk around Knightsbridge thinking he's Cowell." Cowell loved harmless carping so long as nothing disturbed his magic. His personality, he hoped, silenced the critics and secured adoration for himself as the universal hero. One obstacle was *The X Factor* itself: the attraction at the outset depended on humiliating some contestants.

Newspapers were led to Katrina Lee, a twenty-three-year-old Belfast shop worker who Cowell had told five years earlier that ideally her voice should be "in someone else's body." Since then, she had lost thirty pounds, paid for facial laser treatment and dental surgery, and dyed her hair red. "Your comments nearly wrecked my life," she told Cowell in the edited version of an audition, referring to her shingles and an eating disorder. Cowell understood the tabloid readers' appetite for stories of anguish. "He seemed really shocked about how his comments had affected me," said Lee. Her colorful trauma kept *The X Factor* leading the tabloids for days, helped by the *Mirror*'s reports on Hollie Steel, a failed contestant who, it said, after crying on the stage likened Cowell to a playground bully. "Don't do it again," Cowell told journalists in personal telephone calls. "Hollie admits it's not true." Unfair criticism of himself, he explained, was hurtful. "I've ordered the judges to be kind," he said, feeding the tabloids' interest.

Enjoying himself as the executive producer extinguished Cowell's lingering interest in *American Idol.* The combination of Fox's treatment of Abdul, Seacrest's behavior, Fuller's omnipresence, and the frustration of performing rather than producing turned him against staying longer than necessary. With hindsight, Cowell realized that observing Green's negotiations had solidified his antagonism.

At two A.M. one night, he telephoned Green. Accustomed by then to being awoken by his friend during the night, Green assumed that Cowell needed another self-induced therapy session and prepared to doze while Cowell spoke. But the first words snapped his semiconsciousness: "I know it's all done but I'm not doing *Idol* after this season."

"Getting the deal has taken ten months of my life," growled Green.

"I know, but I'm mentally done. I want a clean break to start in 2011." Cowell continued, "The issue is what I want to do. For the first time I'm going to take a risk. It's a red or black moment. I want more on the back end from Fox dependent on ratings rather than big bonuses up front."

This was, Green knew, a seismic change in Cowell's life. Until then, he had always wanted a guarantee of cash up front. Now he was gambling to beat Fuller. Green replaced the receiver. "He got the tuts," he told himself.

Green next called Peter Rice: "My horse has broken its leg fifty yards from the finishing line. You'd better come to London."

Eight weeks into his new job as Fox's chief executive, Rice was sitting with Green at the Dorchester, uncertain why he had rushed overnight from Los Angeles. Cowell arrived late.

"I don't want to do *American Idol* anymore," he announced.

"Really?" gasped Rice, visibly stunned. His Hollywood career had not prepared him for the loss of Fox's biggest star, the foundation stone of the network's bid for supremacy.

Minutes passed and no one spoke. Cowell steeled himself against breaking the silence. "It's so quiet I can hear a pin drop," thought Green. What followed, Green would describe as "the most fascinating moment in my business career." Rice broke the silence: "Is that it?"

"This is very personal for me," explained Cowell. "I've worked nine seasons for you. I'm not entertaining any other offers. It's important for me to be separate now and I don't feel comfortable doing both shows." Rice, he could see, was distressed. He did not want *The X Factor* muddying the waters. This was nothing more than the mutual denigration of two British egos, Cowell's and Fuller's. They were engaged in a gladiatorial contest with Fox haplessly uncertain of the outcome on their own turf.

Normally Cowell was a plate spinner, a man on a wire, occasionally close to falling off, but now his self-confidence was cast iron and he was unusually decisive. He did not imagine how over the following weeks his judgment would be strenuously tested. At the end of fifty minutes, Rice went for a walk with Bryan Lourd in Hyde Park and then flew back to Los Angeles. Within hours, Fuller called Cowell urging him to stay on *Idol.* "It's not personal," Cowell said with an unseen smile.

His income that year would be at least $27 million from *American Idol,* about £9 million from ITV and at least £25 million from Sony Music. With at least another £10 million from other interests, his annual income was heading toward £70 million and would increase. Fuller's was considerably less. Cowell intended to take a gamble and agree that his fees from Fox should depend on the program's audience ratings.

"This is a big turning point in your life," Terri Seymour told Cowell as he approached his fiftieth birthday. "Every decade," Cowell agreed, "is a milestone and a new challenge." Somehow it was appropriate that the celebrations should be organized by Tina Green. In their daily telephone conversations, Philip Green was serving as Cowell's unpaid mentor, advisor, and confessor, so his wife automatically agreed to stage an extravaganza for his birthday. After first suggesting that Cowell "rent three jumbos and fly everyone to New York," Green retreated to something more modest in England. The venue, Tina Green decided, should be Wrotham Park, an eighteenth-century mansion in Hertfordshire, and, after consulting her husband, she chose Cowell's vanity as the theme. A party-planning firm was given a two-million-pound budget.

Not surprisingly, Jackie St. Clair was unprepared to abandon her own plans. Two hundred people, including many of Cowell's former girlfriends, had been summoned to her home in Holland Park. Among the definite exclusions was Louise Payne, his ex-fiancée, and among the diffident invitees were Terri Seymour and Sinitta. St. Clair lived much of her life through Cowell and loved stepping into the limelight with her friend. Aggressive in defending her territory, she disliked her rivals, especially Sinitta, but conceded that Cowell enjoyed competition for his attention. Most guests obeyed her request to bring a mirror as a present. At the end of the evening, 179 mirrors would be stacked in a room.

"I've got a present for you," Cowell said at the outset of his speech, looking at Jackie St. Clair. "It's a picture of someone I greatly admire." Ripping open the paper, St. Clair found a life-sized portrait of Cowell. He also gave her a painting by L. S. Lowry. Anticipating the self-deprecation, she organized that Dannii Minogue, Amanda Holden, Louis Walsh, and Bruno Tonioli (a *Strictly Come Dancing* judge) all wearing Cowell masks, should sing "You're So Vain." The Greens, not invited to St. Clair's "private party for old friends," were surprised to hear that vanity should also have been chosen as its theme, but Cowell had amusingly told the guests after singing some Beatles songs, "Eighty percent of you are not invited to my official party."

That guest list of 450 people included most of the stars associated with his programs, his media allies, his family, friends, and a contingent of his office staff, accountants, lawyers, and professional advisors. Over dinner at London club Les Ambassadeurs two weeks before the party, Philip Green moaned about the absence of a seating plan. "If you didn't have thirty-nine ex-girlfriends it would be easy. And it's growing weekly. They all phone up and ask a variety of 'Can I sing?' 'Can I jump out of a cake?' 'Can I jump off the roof?' You can't imagine."

One week later, Tina Green had still not received a table plan. Her husband called Cowell. "You're crazy," he shouted, "we don't know the people. You've got to tell us where everyone sits." "Right," said Cowell. "I can't do it. Can't get my head around it." The following day he disappeared and resurfaced in the penthouse of the Setai hotel in Miami, one of his favorite haunts. "I couldn't be bothered," he later said. "I didn't want to do it. There were too many fights, so I fled the country to get chilled." Miami was Cowell's natural playground. Latino girls in the nightclubs threw themselves at the generous party animal and within days he had recovered.

Forty-eight hours before the party, he returned to London. On Friday night, October 2, Philip and Tina Green arrived at Cowell's home to find their friend enjoying a facial massage in his bathroom. At first Tina sat on the bathroom floor asking about each name for the table plan. Then, while Cowell immersed himself in a bath, the Greens continued the argument in the adjoining bedroom, spreading the name tags over Cowell's bed. At around midnight the chore was completed.

The next day, before driving to Hertfordshire, Cowell took half a milligram of a sleeping tablet: "I wanted to be slightly dreamy because I was stressed by the thought of nearly five hundred people. I would have to go to the tables and be nice to everyone. I can't bear crowds. It was almost unbearable. The tablet made me relaxed." In the dusk, Wrotham Park was covered by a colored projection of his image with a cigarette. Entering the mansion, he was greeted by waiters wearing Cowell masks and top hats. Peering into the dining marquee with Philip Green, Cowell was impressed at what his three million pounds (the budget had been increased) had bought.

Huge blue satin curtains covered the walls and the curved tables were covered with gold and silver, transforming the room into a debauched boudoir. The waitresses were wearing hot pants and acrobats were hanging from the rafters. The tablecloths were decorated by a profile of the birthday boy. The name plates were cherubs with G-strings and gold crowns. Cowell's own table was decorated by two male porcelain bodies wearing bondage gear and gold angel wings. Hovering over the guests was a replica of Michelangelo's "Creation of Adam" painting on the ceiling of the Vatican's Sistine Chapel, replacing the image of God with Cowell. "Oh my God," exclaimed Cowell. "How camp is this?" From the side, Terri Seymour was watching: "He looked so uncomfortable. He'd lost his usual composure. I expected the evening to be much worse than it was."

Clutching glasses of Cristal champagne, some of London's most beautiful and best-known women, dressed in long, deep-cut couture dresses lit up the room, representing in Cowell's mischievous calculation "half of Britain's Botox consumers." Amid riotous laughter and inevitably the best music, guests were served soup decorated with "Simon" written in cream, followed by fish fingers and shepherd's pie, two of his favorite foods. Everyone was encouraged to smoke.

Cowell was seated by his mother. All of his guests knew about their host's love and support for Julie. Whenever he was in London, he arranged to meet her every week, and usually for Sunday lunch. Some knew that beyond the glowing interviews she gave to newspapers about her son, there was also criticism: his nickname as a child was Mummy Look at Me; she had told a journalist, "Simon gave me a Porsche for Christmas, I wanted a duvet"; and another time she commented, "My best Christmas present ever were my grandchildren by Nick." The insiders suspected that Julie's frustrated ambition to be a star sixty years earlier was an ingredient for her enthusiastic public appearances beside her son.

"It's gone full circle," was Cowell's conclusion. "When I was a child I loved my mother providing access to Robert Mitchum at parties. And now because of me she gets what she wants, the same."

Julie Cowell was scrutinized in particular by the table of journalists.

"This is like *The Godfather*," said the *Mirror*'s editor. "It brings to mind the First Holy Communion party in *Godfather II*—a family event of Michael Corleone's son—a gathering of self-interested parties and not all of them wishing the host well!"

The entertainment was eccentric. Carly Simon joked that her 1972 hit "You're So Vain" was written about Cowell; there was a film of his mother, Nick Cowell, and other friends auditioning on the set of *Britain's Got Talent* mixed with Cowell's derogatory comments; Earth, Wind & Fire had been flown in from New York; there was a rendition of Wayne Newton's 1963 syrupy ballad "Danke Schoen," described by Cowell as "my favorite song"; Ryan Seacrest was pulled from the audience and subjected to mock torture; there were shocks, especially for Julie Cowell, as The Box, a burlesque cabaret from New

York, performed a sex routine dressed as giant vaginas; and finally there was Nicholas Cowell's speech.

Simon Cowell expected "payback for what I did to Nick at both his weddings." At Nicholas's first wedding, to Kim, Simon, during his best-man speech, had quoted from Nick's teenage "diary": "Off to Paris to meet a nice boy; went off with him. Met a nice donkey in the bedroom." Next, Cowell read a "letter for a job application" explaining why, as a boy scout, Nick Cowell had been found giving mouth-to-mouth resuscitation to another scout in a dark room. Then he had quoted "personal letters" describing Nick's love for boys. In the middle of the speech, Kim's father had tried to unplug the microphone.

Undeterred, at Nicholas's second marriage, to Kate, Simon Cowell had again read a series of "letters" sent by a dating agency during their worldwide search for a bride that climaxed in finally unearthing Kate in Eastern Europe. While speaking, Cowell could see Sinitta first holding her head in her hands and then hiding behind a column. Booing broke out and Kate's parents later deleted his speech from the marriage video. "I took it too far," Cowell admitted, "and was meaner and ruder than I intended. They have never forgiven me." After those humiliations, Cowell was expecting his brother's revenge. None of his guests were forewarned.

Nicholas Cowell's body language as he mounted the stage was combative. "Revenge is a dish best served cold," he started. "At my wedding Simon made a dreadful speech, and I was going to wait until his wedding to make this speech. But until they make a law that you can marry yourself, I wouldn't get the chance, so I'll make it now."

His theme was not only his brother's vanity but also his homosexuality. "Simon's favorite animals as a child were elves, goblins, and fairies, and he still likes fairies today," started Nicholas Cowell, "and his favorite group was the Pet Shop Boys." Then he added, "Simon couldn't believe that Terri could be a girl's name as well. . . ."

The side-splitting laughter among insiders was mixed with the bewilderment of those like Philip Green stunned by the brother's venom. Sitting next to Green, Cheryl Cole was fixedly open-mouthed. And since Nicholas Cowell ended without any profession of love, Green wrongly assumed that he had not even wished his brother "Happy Birthday." Looking around the marquee, Green perceived stunned silence and an emotional vacuum. He rose and made an impromptu speech to fill the void.

"Nick was really bad," admitted Simon Cowell, "But I got off lightly." In his own speech, Cowell made no reference to his brother. The most notable mention was warmth toward his guests, including the journalists "who have been kind and balanced," and to Waterman, Lucian Grainge, and Fuller, who was noticeably thrilled with the name check and Cowell's comment "I hope we remain friends for a long time."

The huge birthday cake symbolized Cowell's passion: Carried by two beefy men stripped to the waist, it was adorned by a near-naked lap dancer.

The party ended in disarray. "The best party I've ever been to," said many guests as they left at three A.M. Some guests, including David Hasselhoff, needed help to leave; others cavorted with the scantily dressed waitresses or offered Cowell oral sex, and more, in exchange for a record contract. Some behavior, especially by the former topless model Katie Price, alias Jordan, was so outrageous that newspaper editors spiked the stories.

"I enormously enjoyed the official party," Cowell told friends over the following days, although some were not convinced. Cowell did not like parties and the final bill was more than three million pounds. "I had to earn over five million pounds [before tax] to pay for the seven hours. It was too much, but it was one of the best nights of my life." Cowell did not normally suffer from self-delusion. Beyond his public persona, his confidants knew, was a man who feared toppling into the abyss.

His smugness concealed a nightmare. Etched upon him since his humiliation at school and Arista was an irrefutable law of showbiz: artists' fortunes were either rising or falling. If he was ever to fail, his downfall would be applauded by those on whom he had vowed to avenge himself, including some of his guests. But for the moment his ascendency seemed unstoppable. The music industry had bestowed upon him their highest awards and nominated him for more, but he understood the danger of complacency. After receiving awards, there was always emptiness: "I went home depressed. It means nothing to me when things are based on something that has happened. I am only interested in the future and what I am going to get. Getting there is more fun than being there. . . . I love the journey." Few could understand.

The birthday party had coincided with the audiences for *The X Factor* hitting new records. Cowell credited his success to manipulating the audience's emotions, but continued success, he repeated, depended on reinvention: "The moment that you start assuming that the audience is happy to see the same show again you're dead." Over two hundred thousand people had been auditioned for the next season but not a single contestant had shown star qualities. He feared failing to find another Leona Lewis. Like *American Idol's* curse of sameness since Kelly Clarkson, Britain's *X Factor* had hit a talent plateau.

More than ever, the program depended upon slick editing—crosscutting between the judges' smiles and scoffs, and cutaways of sobs and hugs by anxious families backstage—and quietly dropping contestants who had won the judges' unanimous "yes" votes. They had only "won" to create a feel-good atmosphere but, according to the rules, could be dropped at the producers' discretion. The alternative to talent was a bad singer's "personality," which could serve as fodder until a winner emerged. In 2009, the combination of Cowell's ceaseless ascendency and the dearth of talent sparked a crisis.

As usual, the early episodes had featured hilarious flops—a fat, tone-deaf middle-aged man, screeching youngsters, and singers chosen for their "story" about abuse, drugs, poverty, and tragedy. All were vulnerable to Cowell's "honest" assessment. At the end of October, a set of Irish twins had finally emerged as favorites after what the tabloids called a "shock win," although they were fourth.

John and Edward Grimes were outrageously dressed and unable to sing. "If they win," said Cowell, shuddering about their extravagant hairstyles, "it will be a complete and utter disaster. I'd probably sulk for six months and get on a very fast plane out of the country."

With *The X Factor* at the center of a national debate, Cowell fueled the controversy by damning the duo as "vile little creatures who would step on their mother's head to have a hit." In early November, Lucie Jones, a Welsh teenager, was named the winner of that episode. Before an audience of 16.6 million, Cowell promptly ousted the girl to "save" Jedward, as the twins were now called. Overnight, thousands of fans, including a punter who had lost ten thousand pounds betting that the twins would lose, complained that the program was "fixed," and the tabloids started a campaign against "public enemy number one" for smirking while Dannii Minogue, who had championed Lucie Jones, cried. On November 21, the twins were voted out but Louis Walsh and Sony offered them contracts to produce a song for the following year.

The purists' outrage filled the airwaves and the Internet. Pop music, they wrote, was not about singing—that's opera—but about character, sincerity, and the truth. Unlike Bob Dylan, Leonard Cohen, and Morrissey, who could not sing but were authentic, Jedward were fakes lacking personality, integrity, and real human soul.

The controversy was more profound than merely the promotion of talentless singers. The *Mirror* denounced the program for mixing the background vocals to drown the worst aspects of Jedward's voices.

"Fox will be worried," Cowell told the *Daily Mirror* editor Richard Wallace in a telephone call protesting about a "false" story, insisting on the truth of his report.

"That's not my concern," replied Wallace.

In the days before the *X Factor* finale, Jedward's contract was blamed for fracturing and even destroying the music industry. Creative and aspiring young artists who produced proper music, fumed Cowell's critics, were marginalized on the fringes of the Internet, reliant on downloads, while *The X Factor*'s mediocrities prospered thanks to Cowell's malign influence. He was, they complained, the wrong man in the right place at the right time.

Cowell was pragmatic. Even good artists, he believed, survived for only two to three years. The very greatest could dominate the scene for about ten years, but then their music was no longer played on the radio and they were kept alive on nostalgia. The best—Elton John, Rod Stewart, and Barry Manilow—prospered in Las Vegas, appearing in concerts for $125 a ticket, hoping to promote themselves by guest appearances on *The X Factor.* The irony, as the argument about the soul of music escalated, was ignored.

Even Pete Waterman blasted "the Cowell show" for "ruthlessly" caring only about ratings: "Simon has one fixation and that's being successful, and he'll cut through anything." Waterman was not critical that *The X Factor*'s winner would sing an overproduced, saccharine version of a popular song dripping with melodious emotion; he was irked by "the villainous pantomime host's influence." Especially because the favorite to win, Joe McElderry, was mediocre.

Cowell's consolation was that nineteen million Britons watched the final show over two nights, with live performances by Paul McCartney and George Michael, in front of a studio audience including Prince Harry and his girlfriend, Chelsy Davy. Genuine royalty and pop royalty had accepted his invitation to witness "the nation coming together in an explosion of gloss, glamour and glitter . . . creating good feelings in shameless, mass-market entertainment." As predicted, McElderry won and Walsh gushed, "Joe, you've got everything. You've got the walk, the attitude, the charm. You're a small boy with a big voice." Cowell added, "This is the closest competition I've ever been involved in," although McElderry secured 61.3 percent of the vote. Fortunately for Cowell, his hyperbole was rarely remembered and never thrown back at him.

That night, inhabiting a bubble, Cowell was deceiving himself. More than five hundred thousand people bought Rage Against the Machine's "Killing in the Name," outselling McElderry's "The Climb" by fifty thousand. For the first time in five years, *The X Factor* had not produced the Christmas number 1 hit. Cowell's anger over this was not shared by Sony, however. The company, which also owned "Killing in the Name," effectively increased its profits.

Cowell was stung by the criticism of the show. "We're getting fat, arrogant, and lazy," he told his producers. "This is a wake-up call." Although Leona Lewis had sold six million albums and Susan Boyle had sold millions of albums as well, the program had still not produced a global star like Robbie Williams or Britney Spears. McElderry was certain to disappear. There was just a chance, Cowell thought that Cheryl Cole could evolve into a megastar. Since her appearance on *The X Factor* all her albums were number 1 hits. "People love her," Cowell enthused. "She's unstoppable." Tiffs and teases about her clothes and performance had provoked her tears and even a punch at Cowell during a break, raising her profile and adding strength to his negotiations with ITV. Her dissociation from a serial philanderer was hailed as inspiring conduct by her adoring female fans. The 2009 season had beaten all records since *Pop Idol*'s launch.

ITV had earned an estimated £75 million from advertising and telephone calls during 2009. The following year it was promised more from sponsorship deals and enhanced advertising campaigns. Cowell demanded an additional £3 million for the budget, giving him £1.7 million for each weekend, making *The X Factor* by far the most expensive entertainment program on British television. He also expected ITV to increase Cole's £1.2 million fee. Cowell's demand for perfection made the show seem unassailable, but he sensed exhaustion. "A lot of things are going to have to change next year if we bring the show back," he declared. As Christmas presents, he gave his three fellow judges vouchers for Botox treatment at the Urban Retreat at Harrods. Only change and renewal could guarantee their survival.

"I've walked through a lot of walls to get to the end of the journey," said Cowell as he prepared to fly to Barbados for Christmas. The "end" was not only his last season on *American Idol* but also the prospect of a major change to his bachelor lifestyle.

14

TRUE LOVE

"HE'S MADLY IN LOVE," THOUGHT JULIE COWELL WHEN SHE SAW HER son arrive in Barbados with Mezhgan Hussainy, pronounced Mishcon.

Cowell had met the Afghani makeup artist seven years earlier on the *American Idol* set. While living with Terri Seymour in 2006, he had enjoyed a secret relationship with her, but they had only started openly dating in December 2009. Described as thirty-six years old—although others would say she was forty-one—Hussainy at the age of nine had fled her homeland with her parents and in her early twenties had been forced into an arranged marriage with an older carpet seller. Since her divorce, the attractive brunette had enjoyed life in Los Angeles and, to Julie Cowell, seemed keen to have children.

"Before I go," Julie told her son, "it would be nice if I could see you settled down." "Yes, Mother," replied Cowell with sincerity. Mezhgan Hussainy was special.

During the last months of filming *American Idol*, he later explained, "Mezhgan was helpful to allay my stress. It was difficult in the *Idol* team and she was always at my side. I could confide in her and she was supportive. So we created a real bond." Her presence at his fiftieth birthday party, he agreed with his mother, was "important." Others repeated gossip from the *American Idol* team that Hussainy was "like a kitten and knows what to do in the bedroom." Smitten by the woman's looks and sex appeal, Cowell invited her to join him after Christmas on his chartered yacht.

Exhausted by the prospect of endless conversations with the crowds who flocked annually to Sandy Lane and irritated by the nonchalant staff at Cove Spring House, which he had rented, Cowell decided to stay only with his mother until New Year's Eve. Desperate for privacy and to avoid going out every night, he had chartered *Slipstream.* He planned to leave the island with Hussainy in the early hours of New Year's Day and sail south. Among his guests were Kelly Bergantz, whom he had recently employed to develop a new TV series, and Paul McKenna. He had arranged to meet Philip Green on *Lionheart* in the Caribbean.

Their rendezvous became the gossip on the moguls' grapevine. During the first week of January, a gaggle of billionaires' yachts anchored off Tobago Cays, five uninhabited islands in the Grenadines. Looking from his deck, Cowell mistakenly believed he was miles off Mustique because he could not see any land but he could see *Rising Sun,* one of the world's biggest yachts, owned by David Geffen, the Hollywood film and record producer; Green was on *Lionheart;* his sparring partner, Stuart Rose, the chairman of Marks and Spencer, the retail chain that posed the biggest challenge to Green's clothing shops, was a guest of Elisabeth Murdoch and her family on their own yacht alongside her brother James's *Angel's Share,* a 130-foot sail yacht; and in the middle was Rupert Murdoch's vessel. Nearby, on *Hamilton,* was Charles Dunstone, a retailer and a sponsor of the British *X Factor.* And among that gaggle of the superrich was *Slipstream,* a testament to Cowell's ambition to rise from multimillionaire to billionaire.

To taste the elite's lifestyle, Cowell, Hussainy, and McKenna inspected *Rising Sun,* a 453-foot-long craft with eighty-two rooms on five floors.

"What's the one piece of advice you've got?" Cowell asked Geffen.

"You've got to know when to leave the fair," replied Geffen. "You've got to know when it's time to go."

After a two-hour tour, Cowell sheepishly returned to his 193-foot minnow. "I prefer ours," Hussainy told her depressed host. "It's cozy."

One billionaire's fantasy began before Cowell awoke. Rupert Murdoch stopped by *Slipstream* on his tender delivering that morning's newspapers, published by News International in Britain, America, and Australia. They had been reproduced on a printing press installed on Murdoch's yacht. "The world's most expensive newspaper boy," Stuart Rose had quipped, digging for a coin to tip the deliverer. The surreal party was capped by an evening game of Trivial Pursuit between the guests on Dunstone's and Cowell's yachts. As the tension rose, the game dubbed "Public School versus Showbiz" provoked outbursts of screaming among the contestants. At one game each, the final game would be decided by whether the Dunstone team could name the composer of the *Pink Panther* film score. The entrepreneur was stumped while Cowell was bursting.

"I know," shouted Cowell. "Give up." But at the very last moment, one of Dunstone's team took a wild gamble: "Henry Mancini?" Cowell was devastated as Dunstone's team was declared winners.

Realizing the enjoyment of yachts, Cowell regretted depositing seventeen million pounds for a house to be built on a prime site adjoining the Four Seasons in Barbados, part of a development backed by the real estate mogul Robin Paterson. His neighbors would be Lucian Grainge and Andrew Lloyd Webber, who had recently criticized Cowell's programs. "We nurture, we don't torture," Lloyd Webber had said, attacking "Cowell's gimmicks." A few days later he had apologized. Out of Cowell's super-rich friends, only Green had refused to invest in Paterson's scheme. "I don't like the look of it," he said. Cowell and other investors would later complain that they lost a lot of their money.

During that voyage, Cowell's relationship with Hussainy intensified. For the first time, their relationship was no longer clandestine. The furtiveness of their meetings in Los Angeles was abandoned and in his usual way, Cowell became, his friends noticed, "hot and heavy." Content to listen for hours to Cowell's agonizing monologues about his plans, disputes, and confessions, Hussainy's sympathetic responses drew the two closer together. "She makes me happy," he thought to himself, especially when she ran around the bedroom in her exquisite lingerie. "She's sexy and she's great," he told his friends on the yacht as he endlessly flirted with her.

The big hiccup occurred during a conversation on the voyage about their future relationship. If he refused to commit himself, Hussainy said, she would accept an offer from another person with whom she was also enjoying an affair. Taken aback, he seized her cellphone, where he read messages confirming the existence of another relationship.

Cowell would interpret that scene as banter or "winding each other up," but others believed he was angry. In any event, momentarily he was not genial. To his friends, he appeared unusually vulnerable as he reassessed his position. He spoke to his closest women friends about his fears. They were puzzled by his infatuation and equally bewildered that Hussainy, for no reason, appeared to regard them as enemies. But Cowell, his friends knew, preferred simple, good-looking women who indulged him and enjoyed "fun." The attractions of Cowell for Hussainy were obvious, and she counted her own blessings. He possessed enough money to provide luxury for the rest of their combined lives, and he planned to have even more. On his part, fearing that she could leave, he had persuaded himself that Hussainy's presence during the next stage of his life was ideal.

Introducing *The X Factor* to America meant that he would center his life in Los Angeles rather than London. "I like Los Angeles because of its positivity," he told Hussainy. "I like driving everywhere with the hood down in the sunshine in my Bugatti or Bentley, with girls waving at me." The shouts from strangers on the pavements and the inviting stares from wannabe starlets—even L.A.'s dippy, self-obsessed airheads—were irresistible. "I like the architecture and the great people around me for the shows and hosting great dinner parties for fourteen or sixteen people. I have to pinch myself as I drive into the Fox studios."

In the near future, he would also use a Ferrari being assembled in Italy. The last Ferrari he had driven, on loan from a dealer in London, had ended up in a ditch in the Oxfordshire countryside, the casualty of a reckless reverse. Forsaking London's miserable weather would be a pleasure and he could rebuild the Palm Drive house so that he could live and work in the fresh air. The downside was the city's unfriendliness. Strangely, although he was one of Beverly Hills's most famous stars, he had few genuine friendships. Other than Paul McKenna, Randy Jackson, and Maurice Veronique, a friend from Windsor College with whom he rarely spoke, there were no men he counted as close. His friendships with women were special. Besides Terri Seymour, Sinitta, and Jackie St. Clair, he leaned on Kelly Bergantz and Lauren Silverman. Late at night, he spoke animatedly and honestly about his life and loves, knowing that he could rely on their discreet candor. Hussainy could join the stable. She suited his criteria: tall, dusky, fun-loving, and, most important, tolerant of his needs. She was, in sum, a true friend upon whom he could rely.

His most basic need was relief from a niggling fear of loneliness. Although constantly surrounded by people and compelled to resist the pressure from others demanding his attention, he was sentimental about his parents' happy marriage and half wanted the same. So far, he had chosen women for fun rather than for the intimacy of sharing his life. His success while pursuing his specific goals had depended upon freedom from interference from girlfriends. But now, on the eve of establishing a global empire, he was unusually depressed. Life on *American Idol* had been oppressive. Numbness had replaced his normal excitement. Lacking drive, he was at best on auto-pilot, relying on Hussainy for comfort.

On his return from the Caribbean, Cowell's anxiety reached a new peak. On January 11, 2010, he was due to appear at the Pasadena Civic Center for the start of his final *Idol* season. The media was accurately speculating that Cowell would leave the show and Fox was under pressure to make a public statement. Negotiations for *The X Factor* had been complicated, especially obtaining from Fox guarantees that *The X Factor*'s unique features, including the judges' mentoring, wider age ranges, and huge audiences at the auditions, would not be adopted by *American Idol.*

Cowell's anger with Fuller had not abated. On the one hand, as he told Claudia Rosencrantz, he had sent a letter of condolences to Fuller after his mother's death. In telling the story, Cowell explained his horror of any mother's death. Rosencrantz was impressed. Considering how Cowell hated Fuller, his sentiments showed the way his good nature overcame his deep resentment. But those sentiments and the ones of friendship he had expressed at his birthday party had. disappeared. Now he was fulminating to Fox's producers about Fuller's treachery. To the incredulous Cowell, Fuller explained, "I was in the mood at the party but not anymore."

As Cowell drove from Palm Drive down Santa Monica Boulevard toward Pasadena for the *Idol* presentation, his lawyer called.

"Where are you?" he asked.

"Highland," replied Cowell. "I've just left."

"Do a U-turn and go back," ordered the lawyer. "The contract's not finalized." The last-minute hitch was Fox's insistence on owning all of *The X Factor*'s digital rights. Cowell wanted a 50-percent share.

"Simon's turned round," his lawyer told Peter Rice.

"Okay, fifty-fifty," agreed Rice.

"Do another U-turn and get down to Pasadena as fast as you can," Cowell was told.

Just after midday, Cowell appeared on the stage. The atmosphere in the hall, he sensed, was bad. "There's been a lot of speculation," he began, knowing every word was being carefully scrutinized by journalists in the building, "partly because we didn't have a contract agreement. We reached an agreement formally at about half past eleven this morning." *The X Factor,* he announced, would launch in 2011 and he would be leaving *American Idol* in May. "I was offered a lot of money to stay on but I wanted to do something different. I wanted a new challenge."

The perceptive among the audience understood that Cowell was establishing his own media empire and had declared war against Fuller. None, however, grasped the extent of Cowell's ambitions. He would be satisfied with nothing less than Syco matching Aaron Spelling's corporation as Hollywood's foremost entertainment producer. Thereafter, he did little to conceal his irascible boredom on *Idol*. In what he anticipated would be a poor season, he even criticized good performers, exceeding his own vitriol by describing one contestant in Orlando as singing "like a lawnmower" and watching bemused while the angry performer was forcibly removed from the stage in handcuffs.

Four weeks later, he was back in London to record *Britain's Got Talent*. Coincidentally, St. Valentine's Day was approaching. Cowell's attitude to marriage had not changed since he had broken up with Louise Payne nine years earlier. Marriage, he had often repeated, was an "outdated contract. The truth is you get married and in a year or two they clean you out." But the prospect of bachelor life was no longer so appealing, especially if he could find a woman who, while independent in her own right, was not too independent of him. He wanted someone who was somewhat dependent but not hanging constantly around. "You want someone who's not needy," was the reassuring summary by one of his female confidants. "Someone who's feisty and challenges you but not too independent and doesn't blow smoke up your ass." There was, he believed, little time to lose.

Vitamin injections, special fruits, intravenous drips, piles of pills, Botox, massages, dyes, chest waxing, tooth caps, and cosmetic surgery had limited the evidence of aging, but passing the fifty-year mark had made a bigger difference than he had anticipated. However, the milestone had stirred unusual restlessness aggravated by the relief of leaving *Idol* and risking his career on a successful launch of *X Factor* in America. Preserving his sanity during those tense weeks had meant relying on Hussainy. His hunger for change had been sated at a cost, but now he felt liberated and, most important, happy again. The permanent cure, he suspected, was not only marriage but parenthood. In his search to replicate his parents' happiness, he admitted to himself, "I need to have little Simons running around. Now is the last moment for children or it will be too late." Without confiding in anyone, he made a momentous decision.

At ten P.M. on February 14, St. Valentine's Day, he was in his bedroom in his London home with Hussainy. Days earlier, the manager of Graff, the Bond Street jewelers, had brought six engagement rings for Cowell to see during the *Britain's Got Talent* auditions. He had chosen a rectangular six-carat diamond set in platinum costing £250,000. "I was happy and I wanted her to be surprised," explained one of Hollywood's most eligible bachelors, who enjoyed boasting about his own selfishness. While he lay in bed with Hussainy, he got up, collected the ring inside a box from his dressing room, and proposed marriage.

"Will you marry me?"

"Oh, yes," she replied, thrilled. "Yes, yes."

The following evening, Julie Cowell arrived as usual to stay in his Holland Park home. Although he had become occasionally impatient listening to her complaints, they remained close. Their love did not include Cowell's discussing his girlfriends with Julie and he denied that his change-of-life decision had been influenced by his mother.

"I've got engaged," Cowell told her.

"Have you bought a ring?" Julie asked suspiciously.

"I've bought the ring and have given it to her. And I'm really going to get married."

"I'm so delighted," gasped Julie, relieved that her son had decided to finally "settle down." The ceremony, she imagined, would be held within months in Los Angeles, Barbados, or Brighton and new grandchildren would follow. Two days later, Cowell began telephoning friends.

"I've proposed," Cowell told Lauren Silverman.

"Proposed what?" asked his best friend in New York.

"To marry Mezhgan."

There was a brief pause. Silverman was "completely flabbergasted." Even Cowell's close friend had not "seen it coming."

"Congratulations," said Silverman with little conviction but not betraying her fears. At the end of the call, she told Andrew, her husband, "The whole thing is wrong."

"Guess what?" Cowell asked another female confidant before revealing the engagement. Uniformly, all their congratulations were somewhat contrived. None could quite understand. "I feel I'm losing a friend," sighed another of his holiday companions.

Julie Cowell's doubts began even while her son was telephoning with the news. Unlike Terri Seymour, Hussainy appeared to make only limited attempts to draw closer to Simon's family and, bewilderingly, she never appeared before three o'clock in the afternoon. "What are you doing up there?" she asked. Her future daughter-in-law's replies provoked Julie Cowell to suspect that her peculiar habits were caused possibly by jet-lag. "She's the only American I've ever met," she observed, "who comes to London and doesn't want to see Buckingham Palace and the Tower of London." After another day, Julie exclaimed, "She doesn't seem to be interested in anything." She said nothing to her son about her concerns. His happiness was paramount and she hoped for the best.

In public, Julie played the game. "Turning fifty has changed him," she said. "I'm delighted that he's finally settled down." She also blessed the bride: "She's a lovely woman, She's got a great personality and is perfect for him." Her son would be a "great dad" to their children.

Excited and in love, Cowell and his fiancée returned together to Los Angeles on a private jet and traveled on to meet her parents in Mill Harbour for their blessing. At the end of that day, Cowell was convinced that he had found the perfect wife from an ideal family. He called Terri Seymour. "It's because you're fifty, isn't it?" she asked. "Yes, and why not?" he replied, adding, "We'll see what happens." Energetically, Mezhgan Hussainy summoned Los Angeles's experts to arrange her celebrity wedding.

The event deserved a momentous publicity blast to prove there were no doubts. "She's very special," Cowell told Piers Morgan on his nightly television show on CNN in late February. "You know when you've found someone very special. I'm smitten—I think she's The One." In later interviews, he mentioned how she admired his performance in bed, which he rated as nine out of ten. "She makes me look so handsome," he said of Hussainy's makeup artist who had moved into Palm Drive. In anticipation of marriage and children, Cowell called Brian Biglin, the architect. The extension of the house should be increased.

Six weeks later, the doubts began. In April, Julie Cowell arrived to stay for a week on Palm Drive. Her son's departure from *Idol*, she discovered, had created a crisis between Cowell and some Fox producers. Every night he returned home late for dinner and, to Julie Cowell's distress, Mezghan Hussainy was angry. "Don't say anything," Julie advised Hussainy on the third night. "When he comes in, just give him a kiss and smile and say, 'Hi, I missed you.' Just don't nag him."

Instead, Cowell's arrival sparked a barrage of abuse. "You're late. I thought you'd be here by now," screeched Hussainy.

Cowell's escape was to find "space." Sitting in the garden, he listened to music tracks, smoked a Kool, and drank a beer, interrupted only by texts and telephone calls. Repeatedly Hussainy asked, "What are you doing?"

Hussainy, he realized, was not a feisty woman after all but was suffocating him. She did not understand that she could neither change nor control him.

"The tension was horrendous to me," recalled Julie Cowell. "The way Mezghan behaved made my stomach churn." As they sat down for dinner, Cowell's cellphone rang.

"Who is it?" asked Hussainy in a fiery tone. "Who are you now texting?"

A violent argument erupted. Hussainy got up, screamed abuse, ran upstairs, and slammed the bedroom door.

"Charming," said Julie Cowell.

"Sit down," Cowell told his mother. "We'll eat alone."

"Something's wrong here, Simon. It's not what we thought. I was very happy and now I'm not happy."

"There's a problem," agreed Cowell.

Hussainy, they concluded after lengthy analysis, had clearly not understood that work was her fiancé's priority, and there was a lack of trust.

Soon after Julie returned to London, the Silvermans arrived from

New York. Mezhgan Hussainy, they realized, was clearly unhappy. "There's a lot of tension," Lauren noted. The regularization of their relationship into a daily routine had exposed irreconcilable flaws. Neither the Silvermans nor Cowell could envisage any solution.

Cowell had reached a moment of truth. Late at night, he told Hussainy, "I will always turn my back on you and you won't like it. You have to understand that having a fling with me is different to living with me. Work is my mistress." His fiancée could not understand Cowell's mood as he switched off from her. Most women expected their lover's complete attention, but he focused on work. Unlike other men, he did not need to live with a soul mate. He needed and trusted her as a close friend but living together had proved too difficult.

Ten days later, he celebrated the final *Idol* program: "It was my last season and everyone was in an uncomfortable position. I just wanted the series to end." The sour mood was aggravated by Seacrest.

A few days earlier, Seacrest had been asked in a TV interview how Cowell would cope with marriage. "I hope that if they are building a life together," replied Seacrest, "there aren't too many mirrors around to distract him from his girlfriend." He added, "he's so self-centered." Asked to identify his wedding present, Seacrest replied, "My presence. No, I'm teasing. I don't know that there is a wedding."

Seacrest's perception was followed by his ridicule of Cowell's sexuality live on *Idol*. "Back off," Cowell warned later. "You're trying to set me up."

On the penultimate program, Seacrest had again bantered on the air about Cowell being in the closet.

"You crossed the line," spat Cowell as the opening titles began rolling for the following and last show on May 26, 2010.

"What will you do?" hissed Seacrest sheepishly.

"You'll soon see," threatened Cowell. "I'll do it live." As the program started, Cowell jumped in and created what he called "an awkward moment," telling Seacrest to "forever stay out of my space."

Cowell's relief as the credits rolled at the end of nine seasons was dizzying. "It's been a blast," he told the theater audience. "I want to thank you from the bottom of my heart for the support, the fun, and your sense of humor." Cowell felt bullish as everyone headed for the party at the Mondrian hotel on Sunset Boulevard.

Without him, he expected *Idol* to decline, an unspoken opinion shared by Fuller, who looked edgy when they met at the party. Fuller disliked Cowell's life in the spotlight, always encouraging dramas that were detached from reality. Naturally, his own pretense of staying in the shadows was somewhat contrived. Fuller's publicist employed more than ten people to cultivate his image.

Visitors to Fuller's headquarters on Sunset Boulevard, formerly Playboy's headquarters, were regaled by Fuller with description of global interests in TV, fashion, films, and the Internet. Proud of his "seven homes on four continents," he encouraged his profilers to describe him as a soft-spoken but ruthless negotiator with over a hundred staff members, compared with Syco's eleven employees. In a recent book called *American Idol,* written with Fuller's help, he was portrayed as the cool power broker mobbed by Hollywood's top agents desperate to get world-famous artists adopted by his international empire. By comparison, Fuller told an American newspaper, Susan Boyle was "a freak." Cowell was personified as the underdog fiercely ambitious to imitate Fuller's career trajectory.

Most people spotting the two men chatting at the party that night would have believed that they had reached an armistice, but a subtle tension still plagued their relationship.

Only one curious bystander overheard Cowell's heartfelt utterance of spleen aimed at Fuller: "All I've done—*Britain's Got Talent, X Factor,* and much more—is revenge for what you did to me. And there's much more to come." Fuller stared speechless. That was a defining moment. Fuller's own vulnerability was evident. An original version of *The Hollywood Reporter*'s "power list" had for the first time placed Cowell ahead of Fuller. After representatives of Fuller appealed on his behalf, however, his job category had been changed and the embarrassment avoided. A new reality was emerging as Cowell was personally generating considerably more dollars in revenue than

Fuller, not least because Fuller's collaboration with Sillerman had failed to fulfill the original billing.

In theory, their plan to buy the intellectual property rights of famous icons was inspired. On the basis that "content is king," they planned to unlock various artists' "brand value" to market a catalogue of images and sounds. CKX had bought an 80-percent stake in Muhammad Ali's name and image and a major interest in Elvis Presley's estate. There were plans to acquire Marilyn Monroe's image and to buy the "name" and music catalogues of Elton John and Rod Stewart. Unexpected problems had arisen, however. Living stars rejected Fuller's offers for their estates because CKX, as a public company, would be compelled to disclose their financial secrets. Fuller also discovered that the number of iconic stars amenable to his plan had been exaggerated. Since 2005, instead of a flow of major acquisitions enhanced by a network of production houses boosting CKX's share value, the corporation's ambitions withered. Although Fuller's original puff about a master strategy was unrealized, Sillerman had not lost out.

Thanks to *Idol*'s success, 19's profits had doubled, justifying Sillerman's original risk. Over forty countries had bought the format and Fuller had personally maintained its quality. However, there was nothing to buy with the cash Sillerman was accumulating. At the heart of his dilemma was showbiz's immutable teaser: Was Fuller a one-trick pony?

Fuller's only new invention was *If I Can Dream,* a series sponsored by Pepsi and Ford to be shown on insignificant TV stations across the United States. Contestants living together in a house wired with fifty-six cameras would be shown trying to excel in their speciality. After a stuttering start, it would be abruptly halted in October 2010. His ambition to build an empire was frustrated by the absence of another big idea.

Fuller's parallel strategy, based within XIX, his new corporation, was to become a superagent for stars. His stable was limited to Andy Murray, the disappointed tennis player; the Beckhams, the iconic but fading soccer player and his trusting wife; and Lewis Hamilton, the frustrated Formula 1 driver. To understand the business, he had visited Bernie Ecclestone, Formula 1's supremo. The meeting was unexpectedly curtailed. "I'm not wasting my time teaching you about Formula 1," said Ecclestone, bidding his visitor farewell. Fuller would fail to produce a single new endorsement for Hamilton.

In music, Fuller had done little better. Over the previous ten years, he had failed to pitch any idea with the instant appeal of *Pop Idol*. By contrast, Cowell, as even Paul Jackson acknowledged, remained "a brilliant creative producer."

Days after the *Idol* party, Fuller unveiled his revival strategy—to buy CKX and recover ownership of *Idol*. Fuller had resigned from CKX in January but was retained as a consultant for *American Idol* and *So You Think You Can Dance*, another reality show for which he received 10 percent of the net profits, an annual fee of $1.5 million and an advance of $5 million. His departure followed his failed attempt in 2009 to buy the corporation for $560 million. In May 2010, after Sillerman had also resigned, Fuller renewed his bid, offering $600 million. "You don't mess with Sillerman," observed Cowell, speaking of Sillerman as "a friend, a class guy." After Fuller's offer was again rejected, Sillerman, who owned just over 20 percent of the shares, made a counterbid that, amid controversial media coverage, also failed. Cowell identified Sillerman as a possible future purchaser of Syco.

Eventually, after cutting its overhead, CKX would be sold for $500 million to Apollo, a private-equity investor based in New York. In Cowell's opinion, Fuller was bruised. Without a new idea, his rival risked being beached. Although he claimed to be worth $340 million, the source of the additional $200 million since the sale of 19 was inexplicable, not least because of some losses.

By contrast, in what Paul Jackson described as "a dick-measuring contest," Cowell's empire was growing. Unlike Fuller, Cowell was churning out ideas. Twenty-six countries had bought the *X Factor* format and over forty had bought the *Got Talent* program. Half the income went directly to Cowell, and he earned royalties from all of Sony's record sales and personal endorsements.

His dominance could no longer be ignored. At the annual BAFTA ceremony in May, Britain's film and television industry presented a "special award" to Cowell. Walking onto the stage without a planned speech, he impulsively thanked the "person who had made applause and cheers possible. This is long overdue," and named Claudia Rosencrantz as the begetter of his good fortune. She was not in the theater. His critics, however, sat in front of him, questioning whether the Boyle phenomenon could be repeated. His success in attracting 19.2 million viewers had embarrassed the BBC into pledging to spend more money to recapture viewers. Cowell's critics willed the BBC to succeed.

Many doubted whether Cowell's producers could find sufficient new talent to generate gossip around the watercoolers. Although ITV had invested another million pounds to improve the stage design, the knockers declared, "The talent pool is dry." Even Cowell looked bored watching a burping accounts clerk, a retired teacher impersonating a gibbon, and a woman force-feeding a parrot mashed potatoes. Rolling his eyes, he showed little enthusiasm about another dancing dog and four flabby nude men, alias The Cheeky Boys, holding balloons over their manhood. "It was what it was," he said dismissively and agreed, "The pond has been fished dry." Yet with Ant and Dec oozing charm and the skillful editing of contestants "wanting it" and parading their "journey," fourteen million viewers watched a nonentity win in the finale.

Cowell had flown to London alone. Deliberately, he had decided not to invite his fiancée. To his closest friends he admitted, "I've made a big mistake." In his Los Angeles home, they noticed, he had become unusually silent, as if trapped and uncertain how to escape. Strangely for the self-confident performer, he begged them not to leave him alone in his house with his fiancée. "A light seems to have gone out," thought Lauren Silverman. "He's walking on eggshells." In London, Cowell reflected on his fate.

He was in the midst of his biggest challenge—launching *The X Factor* in America and refreshing Britain's *X Factor*. London was a sanctuary from his emotional stress, but professionally the hecklers were voicing familiar doubts about the British *X Factor*'s revival. The show starting in August would inevitably dominate the autumn schedules, but the legacy of 2009 raised doubts. The public's imagination had been captured by dance, rap, R&B artists, and Lady Gaga, who did not appear on *X Factor*. Cowell's defense was defiant: "Few new artists are signed by labels. We've done more good for the music business by turning up interest in music among the young." The previous Christmas, Cowell had pledged, "A lot of things are going to change." Now, Cowell knew, everyone would scrutinize the program's reinvention. Cowell's publicists promised a revolution.

Sob stories were curbed, "journeys" were outlawed, some songs were banned, and contestants were better groomed. But the cynics smelled desperation. There was a "crisis" because Dannii Minogue was temporarily absent on maternity leave, Cheryl Cole fell sick with malaria, and Louis Walsh was "fired" for appearing on a "stupid TV program" and then rehired after giving "a groveling apology." The drama among the early contestants was predictably tawdry, and compounding the frustrations, Cowell had still not signed a new contract with ITV. On his behalf, Green was demanding a three-year agreement with an additional six million pounds for Cowell but no commitment that Cowell would appear on the programs, and an extra three million pounds for the program budget with a proviso that ITV could cancel the program if ratings fell. ITV's leverage was limited. Huge crowds had appeared for the *X Factor* auditions. The juggernaut was irresistible. Peter Fincham of ITV agreed to a £100-million deal for *The X Factor* and *Britain's Got Talent*. ITV's loss was Cowell's refusal to appear in Britain. "I never begged him to stay," Fincham would say. "We calculated that *X Factor* would work without Simon." To justify the package, Cowell promised new twists to produce a genuine new star.

Cowell was certain a star would emerge. The "dry pool" argument was, he thought, "rubbish." Every year, new teenagers emerged with ambitions to become singers, but as a safeguard, he dispatched talent seekers to the usual venues and decided to create a new group from the contestants. That was one advantage of running *The X Factor*. Record producers risked a fortune to create a boy band without knowing the result. Cowell's lucrative bonus was to do the same cost free. "On the spur of the moment," he had spotted five young boys who had entered the competition individually. He put them together as a group. "Think of a name for yourselves," Cowell told them. They came up with "One Direction." One Direction risked the same fate, predicted the critics, as earlier groups Cowell had put together, like Girl Thing. Their mockery goaded Cowell to wreak revenge. "Embrace the madness" was his slogan. Privately, he called it "playing with my toys." The chemistry was as inflammable as that which he had previously engineered between Minogue and Sharon Osbourne.

"He's gone slightly mad this year," Cheryl Cole told a journalist. "He definitely has a glint in his eye and it's spreading. His influence on people has made them crazy." Sitting next to Cowell on the show with his arm firmly around her, the singer's personality had been transformed as Cowell dismissed Walsh and Minogue with disdain. His emotions were sparked. "Cheryl is complex and I don't understand her," he said with honest awe. "She is distrustful of others but she does trust me."

As the arguments during the program increased, Cole frequently appeared in Cowell's dressing room. He was mesmerized: "She came in dressed in her track suit and slippers, dropped her eyes and played the soulful victim to get around me. She did play me." With roles reversed, Cowell was vulnerable: "When she walked over, I felt I was the mouse with a beautiful cat. I adored her. And as she got her own way, it drove Louis mad."

"These girls are actresses," Walsh warned Cowell. "They'll get you to do what they want." Walsh, Cowell scoffed, failed to understand the wonders of an "intriguing and complex" woman.

"I would have liked an affair with Cheryl but she was uninterested," he admitted in 2011. "She'd broken up with Ashley, and her boyfriend lived in Los Angeles." That, of course, was no barrier to a man who still adored the chase, especially of a woman he deemed to be intriguing. Others would interpret her mournful silences as evidence of a vapid woman with nothing to say, but that conclusion would be rebutted by her shimmering performances on air.

During the programs, Cowell's affections changed every hour. In the battle between himself and the others about the fate of their acts, and especially One Direction, he accused Walsh of being "nasty" and "unpleasant" and then unexpectedly during the transmission swung against Cole: "You've not really got the hang of it this year, have you, pet?" Then, having generated newspaper coverage about their combined hysterics and recrimination, he fostered a barrage of abuse from Walsh and Cole and stormed from the studio. In the national conversation, the tears and tantrums appeared spontaneous, but others saw "the triumph of ersatz working-class culture over real culture. We are all Cowell's children now."

The timing was perfect for Mike Darnell and other Fox executives to visit London. Knowing the history of those who had criticized Fox for staging what they described as an identical rival of America's most popular show—especially Simon Fuller—Cowell had urged Darnell, "You have to taste *X Factor* to see the difference." Darnell arrived to watch the program, discuss Fox's requirements for the American *X Factor*, and sign off the budget. Cowell was nervous about their forty-eight-hour visit.

"Oh Christ, what a day," he wailed on the morning of their arrival. "Fix Factor" was one of the tabloid headlines that day. "They always say it's fixed, but why choose today?" he said. The test was which genius would emerge on top—Cowell or Fuller?

At least Fuller had recently changed his tune, describing *Idol* as a boxing match to *The X Factor*'s wrestling bout. "I like wrestling," Cowell told Darnell in Sony's west London offices. "We're a fun jungle compared to *Idol*'s manicured, polished, protected show where the performances are nice and the pressure is gentle. It's the purity of a meadow versus a showbiz jungle."

On Cowell's agenda was persuading Darnell to hire Cheryl Cole for American *X Factor*. "I've seen the amazing reaction when she walks into an arena," he told Darnell. Ever since her "spectacular" solo performance on *The X Factor* in 2009, Cowell had coached his protégé. "I want to make Cheryl a star," he said.

Six weeks earlier, Cole had met Darnell and Cécile Frot-Coutaz at Cowell's office in Beverly Hills. To Cowell's delight, the pop icon had executed a flawless performance combining amusing banter and professional maturity. Darnell had become infatuated and, after watching some DVDs, excitedly texted Cowell about "this new girl," brushing aside her anonymity in America. The only shadow was Cole's decision to hire will.i.am, a member of Black Eyed Peas, as her agent. Cowell was puzzled but said nothing.

On the eve of Darnell's arrival, Cole was on edge. Excited by the prospect of working in Los Angeles, she imagined that with Cowell by her side, there would be little difference to appearing in Britain. Nothing was said about the cultural differences, especially America's more demanding audiences. "She looks amazing and is amazing," thought Cowell as he watched the singer "parade her assets in front of Darnell."

Cole targeted a man whose line of vision was perfectly aligned with her breasts. "She's in top form and Darnell has been blown away," concluded Cowell. The former actor had already rationalized Fox's dilemma of staging both *Idol* and *X Factor:* "Whichever program wins, Fox wins," he thought. Competition appealed to Darnell. By the end of the visit, Fox's head of marketing was equally excited and Peter Rice, whom Cowell had originally suspected, had become an ally.

Their dinner for twelve people at China Tang in the Dorchester sealed the relationships, although there was one casualty—Ellis Watson, the new chief executive of Syco. Appointed on Piers Morgan's suggestion after a long relationship at the *Mirror,* Watson had argued with Green during the dinner. He sealed his fate at the end of the meal. Idly, Watson spun the Lazy Susan in the center of the table. A lump of ice cream flew off a bowl, landed on Green's face, and fell onto his suit. "I think we'll get the bill," said Green. Darnell's warm farewell confirmed that Cowell's future in America was secured on his terms.

The following morning, Watson's removal was demanded by the chairman of Sony Music in Britain. Watson, it was politely announced, "left for family reasons." Insiders spoke about a man unable to cope with competing interests and personalities. The bloodshed did not stop. Rolf Schmidt-Holtz, CEO of Sony Music, retired and his replacement, Doug Morris, the seventy-two-year-old head of

Universal Music, was urged to reverse Schmidt-Holtz's "dead hand" and improve Sony's music. Cowell hailed Morris, often described as "the Godfather," as "the smartest man in the world and a genius. He knows how to make records. There's no bullshit." Shortly after, Morris fired the Sony chairman.

Survival in the music industry required luck, talent, relationships, and brazenness. Those with only three out of the four qualities would inevitably fail. To climb to the very top, as Cowell had, also required single-mindedness, selfishness, and stardust. BAFTA's acknowledgment of his uniqueness was replicated in November in New York. Rupert Murdoch awarded Cowell the Academy of Television Arts and Science's International Emmy Founders Award for having "reshaped twenty-first-century television and music around the world." Posing for the photographers, Cowell clutched Mezghan Hussainy's hand. He had invited her to come to witness his success and at the same time to quash rumors of a split. In New York, the embarrassed woman found deception hard. "We're still engaged," she told a journalist, adding, without anticipating the reaction, "as far as I know."

Cowell believed their relationship was irreconcilable but she was unpersuaded even after her dispatch alone in early summer from London to Los Angeles. A few weeks later, to the surprise of Cowell and his usual gang of friends, she appeared in the South of France to board *Slipstream* for his annual holidays. The terrible tension, observed a member of the crew, was aggravated by Hussainy's remaining for long periods locked in her cabin and emerging only to engage in arguments. "Simon feels guilty," Lauren Silverman and Kelly Bergantz agreed. Mezghan Hussainy's wedding plans were permanently postponed.

There was a perfunctory kiss as the couple parted—she to return to Los Angeles and he to London for *The X Factor*. As he suspected, during the series no potential star emerged but the competition between the two favorites, Rebecca Ferguson and Matt Cardle, was tight. Neither would be worth promoting, he thought. The certain commercial victor was One Direction. Nevertheless, building on the tabloid frenzy about the judges' warfare, ITV's publicity campaign attracted 19.4 million viewers, one-third of Britain's population and 60 percent of the TV audience to witness Cardle's narrow victory amid strobe lights, dry ice, fireworks, confetti, and raunchy dancers. In truth, everyone was a winner. Except, Cowell calculated, that Cardle's glory would be short-lived, while he could within one year make money out of Cher Lloyd, Rebecca Ferguson, and One Direction. The principal questions posed by the tabloids during the three weeks after Christmas, as Cowell and his friends darted on *Slipstream* between the Grenadines, Mustique, and St. Barts, was which girl was sleeping with Cardle and whether Cowell would receive a knighthood. He did not and Hussainy, in a bad mood, left after two weeks.

Another irritation was spread by Nigel Lythgoe. Cowell's departure had eased the Briton's return as *American Idol*'s producer. In a carefully placed interview while filming the auditions for the next series, he had observed that *Idol* was a "lighter" place with a happier atmosphere since Cowell quit. Incensed, Cowell telephoned Lythgoe. "Nigel, even if you feel that way, you've got to remember that I put nine years of my life into that show, and that was the reason it became such a hit. You're unprofessional, disrespectful, and it's not what you should be doing as a human being and as a producer. It's unnecessary, so just stop it."

The tension before the outbreak of war was irrepressible. Cowell's taste for revenge had never felt more acute and Lythgoe and Fuller shared his sentiments.

15

MAY 8, 2011

AFTER A TORTUOUS NIGHT, SIMON COWELL AWOKE BEFORE MIDDAY on May 8, 2011 in a suite at the Peninsula hotel in Beverly Hills. *The X Factor*'s first audition was due to begin that afternoon.

The previous days had been dominated by brinkmanship that had jeopardized the launch. To relieve the tension on the big day, he called for a masseuse and, while the service of his breakfast was perfectly choreographed, he read text messages and watched cartoons.

Less than one mile away, Mezhgan Hussainy was awaiting his call. She had moved to his hilltop home on Cole Place just before the builders arrived at Palm Drive. Inevitably, she had not been consulted about the plans for the house's latest expansion—this time to fifteen thousand square feet. Cowell, she now understood, forbade any interference in his life. His need for uncomplicated relationships was compromised by the weary baggage of an uncomprehending woman. Her demands for attention and refusal to peacefully acquiesce to total exclusion quite naturally sparked tumultuous arguments. If there was a choice between power, sex, and money, Cowell's priority was power. Amid tears, she had demanded a date for their marriage. Eventually, feeling unusually guilt-ridden, Cowell admitted that he was reneging on his promise. He moved to the Peninsula "to have time without her."

Secure in his "space," Cowell knew precisely how he would extricate himself. His plan was with the best of intentions to "bring Mezghan to the same relationship I have with Terri." Namely, they would not sleep together but remain the very best of friends. His ideal course was to "let things happen naturally and make sure she felt secure." To protect himself from embarrassment and his fiancée from misery, he pledged to provide all her material needs: "I'd put her in the public eye and attracted a lot of attention to her. I had to be sensitive about her position and I didn't want to hurt her family, with whom I had become close."

In Cowell's opinion, he bore a responsibility to provide her with the luxury to which she had become accustomed. To that end, he promised to transfer the ownership of his $8 million home to her. She would laugh when he later joked, "I've found the ideal place for you. I just drove past it."

"I know what you're thinking," she replied.

"Yes," he laughed, "Forest Lawn." The cemetery in Hollywood Hills is a celebrities' favorite.

The loss of the $8 million house was, in Cowell's opinion, a price worth paying. Over the previous months, liberated from *American Idol* and now from Hussainy, he had expunged his demons. "You've weeded out the bad," concluded one of his confidants. "You've grown up a lot, let go of your fears and paranoia, and now you're really excited and happy again."

"I know," replied Cowell. "This is going to be a great year."

To assuage Hussainy's fear of humiliation, they agreed to conceal their separation. At the outset, the deception was not difficult. They met frequently because Cole Place was his office; and because she remained a talented artist, she was hired to apply his makeup for the auditions in Los Angeles. On that morning, she demurely waited, aware that over the previous twenty-four hours, Cowell's threats to abandon his dream had reached a climax.

"Unless she's confirmed today, we're not filming," Cowell had warned Cécile Frot-Coutaz. Thirty years of experience encouraged his taking a risk. Having wagered his reputation on *The X Factor*'s success in America, he would not allow Frot-Coutaz to exclude Paula Abdul from appearing as a fellow judge in the $100-million series.

Ever since Abdul had left *American Idol,* three years earlier, Cowell had pledged to rescue her from the wilderness. "I promised her that she would be on the new show," he told Frot-Coutaz. Viewers, he told the French woman, had been besotted by their fiery relationship and would be excited by their reunion: "I want to get back to those times. Stuff it. Give her a contract."

"Do it with the three of you," countered Frot-Coutaz, meaning that Cowell could start with the two other judges, Cheryl Cole and L. A. Reid, a famous New York–based music producer.

Frot-Coutaz did not believe that firing Abdul was a mistake. She had disliked the hard-nosed bargaining games by an unreliable artist who on one occasion had been asleep while her makeup was being applied.

"No," said Cowell, emphatically pulling on his cigarette. "This deal can be done. Or else cancel the filming."

In the intervening years, Cowell had regularly telephoned Abdul to offer reassurance. Once Fox had bought *The X Factor,* his call was decisive: "I need you on the show." Loved for her vulnerability and empathy, Abdul was an essential ingredient for his glory.

"They're not keen on me," sighed the diva. "They don't want to go back to the old. They fear it'll be a retread. They're not negotiating."

Cowell was adamant. The survivor of humiliation and hubris in showbiz's bitchy jungle trusted only his own judgment. To exact revenge on his foes, the odds needed to be stacked in his favor. Darnell had been as adamantly in favor of Cheryl Cole as Cowell was for Abdul. The compromise, he told Darnell, was to hire both.

At the end of four hours of ceaseless telephone conversations the previous day, squinting in the sunshine on the terrace of the hilltop house, Cowell stubbed his cigarette, took a final sip of his tea, flavored with a slice of lemon, and drove his black convertible Rolls-

Royce down the winding road to Santa Monica Boulevard. Less than one day before the first auditions, Abdul's fate remained undecided.

Even in a hotel suite, Cowell's routine rarely changed. To relieve the tension, he enjoyed a steam bath followed by a massage and finally spaghetti Bolognese, a favorite. The meal was interrupted by a telephone call. Darnell and Frot-Coutaz had capitulated. Paula Abdul would be given a contract. Frot-Coutaz would later say she was never in any doubt that a deal could be done with Abdul, but only on satisfactory financial terms.

Cowell was relieved. Aged fifty-one, he had asserted his primacy as a television mogul, a worthy successor to Aaron Spelling. His dream team was in place.

At lunchtime the following day, Cowell's stretched black Rolls-Royce Phantom was waiting outside the hotel. Polished every week, the limousine had been driven from a vault and sprayed with wax to increase the dazzle. Across Los Angeles, at the Galen Center on the fringe of the University of Southern California campus, over four thousand excited Californians were lining up in the heat. Amid Cowell's endless last-minute concerns, the most pressing were his team's unconvincing assurances about the quality of the talent waiting to be auditioned and whether the audience would understand the process.

Cowell chose a white T-shirt, the second he had worn that morning, and tugged it hard at the bottom. He liked new T-shirts to appear slightly worn. He would change twice more during the day. The last tweaks were honed to a sound bite intended for transmission across the country: "We're here to find a star and give him or her five million dollars, the richest prize in TV history. If we fail to find a star, we'll pack up and go home." In the choreography of arrivals to feed the media, Cowell would arrive last. Abdul was first.

Perched on six-inch stilettos and wearing a light chiffon dress, Abdul's appearance provoked screams from hundreds of women corralled behind barriers: "Paula, we love you." Chanting fans is a celebrity's oxygen and Abdul smiled with relief. "America will get who I am," said the beaming survivor as she disappeared among twenty video cameras. "I'm thrilled, exhilarated—beyond exhilarated—and terrified," she gushed. "It's awkward and wonderful and beautiful all at the same time." Then she headed into the vast convention center. In synchrony, another limousine came to a halt by the barriers restraining over a hundred journalists.

Silence greeted the emergence of Cheryl Cole, the English icon whose mega-stardom owed so much to Cowell. "She has been fantastic to work with," Cowell had recently said. "She is also a complete brat." Unknown in America, Cole had been persuaded by Cowell that her fortunes would soar on his new program. Her first moments in front of the cameras challenged that promise. Dressed in excessively long purple flares designed by Diane von Furstenberg and a frilly peach shirt, her head was cocooned in a strangely elaborate hairstyle like the one favored, quipped an observer, by Chewbacca in *Star Wars.* Another suggested that she had mistakenly dressed for a night out at a disco. Criticized in the media for being an unknown speaking in an incomprehensible accent, Cole also defied Hollywood's mantra for immaculate preening. "I won't be changing my accent," she replied. "I'd be crucified if I did. Americans will understand me." Focus groups commissioned by Fox had confirmed that Cole's accent was not a barrier to success. "I didn't have a contract until yesterday," she volunteered to the press, confirming the last-minute chaos.

The third judge, L. A. Reid, arrived to no fanfare, dressed smartly in a dark suit, white shirt, and tie. He was famous as the one who had signed Justin Bieber, the young global star, to the Island Def Jam label, and for producing Kanye West, Usher, and Rihanna. But as a "face" he was unknown. *The X Factor,* he hoped, would also turn him into a celebrity. "I was happy to get the call from Simon," he said. "It was good for my career at that time." He and Cowell had first met at a BMG music conference in 1999 at the Beverly Wilshire. "When I first saw Simon, I saw a star," he said. Until Cowell's telephone call, Reid had criticized *The X Factor* as "microwave stardom," challenging his trust in nurturing talent. "We've never produced a global artist," Cowell had told Reid. "Selection and mentoring have got better but we've reached the end of improving people. We've got to find some-one special."

Like the other three judges, Reid had seen and heard thousands of aspiring and established singers over the years. Instinctively, he knew good from bad. He had been lured away from a lucrative contract with Universal by Cowell's promise of his own label within Sony and a share of the profits from their new stars. The world's best singers, both believed, were American.

To prevent Reid's defection, at the last moment, Lucian Grainge had offered the producer a place on *American Idol* and over $10 million. Cowell was shocked. Grainge, his old friend, had clearly forged an alliance with Fuller against himself. A peace meeting had been brokered by Philip Green at the Dorchester in London. "You can compete," Cowell told Grainge, "but play fair. I don't like your alliance with Fuller against me. Come into TV with a positive attitude. It's just airtime. Have fun but don't share Simon's obsession to destroy me." They had parted as friends but also rivals.

The next test of Reid's loyalty to Cowell came directly from Simon Fuller. Reid was offered not only Cowell's place on *American Idol* and a huge financial package, but his own new label at Universal Music.

Reid was familiar with Fuller's methods. In 2000, Reid had taken over Arista from Clive Davis. Among the artists on his book was Fuller's client Annie Lennox. Every month, Reid had called Fuller to arrange a meeting and for eighteen months he heard no reply. Eventually, Fuller agreed to visit Reid's New York office. He arrived late.

"You didn't take my call for eighteen months and now you come in two hours late," said Reid, irritated by Fuller's nonchalant, even pugnacious attitude. There was a silent pause as Reid assessed the replies to his placid comments. He then rose and opened his door: "I'd like you to leave my office right now."

Startled, Fuller rose but said nothing. After Fuller left, Reid called his deputy. "I've just kicked Fuller out of my office. Tell him I mean that he should leave the building—now." Lennox's contract with Arista was terminated. Reid did not regret the departure of an artist in decline. Nor did Cowell.

"A monster," was Cowell's reaction about the singer when he heard the story about Lennox's departure, having suffered his own run-in with the singer in the past. Nor was he surprised by Grainge's and Fuller's fury about Reid's final rejection of their offers. "I've made up my mind," Reid told them. "I'm going to Simon Cowell." Those left behind at Universal cursed Reid as driven by narcissism. "He just wants to be famous on the street," grumped one executive, who pledged revenge.

As Reid disappeared into the Center, the architect of this gala event was gliding toward his own grand entrance. Walking down Oxford Street ten years earlier he would have been unrecognized. Now the "Cowell brand" guaranteed thunderous cheers as he stepped from the Phantom. Across the city, he knew, were many who wished him ill fortune. Some, he suspected, had even conspired to block Abdul's contract. Bursting with a mixture of relief and anger, his honest sentiments to the cameras did not celebrate his triumph. "I couldn't have started without Paula. I would have looked ridiculous," he told the cameras. At the eleventh hour, he explained deceptively, "She decided to play hardball. It's a little nuts." Cowell did not deny the chance of failure. "It's the good, the bad, and the ugly in a reality show where so much is made up on the spot. Exciting and unpredictable. That's why we won't know if it's a success until it's done."

Selecting the panel of judges, he continued, was like arranging a dinner party. "It's all down to the chemistry. They haven't all met yet. All the girls get sulky. We'll see if it works within thirty minutes and then it must last for three months. And it will only succeed if it's special. It'll either be great or a train crash." As an afterthought, reflecting his inner turmoil, he said with a smile, "I could walk out in six hours' time and throw myself off a bridge."

Inside the Galen Center, an energetic warm-up man was whipping frenzied excitement among the unpaid audience. Teenage girls dressed in party clothes had been packed in the cameras' view behind the judges. Older people were slotted into the darkness on the sides. In the large "judges room," Cowell was introducing Abdul and Cole to each other and to Reid.

A special bond united Reid and Abdul. In 1988, Abdul had given

Reid his break by paving the way for his first songwriting contract, worth $100,000, with Kenneth "Babyface" Edmonds. The bond between Cowell and Abdul was also special. "Only we understand our relationship," Cowell told Reid and Cole. "Initially I was very shocked by his rudeness and couldn't stand him," said Abdul. "As an artist I thought it was wrong to be critical of other artists. But since then I've grown to love Simon as my hero. He's taught me a lot." Cole sat silently. A glacial freeze seemed to have descended, deterring Reid and Abdul from assuming any familiarity. None of the three doubted Cowell's dominance. As the owner and executive producer of the show, he expected them.to perform to his requirements. In London, Cowell's technique had been monitored by Alan Boyd, a champion of *Pop Idol*. In PowerPoint presentations, Boyd described Cowell as "the benevolent dictator manipulating the judges" whose "golden rule" was "authenticity to keep the public's trust."

"Right. Ready?" asked Cowell thirty minutes after the deadline to start the show. Punctuality was not his priority. Standing unseen at the edge of the auditorium, beneath tiers of seats, he steadied himself. "I go in as a performer, not a producer," he said to himself. Cowell signaled their entry. "Simon, we love you," women began to scream while others embraced Abdul. The uproar relieved his tension. Unlike *American Idol*, where the auditions are conducted in a small room with just the three judges, this extravaganza, he hoped, would start with twenty million viewers and eventually attract thirty million viewers, the same as *Idol* at its peak.

Standing on the stage between Cole and Abdul, casting around at the four thousand spectators, Cowell enjoyed the fascination women showed for him. Underlying the charisma of his supreme self-confidence was the inscrutability of his sexuality. He picked up a microphone: "Hello, everyone. Thanks for coming. I've come here to find a star. Not someone who wants to be a star but someone who is a star. Five million dollars is at stake." Each of the three judges introduced themselves hesitantly. None knew what to expect. Nor did the first contestant, who was greeted by deliberate silence as she walked onto the huge empty stage.

Over the previous months, a dragnet had been cast across America, searching for the talent missed by *American Idol*. In six cities, over a hundred thousand people had lined up for hours to sing for two minutes in a booth to advance to the next stage. Eight hundred hopefuls passed through a single booth every day. In each venue, there were about twenty booths staffed by Syco employees. Their process was identical to *American Idol*'s. As an addition, Cowell had encouraged aspiring contestants to apply on YouTube and in MyStudio booths—mini recording studios set up in malls. Leaving nothing to chance, talent scouts had also been dispatched to clubs, gigs, and schools to find singers prepared to humiliate themselves but who would potentially be good enough to humble *Idol*. Some scouts were seated with Cowell before the session to discuss their strategy to find better contestants over the following days. By May, six hundred contestants were booked to audition on stages in six cities.

Frequently drinking water from a large Pepsi cup—a reward to the sponsor who had pledged $50 million—Cowell would pose similar questions to each of the one hundred contestants to test their grit: "What would you do with five million dollars?" and "This is the chance of a lifetime. What gap in the market are you going to fill? Who are you going to knock out of the game?" Charmless bores were abruptly cut off. He intended to live up to his "Mr. Nasty" image with a succession of barbs. He enjoyed brutal teasing to crush dreams in front of millions: "You should be singing at home, when your children are asleep"; "It was lazy and whining"; "You're limp and forgettable"; "I thought it was totally hideous, total torture. I was waiting for it to end." Appeals for mercy—"I love you, Simon, and have your picture in my kitchen"—were crushed. "You were singing and you looked like you've swallowed poison." To an oddball woman who introduced herself hesitantly, saying, "My name is Carlo but my friends call me Angel," Cowell asked "Why?" "Because I used to be a guy," she replied. There was no mercy. "Imagine the biggest cornfield in the world and multiply that by a million and that's how corny you are." "In five minutes I'll have forgotten you" and "You were born in the wrong body." Hungry for drama, he began ribbing Abdul. On cue, she snapped. "Leave me alone, Simon. You're starting already." "Okay, Cheryl, see if you can do better." "No, I can't," she replied.

Sneering humor was *The X Factor*'s bedrock but Cole was struggling, unengaged. "You're the cutest thing I've ever seen," she repeated to several contestants. At the end of the second session in the evening in front of another four thousand spectators, Cowell returned to the hotel.

After a bath, he ate some vegetable soup, drank the first of four Sapporo beers, lit the first of nearly twenty cigarettes, and began four hours of telephone calls with his producers, publicists, and Fox executives. Cole, everyone agreed, appeared uneasy.

"She's got a great chance and isn't taking it," said Cowell.

"Cheryl's fantastic because she's so sensitive," Shu Greene, the heart of Cowell's production team, said reassuringly. "But she does seem to lack confidence. She's got self-doubt."

The following afternoon, they agreed, Greene would urge Cole to recall her own days auditioning as a contestant. To boost Cole's self-esteem, *The Sun* carried a headline the following morning: "America Loves Cheryl Cole." Cole's performance in the "10,000 seater arena," wrote the U.S. editor, had "dazzled America with her *X Factor* debut." At five in the morning, Cowell took two sleeping pills. His last thought was of a showdown that evening if Cole failed to "up her game."

With the same fanfare, Cowell paraded triumphantly into the screaming auditorium for the second day's auditions. "We're offering five million dollars and don't want a karaoke singer," Cowell told his fans. The venom started soon after. "You're like a goldfish trying to be a piranha," he told a young girl. "This isn't the singing business, it's the entertainment business," said Reid with authority. "People with the X factor are like rough diamonds." Cool and savvy, Reid played the game without revealing that he was on a steep learning curve watching Cowell and Abdul.

After an untalented female singer was booed by the audience, Abdul added, "I could kill her. I want to hear someone worth five million dollars." There were also stunning performances. "You're thirteen," said Cowell to one contestant, "and I like your cocky confidence. I like your incredible arrogance, which I relate to. It's like looking at me when I was thirteen." When one contestant announced that he would sing an Adele song, Cowell said, "As a matter of fact, she's here." Five thousand spectators cheered as the English star acknowledged the applause. *The X Factor*'s critics cited Adele as the opposite of reality TV's products: She was a real, honest woman who wrote her own songs reflecting genuine emotions about life. Her fleeting presence proved the importance of associating with Cowell—uncoincidentally, she was contracted to Sony.

At the end of the afternoon session, Cole was seated in the long, windowless production room with her younger brother and an assistant, picking at a tasteless salad. Speaking occasionally in a timid voice, she had chosen to sit apart from Reid and Abdul. Reid looked across and noticed a glaze over her face. She was isolating herself, keeping everyone at a distance. "It's doing my head in," she had recently said about her domestic crisis, mentioning that she preferred the social company of women since her divorce. To some, the outburst suggested a love-torn woman racked by confusion following the break-up of her marriage. Her producers were more generous. Recalling her success in Britain, they assumed she needed help to become accustomed to her new environment. "Find out what's wrong," Cowell ordered. "She was glued to my hip in England," he laughed. "Is that the problem?" Sitting at her table, his producers tried to fathom whether the problem was the seating. Cowell was now seated beside Abdul. Was Cole, the producers wondered, suffering because she was no longer physically and emotionally close to Cowell during the recording? He was noticeably cheering and sharing moments with Abdul and not with Cole.

Nearby, perched in his makeup chair, eating a turkey sandwich, Cowell was listening to Mike Darnell. Dressed in his trademark high-heeled snakeskin boots, torn jeans, and cowboy jacket, Darnell had been impossible to miss during the afternoon session. Defying his stature, he had frequently jumped onto the judges' plinth and, gesturing animatedly, commanded their attention with his opinions about the contestants and the music. Sensitive about the network executive's power, Cowell had laughed at Darnell's jokes and maintained his rapt attention despite Darnell's disregard of the floor manager's shouts that the taping had started and the show was under way.

More than ever, Cowell needed Darnell's support. *American Idol*'s ratings for the new season, despite Cowell's absence, were higher than anticipated and rising to a five-year peak. Cowell's challenge against Fuller assumed a new dimension. He could not afford any defects, especially a weak judge, and no time could be wasted. The next auditions would be five days later in Chicago. He wanted an immediate solution.

At nearly midnight at the end of the second day's auditions Cowell summoned a meeting of producers, Darnell and Frot-Coutaz in a side room in the deserted Galen Center. "Cheryl's quiet," said Cowell in a toneless voice. "She doesn't look comfortable." Everyone agreed. Cowell wanted a showdown with Cole. "Let's leave it a couple of days," said Frot-Coutaz, a late convert to hiring Cole. Focus groups, she continued, reported a positive reaction to her accent. "America will fall in love with her beauty, her accent, and her incredible chemistry with Simon Cowell," Frot-Coutaz puffed. Darnell agreed. "We should boost Cheryl's self-confidence," he suggested. "Right," said Cowell. "We'll announce, 'The good news is that Cheryl and Paula have bonded together.'"

Still troubled, Cowell seized the first opportunity to pour out his concern to Philip Green in London. Green was not surprised by the early morning call. Coincidentally, Tina Green had been visiting Los Angeles during the auditions and after the first day reported her own impressions and those of the production team. "They say that Cheryl's unhappy and would be happier in England," Philip Green agreed. "I can read the tea leaves. It's time to act the Kissinger and get everybody in place in case she comes back." The timetable was tight. The opening auditions for the British *X Factor* would be ten days later in Manchester, the same day as the next auditions in Chicago. Pleased to offer his services to "manage the accidents" or, as he also put it, "act the wicket-keeper to help things along," Green suggested, "Cancel Manchester and see how she does in Chicago." "Very clever," said Cowell. He hated confrontation and hoped that others would electrify Cole. After conference calls with all the players—Fox, FremantleMedia, and ITV—the *X Factor* trucks were ordered not to drive to Manchester.

As usual Green spent the weekend in Cannes, which coincided with the opening of the Cannes Film Festival, with his wife on *Lionheart,* anchored in the bay. Knowing that Cheryl Cole would be visiting the festival to promote L'Oréal—"You know you're worth it" was the caption over her photograph—Green sent a text that he was outside her hotel and would she like a drink. The billionaire waited for a reply. Puzzled by her silence, he received a call after midnight from Seth Friedman, one of her agents in Los Angeles. "She can't meet you," said Friedman without any explanation. "It doesn't feel right," Green told Cowell. Cowell was not surprised. Cole would not expose herself to difficult meetings. But the truth could not be avoided. In the past, he had targeted Sharon Osbourne, Piers Morgan, and others with "the same complaints, so I did not think a conversation would be unusual." In Cowell's opinion, "Cheryl's position is no different than the contestants whom she is paid to criticize."

Their relationship was special, however. During her first season on *The X Factor* in Britain, she had given him a fifty-thousand-pound watch for his birthday. The gold case with encrusted diamonds was unique. The following year, she had given him a Jaeger watch. In 2010, she had hired a group of dwarves to follow him around the studio singing "Happy Birthday." All that was proof of special chemistry and yet she was so difficult to read. To his regret they had not even enjoyed a "K & C"—and that made her more attractive. He called her in the late morning.

"Are you okay?" Cowell asked. "Look, Cheryl, we've worked together a long time. I've got to be honest with you. I've looked through the L.A. tapes and I've got to tell you, you're not as sharp and focused as before. This is a different country. America is different than England. You've got to raise your game. Once you're in the hot seat there are pluses and minuses. I want you to be as focused as you were when you sang for the first time in *X Factor.*" After a pause, Cole asked, "Do you think you've been as good?" "Probably not," replied Cowell, "but I think I'll get there." After some more talk, Cowell delivered his bombshell. "Do you think you'd be happier if you went back to *The X Factor* in Britain?" Again, Cole paused. The idea was not unattractive, she replied, but added, "I want to come to Chicago to give it another go." If anyone else had been involved, Cowell would have spoken about "no job is safe" and "no one should take me for granted." Had Louis Walsh similarly failed, there would have been no mercy. But this was Cheryl. He smiled about those seductive eyes and agreed to try Chicago.

In London, Peter Fincham received a late-night call from Richard Holloway, who had just returned from L.A. "Cheryl's not working in America," said Holloway. "Simon wondered if she could come back to *The X Factor* here?" After registering surprise that Cowell had so quickly condemned his own decision, Fincham speculated whether the British show should be a refuge for damaged goods. But since no decision was expected yet and Cole was to be given another chance at the next auditions in Chicago, it was agreed to "wait and see."

Paula Abdul was waiting for Cowell at Los Angeles's Van Nuys Airport the following day, Sunday, May 15, at three P.M. Minutes after entering the private plane to fly to New York, Abdul showed Cowell the result of some minor cosmetic surgery on her face. "It doesn't show," soothed Cowell in the friendly manner of a man who would later say, "I saved her career." Bubbly and laughing, Abdul walked to the back of the plane to sit with Mezhgan Hussainy. Cowell hoped that any uncertainties Hussainy had following the recent breakup of their three-year relationship had been healed by her receiving the house and sufficient money to maintain her lifestyle. As the plane took off, Abi Doyle, Cowell's executive assistant, delivered the ratings of the previous night's Eurovision contest in Britain. The global show had been broadcast at the same time as *Britain's Got Talent* and had had a larger audience. Clearly upset, Cowell fumed about Eurovision's ratings victory. "I'm angry," he said. He had watched the Eurovision show live on a Russian station. The German producers, he conceded, "have taken it from the Premiership into the Champions League by using ideas from *X Factor*." Reviewing *Britain's Got Talent* again on an Apple Mac while the jet climbed away from Los Angeles, he condemned his own production: "Boring. It looks provincial." Abi Doyle was summoned to send a message to Shu Greene expressing his un-happiness and demanding a discussion that night about improve-ments. Top of his agenda were production changes to improve *The X Factor*'s appearance to beat Eurovision. He was irritated by the design of the *X Factor* stage in Los Angeles. "It was no good," he dictated. "It's blue and flat and the sound is poor because there's only one mixer."

Sipping a constantly refreshed cup of PG Tips tea with lemon, he ate a turkey sandwich and carrots. "It's all too gloomy," he con-cluded about *X Factor*'s production. He wanted a global extravaganza to compete against Eurovision. Successful shows, he knew, always hit a peak and then fell into a slow decline. *Britain's Got Talent,* he complained, had become "too formulaic." Like all stage perform-ers, Cowell feared failure, but since TV producers can be counted on to recognize trends in advance of an audience, his concerns could be rectified. For the moment, his anger was unanswered. Surrounded by employees apprehensive of his grumpy reaction to any contradiction, no one would put the slide into perspective. He was the center of a flat organization of yes-men bereft of delegated power.

Taking some medicine from vials laid out in a row next to his seat, he suggested a conference call in New York at one A.M. With a com-pulsive need to telephone around the clock regardless of the local time in America or Britain, he demanded instant responses. His only relief before reaching New Jersey's Teterboro Airport was Fox's pro-motion clip of *The X Factor.* He laughed loudly about the reference to his turbulent relationship with Abdul.

Fox's financial lifeblood depended on the choreographed "up-fronts," the network's showcase to advertisers of the best attractions in the coming year. In a heavy downpour, Cowell arrived on Mon-day, May 16, at a dilapidated but packed Broadway theater. Walking into a cramped space backstage, he noticed that Abdul and Cole had unintentionally worn identical red dresses. "Hysterical," thought Cowell, especially because both women were patently embarrassed. "I'm cold," whispered Cole, who had just returned from Cannes. Randy Jackson, still a judge on Fox's *American Idol,* put his jacket over her shoulders. Despite the disquiet about the color clash, Cowell was pleased by Cole's new hairstyle.

"Cheryl's a fighter and wants to win," he confided to an associate, "so she agreed to a makeover." Although he regarded her as a friend, in the showbiz world with so much at stake there was no place for anything other than candor. Cole barely acknowledged Cowell's arrival.

Nearby stood Nicole Scherzinger, the lead singer of Pussycat Dolls, who had just arrived from a show in Scotland. Cowell regarded the dusky beauty as another toy whose professionalism and hunger for success made her "like a panther" but also "the biggest diva I've ever met. She has her water served in a thimble so that it's always the right temperature." In an aside to her female assistant, Scherzinger confessed, "I've never been so nervous and all I've got to do is walk onto a stage and wave. My lips are so dry." Scherzinger and Steve Jones, a Welshman, had been chosen as the "Ryan Seacrests" to host the program.

To cheer everyone in the countdown to their appearance on the stage, Cowell joked as they climbed the steps, "Ready to make animal sacrifices on stage?" The lights were dimmed. A voice introduced Cowell as "the best-looking reality man on TV, and that was just five minutes ago." The lights were reignited as the four *X Factor* judges, along with Jackson, emerged through tacky ice fog. Jackson, as a show of friendship toward Cowell, had agreed with Fox's suggestion to appear in the promotion of a rival. "Randy, you've come to the wrong show," Cowell quipped with weak humor, ordering him off the stage. Then Cowell stepped forward and spoke confidently: "We have just come from L.A., where the two days of auditions were, in my opinion, two of the best I've seen. *X Factor* is going to be fun and this is going to be different." He concluded with an obligatory "special thanks to Pepsi for sponsoring the show."

There was a heavy downpour as the judges headed for Fox's party in marquees at the Wollman Rink in Central Park. "This is like a zoo," complained Cowell, peering into a gloom relieved only by dozens of tiny girls perched on stiletto heels. "I'm not staying for more than an hour." In the perpetual campaign to make *The X Factor* America's most popular show and beat *American Idol,* Cowell engaged with inebriated advertisers and agreed to repeated requests to be photographed together. Next, he was led to a line of television cameras.

"We make the show up as we go along," laughed Cowell as he worked his way down the line. "If it fails, we're out of a job." Before replying to a question about Cole, he noticed that the singer was disturbed by his bantering with Abdul. "I choose people I like, with egos," he said, introducing Abdul. "I gave ammo to Cheryl," added Abdul to extinguish the doubts about Cole, "and she's given ammo to me to make Simon's life difficult." Cole, the scarlet woman, looked on uncomfortably.

As the rain turned to drizzle, Cowell escaped from the dank atmosphere and headed for the airport. On the chartered plane to Chicago he once again watched the rushes of the L.A. auditions. "The set," he dictated to Abi Doyle, "is too flat. It's got the wrong feel. It feels old-fashioned. It should feel more like a spectacular with a documentary sense. I want filmic quality." After a moment's thought he added, "The performances are disappointing. I want a more ruthless feel, as if someone's got to win. I want losers to feel gutted." Next, he listened to a selection of songs for the contestants in the semifinals of *Britain's Got Talent* followed by clips of *Australia's Got Talent,* featuring Dannii Minogue. "It's very good," he said.

Belatedly, he was organizing quality checks of *The X Factor* and the *Talent* programs in over forty countries. Australia's programs would become the template of the best. Finally, he dictated a memo that Syco should bid for the opening music of the London Olympics. Then he relaxed with a beer and a heaped plate of spaghetti Bolognese. "Simon would then like a sliced apple," Doyle told the plane's attendant. "Make sure there's no peel."

Unmentioned during the flight was his unease about Cole. The focus in London, he had been told as he got onto the plane, was on Dannii Minogue, still in Australia. Journalists were asking whether she had been dropped as an *X Factor* judge. The media, Cowell knew, delighted in any damaging news. Someone at ITV, he suspected, had hinted that Cowell disliked Minogue. "We're loyal to people," he insisted, casting his dismissal of Walsh four years earlier as "a glitch." The reality, he knew, was turmoil in Minogue's private life. She was reluctant to travel with her baby and there were "boyfriend problems." But for the moment, Cowell directed that his publicist express his innocence about Minogue's last-minute refusal to fly from Australia to London. "Say, 'We were talking to Dannii Minogue's agent and we've changed the dates to avoid a conflict with her appearance on *Australia's Got Talent.'*" And then later say, if the conflicts can't be sorted, 'We're talking about other projects.' "

Quietly, he had already lined up a substitute for Minogue. To minimize the criticism, he ordered the publicist to arrange telephone interviews with the tabloid journalists the next day.

Cowell awoke in Chicago with a bad migraine. He took a pill to control the pain and abandoned the conference call with journalists in London. At three o'clock in the afternoon, dressed in a gray sweatshirt and jeans, he took another pill to stave off the migraine and left the Peninsula hotel accompanied by a beefy bodyguard who had just secured the security contract for the duration of the *X Factor* show. After twenty-five years, Oprah Winfrey, America's most successful TV celebrity, was ending her show. Cowell had been invited to feature in "Oprah's Surprise Spectacular," her final show. During the fifty-minute drive to the United Center on the outskirts of the city, Doyle repeated the details of the day's events.

"I don't like parties," griped Cowell. "I don't know many celebs or Hollywood stars, so I don't know why I bother to go." By the time he arrived at the giant arena, feeling unsteady, he expressed disbelief that the celebration was not at Oprah's regular Harpo Studios in front of a regular studio audience, but staged in front of fifteen thousand adoring fans.

As Cowell was escorted to his dressing room, a large corporate box overlooking the arena, he passed the rooms assigned to Hollywood's royalty: Tom Hanks, Tom Cruise, Madonna, Beyoncé, Aretha Franklin, Stevie Wonder, and Maria Shriver. He was, he murmured, unprepared for such an extravaganza.

"I feel a bit of a fraud," he told Terri Seymour on the phone, repeating his awkwardness about celebrities. An uncomfortable room, lit by incense candles and decorated with a large photograph of himself standing beside Oprah, was testimony of his own status: the only non-American invited to participate in the homage to a heroine. "It's all about number one," he said, contemplating his status, as Mezhgan Hussainy—having arrived alone—poured a glass of French champagne for herself. "Talking to celebrities is too much effort. They all think the same." He recalled meeting Madonna at an Oscar party and it was "too much" as she brushed past him; and how in 2009, he had said "Hello" to Annie Lennox at another party and she, after staring at him, turned around without a word and walked away. "She just snubbed me," he recalled with a pained smile.

"I'm no good with prompters," he told the producer, who presented his script to be read off Autocue. "And I'll have to wear glasses, which I hate." While he read the script and drank a cup of tea, Hussainy was repeatedly adding makeup. His head was throbbing. "I'm going back to the hotel," he announced, to the organizers' distress. "I'll be back at seven." Two hours later, refreshed, he returned to the dressing room. Peering through the black curtains at the audience screaming replies to the warm-up men, Cowell was unusually mute: "Oprah's pretty incredible. She's going to be very emotional tonight."

His fascination with Oprah's magnetism turned to irritation as he compared the stage below and *The X Factor*'s set. "I like the way they combine the two colors—blue and the pink," he dictated. "I want that. And who's their sound guy? Get his name. How come they can make a stadium work and we can't?"

"Their sound man's called Jeremy," Doyle reported within minutes.

"Get a number for him," ordered Cowell. "And who's their lighting guy?"

"Terra," replied Doyle, anticipating the inquiry.

"Tell them I'm blued out," Cowell ordered, referring to his British production team. "I don't want it anymore, and they should use a bit of red." Peering through the curtains again he saw thousands of glowing Knuckle Lights—handheld jogging lights—waving in the sub-darkness as the audience obeyed the order to move their arms in synchronization. "Get those too," ordered Cowell, eager for wide shots on a thirty-four-inch screen to "show the money" he was spending, overruling his producers' passion for close-ups. Simultaneously Hannah Lamden, his second assistant, was sending images of the stage from her iPhone to *The X Factor*'s producers with the latest instructions: "I want more lights on the judges' desk. And a different color for every city."

To the music of "I've Got a Feeling," Tom Hanks and Oprah walked from opposite sides onto the stage to open the show. Successively, Hanks introduced Tom Cruise, one of Oprah's favorites, Madonna, Dakota Fanning, Rascal Flatts, and many more. Oprah's eyes were glistening. "It's an incredible story, isn't it?" sighed Cowell, gazing at an American coronation. "It looks amazing, amazing. They're the best producers in the world."

Retreating to his room, he watched the show on TV, eating carrots and celery and dragging on successive Kools. Diane Sawyer was announcing that twenty-five thousand oak trees were to be planted in memory of Oprah's twenty-five-year campaign to encourage reading. "I won't even get a bush when I go," said Cowell. "All I'll get is a nettle patch."

Irritated by his script, Cowell asked for an "and" to be deleted and walked toward the stage. On the way, he silently passed Maria Shriver, heavily made up to conceal her emotion. The previous day, the media had disclosed that her husband, Arnold Schwarzenegger, had fathered a son with the family's trusted housekeeper. "Hello," said Cowell as he saw Tom Cruise and Katie Holmes, his wife, holding their daughter's hand. Cruise's smile appeared forced. Waiting in the reception area, Will Smith and Jada Pinkett Smith eyed Cowell warily. Beyoncé looked away. "I've been critical of her, that's why she's frosty," admitted Cowell, mentioning his recent comments about the singer being "out of tune." But, he added, "she was fantastic." He had reached a dimly lit, cavernous waiting room behind the stage.

The grim atmosphere was broken by a tiny blonde, Kristin Chenoweth, hugging Cowell. "You caused a lot of trouble on *American Idol,* kicking your legs in the air," laughed Cowell, referring to her guest performance on the show. "That was only for you," Chenoweth replied, hoping for an opportunity to appear on *The X Factor.* On the side, Tom Hanks seemed to be deciding whether to approach Cowell. Finally, he summoned the courage to introduce himself. To the actor's obvious relief, Cowell was friendly. "Can we have a photograph together?" asked Hanks, as the singer Patti LaBelle approached for an intimate conversation. Admired by Cowell, LaBelle was also hoping for an appearance on *The X Factor.*

Moments later, Hanks walked onto the stage to introduce Stevie Wonder playing "Isn't She Lovely?" followed by Jerry Seinfeld. After four minutes of good jokes, Cowell nervously walked onto the stage to the music of Lighthouse Family's "Lifted." Cowell's task was difficult. After the music, humor, and emotion, he was cast as "Mr. Nasty" to introduce Rosie O'Donnell singing "Fever." After a fluff, cursing his poor eyesight, his words on the retake were not appreciated by O'Donnell: "Oprah, I'm not so sure that this is the most talented group of singers you're going to see tonight. . . ." He left the stage more nervous than during his entrance and was led toward a line of television cameras for interviews.

"What's it like walking onto a stage in front of fifteen thousand?" he was asked.

"Terrifying. Seriously, very intimidating. That's why I sit down for a living." The female interviewer kicked off her shoes to be photographed on a cellphone with Cowell at his height.

After the finale, Cowell stood in the backstage area obviously pleased to be mingling among Hollywood's royalty. He did not anticipate that no British newspaper would include his name in their reports about the extravaganza. Led by his bodyguard, Cowell headed toward his fleet of gleaming black four-by-fours and drove through cheering fans. Hussainy departed by herself.

"Our journey should take twenty-five minutes," said an assistant.

" 'Journey' is a forbidden word," joked Cowell, reflecting his weariness of the word used by *X Factor* contestants to recite their dysfunctional lives. "We say 'trip' now." As he stood in the hotel elevator, a young woman guest was prevented by his bodyguard from stepping inside. "I looked terrible," he complained to his assistant about the incident. "It made me look awful."

The following afternoon his mood deteriorated even more. English newspapers reported that Cowell would need to appear on the British *X Factor* and *Britain's Got Talent* to reverse the falling ratings. In Chicago, the media reported that over twenty million had watched the semifinals of *American Idol* and seventy-five million votes had been registered, some people voting more than once. That unexpectedly high audience was eclipsed by the news of NBC's triumphant debut of *The Voice,* a new competitor to *The X Factor* and *American Idol* that copied *The X Factor*'s mentor style. *The Voice*'s audience of ten million and its good reviews cast Cowell in a bad mood as he drove at four P.M. to the Sears Centre outside Chicago, where *The X Factor* auditions would be held the next day. During the hour's journey, Cowell watched the latest edits of *Britain's Got Talent* on his laptop and issued a stream of criticisms for the producers in London. "The quality of the programs around the world must be improved," he said.

The *X Factor* and the *Got Talent* shows, he believed, needed to appeal more to youth. The prospect of endless discussions with the network executives was unattractive. Bored, he began again cursing the lighting on the *X Factor* set. The comparison with Oprah's set rankled. He anticipated an argument with stubborn technicians at the Sears Centre. Previously he had lost his patience, but he now decided to be less truculent. Overnight, his British production team had responded to his stream of orders to accommodate his preference for purple and gold lighting on the gigantic set, and more illumination on the four judges.

Squeezing into the mobile-studio control truck, Cowell instantly expressed dissatisfaction. "It's still too much like a TV studio. I want scale of enormity like a huge concert." The camera angles were "wrong," he continued. "The floor looks dull, I want it shining." With barely time to inhale he damned a set of low yellow spotlights: "I hate them." To his relief, the surliness he anticipated from the technicians did not materialize. Within minutes, riggers were climbing sixty-foot ropes to adjust spotlights at the top of the scaffolding.

During the return to Chicago, Cowell listened through headphones to selected songs for future *X Factor* shows. "I'm worried about his taste," he complained about an assistant in London who was daily supplying CDs. "Every night my bed is covered with them. It's impossible to take an evening off." He did not equate this problem with his torturous attention to detail and refusal to delegate.

Over the following two days, Cowell concealed his bad mood from the seventeen thousand spectators who packed into the Sears Centre. The original fear that *The X Factor* could attract audiences only if they were paid—and their consequent sullenness—had gone. Paula Abdul was mobbed by women eager for an embrace and a kiss, and dozens of cellphones recorded Cowell's face as he walked amid thunderous cheers to the dais. "I sense an evil crowd and I like that," he said in his self-introduction. "This will be a long three hours. We have barricaded the doors to keep you here. The judges don't know who they will audition. Some will be great, others will be terrible. We'll deal with it. Let us know. You the audience are the fifth judge."

More cheers greeted Abdul, who titillated the crowd with amorous advances to Cowell and then introduced Cheryl Cole. "This is my first time to Chicago," said Cole, "and I'm really enjoying it. And next to me is the amazing and some say legendary L. A. Reid." Reid matched the congratulation: "I'm sitting next to the amazing Cheryl Cole and we're here because I believe there is a superstar still to be found."

"This is a three-minute audition worth five million dollars," Cowell told the first contestant. "Three minutes to change your life. Show me you're worth five million dollars."

His barbs over the two days never faltered as his search for a star was frustrated by freaks and sob stories. "You walk better than you sing," he told one contestant, and to a woman who said, "I've been a singer all my life" he replied, "Then it's time to choose something else." Prompted by the producers, he asked a fifty-five-year-old, twice-married corn farmer's wife from Missouri, "What happened to your first husband?" "I killed him," she replied. "He went for a gun so I went for my gun and shot him." Her fate after the death was left unexplained. Cowell professed not to know.

Equally unexplained was Cowell's late arrival on the second day.

"I wouldn't expect him to apologize," said Reid, who was gossiping with Abdul while Cole morosely ate a salad across the room. Below, thirty-four hundred people had waited for nearly two hours. "Hi," Cowell said. He smiled, concealing his unhappiness. "I was knackered," he later explained. "I don't like traveling and shooting in different cities. I got up dreading the day's filming. And I didn't like the contestants the previous day. There was so much on my mind." They headed down to the auditorium.

"I appreciate your artistic work," Cheryl Cole told a flashy contestant. "But you're camp." The man's face was blank. "Do you understand 'camp'?" asked Cole. The man was clearly puzzled. So was the audience. "What's the American for it?" Cole asked Cowell. The obvious answer was not forthcoming and, after an embarrassing pause, Cole pressed on. "I like your package," she said to the man, who was wearing tight jeans. The double meaning was not lost on the prim Chicago audience. Stung by a few boos, Cole was isolated. Cowell did not come to her rescue.

"I'm a shameless capitalist record executive," Reid was telling the contestant, "and I'm going to say 'no.'" Reid, thought Cowell, "is very competitive. He hates it if I've picked up a point which he has missed." Abdul began sparring with the man, alluding to his life's "journey" assisted by substances. Her understanding of his torment appealed to Cowell. "Paula, you're an L.A. child," he laughed. "You've always lived among rainbows, mountains, and flowers." He silently compared her to Cole: "Paula's a great survivor, with someone always snapping at her heels. It's tough in L.A. But she's got her confidence."

Cole's personal assistant suddenly appeared at the dais to push a paper plate heaped with chocolates and another plate with candies toward her employer. The comfort food reflected Cole's distress. "She wrongly thought that appearing in America would be just like Britain," thought Cowell. She had failed to prepare for the harder challenge. Wilting as her self-confidence sapped, Cole lacked the strength of character and intelligence to rectify her plight. The session ended. The judges returned to their room for dinner.

Philip Green's watch showed it was just after three A.M. in London when Cowell called. Cole had performed badly in the first session, Cowell reported.

"It's a big mess," said Cowell.

"Whatever happens," Green urged, "promise me that at the end of the show you don't have a conversation with her. That you'll go home, have a sleep, and think about it."

Cowell agreed, and returned smiling and waving to the auditorium for the final session. Unusually, the media was unaware of the crisis; also unusually, Philip Green, normally likened to a bull in a china shop, became the mediator, the only person who could bring the disparate parties together. "Simon," he would say, "is my only outside interest."

During the break for dinner, Nicole Scherzinger approached Cowell. "Into here," he said, diving through a curtain into a back room. For ten minutes, the singer hosting the show pitched for Cole's job. She had proved her credibility, she argued, the previous year in the British *X Factor* when she had stepped in while Dannii Minogue had been having a baby. "Nicole wants reassurance that she's important," was Cowell's explanation for the huddle that night. "She wants more involvement in the program." If Cole was fired, Scherzinger was placed to be her successor. Cowell did not commit himself, but his few words were enough for Scherzinger.

At the end of the second audition, the judges were asked to remain to record a promotion tape. "Chicago is a great music town," Reid told Cowell, "a place which changes music, but some of the greatness did not come out. I'm disappointed." Cowell offered reassurance. "We only need two or three potential stars from Chicago and we've got that. And we've got between five or six great hopes from L.A." Reid was not reassured.

"If we can't find one star," continued Cowell, "out of eighty thousand people applying, then we're not doing our job."

Reid still looked doubtful. Cowell explained that the competition process itself turned the raw material into stars. "Kelly Clarkson justified *American Idol*'s 2002 competition and we'll do the same." Even Reid, a highly regarded producer, could not quite imagine Cowell's formula for the judges to mentor their contestants into professionals.

"Cheryl's gone," Doyle told Cowell. "She just left. It'll just be the three of you recording." Cole's unexplained disappearance reminded Cowell that she had attracted some bad reviews in the last season's *X Factor* in Britain. He wondered whether his personal affection had blinded him to her faults.

The driver lost his way to the airport while Cowell wrestled with Cole's fate: "Cheryl has still to find her feet," he told an assistant. "She's instinctive and she's enjoying herself. But here it's hard. She has to start again. In London, she's like Diana arriving but here every Brit that's hired is hired as a complete dick and Cheryl is the first one who's nice." His voice trailed off as the car finally arrived, after midnight, for the private charter to London's Luton Airport. Until three years earlier, Cowell had commuted across the Atlantic on British Airways, but after being mobbed by fans at a shop at Heathrow, he decided to fly private planes, sharing the cost with Fox.

Throughout the seven-hour flight, Cowell could not sleep. "Do I pretend it's okay," he asked himself, "or do I do what in the long term is best for everyone?" Eating an Irish stew and drinking a Sapporo, Cowell discussed Cole's fate with Richard Holloway across the aisle. Their relationship had recently recovered from a breakdown initiated by Cowell and lasting nearly one year. Since then, Holloway had become more eager than usual to oblige Cowell. He agreed that a possible solution would be Cole's return to *The X Factor* in Britain. If necessary, he would approach her, although he was fearful of the media. Holloway then let the chair fall back and fell asleep.

Just before the plane arrived, at lunchtime on Saturday, Cowell revealed that he had not slept throughout the night and was still undecided. Whisked away from the foot of the aircraft in his Rolls-Royce, he anticipated immersing himself in the steam room of his Holland Park house and enjoying a massage before sleeping. "It's all playing on my mind," he said to himself before he finally collapsed at eight P.M.

At four A.M. on Sunday he awoke. By early evening he decided, "It's crazy to delay any longer." Later he would explain, "No one is regarded as having more judgment than me. I had substitutes waiting. I didn't want them to feel second best. I knew that no one else would take the decision. If you're too afraid of the consequences, you'll just get a horrible slow decline. You'd never change and get new people, and it would be a boring world. I had to drop a pebble in the water and take the consequences." He would take responsibility even if the outcome would prove to be an embarrassing mistake.

His first call would be to Mike Darnell and Cécile Frot-Coutaz. Neither, he suspected, would completely understand his reasons but they shared his "consciousness that she wasn't happy." He hoped they would agree that Cheryl should be "eased back into the U.K." No one ever agreed 100 percent with him, but he expected generosity. Compared with others, he had been "a loyal pussycat" toward Fox and FremantleMedia by rejecting the "biggest offer in TV history" from NBC. Frot-Coutaz, Cowell suspected, would be more difficult to persuade than Darnell. Politics and cost rather than quality were her priority. Her usual response to any suggestion was to look down at her shoes and say, "Well, if that's what you want, but Syco will have to pay." *The X Factor*'s success, she had originally feared, would be at the expense of *American Idol,* another program produced by the FremantleMedia machine. Now she hinted indifference to Cowell's torment.

"We're going to make a decision for Cheryl's sake," said Cowell, setting the mood of the conference call. She would be replaced, he continued, by Nicole Scherzinger. To his disappointment, Darnell and Frot-Coutaz both hesitated and seemed unwilling to move from the corporate script. After a long discussion, both shifted. Survival in their world meant keeping the talent like Cowell happy, and Cowell was emphatic. In the end, both knew that success would also depend on instinct and luck. "It's worth a try," Darnell agreed. Cowell next called Peter Fincham. Cole, he explained, would make a surprise return to Britain and should be paid more money. Fincham was doubtful. He was excited by the two women already lined up for the British

X Factor, including singer Kelly Rowland of Destiny's Child. He doubted whether Cole would accept being a pawn on a chessboard.

By the end of Sunday, Cowell was gloomy. "I could feel a sense of unease," he said. "I'd done enough shows to know that people were worried. No one said we must keep her on the U.S. show and I was clear she would be better in the U.K. But no one said 'Great, go for it.'" The burden was placed on Cowell. As a courtesy and to protect Sony's interests, Cowell also called the chief executive of Universal Music, Sony's rival who had taken over the music rights at *American Idol* and to whom Cole was contracted.

With that tepid support, Holloway was delegated to do the dirty work and headed to Cole's temporary home in a hotel outside London. "There were no tears," Holloway reported. "She admitted her disappointment but would think overnight about returning to *X Factor* in Britain." Cowell was optimistic. "I had expected Cole to look at it logically—I had given her a good TV break, produced her well. She would be happier and better in Britain." The deadline for a final decision was Wednesday.

Cole's conversation with Cowell on Monday afternoon started frostily.

"Can I have your dressing room at Wembley?" she asked.

"Yes," he agreed, allocating to her the largest dressing room in the Fountain Studios.

"And I want to keep it quiet," she said, "so I can surprise everyone by appearing live at the auditions in Birmingham."

"I love that," said Cowell. The conversation ended. He had averted a crisis.

"She'll walk onto the stage and be revealed as a hero," Cowell told everyone, assuming that Cole had accepted his plan. Later that day, will.i.am, Cole's agent, called for the beginning of three days of negotiations. The introduction was strained. Cowell was accused of deliberately undermining Cole by reducing the volume of her microphone. The performer-turned-agent, Cowell realized, did not understand his responsibility to put his client's interests first. Instead of understanding both sides of the argument, will.i.am was riding his own ego. Eventually, Cowell pacified him and by the end agreed that

Cole's fee for the British *X Factor* would be increased. "No one from her side has said she wants to stay in America," Cowell reported.

Late on Tuesday, May 24, Cowell was shocked to find that TMZ, the celebrity gossip website, was reporting from Hollywood that Cheryl Cole had been fired from *The X Factor.* The game had completely changed.

"Will doesn't understand the pressures we're under," Cowell was told as the Media's demands for information grew.

"So what's the problem?" asked Cowell. "A leak is not the start of World War Three." Cowell doubted the publicity was damaging. After all, Walsh had been fired and then returned. That was a trademark game he enjoyed playing.

"She's taken her phone off the hook," cursed Holloway. Cole had cut herself off from any calls while her agent furiously screamed "I've been 'mugged'" to Cowell for twenty minutes.

"He doesn't realize we're trying to help them," an aide said to Cowell.

"I've met Will many times," replied Cowell, "and I thought we had a good relationship. He even asked me whether he could be a judge in the British *X Factor.* I refused."

By the end of Wednesday, even Cowell was frazzled by the media storm speculating that the British tabloids' favorite had been ridiculed in America and was a casualty of Cowell's ruthlessness. Navigating around the industry's reptiles was truly horrendous.

"The leak to TMZ was deliberate sabotage by a rival," he concluded. Some speculated that the culprit was Universal, which had a vested interest to get Cheryl Cole off *The X Factor* and onto NBC's *The Voice,* which was contracted to Universal for selling the winner's discs. "They won't have shed many tears about the leak," said Cowell, admitting that he was "naïve to rely on the discretion of agents and managers to keep quiet." Others suspected that the culprit was Cole's agent or someone associated with Nicole Scherzinger, the person who had most to gain by Cole's departure.

The finalizing of Cole's fate was delayed for twenty-four hours by a tortured conference call at three A.M. London time between Cowell, Holloway, Green, and Seth Friedman about some simple legalities. Finally, the hurdles were resolved and Cowell believed that Cole was cleared to return to Britain. The offer was generous. Cole would receive two million dollars for her American contract and would receive a further two million pounds paid out for appearing on the British program.

"Right," Green told Seth Friedman, "we can have a contract finalized in thirty minutes."

"I haven't spoken to my client," replied Seth.

"Why not?" exploded Green. "It's 4:45 A.M. Go and talk to her."

Seth was never heard from again. will.i.am took over. "Can Cheryl have equity in *X Factor*?" he asked.

"It's not mine to give," said Cowell. "But I'll raise her fee from two million to two point five million with a bonus for ratings, and I'll give her the 'executive producer credit' that she wanted." Cowell added, "I'm doing this for her interests, so we can do this cleanly and quickly."

Again, he assumed a deal had been made and that he had her agreement to return to Britain. "I'll consider other options," replied the improbable agent, seeming more interested in himself than his client. Cowell was puzzled. He got on well with Cole. They were personal friends and he understood her vulnerabilities, although there were barriers forbidding any discussion about her boyfriends and marriage. Considering her disappointing performance, he was offering her a generous deal. So he texted her, "Despite the publicity this is all positive. If you like I'll come over and see you." There was no reply. Cole's attitude was a mystery.

As the tabloids heard about her refusal to talk to Cowell or anyone else, they abandoned any reticence about criticizing television's most powerful personality, and the headlines became hysterical about her mistreatment. Her personal refusal to speak did not prevent her family and friends briefing journalists about her "deep depression" while she lived in America, her "major sulk," the tears because "she feels hurt and let down," and her "humiliation," an irony, some would think, considering she was paid two million pounds to tell *X Factor*'s contestants unpleasant truths.

"Cowell under pressure" was the media's kindest description of a man who over the years they had accused of slyly manipulating audiences and criticized for his aggressive promotion of commercial partners, plugs for clients like Leona Lewis and favors for friends like Piers Morgan. Some believed that Cowell, on the eve of his return to British television for the nightly semifinals of *Britain's Got Talent,* was again manipulating the publicity. Cowell could only wish that for once events were under his control.

Cole's refusal to consider returning to Britain had disrupted the plans. The British *X Factor* auditions were due to start on June 1 in Birmingham and the deadline for the judges to be contracted was Saturday, May 28. Under pressure, Cowell could no longer hide behind a screen of publicists. He needed his version to be properly presented.

"My Cheryl Guilt—A Cowell Exclusive" was *The Sun*'s front-page headline on Saturday, confirming the collapse of a miscalculated plot. "I'm sorry it didn't work out," Cowell admitted to the world. Except that Cowell denied the confession. "I haven't a clue how they could say 'My guilt,'" he would say, "because I didn't speak to *The Sun*. I knew I was getting a bashing but I didn't talk."

The rival *Mirror* attacked the "manipulator." "Cowell's monumental blunder," reported the newspaper, arose from his "seat-of-the-pants style of management." The damning quotation from Cowell—"She doesn't travel well. We've made a terrible mistake"—was accurate.

"Are you okay?" his friends texted. "I'm not reading the papers," Cowell replied, tongue in cheek. "Just as well," they agreed. Since outsiders could not understand the root of the crisis, the *Mail* on Sunday identified Mike Darnell as the culprit. Under the headline "Axed by Fiendish Rumpelstiltskin," the report erroneously depicted Darnell as the monster who ruined England's sweetheart because her accent was incomprehensible. "They picked on me because of my height," Darnell laughed, but with the problem slipping out of control of so many interested parties—Syco, Fox, FremantleMedia, and ITV—he was diving to avoid the flack. He suspected that the *Mail* had been briefed by Cowell's publicists. "We're not passing the blame," Cowell told Darnell. "Just don't read the papers."

Cowell was now chain-smoking. The *X Factor* auditions, delayed by two weeks, would start on Wednesday in Birmingham and the judges could be announced only at the last moment. *The X Factor* in America seemed to be a mess, and the *Britain's Got Talent* finals seemed lackluster.

The media were struggling to pinpoint Cowell's position on the curve of the public's feelings. "You always get *X Factor* crisis stories," Cowell told his staff, "but the only crises will be when people stop watching." The intimate circle witnessed a different story: about a man heading toward the edge, hating the delight Simon Fuller would draw from his embarrassment while *Idol*'s ratings rose above twenty-two million. But even Fuller could not assess Cowell's real vulnerability.

Over that weekend, a new solution surfaced from Los Angeles. Darnell and Fort-Coutaz told Cowell that Cole should return to America and appear at the *X Factor*'s next auditions in Newark.

"This is completely crazy," said Green. By then, Cowell was relying on the billionaire to solve his problems and his trust was shared by the other players.

"Is this for real?" Green asked Cowell, bewildered by the somersault.

"You call Mike and Cécile," replied Cowell, shying away from confrontation. The conference call was fractious.

"We want her to return to Newark," said Frot-Coutaz.

"Why?" asked Green.

"Because we're paying her."

"It's a hundred-million-dollar production," exclaimed Green. "Why are you causing so much trouble about a measly two million? What about you, Mike?" asked Green.

"I agree. She should come back."

"Mike, what are you smoking? Why is everyone behaving like this? Can we be sensible?"

Darnell, apparently scared and powerless, was unforthcoming.

"Mike, where is this going?" Green scoffed. "You're four foot already. Do you want to be three foot? Fuck it, I'll pay her."

The call ended without resolution. Cole was still ignoring their telephone calls but had, according to her family, vowed never to speak to Cowell again. "She feels so badly treated," said one relative, "that she has had enough of the showbiz world."

On reflection, Cowell recognized his weakness in America. Without the hinterland, influential allies, or a top-gun American executive, he could only bow to two fearful and superstitious corporate employees who were proposing a ridiculous solution. Quite simply, unlike his earlier arguments in Britain with ITV's chiefs, he lacked any firepower to push through the obvious solution. In the future, he realized, he would need to reinforce Syco and Sony's authority or sell out. In the meantime, he could only play as a meek firefighter.

"48 Hours to Save X Factor" was *The Sun*'s front-page headline on Monday, May 30. "Cowell fears for ratings." Murdoch's newspaper, usually a cheerleader for Cowell, could not resist knocking the man who too often had prevented the publication from running an embarrassing story. "Simon has clearly dropped a massive clanger," wrote a showbiz editor, "and he should be saying sorry." Cowell was described as "shattered" by the end of his friendship with Cole, admitting, "It's a cock-up." Cole herself, "too fragile" because of Cowell's bad treatment, could not consider starting the British auditions on Wednesday. Peter Fincham had allegedly "flown in" to save Britain's *X Factor*. In fact, he was participating in telephone conferences from Calgary in Canada. All of them were baffled at being outwitted by manufactured indignation. As Cowell read the newspaper at lunchtime, he anticipated heading four hours later toward the Wembley studios for the finals of *Britain's Got Talent* and his first public appearance since Chicago. Over the previous days, he had exhaustively ordered the production team to reedit the taped portions.

That afternoon, Cowell chose his clothes carefully. In the midst of a crisis with the excited audience anticipating a drama, he abandoned his jeans and T-shirt and dressed in a gray suit and a white shirt undone to his waist. "They want to see me taking a huge kicking," he said nervously as he entered the Fountain Studios. "There's a bloodbath going on." In the event, there was only one catcall.

"Can you understand us?" asked Ant and Dec, the two hosts with deep north England accents similar to Cole's.

"Am I missing something here?" asked Cowell. "I have just got back. Otherwise, what's been going on?" The answer, Cowell knew, was the prospect of a poor show. "There are too many old acts," he admitted. "It could have been better."

Despite the efforts of his scouts, the contestants were dreary. The show had deteriorated. The only spark was Ronan Parke, an engaging twelve-year-old singer. "At least that answers the cynics who say everything is fixed in advance," said Cowell. The following day's newspapers reported that Cowell's right eye was drooping. Inadequate Botox was blamed. On edge, Cowell explained that the makeup woman had solved the "droop" by removing hair below his eye, he explained, but the damage was done. The only good news was Walsh's excited report that the new *X Factor* panel had done "very well" on its first day, without Cowell and Cole.

Cheryl Cole's exclusion from both *X Factors* seemed inevitable until a nighttime conference call on Wednesday, June 1.

"I'm not comfortable with Nicole," Frot-Coutaz told Cowell. "Mike and I want Cheryl back in the U.S." Cowell suppressed his exasperation. Cécile, he suspected, was still bothered about paying Cole if she failed to appear, and at the same time she had not seen Scherzinger's glittering performance on Britain's *X Factor.* Corporate animals sometimes advocated ridiculous solutions to control potential internal damage.

"I don't want anyone to feel compromised," Cowell replied. "I want a clearheaded decision. If she comes back, okay. If she can get her confidence back, I'll look after her."

While the conversation continued, he was thinking how to remedy the awful lighting on the *X Factor* set.

"Right, that's agreed," Cowell concluded. "Cheryl's coming back." It was decided that Cécile Frot-Coutaz would write to Cole asking whether she wanted to return to America and will.i.am. would be told that arrangements had been made for his client to go to the American Embassy in London on Friday to obtain a new work visa. The crisis, the voices from Los Angeles confirmed, was over.

Cowell's peace was short-lived. When he awoke later on Thursday morning, he was told by his spokeswoman that JustPaste.It, a Polish website, had posted a crucifying blog allegedly written by a Sony Music executive. The anonymous blogger, claiming to work closely with Cowell, described how he had become "increasingly uncomfortable" by the "fixing" of *Britain's Got Talent*. In particular, he asserted that Ronan Parke, the favorite, was not a normal contestant who had worked his way up but the beneficiary of a "grooming and manipulation process to prepare Ronan for stardom." The blogger claimed Parke had been secretly selected by Cowell's scouts two years earlier as part of the strategy to crack the preteen market. Ronan's grooming, wrote the former "executive" not only involved singing and elocution lessons, but also the supervision of his hairstyle, clothes, and poise, and even management of his appearances on YouTube, Twitter, and Facebook. Accordingly, wrote the blogger, all the "oddities, freaks and mentally ill people" who flocked to the auditions at personal expense were being as deceived as the television audience. Even the telephone voting, he claimed, was "manipulated" by those saying, "The public need to be told who to vote for." About 140,000 people had read the wholly false vitriol written by a malicious oddball before Syco's lawyers managed to ensure its removal.

Cowell's return to the front pages of the newspapers—involuntarily because of Cole and the blogger, and deliberately to promote *Britain's Got Talent*—reawakened anger that his huge fortune, estimated at £400 million, had been earned by manipulating the public's taste. To some, the latest sensation about a repeated theme, regardless of its veracity, suggested that Cowell was too powerful and too rich. Some even suspected that the argument was contrived by Cowell to increase the audience. Cowell feared that a bad week could be followed by an even worse one. "Don't give me the newspapers or tell me what's in them," he ordered his assistants, giving the impression that he would remain unswayed by the media. In reality, he regularly looked at his iPhone to read the Google alerts of his name. Everything written was taken to heart.

Cowell was distraught. He suspected a conspiracy. While ITV and Cowell's lawyers hired specialist investigators to track down the crank, Cowell telephoned Ronan's mother.

"Have we ever met? Did we ever help Ronan?"

"No," she replied. "I always wish we had met but we never did and you never helped Ronan."

The media were guided to the woman for interviews: "It is libellous and lies," she confirmed. Within twenty-four hours, Syco's executives were convinced the culprit was living in Germany and his arrest was "just a matter of time."

In Holland Park, Cowell told Jackie St. Clair, who was constantly present, "I've become public enemy number one." The compensation was the certainty of more viewers when he appeared live on the program the following day, Friday, June 3. His bid to make a live statement at the outset of the program was rejected by Fincham. "Don't get dragged down into the tabloid morass," advised Fincham. "It's all hullabaloo." After a brisk discussion, Cowell agreed to confine himself to a short denunciation. "This is a deliberate smear campaign," he told eleven million viewers, "and it is my job to make sure that whoever this liar is, he is exposed and this kid is treated in the same way as everybody else."

Back home after the show, Cowell had his normal massage and steam bath, followed by a burger and chips. "I'm floating," he confessed, buffeted by the media outcry and confused by mixed messages from Los Angeles: "I've got to the point where I've had enough." In public, his staff spoke only about "helping Cheryl" and "wanting the best for Cheryl" although all agreed, "In this crazy world no one knows what she wants." Darnell, Cowell believed, was offering little help. On the contrary, the producer was angry to be dragged into the debacle. Officially, Fox's publicity machine was silent, but Darnell's spokesmen refused to dispel stories about Cole's depression, love torment, homesickness, unconfident performances, incomprehensible accent, and poor bonding with Paula Abdul. To complicate matters, a tape had been released on YouTube showing Cole articulating confident judgments in the auditions.

At two A.M., Cowell started a conference call with Darnell and Frot-Coutaz. Unexpectedly, the mood music from Los Angeles was buoyant. Unburdened by any American media coverage about Cole, neither could grasp Cowell's distress. Although Cole had neither replied to Frot-Coutaz's message two days earlier nor collected her visa, Frot-Coutaz was optimistic. "I'll text Cheryl," she volunteered, expecting a positive reply. They set a deadline of midnight on Sunday, the following day, allowing her just enough time to arrive in New York for the auditions. After daybreak on Saturday, Cowell finally went to sleep. "I must stay focused on the show and not read the papers," he promised himself. Usually he loved publicity but now he admitted, "My life is like reality TV—live TV and live consequences. My private life and business is shared with the world. I'm in a stressful position, trying to make the right decisions. Whatever I do has huge consequences and becomes a massive story."

"It's been an awful week," he admitted, arriving at the Fountain Studios in Wembley Park on Saturday, June 4. "I've spent the whole night on the phone until seven-thirty this morning." In the auditorium, his friends and executives were crowded onto uncomfortable seats listening to a limp warm-up by a former policeman. "I want you to stand and scream and clap," he urged the audience. Some were already weary by the prospect of yo-yoing in and out of their seats over the next three hours. Glancing in the contestants' "holding room," Cowell was overcome by "a huge wave of depression. This is a moment of total pressure. There's no sense of fun. I don't know what's going to happen in the next hour." As a joke he added, "In TV now, there aren't any hard drugs, just prescription drugs to stave off depression. There's not much laughter."

Concealing exhaustion, Cowell entered the studio. He hoped Ronan Parke would win although in his predictions, to be revealed after the show, he had picked New Bounce, four teenage black boys whom he knew had no chance of success even against dreary dancers, an unamusing comedian, and a clutch of tuneless singers. Between the acts, he glanced at his phone. A message from the editor of *News of the World* asked for a call before the newspaper's deadline.

Slipping out of the studio, Cowell made the call. "I've been told from a source in New York," the editor said, "that Cheryl's going back to America. I called Philip Green and he said, 'Be careful. It's not over until the fat lady sings.' But I think it's happening. Is your gut feeling that she'll be in New York on Wednesday?"

"Not one hundred percent," replied Cowell, "but there's a good chance she's coming back, so yes."

The editor ordered the following morning's front-page headline to report Cole's certain return to New York. Cowell was unconcerned about the report's veracity. The public speculation and the pantomime of the nation holding its breath could only enhance his status.

During the show's critical interval, while the peak audience of over fourteen million was voting, Cowell rested in his dressing room with his mother and friends, dipping potato chips into tomato sauce. "There is a twist to the Cheryl story," he confided to his entourage. "A surprise." He smiled as he returned to the studio for the results. How many viewers had been voting remained for the moment a closely guarded secret, known only to the government's regulator to prevent any malpractice.

As the dross got eliminated and the final choice was between Ronan and Jai McDowall, a pedestrian Scottish care worker with a good voice but no star appeal, Cowell closed his eyes. His head jerked with shock when the Scot was named the winner. "It's a dream come true," said McDowall, pledging to use the hundred-thousand-pound prize to buy his house. Clearly disappointed, Cowell praised McDowall as a "worthy winner" and consoled himself that Susan Boyle lost the same competition two years earlier. As he hurriedly stepped over cables and past the cameras toward his Rolls-Royce waiting in a bay next to the studio, he accidentally met McDowall. "You know who you are and where you're going," said Cowell, summoning polite encouragement. The victor nodded mutely to Cowell's offer to "look after him" for the Royal performance.

While the three other judges and the program executives headed to the Dorchester to celebrate, Cowell was driven home, ostensibly for a bath. His more serious purpose was to reply to a text from will.i.am. Thankfully, the agent wanted a conversation.

"She should come back on the American show," said Cowell.

"How do I know this isn't a trick to avoid paying her in case she refuses to turn up?" asked the agent.

"This is ridiculous," exploded Cowell. "Who cares about two million dollars? What does she actually want? Does she want to come back on the show?"

"That isn't your concern," replied the agent. Cowell's suspicions were roused. "Her agent's winding her up," he thought, but he ended the conversation positively.

The deadline was a conference call on Sunday at nine P.M. London time. All the parties were given the telephone number and the code to gain access. He set off for the Dorchester convinced that "it's a complete mess." The party for *Britain's Got Talent* was limp. Having fulfilled his duties and thanked everyone, he returned home after less than an hour.

At nine P.M. the following evening, Cowell, Darnell, and Frot-Coutaz dialed in for the conference call.

"Are you there, Will?" asked Frot-Coutaz. There was silence.

"I don't know why he's broken off," said Cowell. "Perhaps he's negotiating to get her onto *The Voice* in America or even the following year in Britain. She's missed the deadline. That's it. We sign Nicole."

To a man accustomed to win, Cole's tactics were a novelty. Cowell was gearing up to retaliate. Four months later he would gloss over the agony and tell a newspaper, "I had Peter Fincham on the phone saying, 'We'll have her back, we'll pay her more money.'"

The headline in Monday morning's *Sun* appeared one day late: "Cheryl Cole . . . You Have 24 Hours to Save Your Career." The offer to "salvage her career" was described as "her lifeline to return to the U.S. *X Factor*." During that day, Cowell sought to salvage his reputation. "I'm not a monster," he told the *Mirror*, "but I did the right thing . . . she was out of her comfort zone. . . . I was just protecting her." He continued, "The hardest thing to accept is that everyone has painted me as a monster because I embarrassed her, but the truth was I was protecting her."

No one understood the problems, he believed, and few took notice of another story published that day about an investigator having tracked down in north England the Internet imposter who had posed as the "Sony executive" exposing how *Britain's Got Talent* was rigged. The man, supposedly suffering from mental illness, made a public apology.

Cowell had read the newspapers before he arrived at the Harrods executive terminal at Luton Airport to fly to New York. Throughout his life, he had rarely displayed vulnerability after a setback. At school and in the music business, he appeared to shrug off humiliation and move on. This time, he was uncertain about the consequences of the previous two weeks. While twenty-six suitcases were loaded onto the plane, he asked rhetorically, "Have I been damaged? When the general public see what else is happening, they'll see I haven't done a bad thing. The critics aren't producing shows. Every decision depends on audience acceptance and I know when I've done something bad. The impression is that Cheryl was my decision alone but it was a group decision. I've had to take the blame. I've had to be the fall guy, taking the flack. There's always only one name in the firing line. I'm the one sitting in the editing bay and at every audition."

As he walked through the plane he spotted the day's newspapers on a table. "Get the *Daily Mail* off," he told Abi Doyle. Hannah Lamden dropped two bags of fruit in the cabin. "This is just in case Simon asks for a smoothie," she told the hostess. Ever since Cowell had read about the life-enhancing ingredients in a newspaper, he had placed a regular order for rare fruits to be airfreighted to London or Los Angeles. He changed into a track suit, asked for his smelling salts, which he passed under his nose, and continued his discourse. "The public will love Cheryl even more now. She's still a hot property. She can walk onto any show right now." Then he laughed. "The madness this week was unbelievable. They all think I'm manipulating it. I wish."

As the plane crossed the British coastline, he began dictating his latest proposals for new ideas, to move away from reality TV. *Red or Black?*, his latest program bought by ITV, he complained, was poorly produced. Fearful of deterioration or rivals producing better shows, he urged his handful of staff to rejuvenate his programs with the aim of building an empire, like Aaron Spelling. "I can earn money while I'm asleep. Aaron Spelling understood good casting, and he broke stars. He never hired established stars." In the background, Hannah Lamden and Jennie Paine, a third assistant, were searching for the name of a Russian masseuse to book during his two-week stay in Miami after his stops in New York and Chicago. "She had dark hair," he said helpfully. There was no plan for Mezhgan Hussainy to join her fiancé on the East Coast.

Finally, he gave some brief thought to the following day's auditions in Newark. In the state of Frank Sinatra's and Bruce Springsteen's birth, he needed to dispel the gloom. Nicole Scherzinger had won the prize. Paula Abdul, he anticipated, would make a bid to grab the limelight. Cheryl Cole was a ghost.

"After a bumpy week, today is a new beginning," Cowell said, greeting his battered troops. "Enjoy yourselves." Abdul had arrived in the gloomy judges' room to find a large bunch of flowers. The card contained warm greetings from Cole. Sensitive to showbiz turmoil, Abdul was genuinely grateful. In the distant darkness of the room was a basket of fruit for L. A. Reid. The following day, when the circus moved on, the basket and the card from Cole remained, untouched.

16

CRISIS

ALTHOUGH HIS PRIVATE JET WAS PARKED FEWER THAN TWENTY YARDS from the executive terminal at Luton Airport, Simon Cowell made the short journey in his black Rolls-Royce. Not out of convenience but to make a personal statement. To step out of his limousine at the foot of the aircraft steps reconfirmed his fame and wealth.

Two minutes later, the plane was taxiing toward the runway. Lighting up a cigarette, Cowell sipped a cup of tea and told Abi Doyle to start up two laptops. Stretching back, he did not fasten his safety belt.

At the start of the eleven-hour flight to Los Angeles on July 16, 2011, Cowell began watching recordings of the forty-five female singers due to perform at the Pasadena Civic Center four days later for America's *X Factor*. Out of the hundred thousand who had been originally auditioned in six cities, just 262 men and women between thirteen and seventy-six years old had been invited to the "boot camp." After five days of auditions, only thirty-two would survive.

Pulling on the cigarette as the private jet lifted off the concrete, Cowell spoke enthusiastically about his search for a global star who would separate *The X Factor* from the imitation programs sprouting across American television. The countdown had begun to enrich Sony and himself.

"She's pretty and can sing," he commented about Caitlin Koch, a blonde rugby coach from Buffalo, New York.

"I must have been in a good mood on that day," he dictated, terminating the chances of a brunette from Chicago with a flick on the pad.

"Cari Fletcher from New Jersey, she's got potential," he told Doyle.

"She's not going anywhere," he said after two seconds of another brunette, pushing the fast-forward.

"Dani Knights; sexy, good name. I like her a lot."

As Doyle inserted new DVDs into the computers and the plane crossed the British coastline, Cowell grimaced: "They're commercial but they're choosing the wrong songs." On reflection he realized his own error: "The ones I thought were good aren't sounding so good, and those who weren't on the radar are much better than I realized." In Cowell's music business, so much depended on impulse on the night. Stacy Francis, a forty-two-year-old living in Burbank remained his "Susan Boyle replica."

At the end of the viewings, his favorite was an eighteen-year-old blonde from Seattle. "It'll all change," he said, smiling, and noted a few girls who could be forged into a group. Hammering inexperienced singers into four different groups, he decided, would be Paula Abdul's summer chore. The collapse since 2003 of the Dixie Chicks, America's most popular female country band, who sold over thirty million albums until reaction to their anti–President Bush comments left a gap in the market. Before the start of the live *X Factor* programs in October, Abdul would select four attractive women from the dozens heading to Pasadena to shape into a group.

As he ate the dinner sent ahead by Helen, his cook in London, Cowell speculated on the panel's chemistry, especially Abdul's relationship with Nicole Scherzinger. "Nicole," he said with glee, "has become like a panther, ready to strike, which Paula hates because she fears the competition." Their relationship, he envisaged, would crack once they disagreed about the contestants. "I'll encourage it because otherwise the show will be boring." Twenty million Americans, he was sure, would turn on to watch the cat fights. This number, though, was down ten million from his summer prediction.

Cowell's second stretch Rolls-Royce Phantom was waiting outside U.S. immigration's small concrete block at Los Angeles International Airport dedicated to passengers on private jets. After shaking two officers' hands in the empty room, he drove to the house he was renting in West Hollywood. As usual, Abi Doyle had given him fifty dollars in cash, his tip for the driver. Cowell rarely traveled with money. His first appointment the following day was at Palm Drive to see the builders' progress on his house.

To his neighbors' distress, about one hundred workers had been arriving daily since February to transform the exterior, refurnish and redecorate the interior, and expand the house into the yard. The total budget had escalated toward fourteen million dollars.

At two P.M., Cowell drove his convertible Bentley onto the black basalt forecourt. Anticipating his arrival, Zoë, the house manager, had directed four housekeepers and three groundsmen to spotlessly clean the building site. The first glance delighted Cowell.

Over the previous five months, all the exterior white wooden surfaces and many interior shelves and frames had been sanded down and covered by a custom-prepared greeny black oil paint. The last of fourteen coats were being applied. After each coat had dried, the wood had been sanded and another coat painted on.

"It's completely unique," swooned Brian Biglin about the Art Deco style.

"It's great," Cowell agreed.

Since it was Sunday, the usual noise and dirt from excavators and jackhammers was absent. Nevertheless, over forty tradesman were working, many in the garden.

Cowell's idea was an outdoor living space surrounded by plants, water, and fire. Three rooms had been extended to create exterior loggias covered by retractable push-button roof shades if the sun was too strong, and retractable skylights when it rained. Regardless of the weather, Cowell could sit outdoors. Electric heaters in the beams staved off any night chill, and live fires blazed from iron grates.

Along one of the new extensions was a "living wall" for plants.

Amid green foliage, white and magenta flowers would grow verti-
cally as an art piece, watered from permanently moist foam attached
to the wall. Whenever Cowell requested, the wall garden could be
changed within one day. Opposite the living wall was a waterfall gur-
gling into a submerged basin lit up by flames emerging from bubbling water.

To cross between the two seating areas opening into the garden,
Biglin had designed a walkway floating on water. Cowell and his
guests would step on apparently drifting stones linked to black tiles
illuminated by concealed lighting.

At the rear of the yard, in front of the separate gym and guesthouse, was a fifty-foot reflecting swimming pool lined with Italian
Bisazza stone tiles. Colored black with a hint of purple, the water
mirrored the surrounding buildings, the foliage of the nine specially
planted mature palm trees, and the tubs and planters made from European black Absolute granite. "Mine will be the only house in Palm
Drive with palm trees," chortled Cowell.

The unique omission for a Californian home was a barbecue. "I
can't stand them," he had declared, ordering instead two Italian exterior brick pizza ovens. Nearby were racks for various types of wood;
each infused the food with a particular taste. When completed, his
chef would fly from London to confirm that the pizzas could be
baked perfectly in the new ovens, and then return to Europe. Soon
after she fulfilled the task, Cowell decided to employ another cook.

A new feature in the garden was the paving surrounding the lawn.
Seven thousand square feet of limestone had been cut from a quarry
in Vancouver, Canada, found after a long search by Biglin. Cowell
liked the gray color that in sunlight became dark gray with blue
veins.

Persuading the quarry owners to cut the stone in a precise thick-
ness and shape had been difficult because the process would inevitably cause breakages. In anticipation, Biglin had ordered 40 percent
more stone than required. But in the event, so much stone broke that
the quarry lost money on the contract and vowed never to repeat the
process.

Creating this extraordinary garden had irritated Cowell's neighbors. Not only was the quiet road disturbed by noise and dirt but it was clogged by more than seventy vehicles a day. Protests had persuaded the local authority to temporarily ban all building until Biglin organized a shuttle to the site for the workers from two parking lots. "They're neighbors from hell," scoffed Cowell. To fashion reconciliation, he offered the complainants spa treatments and cakes. They would at least be spared his plan to build studios and an office block in Los Angeles if *The X Factor* and *America's Got Talent* were recommissioned.

"When can I move in?" he asked.

"In eight weeks," replied Biglin. "Mid-September."

Five minutes later, Cowell crossed Sunset Boulevard and was driving up Loma Vista, a steep climb into Beverly Hills. His property manager had found a replacement for Cole Place, which was being legally transferred to Mezhgan Hussainy. The house was at the end of a winding road, at the peak of Trousdale Place. It had cost about eleven million dollars. Isolated above the city, the uninterrupted view from the shady yard guaranteed even greater paradise than Palm Drive. Bought from a music producer, the seven-thousand-square-foot house was ornately furnished and lit by crystal chandeliers.

"Get rid of all that," Cowell told his manager.

"It's valuable," he replied.

"Just get it out," insisted Cowell.

The house, to be used as an office, was to be rebuilt as "an eight-thousand-square-foot Asian retreat," which, for Biglin, meant that it would be "warmer, creamy, natural, and relaxed, with a lot of water and wood like a home in Bali." He asked Mezhgan Hussainy to supervise the renovation. "It keeps her involved and happy," he believed, and she was efficient. He had seen an eighteen-thousand-dollar invoice for a month's supply of flowers. Hussainy had negotiated an immediate 30-percent reduction and eventually cut the monthly bill to just $280. "Great," said Cowell. "I can't stand flowers."

At seven P.M., Cowell returned to his rented house. His producers had been summoned to discuss the upcoming five days of auditions. Led by Tim Byrne, Syco's creative director, the British contingent dominated the meeting. Byrne, a former television music producer, had featured Cowell's Fanfare records on ITV's Saturday morning programs, especially promoting the hit "Yell!" by Instant Replay. Reporting to Byrne were the program's producers, music directors, and sound technicians. To tilt the advantage in his favor, Cowell had drawn the best talent from Britain, at the expense of the British show. Thrilled to be responsible for a cast of experts and technicians supporting twenty-four cameras—all at his beck and call—he had hired choreographers, vocalists, stylists, and musical experts to produce a spectacular as different as possible from *American Idol.*

"I'll either be praised as a genius," he told his producers, "or get screwed."

Three days later, Cowell arrived at Pasadena Civic, an imposing theater built in 1931, with more than three thousand seats. The 260 contestants, staying in two local hotels at Fox's expense, were standing on the huge stage facing the empty auditorium. Cowell's introductory sermon was chilling: "Over the next twenty-four hours, you're being tested to see if you're a star. We're going to test your attitudes to teamwork, hard work, and if you've got talent. We will separate the good from the not so good. There'll be no feedback, except that half of you will be going home tomorrow."

The inevitability of expulsions cast a pall. "And more of you will leave over the next days," he added. The gloom was punctured by a promise: "One of you will get five million dollars."

The harsh tone was uncompromising.

"There's one winner up there," said L. A. Reid. "But it's a competitive environment."

"You're competing against one another," agreed Paula Abdul. "This will be a stressful week. Stay true to yourselves. But be amazing. Put your nerves aside. Be bold, daring, unique. There's always a winner, but we are determined to find a star."

"Years ago," concluded Nicole Scherzinger, "I started up there on *Popstars.* This is your time to shine."

Gathered behind the judges was the evidence of Cowell's resolve. Choreographers, vocal coaches, stylists, songwriters, and Sony executives were watching to spot whether any of the raw material bore signs of potential stardom.

Even on *The X Factor,* genuine stars could not be entirely manufactured. The experts searched for talent and character. Within two minutes they could distinguish between actors and those using the song to define their interpretation and identity. Some of those experts spoke about an artist's body as an instrument. True artists used their body to hook an audience. The intense auditions were a pressure cooker, and those overwhelmed by the experience because they lacked talent and character were separated from those using the expertise provided to grow in spurts into a professional.

"I need to see you fighting for the five million dollars," Brian Friedman, the choreographer, was saying as he walked among the contestants. Since his abrupt departure from Britain's *X Factor,* Friedman had been reborn as a creative teacher. "Set your bar really high, and your goal must be to go even higher," he continued. "You must call attention to yourself through the music. It's not about dancing, it's about using the stage." Only a few understood his message.

The first fifteen contestants walked onto the stage to perform.

"Don't stand there like a pencil," Cowell snapped at a hapless male from Dallas. "This was your moment. You've lost it." He called a break.

Smoking in the hot sunshine outside his Star Waggon trailer, Cowell looked at eight containers of antiaging cream placed on a wall for his approval. After a few words with Tim Byrne, he walked into the hall to address the contestants. Alongside him was L. A. Reid.

"The first fifteen were no good," Cowell told the hushed crowd. "They were standing like donuts. You've got two minutes. You need to start thinking about entertaining us. Because a lot of you are going home tonight."

"On the basis of what we've seen," Reid added, "I don't know why we said 'yes' to anyone."

Once the auditions resumed, Cowell's mood darkened. Instead of listening, he and Abdul were engrossed in conversation.

"Thank you for putting me into the show," she told Cowell for the umpteenth time. "It's such a warm, wonderful atmosphere. I feel so appreciated. It's so much better than *Idol*. That's slow, lazy, and underproduced."

On stage, a twenty-two-year-old's fate had been decided. Turning his back to speak to the experts, Cowell expressed his frustration.

"These were good people but they're performing badly. They haven't prepared themselves."

Yet their hunger could not be disputed. One girl stood singing on crutches, two were pregnant, a man sang hours after hearing that his brother had just died, and Stacy Francis performed rather than go to her father's funeral on that same day. "That wasn't good," reacted Cowell and she burst into tears.

"Crunch time," announced Cowell just after eleven P.M. at the end of the second day. The first decisions had been made. Outside the auditorium, 170 contestants were being directed to a long empty corridor. Dragging their suitcases, all wore long faces and, anticipating the worst, some were in tears. They trudged out like doomed refugees in a wartime drama.

Elsewhere, the remaining ninety-two were being corralled into holding areas. While they waited in anguish, the producers discussed the deployment of their cameras to record images of joy and despair.

In a sideshow, four young girls had been taken to a room with their parents to meet all four judges. The group, the Lilas, were being told by Cowell that because one of the girls was one month too young, the group would unfortunately be excluded. Six cameras recorded howls and tears. Their distress caused Abdul and Nicole Sherzinger to also cry. The recorded drama was electrifying but excessively emotional. "We can't use that," Cowell declared, knowing the limits of the public's taste, and headed back into the theater.

Ninety-two contestants were on the stage. "This is not easy for any of us," said Reid, describing the inadequacy of some performances and the rigor of the competition. All believed they were about to be sent home.

"But the good news," continued Reid, keeping a poker face, "is that you're through to the next round." The stage collapsed into cheers.

"I still haven't seen a star," Reid told Cowell at one A.M. "I hope we haven't wasted our time."

"Don't worry," replied Cowell, heading for home and four hours on the telephone.

At six A.M., the survivors were woken up and divided into thirteen groups. Under Cowell's master plan, Paula Abdul, supported by choreographers and vocalists, gave them songs to learn and then instruction on how to sing and dance.

At five P.M., Cowell appeared. Groups entered the stage and while singing together, each contestant stepped forward for a forty-second solo while the remainder provided a choral background. The raw material had been transformed into a disciplined troupe performing compelling entertainment, the small beginning of an intensely micromanaged production process. Cowell would leave nothing to chance.

Spontaneously, Cowell, Abdul, Scherzinger, and Reid burst into animated hugs and high fives. The gaggle of professionals in the vast theater was mesmerized. "We've got some real stars," they screeched. Reid was mightily relieved. There were, he realized, at least six potential stars. Finally he grasped Cowell's insight. There was light at the end of the tunnel.

At 11:30 P.M., after an hour of negotiation, another thirty-two were isolated and brought to the stage. "It's the end," they were told by Abdul. Hurried into a large room, they were filmed crying and even screaming obscenities at Cowell.

Unaware of those scenes, the remaining sixty were summoned back onto the stage. "It's not good news," sighed Cowell mournfully. Twelve cameras recorded misery. Then: "It's great news. You're through." After four minutes of recording, Cowell took the microphone: "Tomorrow we start again. At the end, half of you will also be out of the competition. To stay in, you have to create magic. Think of the five million dollars. Study the songs. Be true to yourselves. In the meantime, we've arranged a party. Enjoy yourselves."

"I'm not going to the party," Cowell whispered to an assistant. "I might do something I regret." One pretty girl might be too attractive to resist.

Twenty-four hours later, just thirty-two people out of the original hundred thousand remained. Divided into four sections—girls, boys, groups, and over thirties—they would be "mentored" over the summer in a "judge's house," which in reality were rented houses in superb locations. Cameras would record the training and the emotions as the judge eliminated and chose which four would arrive for the live shows in Los Angeles in October. Four female country singers who all looked like Taylor Swift were chosen to be trained by Abdul. They decided to call themselves Lakoda Rayne. Optimistic about the four attractive girls, Cowell never understood if the name had a meaning.

In a good mood, Cowell flew with his friends to Nice to board *Slipstream*. During August, his producers would edit the first eight episodes. At the end of the month, *Slipstream* moored in St. Tropez. The news from London was excellent. Forty-eight percent of the TV audience, 11.4 million people, had watched the British *X Factor*. The new panel of judges, which included Kelly Rowland and Louis Walsh, among others, had set a new record. "There's great energy on the show," Cowell concluded. "It's a happy ship." ITV, he noted, "cannot get the press releases out fast enough." Peter Fincham, he heard, was pleased that Cowell had proven to be indispensable.

Over two days, Cowell commuted between the yacht and the rented "judge's house" in St. Tropez where six *X Factor* girls—flown from America—battled for a place on the live shows. At the end, among the two rejected by Cowell was Melanie Amaro, a nineteen-year-old from Florida. Cowell's next stop was London.

Cowell's game show *Red or Black?*, with a daily prize of a million pounds for the winner, whose only skill would be to choose the right color, was starting on Saturday, September 3. Commissioned from Syco by ITV as part of the 2010 contract for *X Factor*, the program was scheduled nightly for one week. Claudia Rosencrantz and other seasoned television executives were surprised that ITV had commissioned a mindless contest which she had unhesitatingly rejected. Fincham was reminded of Paul Jackson's warning that ITV had become too reliant on Cowell. By the second day, the most expensive game show in British TV history, costing about fifteen million pounds, was mired in scandal. The first winner, whose single talent had been to utter a one-syllable word, was exposed as an ex-convict, jailed for brutally assaulting a former girlfriend.

By the fifth day, as Cowell again boarded the jet at Luton heading for Los Angeles, the audience had fallen from 7.2 million to 3.9 million. Cowell's reputation was knocked but he did not appear concerned. Minutes after takeoff, however, he did make a confession.

As the jet crossed the Irish coastline toward the Atlantic, he twice watched Melanie Amaro's performance in St. Tropez on his laptop: "My greatest mistake was not putting Melanie through," he moaned. "It was insane. I don't know why I didn't put her through. I'll bring her back." Shortly after, he flew to Florida and, in a specially taped encounter, invited the tearful girl back into the competition.

His other woman problem that day had also been self-inflicted. Speaking on Howard Stern's radio show, he had admitted to having once enjoyed a threesome with two girls; avoided confirming his intention to marry Mezhgan Hussainy; and, finally, confessed his everlasting love for Terri Seymour. The conversation with the shock jock had embarrassed Hussainy and outraged Sinitta. "Why did you say you love Terri and not me?" she had wailed over the telephone.

Having pacified Sinitta, Cowell planned to tip off "the paps" that he and Hussainy would be walking along Rodeo Drive, Los Angeles's expensive shopping area, later on. "That should wind them up," he thought. A few hours later he abandoned the idea. Instead, his fiancée would be invited to the *X Factor* screening party on September 21.

In Los Angeles, as dinner was served, he cast aside what he considered to be trivial items and considered his challenge during the autumn. With three big shows going in Britain—*X Factor, Got Talent,* and another season of *Red or Black?*—and the launch of *The X Factor* in America, he would be stretched. Simultaneously, he would be supervising Syco's music producers as well as the franchises of his formats in over forty countries. Overshadowing all that was the resilience of *American Idol*'s ratings, attracting over twenty-two million viewers. Normally he loved competition, but criticism of his power to dictate public taste in television and pop music had become irritating. Too many were speculating whether cracks would soon show.

Among the latest critics were Lohan Presencer and James Palumbo at the Ministry of Sound record label. The producers complained that Syco had seized without their agreement "Collide," a song written by Avicii, to relaunch Leona Lewis. Cowell denied their claim and the dispute was destined for an expensive High Court battle. The more profound issue, Cowell knew, was the argument about Leona Lewis's integrity. Compared to Adele, who wrote her own songs, Lewis lacked an intimacy with music and, like an actor, relied entirely on others for her material.

Presencer and Palumbo were trenchant opponents of *The X Factor*'s manufactured pop. Lewis's inability to write her own music, they argued, and her unmemorable interviews, guaranteed a "short play" for her career. *The X Factor,* wrote Palumbo, is "a cruel illusion that karaoke crooners can become stars." Lewis, he predicted, would "soon be finished." Her first album had sold seven million copies, her second sold one million copies, and the third, he predicted, would crash.

Both "snobs" infuriated Cowell. "How many songs did Frank Sinatra write?" he asked rhetorically. His opponents had briefed the *Guardian* and *Daily Mail* to publish prejudiced reports about the Avicii dispute under the headline "Rip-off Factor." Unfortunately, Lewis's relaunch singing the Avicii song on *Red or Black?* had failed. The song was poor, confirming Lewis's problem that no one was writing suitable music for her. Commercially, Lewis's fate was unimportant to Cowell. Cher Lloyd, a runner-up in the last *X Factor,* would be a hit by Christmas. The truncated careers of pop stars caused him little concern.

In the big picture, Palumbo was a pinprick for Cowell. The real challenge was posed by Lucian Grainge. Cowell's old friend had successfully plotted to sell *The Voice* to the BBC starting in 2012. "I bit like a dog on a bone when I got the offer," admitted Grainge. Eighteen months after becoming Universal's global chief, he was proud to have become Cowell's principal rival, owning the international record rights for *American Idol* and now *The Voice.*

Sipping a red smoothie on the plane, Cowell spoke dismissively about Grainge's previous failures "with his other TV shows—*Fame Academy* and *Britannia High.*" He was also flippant about the failure of *Idol* and *The Voice* to produce any hit records in 2011. "*X Factor* U.S.A.," he pledged, "will produce stars."

Cowell was, however, irked by the BBC spending about £24 million of the public's money to pitch *The Voice* against him. "The BBC is obsessed with destroying one of my shows. That's why I'm going back to Britain. I'm going to throw everything at them."

One piquancy was not lost on Cowell. Twenty years earlier, he had been persecuted at Arista by Nigel Grainge. Now his estranged brother had declared war. And, Cowell suspected, Fuller was lurking in the shadows as an advisor. Eager to get his own revenge, Fuller might have encouraged will.i.am and Will Young to join *The Voice*'s panel in Britain. He predicted that twenty million viewers for *The X Factor* on September 21 would silence Grainge, Fuller, and the rest. "It's got personal," he said about *The Voice.* "I'm going to kill them."

His self-confidence was boosted as his chauffeured Rolls-Royce drove north up Interstate 405 from Los Angeles Airport. The huge billboards along the freeway featuring his photograph to promote *X Factor*'s launch were comforting. Even Ryan Seacrest had sent a text admitting irritation about Cowell's looming presence across the city.

The countdown to the first night was an unprecedented party for fifteen hundred guests at the ArcLight Cinema in Hollywood to premiere the first episode, followed later that night by a second party for two hundred at the Redbury hotel. By three A.M., even hardened critics spoke admiringly about *X Factor*'s "European edginess compared to *Idol*'s schmaltzy, shameless pulling of heartstrings."

At five P.M. on September 21, the program's producers and stars met at Syco executive Simon Jones's home in the Hollywood Hills to watch the live transmission on a big screen in the garden. Forty people left in high spirits, boosted by the Twitter reaction on the East

Coast. Early the following morning, the same people were reeling. Only 12.2 million had watched, and *X Factor* had ranked only as the third most popular program that night.

"I feel bruised," Cowell told Bryan Lourd in one of his first calls.

"You've set your bar too high," replied his agent. "Twenty million for a new show in the fall was impossible."

"I wish I'd kept my big mouth shut. I should have been less lippy."

"If it falls by thirty percent tonight," warned Lourd about the results episode, "you've got real problems." No one else, Cowell thought, steeling himself, would be allowed to see his unease.

During a hastily summoned meeting, Cowell urged his producers, to "work hard to put on a good show." The blame, he announced, was not *X Factor* but fatigue with singing competitions and similar formats. *Idol,* he consoled himself, had started without any competition.

"It's hard to accept that there are people who will celebrate your failure" was his only concession of vulnerability.

Unlike earlier crises, he could cope with the fear of failure, but when his team departed he admitted to a confidant: "If it's bad tonight, we're toast. It'll be the end of my TV career in America."

Other channels were swiftly cancelling series like *Pan Am* and a remake of *Charlie's Angels* "on air" after a few episodes. Even Cowell was shocked by the brutality. Still blistered by his failure to secure twenty million viewers, he mentioned to his confidants his genuine fear of a similar fate if his audience collapsed. Bitter memories of his Arista days revived but naturally remained unspoken. Only his father could have understood his invisible pain and now no one would sympathize with a man whose fame relied on nonchalance toward the downfall of others.

At six A.M. the following morning, Cowell telephoned Darnell. To his relief, the ratings were steady. Not only had nearly twelve million watched, but critically, *The X Factor*'s audience was top of the eighteen-to-forty-nine demographic that advertisers targeted. The collapse had not occurred.

The relief was short-lived. The news from America about Cowell's failed prophecy had encouraged his critics in Britain to ask, "Who needs Simon?"

Cowell interpreted the reaction as "the media are waging a vendetta against me." Even Walsh fueled the fire, saying about the British *X Factor,* "Everyone's happy because it's really working. There's less pressure because Simon's not here." The reports, Cowell admitted, were "not great for the ego. I always thought it would happen one day. I'm not feeling sorry for myself." *America's Got Talent,* too, was under a microscope, even though it had received the highest summer ratings. Piers Morgan would not have his contract renewed by NBC in favor of Howard Stern. NBC cited Morgan's duties for CNN in an election year as the reason, but in reality they wanted Stern to increase the advertiser's target audience of eighteen- to forty-nine-year-olds. To win that so-called demo, NBC was prepared to spend an additional twenty million dollars to move the production to New York to feature the American star. "He's too dangerous for a family show," Cowell told the NBC executives. "We could lose sponsors if the pressure groups start going." But after Stern's assurances—"I know what I can and what I can't say," he promised—the move to New York was agreed. The presenter would be paid just over ten million dollars for the season.

Seeking a break, Cowell flew to Miami to celebrate his fifty-second birthday. In a conference call with his *X Factor* producers he agreed, "I'll change the program on the basis of feedback but I'm sticking to the principles I believe in. We must do what interests me and I won't be swayed." At issue was nothing less than Cowell's micromanagement of every aspect of the show. Not only the lighting and sound, but also the contestants' appearance and the music. At later stages he would allow them and their "judges" to choose their clothes and songs, but his eye on the production values of the showbiz extravaganza was, he believed, essential. No one dared to voice any contradiction, such as that the show risked appearing overproduced, undermining its credibility.

In his absence, Cheryl Cole hired a plane with a trailing banner to fly over Palm Drive with barbed congratulations: "Simon Cowell is 52 today. Ha ha ha! Love Cheryl xoxo."

"I must admit the show is incredible," she texted Cowell.

He was thrilled. Always intrigued by the woman who eluded him romantically, he immediately telephoned her. During an hour's conversation, she confirmed that she wanted to resume their working relationship.

"Thanks for making me look so good on the show," Cole said, grateful that her brief appearance had been well edited. Taking the cue, he hoped she could be persuaded to return to one of his programs.

"Come back to *X Factor* in London," said Cowell. "It'll be your Princess Diana moment. You'd do a great entrance."

"Okay, I'll do it," agreed Cole.

Soon after, will.i.am, her agent, vetoed the idea.

The rebuff incited Cowell to consider retaliation. If will.i.am was to appear on BBC's version of *The Voice* in early 2012, he would appear against him on *Britain's Got Talent*. He called Cheryl Cole again. Would she, he asked, like to join him. "No way," she replied. His next call was to Dannii Minogue to get her on to *Britain's Got Talent*. "She's a real man's girl," he thought. "Very feminine. I miss her." The conversation was positive.

"She's like a greyhound out of a trap," he chuckled. All that remained was a conversation with Peter Fincham to agree on the judges.

The possibility of easy negotiations disappeared at the end of the week. The pincer came from two fronts.

In Britain, *The X Factor*'s audience for the live shows had fallen by seven hundred thousand in one week and it was heading to fall five hundred thousand below the BBC's *Strictly Come Dancing* for the first time in four years. Most commentators blamed Cowell's absence from the program as the reason.

"I can see the trap they've fallen into," said Cowell, watching in Los Angeles. "They've chosen the wrong songs, wrong styling and choreography. I can't change the problem of the talent." The contestants, everyone agreed, were uninteresting.

On October 15, he spoke to each of the judges for thirty minutes, then to the producers, and finally sent detailed notes. "I need ten percent improvement each week," he concluded. "But I can't be too hard on them because it wouldn't be the best thing to do." The following day, the tabloids' headlines dramatized Cowell's "explosion" after two million viewers had switched off. "This series of *X Factor*," said Fincham grittily, "is still the second most popular series in its history and is still getting the same advertising revenue."

Battered in Britain, Cowell was painfully learning about the difference of cultures between British and U.S. audiences, not least among teenagers. "It's obvious it's going wrong," he admitted. Ratings in America remained stubbornly below twelve million. His bid to attract younger viewers had alienated the middle-aged. *The X Factor* had little appeal among the mid-American audience, especially for family viewing. Most of the contestants came from the two coasts and there was not enough country music.

In America, the momentum of the recorded shows, Cowell acknowledged, was slipping. The show's appearance and even the songs were "wrong." The recorded episodes were predictable and lacked suspense. The contestants seemed too similar and the audience was unable to understand the differences from other shows.

"There have been a few blunders and I'm learning from the mistakes. I thought I could start where we ended in the U.K. It was arrogance on my part. We're adapting, not panicking."

He was reconciled to the idea that an audience of eleven million for a new show was respectable, but pledged that sixteen million would watch the finale in December. The turning point, he hoped, would be the first live two-and-a-half-hour show on October 25.

One day earlier, he arrived in his Bentley for the dress rehearsal at the CBS studios. He parked outside his new double-decker $1.6-million trailer, rented in the confident days of a star anticipating twenty million viewers. "It's all worse than I've ever seen," he exclaimed, "It's not what I wanted." The graphics and sound were "wrong." The lighting—the most complicated ever constructed on the CBS set—was "awful." The music was "badly mixed." The contestants, he protested, looked phoney. "I don't want stylists jumping all over them, sucking their identities out of them. The kids won't buy into acts if they're changed out of reality." His problem, he thought, was working with strangers—like the lighting director—so "messages were mixed." Twenty hours before the live show began he spoke about a "meltdown."

The burden was entirely on Cowell. Although L. A. Reid was "my rock—he's amazing," only Cowell could save his show. "As producer, I've got to do all the work. Everything depends on the feel on the night when I walk into the studio."

Over twenty people were summoned to his trailer. "We came to America to raise our game," he started. "I feel let down. We've got to improve." Over five tense hours, he unpicked and rebuilt every aspect of the program. "I don't want the show to be an identikit to the U.K.'s. It must be different. I want the set to be like an infinity pool so you don't see the beginning and end."

The team was dispatched to work through the night. He returned to his rented house. After two beers, he called with a new list of improvements.

"This isn't the usual karaoke with just one good singer," he told Tim Byrne. "We've got six great potential stars. I want them all to look different. They mustn't sound like a talent show. We've got to play to their strengths. Think hard what they should sing."

Once he ended the conversation, he became maudlin: "I'm learning on the fly—I'm learning something new—that you don't win in America unless you deserve to win. I'm working under difficult conditions. I've got sharper awareness than before. But I feel freer than I have for a long time. We're going to make it with this group of people."

At two P.M. the following day, Cowell returned to CBS's Television City. Overnight, another crisis had erupted on Britain's *X Factor*. Kelly Rowland had argued with the other female judge and had abruptly flown to Los Angeles. She was pleading that sickness would prevent her return to London. The tabloids were speculating that Louis Walsh would be fired as the program spiraled down. "I have not arranged for the judges to argue," Cowell scoffed. "I don't want a panto," meaning a slapstick show. But as usual he regarded the drama as a godsend: "I love it. We're all at war now."

Nor was he worried by the bad publicity. Fincham might complain about the "tabloid morass," but the speculation about Kelly Rowland's antics would add to the ratings. He texted Walsh some reassurance and called Cheryl Cole to beg her to return for a guest appearance on the British show. "No way," Cole replied, changing her mind once again. As he predicted, the headlines did push the British show back up to a peak audience of 13.5 million. His self-confidence was restored. Even when he had been down, Cowell had never revealed his anguish.

"What shall I wear?" he asked himself, looking at six suits and six white shirts hanging on a rack in the trailer.

"I'm going to touch you up," said his new makeup artist, who was hovering nearby. Cowell laughed—looking down he realized that he had just completed a magazine interview with his fly undone. The attractive female journalist had said nothing while he chewed a raw carrot.

"Ginger tea, please," asked Cowell. A half-sentence conversation had recently persuaded Cowell about the medicinal benefits of strong herbal tea, and he now had it made with filtered water brought from his home. A conversation with his makeup artist had persuaded Cowell to buy a Kangen water filter. "It makes your skin a lot better," she had promised. "It filters all the toxins out of the water and adds vitamins and alkaline." For $4,800 plus $130 for each filter, Cowell snapped up another remedy to prevent aging.

At 4:50 P.M., the studio was packed, the audience was wild and the program was ready to go live. Cowell's favorites to win were constantly changing. On that evening, his male choices were Chris Rene and Astro, a fourteen-year-old black rapper from Newark. "The most arrogant kid I've ever met and he looks like a star," Cowell said. He was no longer sure about Rachel Crow—"probably too sweet," he thought, "and doesn't love pop music like Justin Bieber"—and was hankering for Melanie Amaro and another contestant, Drew Ryniewicz. "Stacy's probably going home," he speculated.

Just how he had shifted his allegiances toward Crow and Francis was baffling. "I'm a bit of a flake," he admitted in his trailer. "One minute I love someone and then I switch. It's easy to fall in and out with a contestant. They're bubble moments. In the auditorium, the song is good, the audience are on their feet, and you lose your sense of perspective. I didn't realize the difference between a TV moment and a future star. At the beginning, Stacy was okay and then it was, 'You're getting on my nerves now. You're too whimsy and misunderstand the audience.' Eventually there are too many TV moments and the public saw limitations which I didn't."

The real test was the public's verdict about him. For the umpteenth time, Cowell looked at himself in the mirror: "If I go down, I'll go down in flames." He walked in the sunshine toward his fate.

The following morning, the world had not changed. The show's audience had barely increased and media interest was mute. Unlike in Britain, there were no raging tabloid headlines highlighting a scandal to generate new interest. Despite all his efforts, *The X Factor* was static.

On the eve of the following week's show, Cowell had dinner with Peter Rice and Mike Darnell. Unexpectedly, at the end he was told that Fox would commission the series again for 2012. He returned home "bouncing." Brian Biglin had called: "Your house is ready." He drove straight to Palm Drive. Frantically, his staff had removed every last wrinkle. On November 3, he entered a perfect home.

"Bouncing around like a kid," repeated Biglin as Cowell rushed around fifteen thousand square feet of bliss. Everything, he declared, was "great," except the grass in the yard. "It's too smooth, like for bowling." He ordered it to be ripped out and replaced with normal grass.

Then, wanting to share his pleasure, he summoned Terri Seymour and Mezghan Hussainy. Within minutes both drove down from the houses he had bought in Beverly Hills. In a surreal snapshot, Cowell was showing two rival ex-lovers his stunning but, to a feminine eye, sterile home. On cue, both admitted their admiration and both chanted their demands for similar furniture and features in their own houses. After a time, their paymaster's enthusiasm for his guests was sated and he bid them farewell. Thankfully, alone again in his house, he could enjoy the solitude of his "space."

At 1:30 A.M. on the same night, he was linked to the *X Factor* contestants in London by Skype. "The contestants are not being given enough guidance," said Cowell. "They need renewed confidence." Even Denise Beighton had told Sonny Takhar that the independent labels were not interested in the contestants. The only choice, some suggested, was to bury the series and start afresh in 2012.

Cowell had wanted to fly the contestants to Los Angeles from Britain but Fincham had vetoed the idea.

"I don't want Cowell interfering," he said. "The show should stand on its own feet."

Cowell's return to *Britain's Got Talent* the previous summer, Fincham thought, had been disruptive, and any future return would be "part of a big conversation." Fincham was not pleased by *Red or Black?*, which he had bought for his channel, but the viewing figures were poor and the publicity about the first winner—a man jailed for beating up a girlfriend—was unhelpful. "Cowell is spinning too many plates," Fincham told his staff, who were also irritated by *Red or Black?* The crisis was growing. Even *The Sun* was hostile.

"We're not going to bury the show," announced Cowell. "I'm going to do something to get it back on the road. We fight to the end." If Fincham blocked a trip to America, he would find another way to speak directly to *The X Factor*'s remaining contestants. He imagined a jokey fifteen-minute session on Skype.

The vision on the huge screen in his new media room shocked Cowell. Staring at him from London was a surly group. "Why are you hiding your face?" he asked one young man with a hood over his head. "That's disrespectful."

"Why," he asked another, "don't you speak to me?" There was a nineteen-year-old who could neither sing nor dance but whose sex life and drugs made him as attractive as Johnny Rotten—with matching publicity.

"Why are you putting your hand up to speak to me?" asked Cowell, perplexed by the lack of attitude. "You all need to get your game up." When one of the Little Mix girls asked, "What should we do?" Cowell could not swallow his anger.

"The Spice Girls never asked 'What should we do?' They said what they were going to do. If you don't know, you're lost."

At the end of ninety minutes he cut the link.

"This is the worst group there's ever been," he told his producers. "We need a complete change."

At 5:30 A.M., he took a sleeping pill and went to bed in his new house. At midday, he woke up and tried to open his bedroom door. Concealed bolts, installed for his protection, prevented his exit. Locked in the room, he called his housekeeper. "There's a hidden button to release the bolts," he was told. Concerned for his safety, he had also pledged to buy two Doberman pinschers to supplement the permanent security guard.

After drinking three glasses of filtered water and three smoothies, followed by a small plate of pills, some oatmeal, and other nutrients, he summoned an emergency meeting of producers at his house at 3:45 P.M. Overnight, the shock from London had sparked doubts about the American show.

"It's all bad," he told his employees standing in the garden. "Last night was the worst program I've ever been on." Not only was the music and lighting "bad," but he was disappointed that L. A. Reid and Nicole Scherzinger were unengaged. "They need to work hard for their artists," he ordered. "The show must have more star appeal, and more American appeal." Steve Jones, the Welsh host, he declared, was incomprehensible for Americans and should not be rehired. Everything needed renewal.

The crisis, however, was no reason to abandon enjoyment. To celebrate the twenty-ninth birthday of Kelly Bergantz, the executive producer responsible for developing new programs, Cowell flew her and Ben, her boyfriend, along with Lauren and Andrew Silverman to Las Vegas by private jet. To celebrate Halloween, the casino magnate Steve Wynn had allocated villas in his private compound to the group. He also provided five bodyguards to escort them to the party at the XS nightclub. It proved insufficient to fend off dozens of women who threw themselves at Cowell. Repeatedly, he agreed to pose for photographs and be kissed. At two A.M., in the midst of a rousing party, he led the way to the Las Vegas branch of Spearmint Rhino. For three hours, three lap dancers focused on Cowell. When he left at six A.M., he appeared to be attracted to one of the girls.

"Leave them," ordered his friends. "You don't need any bad publicity."

Earlier that week, after a good evening at Drai's, a nightclub in Hollywood, he had taken a girl back to his bungalow at the Beverly Hills Hotel. He awoke in the morning to discover not only the theft of money but also of his laptop filled with commercial secrets. The local police, using images from the club's and hotel's security cameras, had traced the girl, who was persuaded to return the computer in exchange for keeping the cash. No one thought it worthwhile to repeat the risk in Las Vegas.

"It's warfare in the jungle now," Cowell said, surveying his fate on his return to Los Angeles. Amid the postmortems and plans to increase *The X Factor*'s audience, Cowell had separately met Ryan Seacrest and Nigel Lythgoe for dinner. The one with Seacrest was uneasy, the one with Lythgoe was "relaxed," but both failed to rekindle the old friendships. Meeting the enemy, however, had reignited his quest to understand his mistakes.

Frustrated that his producers could not provide the answer, he had paid $250 to Mezhgan Hussainy's fifteen-year-old nephew to write a merciless critique of the program's failures. The unorthodox report was damning. The contestants, he was told, failed to connect with the audience, the "reality" was unreal, and, most important, Cowell had mistakenly assumed that American audiences would immediately understand what had taken seven years to develop in Britain. "It's taking too long to sink in," realized Cowell. His British producers, Cowell concluded, were paid too much and were "too safe and too cozy." The four girls of Lakoda Rayne symbolized the problem: "They've got no clue who they should be, and no clue about the music business." They would be rightly voted off the program, he decided, because "they look too manufactured." In the weeks before the finals in Britain and America, he had taken his critics' remarks to heart. He would need to renew everything for the following year: producers, judges, and the entire format.

17

REVENGE IS SWEET

AS RACHEL CROW COLLAPSED, SOBBING, ONTO THE STAGE AFTER
being unexpectedly voted off the competition, Cowell rushed toward
the helpless fourteen-year-old. The audience in the CBS studio—
already hyped-up by an energetic cheerleader—spontaneously erupted.
Screams filled the vast hangar. Even for Cowell, the drama was unexpected.

Crow, he knew, was convinced she would win. In the backstage
area, she and her mother had skipped around, confident about her
destiny. Enjoying the fussy attention of the wardrobe, makeup and
personal assistants, Crow had assumed the demeanor of a star. Now,
she risked self-destruction.

"Her mum's going to have a nervous breakdown," Cowell said as
he watched the crumpled teenager being helped to her feet.

"You promised I would win," Crow howled reproachfully at her
mother.

The girl's fate, Cowell knew, would be decided within seconds.
Any mistake as millions watched live, and later by countless more on
the web, could destroy a talented TV artist who over the previous
weeks had played the media, in his words, "incredibly well."

The broadcast cut to a video showing the highlights of Crow's past performances. In the studio, the tension was near breaking point.

"I can't breathe," Crow cried out. "I was supposed to win this. I was going to make history." With seconds to go before the live transmission resumed, Cowell formulated a harsh message.

Viewers saw him speaking to the stricken girl. None could have imagined his precise words: "Stop crying. You can't change anything. You were at the bottom of the votes. Now you must act like the person every record company wants to work with. Disney will not want to work with a sore loser. Say something gracious. It'll make you more interesting, darling."

Mercilessness rather than compassion would have reduced others to renewed hysteria but Cowell understood the girl whom he described as "an actress with a thirty-year-old's mind." Crow quickly recovered as Nicole Scherzinger, whose vote had triggered her expulsion, mounted the stage. As boos from the audience resounded across the studio, Scherzinger tearfully apologized. Crow now hugged and consoled the singer. Puffing out his cheeks, Cowell stood transfixed. "Bloody hell," he repeated to himself. "I hope she says the right things."

On cue, Crow looked into the camera and sweetly but tearfully told the audience "I love you" and other platitudes. The broadcast ended. The wounded were led from the spotlight into the darkness of backstage.

Ten minutes later, searching for Crow, Cowell arrived in Scherzinger's dressing room. The two were together—the target of a hyperactive photographer. "The room's soaking wet," said Cowell, smiling. "Mostly from Nicole."

The drama, Cowell knew, was TV magic. The viewers had been hooked. This, he hoped, would be the breakthrough to get a bigger audience. Instead, *The X Factor*'s ratings the following week stayed stubbornly below eleven million.

"I misunderstood America," Cowell admitted yet again. "I cocked up."

He had arrived in Los Angeles accompanied by his prized British production team. Together, they convinced themselves, they would beat *American Idol*. But by December 21, the eve of the final episode, with an audience below ten million, Cowell acknowledged a heap of mistakes.

The program had too many gimmicks, too many dancers, strobe lights, and bursts of flames. What it lacked in a saturated market were contestants who grabbed mid-America's interest. In a series of late-night telephone calls, he blamed himself for overproduction and for preventing the contestants from "being themselves." To please the advertisers, he had focused too much on teenage stars who pulled in the young audience, but ignored mid-America's passion for country music.

Even chasing the youth audience had not been an outright success. The fourteen-year-old Drew Ryniewicz and thirteen-year-old Rachel Crow had originally been among his ideal winners, but both had been expelled, first by the audience's votes and then by Paula Abdul and Nicole Scherzinger voting for deadlock.

"At least it proves I don't fix the shows," he said without bitterness.

Now he pondered whether both judges should be dropped from the next series. Scherzinger, cursed by what he called "her flakiness," had attracted no extra viewers, and even Abdul's initial attractions had waned. To Cowell's surprise, during live performances his old partner had been reading on her phone suggested comments composed by a scriptwriter. He would never allow sentiment to interfere with his decision whether to part with Abdul. But as usual, he would not make a decision until the last moment. He enjoyed cultivating peoples' insecurities. Instead, his focus was on the final episode.

Even before Crow's departure, Cowell had switched his support to Melanie Amaro. At first, he had been suspicious about the nineteen-year-old's ability to engage. A good voice was not enough. Genuine artists won an audience's sympathy by displaying their understanding of music through their character and personality. Gradually, he noticed, Amaro understood his message. Unlike the others, she was learning particular tricks from her coaches and, more important, displaying the willpower needed to become a star.

The change had started six weeks earlier. Concerned about Amaro's attitude, Cowell had invited the girl from a poor background to visit his house, now revalued at $34 million, for a pep talk over tea. "Start working hard," he told her in the loggia flanked by the living wall on one side and a waterfall on the other. "Get into your head that you're going to win. You've got to show how much you want to be a star. Kelly Clarkson has had a ten-year career because she's a killer."

Unfortunately, during the competition, Amaro had ballooned two sizes. She required three corsets and elastic tights to constrain her figure. Despite her exceptional voice, making her attractive to America would be a challenge, not least because her music was unfashionable. Songwriters were not offering new material or diva ballads for singers like Leona Lewis because pop radio stations refused to play those records. Finding hit songs was a challenge, Cowell decided, that L. A. Reid would have to overcome to relaunch Epic, the label he now ran. At least, during the last days of the competition, Amaro had fully understood Cowell's lessons and convinced herself that she could become the new Mariah Carey. By contrast, her two male competitors, Josh Krajcik and Chris Rene, lacked serious commercial potential. Their music would not attract big sales.

In Britain, Cowell's problems were worse. The *X Factor* winners, the four Little Mix girls, were, many thought, unattractive, uninteresting, and could not sing. Sales of their Christmas single, which normally would have been an automatic number 1, were poor. "Before I decide what to do with them," said Cowell, "I'll have to look into their eyes." Compared with the dazzling American show, Britain's *X Factor* was dowdy and no longer the country's number 1 program. BBC's *Strictly Come Dancing* had snatched that prize after *The X Factor* had attracted only 13.7 million viewers for its final show, compared with 17.7 million in 2010. Cowell's absence was blamed for that decline. He had now decided to drop at least two of the judges, replacing one with a former record executive. "I need someone who naturally understands production and the music business," Cowell said.

In London and Los Angeles, Cowell's critics were reveling in his misfortunes. He shrugged off the doomsayers. Both *X Factor* and the *Got Talent* programs remained top-rated shows and, after thirty years in the music business, he knew how to cope with setbacks. He already had plans for major changes to the programs' formats—and to Syco's staff. Too many of his producers—British and male—had become complacent and were reluctant to embrace radical change. He needed younger, wittier, and less predictable producers on his team.

Confident that he could fix the problems and increase the ratings over the following two years, and certain that he still enjoyed the support of the broadcasters and sponsors, Cowell refocused on those who were relishing his discomfort.

Simon Fuller, he concluded, was no longer his principal rival, as he hadn't had a new successful program on the U.S. or British networks for ten years. Cowell spoke about Fuller as the past. "*Idol*'s in decline," he mischievously told Fox's executives. The new target, he explained, was *The Voice*. "That's the new kid on the block," he told Peter Rice, "which threatens *Idol*'s supremacy in 2012." American TV, he continued, with a diminishing pool of talent, could not sustain three major music reality shows; there would, he said, be a battle for survival and one show would be axed. "There's going to be a bloodbath," he predicted, with *The X Factor* emerging on top—if, and only if, he could persuade Fox "to prioritize *X Factor* in its battle against *The Voice,* and let *American Idol* wither."

His reasoning was clear. Unlike *Idol*, *The X Factor* and *The Voice* were reinventing themselves using TV programs to sell more than music. According to *The Voice*'s rules, artists under contract to a record label would be allowed to participate in the TV competition. Theirs was no longer a talent contest for amateurs. He would consider the same for his revamped shows in 2012. In his battle for supremacy, his biggest rival had become Lucian Grainge and Universal Music, associated with *American Idol* and *The Voice*. "I've now got two TV series," Grainge had boasted, "against Simon's *X Factor*."

Cowell was looking for what he called a "game-changer." *Pop Idol* and its successor programs had replaced radio as the key marketing tool of pop music. Now, he believed, was the moment to develop a new format as an alternative to *The X Factor,* and to revolutionize the business.

To plan the future battle, he invited fifteen managers of Sony's global music business to a meeting on December 2 at Soho House in Hollywood. There would be a presentation about what Cowell described as a "defining moment" for Syco.

Across the world, sales of *The X Factor*'s format had overtaken *American Idol*'s. About forty broadcasters were buying *The X Factor* compared with about fifteen sales of *Idol,* down from thirty-five. The *Got Talent* format was sold by FremantleMedia in thirty-six countries. Depending on the country's population, Syco earned in 2011 between thirty thousand dollars (in Estonia) and three million dollars (in Australia) from each broadcaster for *X Factor* and *Got Talent.* In addition, the American *X Factor* program was broadcast in 130 countries. Syco's income from those sales was about fifteen million dollars, a small amount compared with the major earnings from the sale of Sony and Syco records promoted by *The X Factor.* That was the principal difference between music reality shows from the rest of TV's output. Namely, the TV programs spawned profits from music that belonged to Syco and Sony. Increasing that income was the reason for the meeting in Soho House.

Over ten years Cowell had built a sustainable business, but he had now reached a crossroads. His challenge was to avoid becoming a casualty of the industry's appetite for sucking out the best and discarding the corpse of a fading star. His longevity depended upon not being a "lollipop." The future, he decided, was using music reality shows to exploit Sony's electronic products and those of his sponsors, Pepsi and Verizon. But first he needed to reassess his relationship with Sony, a damaged corporation recovering from the Japanese earthquake and serial hacking attacks in which customer IDs and passwords were stolen. "Sony's become too passive," Cowell complained.

Syco's agreement with Sony negotiated by Philip Green in 2010 was to end in 2013. At that stage, both sides would have the option to sell their 50-percent share. Cowell was spinning the thought of selling out if Sony did not become more aggressive against Universal. His business, he calculated, was worth around $700 million.

"You must take an interest in the battle to support *The X Factor,*" Cowell urged Sony's managers. "*The Voice* has given us a kick up the ass. The battle is international. The common enemy is Universal Music. To beat *Idol* and *The Voice* we must take control of the music from FremantleMedia and defeat Universal." If Sony failed to engage in the battle, he hinted, he would sell his 50 percent to Apollo, Bob Sillerman, or to another investor and start afresh. Unspoken was his idea to manage *Idol, X Factor,* and the *Got Talent* programs as a director of Apollo.

An opportunity to engineer a dramatic change had started during a chance meeting backstage at *The Oprah Winfrey Show* in May. He had been impressed by Jada Pinkett Smith. Jada spoke about her ideas for a new music show. "We must work together," Cowell suggested. "I'll give you fifty percent of anything we do." Soon after, as a token of her affection, Pinkett Smith gave Cowell a Can-Am three-wheeled motorbike. "My latest toy," he chirruped as he roared around Beverly Hills. In return, he sent Pinkett Smith a custom-built Smart car, similar to one he had just bought, equipped with gull doors and leather seats supplied by Bentley. He also gave her an idea to develop.

The result was unveiled on the eve of the *X Factor* finale in Cowell's trailer on CBS's lot. *In the Mix,* Pinkett Smith explained, was a competition to find the best disc jockey in America and Britain. Music's new stars were the handful of DJs commanding a million dollars for a single night's session. *In the Mix* would be a competition between those DJs playing different music to three thousand clubbers invited either to Sony's studio in Culver City or to one of the fifty major nightclubs in America and Europe. To save money and enhance the visual experience, virtual stages would be generated by computer for the TV viewer.

"The tribes in the clubs," Pinkett Smith told Cowell, "will rate the DJs' music by the amount of noise they generate. By clapping, shouting, and stomping." Interspersed between the dancing, the DJs would reveal their life stories. On the back of the shows, Sony would sell not only music but also equipment to clubbers wanting to be their own DJs. "I think it's genius," trilled Cowell. "I'm blown away." Fearing competitors would steal the idea, he wanted a formal proposal written by January. "We'll have a few days to develop it. Sony can either come in or sell out," he believed. Fizzing with excitement, Cowell was sure he had seen the future. (In early 2012, their relationship would acrimoniously crumble.)

One hundred yards away, the three contestants were finishing rehearsals for the next day's American *X Factor* finals. Cowell walked confidently to the studio from his trailer. Anyone taking his passion for fun, money, and celebrity as flippancy would be mistaken. One of his strengths was to disguise the seriousness of his ambitions.

From the stage, Amaro's powerful voice filled the empty studio. In six months, she had been transformed by Cowell's team. Sitting among his producers, stylists, choreographers, singing coaches, and record executives, Cowell wondered whether his latest manufactured star could become as credible as Adele. Amaro's new steely resolve certainly glossed over the emptiness of reality TV.

There was nothing phoney about her singing, but no one in Cowell's entourage at the rehearsal said with certainty that the likely winner from the original hundred thousand applicants had the depth to match the billing of an enduring five-million-dollar star. Rather, they spoke about the short term. Amaro and her two male competitors would undoubtedly earn profits for Syco from recording contracts. And Cowell also expected income from Drew, Rachel Crow, Astro, and one of the expelled groups. That alone, said Cowell, was far better than the miserable revenue earned by the winners of that year's *American Idol* and *The Voice*. At the end of the day, he could launch at least six artists from the series with no cost to Syco and Sony.

Cowell had left nothing to chance. Despite his professed disdain for gimmicks, he had included every trick to make a breathlessly exciting show: dancers encouraged by Brian Friedman to be "real sexy," flashing beams of light, shooting flames, Knuckle Lights for the whole audience, and a ton of tinsel cascading from the heights. The credits would roll for a show that also included Alanis Morissette, Justin Bieber, Stevie Wonder, and R. Kelly. The producers had conjured up a true spectacular—dazzling, loud, humorous, and tense—but for many the enjoyment lacked emotion. Amaro was declared the winner with 42 percent of the forty million votes. The show was watched over two days by between 11 million and 12.5 million viewers, lower than all his predictions. "Thank God she won," sighed a Cowell aide. "Otherwise Simon would have been in a grump for three months."

Backstage at the end, the atmosphere was relief rather than excitement. Cowell had secured credibility for the next series but had failed to make himself or *The X Factor* the hot topic in America's conversation.

In Cowell's trailer after the finale, Peter Rice and Mike Darnell stood close by as a bottle of champagne was hesitantly opened. Cowell appreciated the support of Fox's executives.

"Mel's mother's home has been foreclosed," Cowell revealed, referring to the winner, "so the five million dollars will save them." His visitors nodded.

"I make popular dreams come true," Cowell said. He truly believed it. The singer, he had decided with L. A. Reid, would be sent to a health spa for a month to lose weight and enhance her appearance.

"There have been a lot of references to *X Factor* in Fox's meetings this week," muttered Rice—this was corporate jargon for congratulations. Cowell crunched a carrot while the glasses were raised and put down without a drop drunk. All three had reason to be satisfied. Cowell could be relied upon to improve the ratings in 2012.

Outside the trailer, Nicole Scherzinger was standing with a carton of expensively wrapped presents for the two executives and Cowell. Rushing to get away, all three were underwhelmed as she distributed the boxes. Without opening his gift—a specially made pair of *X Factor* cufflinks—Cowell chuckled as he walked toward the waiting media: "I know what you're thinking," he told a friend. Scherzinger's fate had been sealed long before.

After a raucous "wrap party" for five hundred people at Drai's club, Cowell returned to his house at four A.M. Several women had waited for an invitation to accompany him. More self-confident and more relaxed than previously, he was not in the mood for a one-night stand. He did not exclude at some stage the possibility of a permanent relationship. "But," he said without regret, "it's no use looking." (A few weeks later he would abandon the idea.)

Underneath the Christmas tree were about twenty parcels of all sizes. "They're all for me," said Cowell jokily. There was unusual mayhem in the house as he prepared to depart for Barbados later that day. Among his many calls was one to Peter Fincham at ITV. He needed Fincham's agreement to offer a starlet on BBC's *Strictly Come Dancing* over £300,000 to appear with him on *Britain's Got Talent* in early 2012. "We've got to beat *The Voice*," argued Cowell. He himself would be returning to the program on his terms to resurrect his status as British TV's number 1. Everything had to be tilted in his favor, ready for the next battle. Just as Cowell expected, Fincham finally agreed, but his relationship with ITV had become uneasy.

Delayed by calls and last-minute instructions, he left his Los Angeles home and headed for the private jet. He would not return until May. Among the crowd waiting for him in the Caribbean was Lucian Grainge, his old friend and new enemy.

"Come for tea," Cowell suggested to Grainge when they met in Philip Green's suite at the Sandy Lane Hotel. Grainge arrived at Cowell's rented apartment looking somewhat suspicious. Cowell was deliberately emollient. The music business was tough, both knew, and Cowell wanted to disarm his rival by holding out the possibility of Grainge joining Syco.

"You won't be working at Universal forever," said Cowell, hinting at the inevitable corporate power struggles. "We're friends, so don't rule out that one day we'll be working together."

"We'll see," replied Grainge warily. Like Cowell, he was looking forward to the next round of the battle in Britain, aware that one of them would certainly be humiliated by defeat. Cowell's cheery self-confidence was irritating, but Grainge was reassured by BBC's commitment to win the battle.

"I know what works," said Cowell. "I can do it better."

They put aside their conversation for the time being and enjoyed the hotel's New Year's Eve party. "The best ever," agreed Cowell and his friends. Unlike previous years, Cowell remained long after midnight and continued celebrating in his apartment. The following afternoon, he bid farewell to his mother and flew to St. Barts to board *Slipstream* for a three-week cruise around the island. Joined by Sinitta; Zeta Graff, a Greek divorcee; Lauren Silverman; and Kelly Bergantz, he appeared more relaxed than he had in many years. "I feel free," he told his friends. "I've got my energy back and I'm not frightened anymore. Not even of the paparazzi."

Looking over the blue sea, he reflected that he was finally in command of his own destiny. He knew how to improve *The X Factor* in America, his *Got Talent* program would beat *The Voice* in Britain, he had found enough potential stars to score hits on the charts, and he would rebuild his organization to meet his challengers. And above all, he felt that he had scored his revenge against Fuller.

At the end of one high-spirited night at the island's yacht club fuelled by champagne and vodka, he had invited a group of Brazilian girls onto *Slipstream*. By five A.M. he was intimately embraced with a well-known international model. At teatime later that day, she had flown back to Sao Paolo on a private jet and texted her intentions. "She's coming to London soon," he announced at dinner. "That should be fun."

Over the last days of his holiday, he bought a reconditioned blue vintage MG sports car for spinning around London, posed on the sun deck speaking into a banana for an invisible paparazzi, and confirmed his first appointment upon returning home: a forty-minute colonic irrigation session. "It's so cleansing," he told his friends while sitting on *Slipstream*'s aft deck at three A.M. "And it makes my eyes shine brighter, and the whites of my eyes whiter." His first meeting would be with Philip Green to plan the expansion of his empire. "I know I can do the shows better than anyone," he repeated as Frank Sinatra sang "Witchcraft" and he lit a Kool. "The wheel is going to be turning faster than ever. I'll win."

ACKNOWLEDGMENTS

———

I AM VERY GRATEFUL TO HELEN DANN, ROBIN DENSELOW, AND ADAM White for their help at the beginning.

Robert Barrett produced outstanding research about the Cowell family's history.

I am grateful to all members of the Cowell family. Among Cowell's close friends, I am grateful to Lauren Silverman and Kelly Bergantz. Among his staff, thanks to Abi Doyle, Sarah Jane Ingram, Hannah Lamden, Jennie Paine, and Ann-Marie Thomson.

In Los Angeles, the staff of the Petit Ermitage, especially Chris, Josh, and Lena, made my stay very comfortable.

As always I owe a lot to the publishers. Angus Cargill, Ian Bahrami, and Will Atkinson at Fabers; Pamela Cannon, Ratna Kamath, Mark Maguire, Liz Cosgrove, Amelia Zalcman, and Crystal Velasquez at Random House in New York; and the copyeditor, Kate Norris, were all invaluable.

David Hooper has been my libel lawyer since 1987. Thanks to him, so much truth that others would have suppressed has been courageously published. He is a champion of free speech.

I owe a similar debt to Jonathan Lloyd, my agent at Curtis Brown.

Always in a good mood, Lloyd combines friendship with honest criticism.

Above all, I owe so much to my family. My mother, Sylvia, my children, and especially Veronica, an amazing friend and supporter.

AUTHOR'S NOTE

———

I FIRST TOOK AN INTEREST IN *THE X FACTOR* JUST BEFORE CHRISTMAS 2010. A friend, knowing my track record of writing about men with power and money, had suggested I should write Simon Cowell's biography. "Why not watch the final with me," she suggested, "and see what you make of it?" Shortly after, I started serious research for an unauthorized biography. Then, out of the blue I received a telephone call. "Would you like to meet Cowell?" I was asked. Subsequently, I accepted his offer of cooperation subject to the condition that I would publish both criticism and any evidence of wrongdoing. After May 2011, we met regularly in London and Los Angeles or spoke for hours on the telephone at all times of the day and night.

Although Cowell answered my questions in his own fashion and did arrange for me to meet several members of his family and some friends, there were limits to his cooperation.

He accepted my stipulation that he had no copy approval and certainly would not read the book until publication. He did place barriers to my access to some people. I did my best to overcome those attempts. Sometimes I succeeded, but other times I discovered that individuals who had worked with him were just too fearful of the damage to their own reputations to speak to me—and sometimes their fears were understandable, because they had treated him badly. Others feared his wrath if they risked speaking.

Cowell was particularly sensitive about his relationships with some women, especially those confidants who still hear his intense confessions about fears and phobias. Fortunately, the obstacles he raised were not always successful. To his credit, when I did ask for a comment about any embarrassing information I had discovered, he answered my questions without any rancor.

As time passed, I realized how many mysteries remained. After experiencing many pitfalls, Cowell is even more wary than most in show business to protect his reputation. One false move, he knows, could end a remarkable career. Despite the constant glare of the media, with which he actively cooperates, he has successfully preserved many secrets about his life. Occasionally, when I asked for a confession about a particular "skeleton in the cupboard," he created a shield of perplexed innocence, but eventually he did admit to "unknowns," which are unraveled within this book. Considering that he had no control over the outcome, he was remarkably candid.

Even under scrutiny, Cowell is good company. He likes to be entertained and is himself entertaining. Our relationship was harmonious. Many may suspect that Cowell is simply an outstanding manipulator, but after a forty-three-year career of chasing criminals, cheats and con men, I don't think Cowell fits into any of those categories. Nor am I vulnerable to the charm of a man who is undoubtedly civilized but who describes himself as "odd."

Significantly, Cowell did not initially steer me and help me to understand his quest for revenge. On the contrary, he initially refused to speak about his enemies and rivals. He waited until I had accumulated the evidence from others, often without his knowledge. I arrived unaided to my own conclusions. Only then did he explain to me his motivation and offered information which was until then unknown.

Irrefutably, he is a master of our celebrity culture. He also has ambitions to become a TV mogul with an empire stretching across the globe. At the moment, his quest seems realizable. How he achieved that status is the essence of this story.

I have not listed individual sources in endnotes for this book. Unless indicated to the contrary, most direct speech was obtained by me in interviews. I have naturally relied on the huge volume of newspaper and other media reports. I am grateful for the insight provided by the following books:

American Idol (Richard Rushfield. New York: Hyperion, 2011)
Desperate Networks (Bill Carter. New York: Doubleday, 2006)
Hit Men (Frederic Dannen. New York: Times Books, 1990)
I Don't Mean to Be Rude, But . . . (Simon Cowell. New York: Broadway Books, 2003)
The Mansion on the Hill (Fred Goodman. New York: Times Books, 1997)
Simon Cowell (Chas Newkey-Burden. London: O'Mara, 2009)

As usual, many sources wish to remain anonymous, and to them I express my genuine gratitude, as I do to the sources I can mention. These include:

Paula Abdul, Denise Beighton, Brian Biglin, Keith Blackhurst, Alan Boyd, Iain Burton, Tim Byrne, Mike Darnell, Clive Davis, Stephen Ferrera, Marc Fox, Cécile Frot-Coutaz, Tanya Gold, Hugh Goldsmith, Diana Graham, Lucian Grainge, Nigel Grainge, Richard Griffiths, Chris Herbert, Chris Hill, Claire Horton, Denis Ingoldsby, Simon Jones, Jonathan King, Jeremy Lascelles, Ian Levine, Camilla Long, Jeremy Marsh, Korda Marshall, Ron McCreight, Lohan Presencer, John Preston, Steve Redmond, L. A. Reid, Claudia Rosencrantz, Richard Rushfield, Dan Sabbagh, Terri Seymour, Robert Sillerman, Nigel Sinclair, Marty Singer, Rav Singh, Jackie St. Clair, Mike Stock, Louis Theroux, Maurice Veronique, Louis Walsh, Pete Waterman, Tom Watkins, and Paul Williams of *Music Week*.

INDEX

ABOUT THE AUTHOR

TOM BOWER has a distinguished reputation as an investigative historian, broadcaster, and journalist. After earning a law degree, he spent twenty-five years as a producer and reporter for BBC Television, where he covered war, politics, intelligence, and finance. He is the author of nineteen books, including biographies of Robert Maxwell, Mohamed Al Fayed, Gordon Brown, Richard Branson, and Conrad Black. He lives in London, England.

ABOUT THE TYPE

This book was set in Stone, a typeface designed by the teacher, lecturer, and author Summer Stone in 1988. This typeface was designed to satisfy the require-ments of low-resolution laser printing. Its traditional design blends harmoniously with many typefaces, making it appropriate for a variety of applications.